SLAVERY ATTACKED

SLAVERY ATTACKED

SOUTHERN SLAVES
AND THEIR ALLIES
1619 – 1865

Merton L. Dillon

LOUISIANA STATE UNIVERSITY PRESS
BATON ROUGE AND LONDON

Designer: Diane Batten Didier
Typeface: Aster
Typesetter: G & S Typesetters, Inc.
Printer and binder: Thomson-Shore, Inc.

Library of Congress Cataloging-in-Publication Data

Dillon, Merton Lynn, 1924–
    Slavery attacked : Southern slaves and their allies, 1619–1865 /
Merton L. Dillon.
        p.   cm.
    Includes bibliographical references (p.   ) and index.
    ISBN 0-8071-1614-9 (alk. paper)   ISBN 0-8071-1653 (pbk.; alk. paper)
    1. Slavery—Southern States—History.   2. Slavery—United States—
Anti-slavery movements.   3. Southern States—History—Colonial
period, ca. 1600–1775.   4. Southern States—History—1775–1865.
I. Title.
E441.D55   1990
975'.03—dc20   90-6067
                                                                          CIP

The paper in this book meets the guidelines for permanence and durability of the
Committee on Production Guidelines for Book Longevity of the Council on Library
Resources. ∞

Contents

Acknowledgments

A book as long in the making as this one inevitably incurs heavy obligations on the part of its author. The greatest of these is to the many persons, past and contemporary, whose work has made possible my own. I hope that the footnotes and bibliography adequately convey the extent of my debt to them. Other obligations come to mind. The Graduate School, the College of Humanities, and the Department of History of the Ohio State University provided a grant-in-aid and allowed me time that facilitated my research and writing. A senior fellowship from the National Endowment for the Humanities, awarded some years ago for a different project, contributed in important, unforeseen ways to this one. I am grateful to all the staff at Louisiana State University Press for their courtesies, but especially to Margaret Dalrymple, editor-in-chief, for encouraging my project from the time she first learned of it, and to John Easterly, production editor, for his exceptional competence in editing my earlier book and coordinating the editing of this one. I am also grateful to Joan Seward, my copy editor, for planing rough places in the manuscript. Finally, my appreciation goes to Marjorie Haffner and Janice Gulker, valued members of the office staff of the Ohio State University's history department. Their cheerful assistance helped me through many a crisis during the final stages of preparing the manuscript for this book.

SLAVERY ATTACKED

Introduction

North American slaveholders strove for the absolute submission of their labor force and also its isolation from any group with which it might make common cause. But those were goals difficult if not impossible to attain, and probably few truly expected to do so. An approximation must suffice. With some success, slaves contrived to resist demands for submission and, despite all precautions, succeeded in finding people who welcomed and even encouraged their resistance. For generations such subversion proved manageable, but with nearly every passing decade it became more troublesome and more ominous. Eventually, after many years of vigilance, slaveholders faced in the slaves and their allies a combination too powerful to be overcome. The result was the fall of their regime.

From one point of view, this outcome seems surprising, for though West Indian and Latin American slaves challenged their owners with devastating rebellions and extensive, long-lasting maroon settlements, slaves in North America appeared comparatively docile and reconciled to bondage. Never throughout their long history did they carry out a large-scale insurrection. The three major rebellions that did occur—in South Carolina (1739), in Louisiana (1811), and in Virginia (1831)—had relatively few participants (a few hundred at most), were confined to small areas, and were of short duration. It is true that some conspiracies to rebel, particularly in New York (1741), in Virginia (1800), and in South Carolina (1822), purportedly gained more adherents—thousands, it was said—and thus may have had greater potential. But we shall never know, for each was exposed and its leaders were tried and executed before their plans could be carried out. Slaveholders seemed to have met every challenge successfully.

Yet the apparent stability of the North American slave system masks the danger contemporaries saw in it and belied its vulnerability. Slavery contained within itself the seeds of its own destruction. Few owners could fail to know that their labor system rested ultimately on force—the threat of reprisal—and the willingness of slaves, however extorted, to remain in bondage. Slaveholders must have realized that slaves continued to work at their assigned tasks, finally, because coercion—and the absence of formidable allies—compelled them to do so. And the owners also must have known that it was to secure that labor and to preserve their own dominion that they kept the slave population under steady surveillance and ruthlessly punished transgression. It was similarly obvious that on the day their power to dominate disappeared, their regime would fall.

The necessity for force was not theoretical. Only with unremitting effort could slaves be kept at work on the masters' terms. Many ran away, and everywhere owners were faced with workers who malingered, ignored orders, and otherwise resisted exploitation—even to the point of violence. Although such subversive behavior was far from universal, it occurred often enough to make the potential for massive disorder and consequent ruin a constant dread.

Overwhelming evidence shows that slaves sought not so much advantage within the system as escape from it, even its destruction. However, their own energies might not be enough to achieve those ends. In this conflict, as in any other, outside aid would be useful, if not essential. Accordingly, slaves welcomed allies in their struggle for autonomy. Likewise, enemies and rivals of the owners, whatever their attitudes toward blacks or toward slavery itself might be, repeatedly made use of the slaves as a means of attaining their own ends.

For many years, circumstances allowed slaveholders to keep their slaves adequately in check and to counter the menacing outside forces. But, eventually, the two sources of opposition—the slaves themselves and the owners' rivals and enemies—joined forces to bring ruin to the slaveholding South.

This book, then, is about the slaveholders' long travail and their ultimate failure. It is about the changing relationship of slaves to other groups within the South and beyond it. It is about the ways in which slave resistance was linked to foreign relations, war, and invasion, and to internal social and political conflict.

1

☒☒☒☒☒☒☒☒☒☒☒☒☒☒☒☒☒☒☒☒☒☒☒☒☒☒☒☒☒☒☒☒

A Worrisome People

The English who settled at Jamestown in 1609 faced a hostile environment. Hunger, disease, and early death were the fate of most of them. Indians and Spaniards threatened the colony. Factionalism plagued it. To these misfortunes (each of them arguably unavoidable) the Virginians soon chose to add slavery. This eventually proved to be a source of disorder and insecurity fully as grave as any of the other ills that beset them.

Sometime in the summer of 1619, a Dutch man-of-war landed "20. and odd Negroes" at Point Comfort, where the James River empties into the Chesapeake. So reported John Rolfe, future husband of Pocahontas, shortly after the ship had sailed away. If, as has been argued, the white settlers wavered for a while between holding the new arrivals as slaves and treating them as indentured servants, the indecision did not last long. By 1640 some, perhaps most, of the Africans in Virginia undoubtedly had been enslaved, and just as quickly as more became available, those white proprietors who could afford to do so added to their numbers.[1]

Practice and custom soon were codified in law. During the 1660s,

1. Susan M. Klingburg (ed.), *Records of the Virginia Company of London* (Washington, D.C., 1906–35), III, 241–48; Wesley Frank Craven, *White, Red, and Black: The Seventeenth-Century Virginian* (Charlottesville, Va., 1971), 73–103; Wesley Frank Craven, "Twenty Negroes to Jamestown in 1619?" *Virginia Quarterly Review*, LVII (1971), 416–20; Robert McColley, "Slavery in Virginia, 1619–1660: A Reexamination," in Robert H. Abzug and Stephen E. Maizlish (eds.), *New Perspectives on Race and Slavery in America: Essays in Honor of Kenneth M. Stampp* (Lexington, Ky., 1986), 11–24.

the colonial assemblies of both Virginia and Maryland defined slavery as a lifelong, inheritable condition and provided legislation designed to protect it. In South Carolina, founded in the 1670s by proprietors familiar with the slave-labor system of both the Barbados and the Chesapeake area, no period of indecision was evident. There the institution unquestionably existed from the first settlement. And in Georgia, where the trustees had planned to keep slavery out, popular demand soon led to its introduction. In the New England colonies, as well as in New York, Pennsylvania, and New Jersey, blacks were introduced at an early date with little if any controversy regarding their slave status.[2]

Nowhere in the English colonies did any effective counterforce exist to prevent white settlers who could afford to do so from taking full advantage of the alluring economic opportunities offered by the exploitation of blacks. The Europeans were free to do with them as they liked. It is hardly surprising, then, to find that well before the end of the seventeenth century, the great majority of blacks in English America were slaves in law as well as in practice and that continued importation steadily increased their numbers. At the same time, the supply of indentured white servants diminished. There were only about three hundred blacks in Virginia in 1648, out of a total population of fifteen thousand, and only two thousand (or 5 percent of the population) in 1670, but by 1710, about one-quarter of the population of Virginia and Maryland were black slaves. In South Carolina in 1720, they made up 40 percent of the population, and importation continued undiminished.[3]

We can be reasonably sure of the motives that led profit-seeking colonists up and down the Atlantic coast to hold blacks as slaves and to import more of them. Equally important for understanding the southern past are the anxieties and dangers that resulted from those decisions. The profits and convenience of slave labor never entirely disappeared, but neither did its constantly unfolding haz-

2. Paul C. Palmer, "Servant into Slave: The Evolution of the Legal Servitude of the Negro Laborer in Colonial Virginia," *South Atlantic Quarterly*, LXV (1966), 355–70; James Curtis Ballagh, *A History of Slavery in Virginia* (Baltimore, 1902), 31; James H. Brewer, "Negro Property Owners in Seventeenth-Century Virginia," *William and Mary Quarterly*, 3rd ser., XII (1955), 575–80; Carl N. Degler, "Slavery and the Genesis of American Race Prejudice," *Comparative Studies in Society and History*, II (October, 1959), 49–66; Edgar J. McManus, *Black Bondage in the North* (Syracuse, N.Y., 1973); Lorenzo J. Greene, *The Negro in Colonial New England, 1620–1776* (New York, 1942).

3. David W. Galenson, *White Servitude in Colonial America: An Economic Analysis* (Cambridge, Eng., 1981), 118–68; U.S. Bureau of the Census, *Historical Statistics of the United States, Colonial Times to 1970* (2 vols.; 1975), II, 1168.

ards. At no time could American slaveholding society be called secure. Efforts to eliminate threats to its survival failed. No sooner
had challenges in one form been dealt with than they reappeared in
different shape. Never for long could slaveholders escape the need
to defend their interests from both internal and external foes. The
constant need to be on guard helped set the course of southern history and in that manner influenced the development of the nation.

An internal threat appeared almost as soon as slavery was instituted. Native Americans, attempting to defend themselves against
relentless European encroachment, might use dissident blacks
within the European settlements as military instruments to destroy
the invader; likewise, blacks might view Indians as allies in their
own struggles for freedom. Even if no such political connections
were made, backcountry Indians still might harbor runaway slaves
and thereby add another element of insecurity to a valuable but
unstable institution. Those possibilities—absent nowhere—seemed
most alive in the Southeast, where potent Indian tribes lived close
to large concentrations of slaves. Accordingly, authorities there took
steps designed to prevent the unthinkable—an Indian attack coordinated with a slave uprising. Everything possible was done to
prevent the two threatening groups from recognizing and taking advantage of their common interest. Indians and blacks were encouraged to view each other as enemies, and Indians were rewarded
for returning runaways. For example, in South Carolina, Indians
helped round up insurgents after the great rebellion at Stono in
1739. But these efforts were not completely successful, for in Georgia and South Carolina in particular, runaway slaves continued to
find refuge in the Indian country. In South Carolina, the point of
greatest danger, officials decided—though their efforts proved futile—to encourage the importation of indentured servants rather
than black slaves on the ground that white servants would help
guard the frontiers against Indian attack while also defending against
slave insurrection.[4]

Potential danger appeared within the white settlements as well.
Living among the ambitious importers of black labor was a mi-

4. William S. Willis, Jr., "Divide and Rule: Red, White, and Black in the Southeast," *Journal of Negro History*, XLVIII (1963), 157–76; William S. Willis, Jr., "Anthropology and Negroes on the Southern Colonial Frontier," in James C. Curtis and Lewis
L. Gould (eds.), *The Black Experience in America: Selected Essays* (Austin, 1970),
42–46; Robert L. Meriwether, *The Expansion of South Carolina, 1729–1765* (Kingsport, Tenn., 1940), 17, 18, 27; Lathan A. Windley (comp.), *Runaway Slave Advertisements: A Documentary History from the 1730s to 1790* (Westport, Conn., 1983), IV, 36,
40, 43, 102, 104; III, 94, 265, 638.

nority of whites who, though seldom openly opposed to slavery, were not committed to it either. They were exasperatingly slow to adopt the attitudes essential to maintain it. Their hesitancy posed a problem for ambitious planters, for a persistent absence of internal consensus would threaten the masters' control of increasingly valuable property. The disciplining of slaves—always a challenge—would be made even more difficult if part of the white population failed to treat them as members of a base class or—still worse—if they helped them escape or in less drastic ways encouraged them to resist the owners' authority.

In the seventeenth century, especially, there were signs that these things were happening. Instead of quickly developing closed societies, the southern colonies for a long time left room for much diversity in attitude and practice with respect to slavery, and whites remained far from united in resolve to debase the growing black population. So long as this situation continued, the owners' social position and their property would be problematic.

Race consciousness, with its attendant bias, developed more slowly than is sometimes supposed. Whatever degree of prejudice the colonial elite felt against blackness—and Winthrop Jordan has proved that the bias was deep and of long standing—the white indentured servants, who supplied most of the labor in seventeenth-century Virginia and Maryland, were less quick to interpret their own color as a badge of superiority over their black fellow bondsmen. Although in outward appearance and cultural traits the two groups markedly differed from each other, this finally mattered less than a later generation might expect. And in any case, until late in the seventeenth century, blacks in the Chesapeake Bay area and even in the Carolinas remained too few to be perceived as a threat to white cultural dominance. Under such circumstances, lower-class white colonists—servants and even small farmers—could ignore racial barriers without feeling they courted danger or violated taboo. The blacks' condition as slaves unquestionably was wretched, but so was that of many white servants. The burdens and griefs of bondage were not confined to blacks alone.[5]

Relationships between members of the two oppressed groups

5. Winthrop D. Jordan, *White over Black: American Attitudes Toward the Negro, 1550–1812* (Chapel Hill, N.C., 1968), *passim*, but esp. x–xi, 91–98, 110; Gerald W. Mullin, *Flight and Rebellion: Slave Resistance in Eighteenth-Century Virginia* (New York, 1972), 187n, 191n, 192n; Warren Billings (ed.), *The Old Dominion in the Seventeenth Century: A Documentary History of Virginia, 1606–1689* (Chapel Hill, N.C., 1975), 145, 151–59; Peter H. Wood, *Black Majority: Blacks in Colonial South Carolina from 1670 Through the Stono Rebellion* (New York, 1974), 54–55, 97–98.

were sometimes close, even intimate. Blacks and lower-class whites who worked together at their masters' tasks did not in every instance end their association when they left the fields at day's end. Apparently they enjoyed each other's company, for, we are told, they drank together, slept together, ran away together—all with more awareness of shared predicament than of racial difference.[6] By breaching the wall of racial solidarity, such waywardness threatened the masters' control over their black property and thereby imperiled development of a slaveholding society.

But the gradual decline of white servitude in the eighteenth century and the improving economic lot of small farmers lessened the likelihood of such collusion, while the rapid increase in the numbers of blacks, many of them newly arrived from Africa, sharpened awareness of cultural differences and, in some instances, of economic competition. Yet some free white persons, especially those in the lower orders—David Brion Davis has called them "independent and irreverent fraternizers"—long continued to relate to blacks in ways suggesting either ignorance of the racist implications of proslavery laws and customs, disagreement with them, or outright defiance. Testimony of slaves implicated in an alleged conspiracy in South Carolina in 1739 revealed that white agitators—all of them lower-class and some of them itinerants—understood the slaves' grievances and had encouraged them to revolt.[7] Slavery obviously did not serve the interests of all white persons equally. Not everyone could grasp its purported social and political necessity, and even fewer persons were in a position to reap its economic benefits.

The area in which early lower-class white colonists most conspicuously evidenced their lack of concern for the proscriptions of slavery was that of sex. While in principle the races from an early day may have been expected to remain biologically apart, in practice whites and blacks appraised each other from the beginning as potential sexual partners: One of the earliest pieces of evidence testifying to the presence of blacks in Virginia is the record of the pun-

6. Ira Berlin, "Time, Space, and the Evolution of Afro-American Society in British Mainland North America," *American Historical Review*, LXXXV (1980), 44–78; Edmund S. Morgan, *American Slavery, American Freedom: The Ordeal of Colonial Virginia* (New York, 1975), 325–27; Billings (ed.), *Old Dominion*, 159.

7. Timothy H. Breen, "A Changing Labor Force and Race Relations in Virginia, 1660–1710," *Journal of Social History*, VII (1973), 3–25; David Brion Davis, *The Problem of Slavery in the Age of Revolution, 1770–1823* (Ithaca, N.Y., 1975), 279n.; Philip D. Morgan and George D. Terry, "Slavery in Microcosm: A Conspiracy Scare in Colonial South Carolina," *Southern Studies*, XXI (1982), 120–23, 138–41.

ishment assessed a white man named Hugh Davis for the offense of "lying with a negro."[8]

Some legal interracial marriages took place in seventeenth- and eighteenth-century America, though so subversive of social order and economic interest did the ruling classes think these to be that the colonial legislatures soon outlawed them. Not surprisingly, a considerably higher incidence of irregular sexual activity character- ized relations between the races. This did not in every instance in- volve white men and black women and thus cannot reasonably be ascribed to the aggressive, brute force of the master class. In 1681, for instance, Mary Williamson of Norfolk County, Virginia, commit- ted the "filthy sin" of fornication with William Bassett's slave named William, for which offense she was assessed a heavy fine. William, in his turn, refusing to display either shame or contrition for his deed (on the contrary, he "very arrogantly behaved himself in Linhaven Church in the face of the Congregation"), was punished with thirty lashes.[9]

An incident that occurred in late summer of the same year in Henrico County provides a still more revealing illustration of re- laxed racial barriers in early Virginia. There, several white men and women, presumably from the class of small farmers, gathered at Thomas Cocke's farm, where the slaves were clearing the orchard of weeds. No thought of maintaining distance between the races was evident when, as the afternoon wore on, all adjourned to drink to- gether in Cocke's house. The conviviality of the occasion led a Quaker woman named Katherine Walker to fling aside every consid- eration of racial distance as well as of propriety. She embraced and kissed the slave Jacke while reproving him for not more often visit- ing her and her husband's home. She became much more familiar with the slave Dirke, even lifting his shirt and commenting admir- ingly on the dimensions of what she saw there. Then when Jacke, who clearly was her favorite, passed near her on his way to draw more cider, she "putt her hand on his codpiece, at which he smiled." Soon after, having retired to a bedroom, she was seen behaving in a like, but still more brazen manner, with a slave named Mingo. How- ever one explains this episode—if only by reference to cider imbibed by a motley gathering in August heat—the sociability manifested

8. Jordan, *White over Black*, 78.
9. *Ibid.*, 161. The theme is explored in James Hugo Johnston, *Race Relations in Virginia and Miscegenation in the South, 1776–1860* (Amherst, Mass., 1970), esp. 175–76, 179–81.

by the entire company, not by a wanton Quaker woman alone, demonstrated a degree of interracial comity perilous to slavery and nearly unthinkable in a later time.[10]

In seventeenth-century Maryland, a similar laxity evidently prevailed. There, some white people who were well advanced on the social scale evidently saw nothing wrong with intimate relationships between their female white servants and male black slaves and may even have encouraged them, a practice the colonial assembly took outraged note of and felt obliged to prohibit.[11]

If interracial liaisons of this and more conventional kinds had represented simply one more means to exploit a subject people, they would have been seen as strengthening the bonds of slavery rather than as weakening them, but they were not so regarded. Instead, such relationships were viewed as a major threat, because notions of caste did not accompany them. They demonstrated that some white persons considered racial differences irrelevant. In a society in which slavery was based on race, such disregard obviously would prove fatal. Interracial sex, which in another setting might have been seen as a matter of personal choice, of instinct, of pleasure, in a slave society early acquired a political aspect from which it never could be free.

In an effort to strengthen the white colonists' sense of racial exclusiveness, the Virginia House of Burgesses in 1661 imposed a fine on interracial fornication; other colonial legislatures in due course enacted similar laws, and children of slave women, however "white" they might appear, were ruled to be "black" and enslaved. When lawmakers placed the stamp of illegality on interracial sex, it became disgraceful as well as risky. The shame attending mixed-race liaisons, especially those between black men and white women, became so overpowering that eventually such activity came to be associated only with the very lowest class of white women, although, in the nature of things, others sometimes indulged as well. And, as is well known, the sexual exploitation of slave women by free white men continued unabated, almost as though prohibitory laws did not exist.[12]

10.   Billings (ed.), *Old Dominion*, 161–63.

11.   Johnston, *Race Relations*, 165–90; Helen T. Catterall (ed.), *Judicial Cases Concerning American Slavery and the Negro* (Washington, D.C., 1924–26), IV, 28, 49, 52, 61–62, 370; *Archives of Maryland: Proceedings and Acts of the General Assembly of Maryland, October 1678–March 1683* (Baltimore, 1889), 204.

12.   John Codman Hurd, *The Law of Freedom and Bondage in the United States* (Boston, 1858), I, 236–37, 242, 249, 250, 251, 253, 263, 290, 292, 295, 298, 301, 302; Johnston, *Race Relations*, 187–88; Jordan, *White over Black*, 137–42, 473.

Perhaps more indicative of the depth of interracial sympathy, because it occurred outside the tangled thicket of sexual expression, was the frequency with which blacks found among colonial whites ready accomplices in their resistance to slavery. Here, too, individual desires and calculation took precedence over the demands of state and society. As we have seen, slaves and white indentures working together at the planters' tasks found racial differences easy to ignore. Not surprisingly, their shared predicament sometimes led them to join forces to resist intolerable treatment, as in 1663 in Virginia, where a reported plot in Gloucester County involved both white servants and black slaves, and in 1711 when a colonist complained that "the negroes and other servants grow so intolerant that I am afraid what the issue will be." The danger was judged especially great in Maryland, where in the first half of the eighteenth century Catholics fell under suspicion of such intent.[13]

Worrisome as were the racial attitudes of dissidents and lower-class whites, the day-to-day response of blacks to their enslavement understandably more immediately concerned the owners. To no one's surprise, newly arrived Africans were slow to be reconciled to a life of captivity. "Seasoning" and acculturation failed to eliminate—may even have increased—their desire for personal autonomy. One of the most common and most nearly complete forms of resistance by both "new" and acculturated blacks was to declare themselves free by simply running away, a practice that would plague owners as long as bondage lasted. Almost as soon as they arrived in America, blacks began fleeing the places their owners wanted them to be. To the planters' dismay, white settlers sometimes helped them do this, thereby adding a political dimension to a persistent problem.

Often runaways absconded only to satisfy some transitory purpose—perhaps to escape punishment—and then, having found no better place to be, soon returned. But others fully intended to make the parting permanent. Some of them retreated in groups separate not only from the master but from all white society. Evidence of such maroonage is abundant, especially in the Carolinas and Georgia, but in Virginia as well. Runaways, when gathered in numbers in maroon settlements, constituted a grave social problem and

13. John Cotton to Rowland Cotton, October 27, 1711, in Miscellaneous Manuscripts, New-York Historical Society, New York, N.Y.; Herbert Aptheker, *American Negro Slave Revolts* (New York, 1943), 164–65; Ulrich B. Phillips, *American Negro Slavery: A Survey of the Supply, Employment and Control of Negro Labor as Determined by the Plantation Regime* (New York, 1918), 472; Billings (ed.), *Old Dominion*, 159.

sometimes a military threat, for armed as they often were, they were likely to menace white settlers and their property. In the 1690s the slave Mingo fled from his master in Virginia to take up a separate existence and then together with several followers lived by ravaging the plantations of Rappahonic County. In 1729 Governor William Gooch reported to the Board of Trade that another band of fugitives, apparently intending to become self-sufficient and sever all connection with white society, had retreated into the Blue Ridge Mountains with arms and farm tools, but that pursuing colonists had attacked them and reenslaved the survivors. A few years later, in Virginia, six slaves in Accomac County fled their owners: "They are armed with Guns, &c and have broke open several Houses. . . , committed Felonies, have taken a Canoe." With the spread of white settlement into the West, the isolation upon which maroonage depended lessened and its incidence, accordingly, declined. Yet, as late as 1830, a group of thirty or forty such persons was found in the Dover Swamp in North Carolina, and in Florida the allied Seminoles and blacks managed to resist white encroachment for decades.[14]

Such fugitives, who in the eyes of white colonists were bandits, constituted a drain on the white economy as well as a source of disorder. They also undermined slavery itself, for they were living proof of the enmity of the blacks and of their daring, skill, and strength. Further, they sometimes enticed other slaves to join them. In Georgia in 1767, a slave named York was thought to have been decoyed from his master by members of a maroon settlement. Soon afterward, three newly imported blacks were "supposed to be carried away from the bluff (where they were fishing) by some runaway negroes in a canoe." And when, in 1774, six "new" blacks disappeared from a Georgia plantation, their owner took for granted that they "got in with a parcel of Mr. Elliot's negroes who have been run away for some time."[15]

As colonial society matured and its economy became more complex, runaways, especially those with marketable skills and thus less likely to be inclined toward maroonage, could reasonably count on making a living in the developing market economy, free from a master's supervision. The prospective cooperation of white persons

14. Aptheker, *American Negro Slave Revolts*, 167, 179; Windley (comp.), *Runaway Slave Advertisements*, I, 21; J. Burgwyn to the Governor, November 15, 1830, in Governor John Owens Letter Book, 1828–30, in Governors' Papers, North Carolina Division of Archives and History, Raleigh.

15. Windley (comp.), *Runaway Slave Advertisements*, IV, 23, 37, 58–59.

was implicit in slaves' calculations as they planned their escape. Thus, when Will fled, he took with him the tools he used for making wooden bowls. Sandy, who, though much addicted to drink and given to profanity, nonetheless had served Thomas Jefferson as shoemaker, carpenter, and horse jockey, carried off his shoemaker's tools when he quit Jefferson's plantation, and Cudjoe, age eighteen and Angola-born, took his bricklaying tools with him. Such skilled slaves probably intended to blend into the growing free black city population as independent workmen or, perhaps, to attach themselves to white craftsmen who would pay them for their skills. In either event, if they made good their escape, they and the whites who connived with them would have established a relationship incompatible with slavery as southern planters knew it. The political potential of such a development was incalculable.[16]

When fugitives took to woods and swamps, whether as solitaries or maroons, they had little need to seek help from anyone except perhaps potential fellow runaways. But if they chose a less isolated life, aid would be welcome—and it was not impossible to come by. Here, too, the planters discovered, racial solidarity was incomplete. Doubtless, other slaves and free blacks were the first persons a fugitive ordinarily appealed to, for they were innately subversive, but slaves also found that some whites were willing to ignore what the leaders of society insisted was their racial interest. White colonists, even though living in emerging slaveholding societies, wrote passes to help runaways satisfy challenges from the suspicious and the vigilant; they hid them from pursuers; they arranged passage on ships bound for faraway places.[17]

The master of Tom Flute, a slave who was fond of cards and even in bondage somehow had accumulated cash, supposed that "he has got a forged Pass, as he has been concerned with some white People of the same Stampe." Flora was thought "to be harboured under the Bluff by sailors." William Wood, a former sailor, helped Betty and her white servant friend escape. Davy's master suspected that he "has had dealings with a woman of infamous character in this neighbourhood, named Anne Ashwell, and that she has advised him to run away." Sall Cooper, "for some Time past much in the Company of a white man," presumably followed him to Norfolk. A white man named Peter Gossigon, recently a sailor on board a man-of-war's tender, was said to make a practice of trying to persuade

16. *Ibid.*, IV, 38; I, 73; III, 126.
17. Wood, *Black Majority*, 243–44; Julia Floyd Smith, *Slavery and Rice Culture in Low Country Georgia, 1750–1860* (Knoxville, Tenn., 1985), 187.

slaves to go off with him on the promise of freedom; the slave Jack evidently accepted his offer. Tom was seen working on board a ship bound for Liverpool. A white oysterman in Virginia used his boat to help a slave and a white servant escape.[18]

The circumstances of abandonments such as these suggest that the motives for extending aid often were not purely altruistic. In cities in particular, where slavery early displayed a flexibility and variety rare in rural settings, whites secreted runaways and helped them ply their crafts, expecting to profit from the transgression. Bob's master, knowing he was a very good blacksmith, supposed someone of that trade harbored him. The owner of the shoemaker Tom speculated that he "may probably be concealed and kept at his trade in Annapolis . . . by some white people, who make too familiar with my slaves to my great prejudice." In South Carolina, January's master supposed "some evil white person" employed and concealed him. And in that colony Barnaba, too, was thought to be "harboured by some evil disposed white Persons being a remarkable fine Seamstress, and easily kept at her Work, without Discovery."[19]

The small farmers of colonial North Carolina made themselves notorious by harboring fugitives from the plantations of their richer neighbors to the north and to the south. But even in the heart of Virginia and South Carolina—bastions of slavery—white proprietors sometimes employed black laborers whom they must have known to be fugitives, and helped them elude their lawful owners. Here, as in the cities, the display of generosity may have been in large part self-serving, for the slaves' labor skills tempted enterprising whites, almost always in need of extra hands, not to ask too many questions about the past of the men and women who arrived at their door seeking asylum and work. In South Carolina, Henry Laurens found that his runaway Sampson had been harbored by "a poor worthless fellow," who, nonetheless, taught him to process indigo and "to speak tolerable good English."[20] Another South Caro-

18. Windley (comp.), *Runaway Slave Advertisements*, II, 63; IV, 53; I, 4, 84, 104, 107; III, 504.

19. *Ibid.*, I, 305; II, 112; III, 205, 328.

20. Jeffrey J. Crow, *The Black Experience in Revolutionary North Carolina* (Raleigh, N.C., 1973), 40–42; William M. Wiecek, "The Statutory Law of Slavery and Race in the Thirteen Mainland Colonies of British America," *William and Mary Quarterly*, 3rd ser., XXXIV (1977), 277; Gerald W. Mullin, *Flight and Rebellion*, 110–15, 190n, 191n; Wood, *Black Majority*, 243, 245, 253n, 264. See the case of Sampson in Henry Laurens to Joseph Brown, June 28, 1765, in Philip M. Hamer *et al.* (eds.), *The Papers of Henry Laurens* (Columbia, S.C., 1968–), IV, 645. For a like incident in New York, see Edgar J. McManus, *A History of Negro Slavery in New York* (Syracuse, N.Y., 1966), 113–14.

lina planter complained, "It is a customary thing for the back settlers of this province, to take up new negroes, and keep them
employed privately."As early as 1763 this had become a "pernicious
custom."[21]

Such illicit activity probably contributed to the immediate welfare of individuals and, in a small way, aided the development of the
colonial economy. But this made the practice no less damaging to
the masters' interests and no less subversive of slavery. Blacks and
whites were partners in deception, and their deception was at the
expense of the master-slave relationship.

Parallel events occurred at the subterranean level of colonial society. There in the American underground, whites joined blacks in a
life of crime, with thievery being the most common activity. Blacks,
slave or free, generally did the stealing, and whites, less likely to be
suspected, arranged to receive and sell the stolen goods, though
roles might be shared or reversed. In any event the biracial broth-
erhood of thieves forged in colonial America enjoyed a long and
flagrant life. Suspicions concerning interracial thievery weighed
heavily in the trials growing out of the New York slave conspiracy
of 1741. In 1759 in Charleston, an exasperated John Paul Grimké
charged that his slave boys Cuffee and Sharper made a practice of
robbing him and then running away, "being harboured and entertained by some evil-disposed persons in this town while their money
lasts." The practice did not stop. More than a half century later,
South Carolina citizens still complained that "fugitive slaves are
harboured . . . by unscrupulous people who encourage them to rob
and steal from their industrious neighbors." Corruption entered
even the machinery authorities devised to maintain the slave system. Members of the slave patrols, a black refugee reported many
years later, sometimes struck deals with the persons they were supposed to discipline, agreeing to "take whatever the slaves steal paying in money, whisky, or whatever the slaves want." Slaveowners
seldom were allowed to forget that white persons who lived on the
fringe of society could not be trusted to maintain the behavioral
patterns that were required to preserve slavery. They always were
seen as potential allies of the blacks, and the blacks, it is clear,
viewed them that way as well.[22]

21. Windley (comp.), *Runaway Slave Advertisements*, III, 151–52, 227, 604.

22. *Ibid.*, III, 170; Gerald W. Mullin, *Flight and Rebellion*, 60–61; Wood, *Black
Majority*, 243; Catterall (ed.), *Judicial Cases*, III, 20; IV, 27, 34, 36, 38; Ferenc M. Szasz,
"The New York Slave Revolt of 1741: A Re-examination," *New York History*, XLVIII

The variety of collusive and wayward activities indulged in jointly by blacks and whites, free persons and slaves, suggests that neither slavery nor freedom in early America had developed the full meaning those words eventually would acquire. It also suggests that the concept of race as yet exercised only limited prescriptive power and that slavery as an institution was slow to manifest the domineering quality that later would emerge as perhaps its most telling characteristic.

This fluid circumstance—when much in interracial relationships was still unsettled—would not last long. As eighteenth-century white southerners committed themselves to plantation agriculture, the black element in America came to constitute an increasingly valuable economic asset whose possibilities would be fully exploited. White farmers in ever increasing numbers joined the slaveowners' ranks. This meant increasing importation of blacks as well as more efficient use of them.[23] The result for many white colonists was wealth and expanded opportunity. Yet, the ever-growing servile population generated anxieties even as it created fortunes and solidified the social position of the white proprietors. This was so because, quite apart from such disquiet as the slaves' distinctive racial and cultural characteristics produced, it was obvious that their interests clashed with those of their oppressors. No special gift of prophecy was needed to foresee the probable result. Slaves did not accept the restrictions and brutalities to which they were subject without resisting, sometimes to the extreme of violence against owners and overseers. Accordingly, the society that grew and prospered as a result of the exploitation of slave labor produced individuals who warned of the disaster that awaited a people who relied upon such an explosive labor system.[24]

Although white colonists found their slave property virtually indispensable, they also distrusted it. They had no difficulty in seeing that blacks shared the common human desire to be free of restraints

---

(1967), 217, 227; Grand Jury Presentment from Georgetown District, November 6, 1799, in Grand Jury Presentments, South Carolina Department of Archives and History, Columbia; Benjamin Drew, *A North-Side View of Slavery: The Refugee; or, The Narratives of Free Slaves in Canada* . . . (Boston, 1856), 157; [George Ball], *Fifty Years in Chains; or, The Life of an American Slave* (New York, 1858), 220–24; John Brown, *Slave Life in Georgia: A Narrative of the Life, Sufferings, and Escape of John Brown, a Fugitive Slave, Now in England* (London, 1855), 57–58.

23. These changes and their profound implications are discussed in Michael Mullin (ed.), *American Negro Slavery: A Documentary History* (New York, 1976), 10–24.

24. Jordan, *White over Black*, 111–15.

and to pursue their own welfare. Colonial masters may have been racially prejudiced, but they seldom contended, as their descendants often did, that slaves willingly accepted their lot or that blacks as a race possessed inborn traits peculiarly fitting them for bondage.

Little in their experience could have led them to such a conclusion. In the pioneering stage of colonial development, before a paternalistic plantation society evolved, slaves regularly displayed—and were valued for displaying—unslavelike qualities of independence and resourcefulness. But the time soon passed when the slaves' autonomous behavior could be used to work to the benefit of the master. Directors of more settled slave-staffed enterprises understood that such characteristics, if channeled in the wrong direction, might subvert the slave-labor economy and destroy white-dominated plantation society.[25] And the subversion certainly would be hastened if the slaves found allies among the white population.

Some entertained the frightening possibility of a massive, coordinated slave uprising. Others judged this event unlikely, noting that slaves in America were not intimately bound together by cultural ties, since they came from a variety of African backgrounds and for a time lacked even a common language. But as astute colonists understood, this diversity provided no guarantee against slaves combining to resist an increasingly oppressive bondage: "Freedom Wears a Cap which Can Without a Tongue, Call Togather all Those who long to Shake of the fetters of Slavery," warned Governor Alexander Spotswood in 1710 as he urged the Virginia assembly to enact stern laws to control the colony's slaves. The governor of South Carolina in 1711 expressed similar misgivings about the course of that colony's development. And in 1732 the trustees of Georgia, perhaps mindful of unsettled social conditions elsewhere in America, prohibited slavery in their new colony, partly on the ground that an enslaved population would imperil it.[26]

Danger of rebellion could not be eliminated by strict laws of the sort Spotswood proposed for Virginia. On the contrary, as colonial

25. Peter Wood makes this point for South Carolina (Wood, *Black Majority*, 95–103). Gerald W. Mullin finds Virginia planters almost from the beginning "patriarchal" and thus unsympathetic with slave autonomy (Mullin, *Flight and Rebellion*, 3–33). See the suggestive comments in Duncan J. MacLeod, "Toward Caste," in Ira Berlin and Ronald Hoffman (eds.), *Slavery and Freedom in the Age of Revolution* (Charlottesville, Va., 1983), 225.

26. Alexander Spotswood quoted in Jordan, *White over Black*, 111; Allen D. Candler (ed.), *The Colonial Records of Georgia* (1904; rpr. New York, 1970), I, 50–51.

society became more cohesive and the bonds of slavery correspondingly tightened, resistance gained the focus it previously had lacked, and the possibility of slave combination grew. Continued expansion of the black population throughout the eighteenth century added to the danger. The facts were unsettling. After the 1730s, blacks consistently made up between 40 and 50 percent of the population of colonial Virginia. In South Carolina, from an even earlier date, they constituted an absolute majority.[27]

With white dominance so precarious and distrust of slaves so intense, a white colonist need not have been unnaturally timid or afflicted with morbid imagination to experience doubts about the security of life and property and the stability of the American social order. No slave upheaval occurred in the mainland colonies on anything like the scale of racial disorders that enflamed the Caribbean islands, but white Americans learning of them shuddered at the perils faced by societies that resembled their own. Knowledge of slave rebellions reached American slaves as well. It could not have been otherwise, for slaves continued to be imported from the West Indies, where turbulence was endemic. In some instances, participants in the island revolts were sold to the mainland colonies rather than executed.[28]

The importation of a radical tradition was only one source of the planters' concern for the stability of their labor force. Most of the Africans adapted with remarkable facility to the new country, but instead of assuring subordination, acculturation was itself a source of instability. Acceptance by blacks of ideas and institutions common to white Americans threatened to undermine their slave status.

Almost as soon as they learned English, many slaves became Christian, a process encouraged by pious planters as well as by the Anglican church. However, this achievement sometimes increased discontent, for seventeenth-century Americans—both black and white—naïvely supposed that by accepting Christian baptism, slaves automatically became free. So alarmed were slaveholders at this notion that by the end of the seventeenth century, Maryland, New York, Virginia, the Carolinas, and New Jersey had passed laws

27. Gerald W. Mullin, *Flight and Rebellion*, 16; Jordan, *White over Black*, 102–103; Wood, *Black Majority*, 36; U.S. Bureau of the Census, *Historical Statistics*, II, 1168.
28. Wood, *Black Majority*, 221–24; Daniel Horsmanden, *The New York Conspiracy; or, A History of the Negro Plot, with the Journal of the Proceedings Against the Conspirators at New York in the Years 1741–42* . . . (2nd ed.; New York, 1810), 73, 128, 170, 209, 226.

assuring masters—and advising slaves—that conversion did not release slaves from bondage.[29]

Slaves, nonetheless, only reluctantly gave up the notion that baptism made them brothers in Christ with the white population and entitled them to freedom.[30] They persisted in believing they had been wronged—a belief Christian doctrine did nothing to dispel—and that justice rendered by a far-off authority someday would overrule their oppressors and set the grievance right. Thus, when Alexander Spotswood came to Virginia as royal governor, slaves imagined he brought with him the king's order "to sett all those free that were Christians" and to free those who afterward accepted baptism. When nothing of the sort happened, they held "unlawful meetings" and engaged in "loose discourses" aimed, some whites feared, at rebellion. Shortly afterward, in New Jersey, slaves expressed the same complaint: In defiance of the king's edict of emancipation their masters refused to free them.[31] Slavery, these incidents suggest, was felt by at least some slaves to be a temporary state and one that defied a just ordering of society. Somewhere there must exist a power sympathetic to their welfare. Whether they sought that ally in earthly or supernatural form, they never abandoned their search. It naturally followed that as long as the Old South lasted, southern whites would be preoccupied with preventing that ally from being found.

In becoming more like white Americans, blacks made slavery harder to maintain and to justify. At no time could colonial masters count on slaves to accept bondage willingly or to behave in slavelike manner. No one could be surprised when unbroken, unseasoned blacks fresh from Africa disobeyed their owners and tried to run away, but it was more troubling to find that some of the most acculturated slaves proved to be unruly, violent, and willful property. Even the ablest and most valued of them might stubbornly insist on exercising an independence of judgment that did not reconcile with the subordination demanded by both the evolving rigid concept of slavery and the developing paternalistic ideal of the planter. Landon Carter's slaves regularly behaved in ways he found exasperat-

29. Edmund S. Morgan, *American Slavery*, 331–32; Jordan, *White over Black*, 92–93, 180–87, 190–93.
30. White colonists considered this belief a major source of unrest; thus the evangelist George Whitefield was accused of being the "cause of all the disturbance" among New York slaves in 1741 (Horsmanden, *New York Conspiracy*, 360).
31. Aptheker, *American Negro Slave Revolts*, 79–80.

ing, but one of their most curious transgressions—from his point of view—was their practice of performing tasks in a better and more thorough fashion than he had intended.[32]

These problems were vexing and likely to make persons short on patience regret their dependence on slave labor, but even had planters not been surrounded by "outlandish" and intractable blacks restless under the yoke of slavery, they might still have had misgivings about the direction in which their society was moving. Certainly, many deplored the presence of allegedly inferior beings toward whom they felt prejudice, but more important, they were apprehensive about what the future might bring from them. The slave upheavals that periodically disrupted the West Indies gave ample cause for alarm, but the reflective found still other grounds for concern that had little to do with passing events.

Americans who read the Bible were familiar with the bondage of the Israelites and the fate that befell their Egyptian captors. Those whose education extended to the history of Greece and Rome knew that in antiquity, as in modern times, slaves constituted a major element in the population. They also could not forget that the ancient world had been wracked by slave rebellion. Americans understood that however harmless and compliant their bondsmen at any given moment appeared, they nonetheless *were* slaves. And slaves at all times and in all places had a historically defined part to play. Obedience and unrequited lifelong labor ideally characterized that role, but it might also be punctuated by rebellion. Greek and Roman writers had told the dreadful story.[33]

We know now that such fears were groundless, but white colonial Americans had no reason to be confident they would be spared the fate suffered by slaveholding peoples in the remote past. There was enough evidence of slave discontent on any plantation to suggest that the experience of antiquity might be repeated in colonial North America. And above all, mainland colonists could not ignore the revolts that punctuated the history of the West Indies. Comforting, but largely irrelevant, was the impression that the vast majority of slaves were faithful if sometimes exasperating workers, harmless and loyal to their owners. The fact remained that the explosive material long ago introduced into America constantly grew in quantity and thus in potential danger.

32. Jack P. Greene (ed.), *The Diary of Colonel Landon Carter of Sabine Hall, 1752–1778* (Charlottesville, Va., 1965), I, 369, 568.
33. For William Byrd's awareness of the classical precedent, see Jordan, *White over Black*, 111.

Another disturbing prospect must also have occurred to thoughtful persons. Slaves constituted not only a military threat but also a political one that might be manipulated to overthrow the social order. The Virginia slavemaster William Byrd in 1736 alluded to the danger as he looked back at the factional political and social strife that in earlier decades had afflicted his colony. Especially pertinent was the record of the great rebellion of 1676, when Nathaniel Bacon, at a desperate moment in his dispute with Governor William Berkeley, had sought new recruits by offering freedom to the servants and slaves owned by Berkeley's followers. Such events gained in pertinence when it was recalled that absolute unity among the white population in support of slavery had not been achieved. Poorer whites—or any other disaffected group—their racial pride not yet fully developed, might forge an alliance with slaves based on common interest.[34]

Yet all such threats were prospective only. These horrors had not happened in mainland America, and they might never happen. Of more pressing concern to officials and to the majority alike were immediate dangers looming from beyond colonial borders. English settlers lived alone in a perilous world. While internal factionalism threatened to shatter their still fragile societies, external enemies— Indians, Dutch, French, Spanish—might encroach upon their frontiers at any moment. If that happened, then enslaved blacks likely would respond in ways fatal to their English masters.[35]

In time of war, persons not fully incorporated into society and shut out from its benefits could not be counted on to come to its defense; they might even join its enemies. The English colonists' vulnerability in this respect was no secret. Thus, enterprising foreign foes could be expected to exploit the opportunity of making common cause with slaves, their natural allies living in the very heart of the English colonies. "Insurrections against us have been often attempted," said the council of South Carolina in 1734, "and would at any time prove fatal if the French should instigate them (the negroes) by artfully giving them an expectation of freedom."[36]

Eventually white southerners would conclude that the chief source of danger to their institutions was not to be found in the slave

34. Stephen Saunders Webb, *1676: The End of American Independence* (New York, 1984), 6–7, 66, 86, 110, 121, 123.

35. Ballagh, *History of Slavery*, 79.

36. Quoted in William A. Schaper, "Sectionalism and Representation in South Carolina," in Vol. I of American Historical Association, *Annual Report . . . for the Year 1900* (Washington, D.C., 1901), 310.

dissatisfation that was inevitably generated by bondage—in fact, they came to deny that such discontent existed—but rather in hostile outside forces seeking to bring them down by inciting racial discord. In the nineteenth century, northern abolitionists would be identified as the great external fomenters of slave rebellion. But during most of the colonial period, it was the Spanish located to the south of the English colonies who appeared to be the instigators of slave resistance.

The English had planted their settlements overseas in part as a challenge to Spanish dominion in the New World. In the West Indies and on the southeastern shores of North America—places where slavery was a key factor in economic growth—the persistent Anglo-Spanish rivalry found its focus. Spanish Florida was a long-standing irritant to the English settlers, a source of hope to slaves, and a drain on the resources of the South Carolinians, who for a long time were its nearest neighbors. The perilous circumstance in which southerners thus found themselves hampered whites in Georgia in their campaign for permission to acquire slaves, an effort James Oglethorpe suspected the Spanish of encouraging precisely because slavery would weaken the colony. One Captain Dempsy predicted in 1738 that if Georgians realized their ambition to become slaveholders, in two months time not fifty of five hundred slaves would remain, "for they would fly to the Spaniards, wherefore it would not be fit to allow of them until all Florida be in our hands for then they would have no place to retreat to."[37] It was a lesson all southerners eventually would learn: No slave region could be secure if a hostile state bordered it.

Two years later, a great slave rebellion having erupted in South Carolina, objection to introducing slavery in Georgia seemed still more compelling. In conversation with a Charleston merchant, Georgia's governor revealed his concern that "Negroes might cut the throats of our people and run to the Spaniards." Ignoring evidence offered by his own colony's recent experience, the South Carolinian answered that "if Negroes are well used, they never run." Such unjustified confidence was too much for the governor. He heatedly contradicted his guest: "Liberty, protection & lands which the Spaniards have proclaym'd to all Negroes that run to them, and the nearness of Augustine to Georgia would prove a great temptation . . . and . . . in Carolina some who were thought so faithfull as to be made Overseers of others . . . had made their escape to Augus-

37. Candler (ed.), *Colonial Records of Georgia*, V, 315.

tine, and headed rebellions, & this very lately." The taunt silenced the Charleston merchant, and he "reply'd nothing."[38]

For generations, Anglo-Americans regarded the Spanish fort at St. Augustine as an extreme peril to their own settlements. Slaves could not be kept ignorant of the significance to themselves of the Spanish presence. White South Carolinians often worried about the possibility of their slaves absconding to the refuge of Spanish Florida, and a distressingly large number did so. As early as the 1680s, a group of "diverse negro slaves" ran away from their South Carolina masters to St. Augustine. The exodus continued, an Underground Railroad toward the South. The Spanish lure extended even to New England, where in 1741 five slaves stole a boat in Boston harbor, planning, so it was said, to make their way to Florida.[39]

The danger appeared to increase, and anything might be believed. Slaves became pawns in the Anglo-Spanish struggle for empire. In 1733 an edict of the Spanish king promised freedom and protection to all fugitive slaves arriving in St. Augustine from the English colonies. When one such group eluded their pursuers and reached Florida, so the English ruefully noted, "They were received with great honour, one of them had a Commission given to him, and a Coat faced with Velvet." In 1737 reports reached Charleston that the Spanish planned a full-scale assault against their English neighbors, intended, in the words of South Carolina's lieutenant governor, to "unsettle the colony of Georgia, and to excite an Insurrection of the Negroes of this province." The governor alerted the colonial militia, and the General Assembly established patrols to keep the slaves in order.[40]

In February, 1739, rumors spread through Georgia that large numbers of South Carolina slaves were about to escape to Florida. Later in the year—on the very weekend when news reached Charleston that war between England and Spain finally had begun—the long-feared uprising materialized. Early Sunday morning, September 9, in St. Paul's Parish, near Charleston, the slaves began to gather. Reportedly of Angolan origin, the rebels also were said to speak Portuguese and to be Roman Catholic converts, factors which, if true, suggest possible exposure to revolutionary experience unknown to most North American slaves. Some twenty of them, led by

38. *Ibid.*, 476.

39. Wood, *Black Majority*, 51, 239, 305; Lorenzo J. Greene, *Negro in Colonial New England*, 150.

40. Wood, *Black Majority*, 305; Candler (ed.), *Colonial Records of Georgia*, Vol. XXIII, Pt. 2, pp. 232–33.

the slave Jemmy, started their march. At Stono Bridge they beheaded the keepers of a store—the means of death typically employed by warriors lacking firearms—and seized small arms and
powder. Then they made their way southward toward the road that
led to St. Augustine, gathering recruits and plundering, burning,
and killing as they went. A wholesale desertion to the Spanish was
under way. Late in the afternoon the rebels, then numbering fifty or
more, halted in a field near the ferry on the Edisto River. There they
danced and beat drums while they awaited the arrival of more recruits. By that time, alarm having been raised throughout the countryside, armed and mounted white men prepared to move against
the rebels. Against such odds the blacks' main force was scattered,
and the flight was stopped, though remnants of the band remained
unsubdued and at large for many weeks afterward. Nearby Indians
helped round up the survivors, thereby testifying to the colonists'
success in preventing an Indian-slave alliance.[41]

   Not surprisingly, in view of that close call, rumors of conspiracies
periodically swept the colony for years afterward, eventually making antebellum South Carolinians perhaps the most sensitive of all
Americans to the safety of their institutions, the most resentful of
criticism, and the most ready to resist external threats. They had
learned that as long as outside enemies existed and as long as slaves
had allies, not even the most repressive regime could make slavery
secure.

   English settlements farther north shared the southern concern for
slave loyalty, though their greater distance from Spanish Florida
made the danger less acute. In the late 1730s, informers in Maryland
exposed a purported conspiracy by blacks to seize control of that
colony. Officials charged Roman Catholics—allies of the Spanish
crown—with inciting slave unrest and masterminding the plot. Not
even New York escaped the Spanish fear. In the spring of 1741,
while the Anglo-Spanish war still raged and New Yorkers lived in
dread of attack by a Spanish fleet, about 150 slaves and 25 alleged
white accomplices were arrested and charged with setting fire to a
number of buildings in the city, the first stage, authorities suspected, of a full-scale uprising that would be coordinated with a

    41. Wood, *Black Majority*, 308–20; Aptheker, *American Negro Slave Revolts*,
187–89; Michael Mullin (ed.), *American Negro Slavery*, 84–86. Oral tradition of the
revolt evidently persisted among blacks in South Carolina, for in the 1930s a former
slave claimed to be descended from the revolt's leader. George P. Rawick *et al.* (eds.),
The American Slave: A Composite Autobiography: Supplement, Series I (Westport,
Conn., 1977), XI, 98–100.

Spanish invasion. The courts accepted the reality of the charges. In furious retribution thirteen slaves were burned alive, eighteen were hanged, and seventy were banished. Four of the accused whites, including one woman and a man reputed to be a Spanish priest, also were executed.[42]

A degree of hysteria no doubt accompanied these and similar incidents, and the extent of the conspiracies may have been exaggerated. Yet there could be no denying the presence of revolutionary material in American society, nor could one dismiss the possibility that an impulse from either within the colonies or outside them might at any moment produce upheaval. The dread of slave alliances with an outside power or with an internal faction persisted as long as slavery itself endured. It would have momentous consequences. It encouraged American expansionist policy and Indian removal, it generated fear of northern abolitionists, and it served finally as a principal ground for southern withdrawal from the Union.

The Spanish threat that loomed so large in the minds of Americans early in the eighteenth century gradually subsided as political conditions in Europe changed. Still, slavery in English America was to enjoy no respite from outside interference, for the French menace grew as the Spanish threat declined. Northern colonists had clashed with the French and their Indian allies on several previous occasions, but those faraway battles, most of them fought in Canada, had brought little disruption to the South. In 1754, however, war with France broke out again, with inescapable effect. This time the conflict started in the Ohio valley, so near to concentration of blacks that its impact on southern society was immediate and severe. Early the next year, a white servant named James Francis and the slave Toby ran away from a Maryland plantation, taking with them a gun, powder, and shot. Their master drew the appropriate conclusion: "It seems to be the Interest, at least of every Gentleman that has Slaves, to be active in the beginning of these Attempts, for whilst we have the French such near Neighbours, we shall not have the least Security in that kind of Property."[43]

In the summer of 1755, General Edward Braddock, commander-in-chief of the British army in America, marched his troops from headquarters in Maryland toward French-held Fort Duquesne at the

42. Thomas J. Davis, *A Rumor of Revolt: The "Great Negro Plot" in Colonial New York* (New York, 1985), *passim*. The trial records are in Horsmanden, *New York Conspiracy.*

43. Windley (comp.), *Runaway Slave Advertisements*, II, 23.

fork of the Ohio River, site of the present city of Pittsburgh. When his splendid force of regulars and Virginia militiamen neared the fort, they ran into an ambush of French and Indians sent to delay the British advance. In the ensuing battle, Braddock and many of his men were killed, leaving only a remnant of battered survivors to return in disarray to the security of Fort Cumberland in Maryland.[44]

Persons who had seen the proud army march off to engage the French now witnessed its humiliating retreat. The implication of that sudden change in fortune, whites suspected, would not be lost on the blacks who observed it. Although the maintenance of slavery rested ultimately on force, it depended in its day-to-day functioning on the slave's recognition and acceptance of the master's position of power. There could be little doubt that when the English and colonial forces experienced defeat, their own self-esteem suffered. How much more grievously, then, must they have been wounded in the eyes of blacks? Colonial officials believed they must expect dissident elements within their borders to take advantage of the changed balance of power resulting from military disaster.

In the wake of Braddock's defeat, officials in both Maryland and Virginia prepared to resist the expected slave uprising. Maryland's governor, Horatio Sharpe, wrote "Circularly Letters to have the Slave, convicts &c well observed & watched & [gave] Orders for the militia . . . to be prepared to quell it in case any Insurrection should be occasioned by the Stroke." In Virginia the possibility of slave unrest was judged grave enough even to affect deployment of the colony's military forces. The number of militiamen who could be spared to fight the French must be limited, said Governor Robert Dinwiddie, on account of the necessity to leave troops in each county "to protect it from the combinations of the negro slaves, who have been very audacious on the defeat on the Ohio." The governor explained why this was so. "Those poor creatures," he told the Earl of Halifax, "imagine the French will give them their freedom."[45]

Concern for the effect of war on the slaves even reached across the Atlantic Ocean to trouble the composure of Englishmen. As soon as

44. Stanley M. Pargellis, "Braddock's Defeat," *American Historical Review*, XLI (1936), 253–69.
45. Jeffrey R. Brackett, *The Negro in Maryland: A Study of the Institution of Slavery* (Baltimore, 1889), 94–95; *Archives of Maryland*, VI, 251; Robert Dinwiddie to the Earl of Halifax, July 23, 1755, in John C. Fitzpatrick (ed.), *The Writings of George Washington* (Washington, D.C., 1931–44), I, 151n. See also Dinwiddie to Charles Carter, July 18, 1755, in R. A. Brock (ed.), *Official Records of Robert Dinwiddie, Lt. Gov. of the Colony of Virginia, 1751–1758*. Virginia Historical Society Collection, n.s., III and IV (2 vols.; Richmond, 1883–84), II, 102.

word of Braddock's defeat arrived, the Reverend Benjamin Fawcett, a prominent dissenting clergyman, prepared *A Compassionate Address to the Christian Negroes in Virginia*, in which he appealed for the blacks' continued loyalty: "At one Time or other it will probably be suggested to you that the *French* will make better Masters than the English. But I beseech you to consider, that your Happiness as *Men* and *Christians* exceedingly depends upon your doing all in your Power to support the *British Government*."[46]

As it turned out, concern for slave allegiance was less necessary than Fawcett and the colonial governors supposed. Whatever potential for social disruption existed in the war with France was not to be realized. The French exerted little military effort in southern regions, and the extensive campaigns that finally brought their resounding defeat were fought in Europe, India, and Canada rather than in the American South. After 1763, English power in North America faced no serious challenge from any European rival; thus colonial slaveholders temporarily were freed from imminent outside danger.

But while revolts, conspiracies, and foreign threats had been distracting mid-eighteenth-century Americans, new ideas about human rights had begun to transform attitudes toward slavery itself and quietly to erode its legitimacy. The spread to America of Enlightenment theories shattered the ideological innocence of slaveholders. Experience already had taught that slavery was a fragile and unstable institution with unavoidable political implications. Now, in the 1750s, some began to suspect that it also was wrong. A new force had appeared whose effect could only be subversive. The right of individuals to autonomy, to independence, became a widely accepted principle as Americans developed arguments to justify their rejection of British control over the economic and political aspects of their lives. When these arguments gained currency as truth, it became hard to believe that independence and personal autonomy were rightfully the monopoly of a master race. White Americans questioned slavery as never before. The new ideas also changed the attitude of slaves toward their bondage. Even to the least reflective of them, freedom, however it was defined, always had been desirable. For some, it now became a right. And in the hope of enjoying that right, some slaves, like their white countrymen, would accept the use of force.

46. Benjamin Fawcett, *A Compassionate Address to the Christian Negroes in Virginia* (London, 1756), 17–18.

2

The Disruptive Power of Ideology

Creation of a natural-rights ideology forever altered perspectives toward slavery on the part of Americans, both slave and free. White colonists long had viewed the growing black population with misgiving. Now, with increasing concern for the welfare of individuals and for the proper limits of power, whites begain to doubt the justice of their actions and to question even the moral basis of their society. The effect of the new ideas on the slaves was as profound. Slaves, who always had found subjugation and forced labor painful to bear, now learned that bondage was wrong and that they, too, held claims on the newly discovered store of human rights. When resistance became linked to ideology, it took on new meaning and led to a prolonged period when slavery was subjected as never before to questioning, challenge, and disruption.[1]

Slaves saw the connection between their hopes for freedom and colonial claims for autonomy about as soon as their masters did. Parliament's passage of the Stamp Act in 1765 awakened white colonists' concern for their political rights, which they acted in concert to defend. Resistance to tyranny proved contagious. With little prompting from whites, slaves, too, learned the language of the Revolution and understood that their long-standing desire for liberty harmonized with the spirit of the new age. The sight of blacks parading through the streets of Charleston in January, 1766, and

1. David Brion Davis, *Problem of Slavery*, 488–89.

shouting "Liberty!" must have been unsettling indeed, for white South Carolinians surely knew that if such sentiments spread, if plantation slaves self-consciously linked the new ideology to their day-to-day resistance, the result would be disastrous.[2]

While colonial statesmen drafted petitions to King George III asserting American rights within the empire, slaves appealed to similar doctrine to justify their own claims to freedom. A few in New England did this by presenting formal petitions to governing bodies. "The divine spirit of freedom, seems to fire every *humane* heart on the continent," observed certain Boston slaves in 1773 as they beseeched the General Court for emancipation. A year later, other blacks in Massachusetts pursued the logic of equal rights in the rhetorical conclusion of an appeal to Governor Thomas Gage and the General Court "Shewing That your Petitioners apprehend we have in common with all other men a natural right to our freedoms."[3]

Blacks in the 1770s were as unwilling as other Americans to limit defense of personal liberty to the mere drafting of formal appeals to an abstract system of rights. A few of them tried to forge a political antislavery strategy that would implement liberal ideology. In the fall of 1774, when Boston appeared to be approaching a state of insurrection, slaves corresponded with the royal governor of Massachusetts. If Governor Gage gave them arms, they wrote, they would join the British in putting down the impending rebellion. Their price? Freedom.[4]

Although nothing apparently came from the proposal, its significance should not be underestimated. The overture to Gage was one of the earliest and most politically innovative efforts by slaves to participate in the revolutionary movement. Above all, it evidenced awareness of the part they might play in any struggle between competing groups of whites, a possibility that had long troubled southern slaveholders.

At almost the same time—November, 1774—rumors spread that slaves in Virginia also saw in the political turmoil a chance to better their condition. The planter and revolutionary war leader James

2. Pauline Maier, "The Charleston Mob and the Evolution of Popular Politics in Revolutionary South Carolina, 1765–1784," *Perspectives in American History*, IV (1970), 176; Henry Laurens to John Lewis Gervais, January 29, 1766, in Hamer *et al.* (eds.), *Papers of Henry Laurens*, V, 53–54.
3. Herbert Aptheker (ed.), *A Documentary History of the Negro People in the United States* (New York, 1951), I, 8.
4. Charles Francis Adams (ed.), *Letters of Mrs. Adams . . .* , (4th ed; Boston, 1848), 20. The difficulties inherent in such efforts are discussed in Phillips, *American Negro Slavery*, 117.

Madison outlined the contour of their expectation by noting that "if America and Britain should come to an hostile rupture, I am afraid an insurrection among the slaves may and will be promoted." Already, Madison believed, blacks had laid their plans: "In one of our Counties lately a few of those unhappy wretches met together and chose a leader who was to conduct them when the British Troops should arrive."[5] Again in the 1770s as in the days of the Spanish and French wars, an external enemy offered slaves an opportunity for freedom.

Planters soon discovered that political and social divisions among whitès at home also might encourage slave unrest. In May, 1775, a grand jury in Dorchester County, Maryland, found that disaffected whites had talked of forming coalitions with slaves to promote a revolt against the great landlords. Some months later, a county committee complained of the growing "insolence of the Negroes" and reported on efforts to disarm them. "The malicious and imprudent speeches of some among the lower classes of whites," the committee explained, "have induced them to believe, that their freedom depended on the success of the King's troops." White solidarity with respect to slavery and the subordination of blacks may have been stronger in the 1770s than a century earlier, but it still could not be taken for granted.[6]

In the developing imperial crisis, the slaveholders' vulnerability fascinated the makers of English policy as much as it alarmed white Americans. When overt warfare began to loom as a distinct possibility in 1773, a British observer assessed as minor the role the South would be able to play in the mounting resistance. "The Southern Provinces may be entirely thrown out of the Question," he explained, "not only as being thinly peopled & enervated. But from the great Majority of Negroes intermixed, which exposes them to immediate ruin whenever we detach a small Corps to support an insurrection." Early in 1775, while colonial leaders debated means to resist British policy, Governor Gage, from his post in Boston, offered advice and warning to South Carolinians: The colony should make sure it sent only moderates to the forthcoming Second Continental Congress, for "it is well known that if a Serious Opposition takes place, you can do but little—You have too much to take care

5. James Madison to William Bradford, November 27, 1774, in William T. Hutchinson and William M. E. Rachal (eds.), *The Papers of James Madison* (Chicago, 1962–), I, 129–30.

6. Ronald Hoffman, *A Spirit of Dissension: Economics, Politics, and the Revolution in Maryland* (Baltimore, 1973), 147–48.

and think of, but should you proceed [to] much greater lengths it may happen that your Rice and Indigo will be brought to market by negroes instead of white People." In Virginia, too, as the revolutionary movement proceeded, the slave population continued to evoke apprehension and was considered an obstacle to effective colonial resistance. James Madison, who a year earlier had expressed fear of slave revolt, now, in June, 1775, considered incitement of slaves by an enemy to be "the only part in which this Colony is vulnerable; & if we should be subdued, we shall fall like Achilles by the hand of one that knows the secret."[7]

Already rumors had reached America suggesting that the British planned to enlist both Indians and blacks to help subdue dissident white colonists. Lord Dunmore, the Virginian William Lee believed, had informed the ministry of an impending slave uprising. Slaves, Dunmore allegedly reported, looked favorably on the British, for they believed the king intended to free them. Whether Dunmore actually had so informed his government or not, it was true that he boasted to the Earl of Dartmouth of his ability to "collect from among the Indians, negroes and other persons" a force sufficiently large to quell the brewing white rebellion. In England such suggestions encouraged confidence in British ability to cope with colonial resistance. On his visit to the House of Commons in October, 1775, Ralph Izard, the South Carolina rice magnate, listened to a speaker who "was particularly rancorous against Americans and plumed himself much on the expedient of encouraging the Negroes in the Southern colonies, to drench themselves in the blood of their masters."[8]

American suspicions of British objectives account for the section of the Continental Congress' Declaration of the Causes and Necessity of Taking up Arms (July 5, 1775) that cites General Guy Carleton's effort to provoke the Canadians "and the Indians, to fall upon us," and adds, "We have but too much reason to apprehend that schemes have been found to excite domestick enemies against us." A year later, Thomas Jefferson immortalized that charge in the Decla-

7. Hugh F. Rankin, *The North Carolina Continentals* (Chapel Hill, N.C., 1971), 29; John R. Alden, "John Stuart Accuses William Bull," *William and Mary Quarterly*, 3rd ser., II (1945), 318; James Madison to William Bradford, June 19, 1775, in Hutchinson and Rachal (eds.), *Papers of James Madison*, I, 153.

8. Worthington C. Ford (ed.), *Letters of William Lee* (Brooklyn, 1891), I, 143, 144; Ralph Izard to a Friend in Bath, October 27, 1775, in *Correspondence of Mr. Ralph Izard of South Carolina, from the Year 1774 to 1804* (New York, 1844), 58, 125; Robert A. Olwell, "'Domestick Enemies': Slavery and Political Independence in South Carolina, May 1775–March 1776," *Journal of Southern History*, LV (1989), 21–48.

ration of Independence by including in his catalog of George III's crimes the allegation that "he has excited domestic insurrections amongst us." More than likely, their dread of British intentions toward Indians and slaves persuaded some otherwise reluctant southerners to support the Patriot cause.[9]

Despite British expectation and American concern, slaves proved less than unanimous in support of the British cause. When fighting finally broke out between rebellious colonists and imperial forces in 1775, blacks could be found on both sides of the conflict, as painfully divided in allegiance as were their white Patriot and Loyalist countrymen. For slaves, the British occupied an ambiguous position. As Americans, they were likely to fear the British as invaders and oppressors; as slaves, they welcomed them as liberators.

In numerous instances slaves aided, sometimes even served in, the Patriot armies and in other ways contributed significantly to the revolutionary war effort, for which service they customarily were rewarded with emancipation. But wherever British armies appeared in plantation country, nearby slaves were tempted to join them. Owners were distressed by such desertions, but they were not surprised. Scarcely twenty years earlier, the war with France had disclosed wavering slave loyalties, and memories of still earlier Spanish intrigue could not yet have totally faded. Now a new generation of white Americans prepared to confront a like situation.[10]

In April, 1775, after news of the battles of Lexington and Concord reached Maryland, "six gentlemen of respectable characters" called on Governor Robert Eden to report their "great apprehensions of some attempt being made by the servants or slaves for their liberty." With some show of reluctance, the governor agreed to supply "arms and ammunition to keep the servants and negroes in order." A few months later, two delegates from Georgia to the Continental Congress revealed a similar concern to John Adams: If the British should land on the coast of South Carolina and Georgia and proclaim freedom to the slaves, twenty thousand blacks would flee their owners and join the invaders. As a Massachusetts resident who never had lived among a large slave population, Adams had trouble crediting such a grim forecast. How could slaves located far in the

9. Sidney Kaplan, "The 'Domestic Insurrections' of the Declaration of Independence," *Journal of Negro History*, LXI (1976), 243–55; Olwell, "'Domestick Enemies,'" 21–48.

10. For the slaves' response to the Revolution, see Benjamin Quarles, *The Negro in the American Revolution* (Chapel Hill, N.C., 1961), and Gerald W. Mullin, *Flight and Rebellion*, 130–36.

interior learn about the British presence and coordinate their flight? "The negroes have a wonderful art of communicating intelligence among themselves," he was told. "It will run several hundred of miles in a week or fortnight." Still direr prophecies of black disaffection were voiced in those anxious days. Some whites in Georgia in July, 1776, confessed that they feared much worse at the hands of slaves than mere bloodless abandonment.[11]

Nowhere on the continent did slave flight occur on the scale predicted by the Georgians; still less did slaves rise up and slaughter their masters. But as white Americans had feared, ruinously large numbers of them chose to seek sanctuary within British lines. Defections along the South Carolina and Georgia coasts were especially large, with one owner reporting the loss of three dozen slaves in a single day. No place or person was exempt. When General Cornwallis left Thomas Jefferson's plantation after using it as headquarters for ten days, some twenty of Jefferson's slaves accompanied him. (Three of these returned, Jefferson remembered, only to die of "camp fever.") A report from a woman in North Carolina suggests the British attraction for slaves of every age and condition: All but two of those owned by her brother were "determined to go to them—even old Affra." And in South Carolina in May, 1779, with a British army operating nearby, Eliza Lucas Pinckney found she could no longer control the blacks at Belmont. If the slaves decided to join the enemy, she concluded, there was no use whatever in trying to stop them, "for they all do now as they please everywhere." The appearance of a force not amenable to planter control disrupted the slave-master relationship and sometimes destroyed it. A slaveowner in Charleston reported his discomfiting exchange with seventeen-year-old Quamerin shortly after British armies had won notable successes in the South: He "told me to my face, 'he can go when he pleases, and I can do nothing to him, nor shall I ever get a copper for him.' "[12]

11. Hoffman, *Spirit of Dissension*, 146–47; Charles Francis Adams (ed.), *The Works of John Adams, Second President of the United States, with a Life of the Author* (Boston, 1856), II, 428; *The Lee Papers . . . 1754–1800*, New-York Historical Society Collections, 1871–74 (4 vols.; New York, 1872–75), II, 115.

12. Julian P. Boyd (ed.), *The Papers of Thomas Jefferson* (Princeton, N.J., 1950–), VI, 224; XIII, 363–64; Jean Blair to Hannah Iredell, May 10, 1781, in Don Higginbotham (ed.), *The Papers of James Iredell* (Raleigh, N.C., 1976), II, 239; Mary Beth Norton, " 'What an Alarming Crisis Is This': Southern Women and the American Revolution," in Jeffrey J. Crow and Larry E. Tise (eds.), *The Southern Experience in the American Revolution* (Chapel Hill, N.C., 1978), 214; Windley (comp.), *Runaway Slave Advertisements*, III, 577; IV, 84, 85.

The mass desertion brought financial disaster to some planters, but not to be omitted in tallying cost was the anguish owners felt when they saw close associates whom they had imagined to be grateful and loyal abscond to the enemy. Surely it was more than the red ink in their ledgers that caused the sleep of the great Virginia planter Landon Carter and his daughter Judy to be troubled night after night by dreams of their lost slaves. The blow to the assumptions of paternalism was in itself a painful incident of war.[13]

The British would have been unenterprising indeed had they not capitalized on the military advantage offered them by the slaves, much as the Spanish had done a generation earlier. In November, 1775, Lord Dunmore, the last royal governor of Virginia, proclaimed freedom to all adult males who would flee their masters and come under his protection. The exact number who responded—mostly from the Chesapeake Bay area—remains a matter of dispute, but whatever its magnitude, the loss was large enough to bring their owners all the distress the British intended, and to demonstrate again that the slave population offered an enemy easy means to derange the American society and economy.[14]

But that was not the whole of it. Slavery also weakened the Patriots' war effort by requiring diversion of troops and supplies to protect the home front. In April, 1776, Charles Lee, writing from Williamsburg, warned of an imminent "piratical war" and slave insurrection. He called upon northern states to dispatch immediate military aid to Virginia, not to drive back the British but to maintain domestic order. Lee explained why this must be done: "An infinite number of slaves are to be watched over." Shortly afterward, officials in Maryland found that men on the Eastern Shore "reluctantly leave their own neighborhoods unhappily full of Negroes who might, it is likely, on any misfortune to our militia become very dangerous." In September, 1777, the Patriot lawyer William Pace offered advice: Maryland's forces on the Eastern Shore should remain there in order to control both the white Loyalists and the slaves who came down from the interior hoping to make contact with the British. In Hartford County, too, the militia was employed not to fight the British but "to prevent the Negroes, servants, and disaffected peoples from going to the enemy." Again as in earlier times slaves

13. Jack P. Greene (ed.), *Diary of Colonel Landon Carter*, II, 1064.

14. Benjamin Quarles, "Lord Dunmore as Liberator," *William and Mary Quarterly*, 3rd ser., XV (1958), 494–507.

joined with marginal persons in recognition of a common interest that was at odds with the dominant part of society.[15]

The emergency seemed as great in states farther south. In February, 1777, General Robert Howe urged the president of Congress to station a large body of troops in South Carolina expressly to counteract the slaves' temptation to join the British. In 1778, when the British increased their influence on slaves by moving their military operations to the South, the Georgia legislature ordered one-third of the troops in each county to remain where they were as a permanent slave patrol. In March of the next year, a committee of the Continental Congress found that South Carolina was "unable to make any effectual efforts with militia, by reason of the great proportion of citizens necessary to remain at home to prevent insurrections among the negroes, and to prevent the desertion of them to the enemy." The problem persisted. In early 1782 the South Carolina legislature required each militia company in the state to organize a six-man patrol whose sole duty would be to maintain order on the plantations.[16]

Even though insurrection in the bloody and destructive form white Americans most dreaded failed to materialize during the war, the close watch they placed on slaves did not prevent a species of revolt. When slaves joined the British forces, served as spies and informers, bore arms, and fought the Americans, as some did, they were in effect engaged in armed rebellion against their former masters. One example of such activity, which understandably horrified slaveholders, also illustrates the danger of generalizing about slave response to the conflict. In the winter of 1781 a unit of some 150 white and black soldiers swept into the interior of South Carolina. Only "by the intervention of their own slaves," the governor was told, were some whites saved.[17]

In time of war, with the balance of power among whites drastically changed, slaves simply could not be controlled, and the loyalty of none could be taken for granted. White Virginians later suspected

15. Charles Lee to Robert Morris, April 16, 1776, in *Lee Papers*, I, 425–26; Hoffman, *Spirit of Dissension*, 185, 204.

16. Quarles, *Negro in the Revolution*, 125–26; Worthington C. Ford *et al.* (eds.), *Journals of the Continental Congress, 1774–1789* (Washington, D.C., 1904–37), XIII, 386.

17. Judge Burk to Governor Guerard, December 14, 1785, in Governors' Message to the Senate, January 24, 1786, in Governors' Messages, 1791–1800, South Carolina Department of Archives and History, Columbia.

that even some who from outward appearance remained faithful to their masters secretly had aided the British by committing acts of sabotage. Some of those who fled to the British and then returned were thought to be principals in later conspiracies to revolt.[18] Much of the difficulty Americans experienced in these respects resulted from their loss of mastery in the eyes of slaves. Although slavery ultimately rested on brute force, it also depended to large degree on the slaves' acceptance of its legitimacy, on their acknowledgement of the "right"—even though extorted by coercion—of the whites to rule. But such compliance was fragile. Evidence that the owners' power had declined could destroy the institution of slavery by crumbling its foundation of legitimacy.

The British were able to land on the coast at almost any point they chose and to occupy almost any territory. White Americans thus appeared weak, their soil at the mercy of an invader. Some planters who had closely identified themselves with the Patriot cause—Thomas Jefferson among them—fled at the approach of the British. Others, even though less tainted in British eyes, tried to save themselves and their slave property by avoiding the routes armies were likely to take. Such behavior severely tested slave faithfulness. Through inability to hurl back the invader, planters lost their commanding air, and slaves responded accordingly. The import of the phenomenon was not lost on American strategists. Charles Lee, for one, warned of the stunning effect the fall of Charleston would have on slavery throughout the South Carolina low country. The city must be defended, he explained, not only for its own sake but because its loss would signal to slaves the impotence of their masters. When the city finally was taken, reports of slave flight by owners in the region proved the prediction accurate.[19]

As the war progressed and British armies campaigned through the southern counties of Virginia, perhaps as many as 30,000 slaves were lost to their owners. The story was repeated elsewhere. One estimate places the number of blacks throughout the colonies who

18. John Clarke to James Monroe, June 12, 1801, in William Palmer, Sherwin McRae, and H. W. Flournoy (eds.), *Calendar of Virginia State Papers and Other Manuscripts, 1652–1869, Preserved at the Capitol in Richmond* (Richmond, 1875–93), IX, 201; John B. Scott to James Monroe, April 22, 1802, in Executive Papers, Virginia State Library, Richmond.

19. Charles Lee to Richard Henry Lee, April 5, 1776, in *Lee Papers*, I, 379, 410; Windley (comp.), *Runaway Slave Advertisements*, III, 584.

made good their escape at 100,000.[20] The statistic, even if accurate, is not entirely satisfactory, however; for by no means can all slaves who fell into British hands be presumed to have acted voluntarily or to have accepted willingly the British disposition of them. An undetermined number of those captured were sold elsewhere as booty of war. The British, slaves learned, in some instances proved as careless of their welfare and desires as their American masters. In early July, 1776, Landon Carter reported, the British commander in Virginia sent a load of blacks "to one of the Islands which so alarmed the rest that the County of Gloster [*sic*] was disturbed by their howlings."[21] It does not seem likely that the 2,500 whom the British took from Charleston to Jamaica or the 2,000 sent to East Florida, whether sold as slaves or not, found their circumstance significantly bettered by the change. Despite such perfidy, the opportunity offered by the British presence was tempting to slaves, and nothing owners did could prevent the venturesome from taking advantage of it. The slaves' response to warfare strikingly demonstrated both southern vulnerability and their own urge to escape from bondage.

The fate of the many thousands of blacks who cast their lot with the British no doubt varied greatly and in most cases cannot be determined. But the fortunes of some are matters of record. When the Tories fled Boston after the Battle of Bunker Hill, their own slaves and some others accompanied them to Canada. Probably a few of these eventually found themselves in England; later, following independence, some who had remained in Canada, or their descendants, returned to Boston to swell that city's already sizable free-black community. An uncertain number of absconding southern blacks also found a haven in the northern states.[22]

Some blacks voluntarily returned to their owners after a season with the British, but sojourn in the British camps was likely to strengthen the self-confidence that had inspired flight in the first

20. Herbert Aptheker, *The American Revolution, 1763–1783* (New York, 1980), 218. Quarles, *Negro in the Revolution*, p. 172, tallies some 19,000 slaves evacuated with the British.

21. Quarles, *Negro in the Revolution*, 167; Jack P. Greene (ed.), *Diary of Colonel Landon Carter*, II, 1056. The sufferings of slaves who escaped to the British are detailed in Sylvia R. Frey, "Between Slavery and Freedom: Virginia Blacks in the American Revolution," *Journal of Southern History*, XLIX (1983), 388–97.

22. James Oliver Horton and Lois E. Horton, *Black Bostonians: Family Life and Community Struggle in the Antebellum North* (New York, 1979), viii, 137n.

place. Probably the transformation that his master noted in Stephen was not unique: "He affects to be free . . . he is very specious and knowing, having been some time with the British." Others, finding themselves emancipated by their flight, left the British camps and managed to blend into the growing free-black population that flourished in such cities as Savannah, Charleston, and Richmond. The experience of freedom predictably led to the resolve never to be enslaved again. Nanny, who ran to the British in May, 1779, and at the end of the war accompanied them to St. Augustine, managed to escape from her master's agent while he was trying to bring her back to South Carolina. Stepney, who went with the British forces from South Carolina to Virginia, was somehow returned to his owner, only to flee again. A family of five slaves left James Island with the British in 1779. After being in Savannah for a while, they disappeared from white society altogether, probably retreating into Indian country.[23]

To the chagrin of patriotic slaveholders, many blacks chose to remain with the British after military victory at Yorktown confirmed independence. Others left with the French. Perhaps as many as ten thousand blacks crowded aboard British ships as they sailed from Savannah and Charleston in 1782. When British armies withdrew from Virginia after their defeat at Yorktown in October, 1781, three thousand former slaves left with them. With their anguished owners vainly protesting and seeking intercession from every available authority, the blacks were taken first to New York, and then, in violation of the Treaty of Paris, to Halifax, where they were lost to their Patriot masters forever.[24]

The revolutionary experience gave white Americans new reason to understand that the loyalty and docility of the slave population could not be taken for granted. "In a time of war, slaves rendered a country more vulnerable," was the painfully learned lesson William C. Davies of North Carolina conveyed to his countrymen in 1788. While the Patriot soldier surely knew that in regions distant from British armies the great majority of slaves remained with their owners throughout the war and that impressive numbers supported the American cause even to the extent of serving in the Continental

---

23. Windley (comp.), *Runaway Slave Advertisements*, III, 380, 408, 712, 713, 718, 735, 740; IV, 104–105.
24. Their saga is told in James W. St. G. Walker, *The Black Loyalists: The Search for a Promised Land in Nova Scotia and Sierra Leone, 1783–1870* (London, 1975), 1–18 and *passim*.

armies, this knowledge inspired little confidence for the future. As early as 1785, Charles Thomson, secretary of the Continental Congress, remarked to Jefferson that he feared America's slaves more than Algerine pirates or potential European foes. If slavery were not ended by "religion, reason and philosophy," he predicted, it would someday end "by blood."[25] The commonly held opinion that eventually a slave-inspired disaster was inevitably going to happen was a powerful incentive for the several gradual emancipation schemes put forward following the Revolution, including that of Jefferson. In a hostile world, American national security would be imperiled by its slave population. And no slaveholder, as events soon proved, could be certain that any quarter, even within his own country, was immune to subversion.

British wartime policies designed to disrupt slavery were predictable. Such timeworn tactics were regarded as an unavoidable, if odious, technique of war. Far more startling to southern slaveholders and ominous for their future security was an incident occurring in Massachusetts during the Revolution. When some thirty-four slaves from South Carolina were carried off by the British and then recaptured by two Massachusetts vessels, the *Hazard* and the *Tyrannicide*, the Massachusetts Supreme Court refused to order them returned to their owners and eventually set them free. The judges' decision infuriated South Carolina's Governor Benjamin Guerard: "No act of British Tyranny could exceed the encouraging the negroes . . . to desert their owners to be emancipated." The decision, added the governor, "seems arbitrary and domination [*sic*]." He found in religious differences between North and South an explanation for the court's perverse judgment. But understanding did not bring forgiveness: "The liberation of our negroes disclosed a specimen of Puritanism I should not have expected from gentlemen of my Profession."[26]

The incident bore alarming implications for white southerners. To have defeated one enemy, it appeared, was only to have acquired another. The British were unlikely soon to renew their interference with American slaves, the Spanish menace had lessened, the French were gone. But what if revolutionary and religious ideology, rein-

25. Jonathan Elliot (ed.), *The Debates in the Several State Conventions, on the Adoption of the Federal Constitution* . . . (Philadelphia, 1907), V, 31; Charles Thomson to Thomas Jefferson, November 2, 1785, in Boyd (ed.), *Papers of Thomas Jefferson*, IX, 9.

26. Benjamin Guerard to John Hancock, October 6, 1782, in George Henry Moore, *Notes on the History of Slavery in Massachusetts* (New York, 1866), 173.

forced by sectional political ambition, should someday lead northerners to assume the liberating role recently played by European
powers? The prospect for the South in that event would be ominous
indeed.

Some leading southerners, aware that in parts of the North attitudes toward slavery conflicted with slaveholding interests, felt uneasy at the prospect of creating a stronger union in 1787. Northern
and southern economic interests had already clashed in the Continental Congress. Some individuals, still relishing their shedding of
British restrictions, wished to remain free to carry out private pursuits without interference by others through the instrumentality of
the state. On that account they found the decentralized government
created by the Articles of Confederation ideal and might be expected
to resist proposals to expand the power and efficiency of government. Yet in the 1780s, despite such sentiment, the need for a more
effective union to replace the Confederation was widely acknowledged by public-spirited Americans of all sections.

Thus Southerners, including great slaveholders, joined in ini-
tiating the movement that led to the Constitutional Convention in
Philadelphia in 1787. But even while some of them were conceding
the necessity for stronger government, others opposed the new
political creation, which under hostile leadership might disregard
southern interests and use its augmented power to doom their peculiar institution.

A taste of things to come was provided in 1787 when representatives from all parts of the country met in deliberation at Philadelphia, where the issue of slavery, in the words of Abraham Baldwin,
delegate from Georgia, caused the Constitutional Convention "pain
and difficulty." Its power to irritate, slaveholders must have realized, would be no less in the new union. Delegates to the convention
managed to compromise their large differences on slavery, but they
could not hide them. They accepted its existence, agreed to count
three-fifths of the slaves for both apportioning representation in
Congress and levying direct taxes, authorized a fugitive slave law,
prohibited restriction on importation of slaves for twenty years, and
gave the new government power to aid in putting down insurrections. Yet to the slaveholders' dismay, some northerners insisted on
viewing the new constitution as an antislavery document.[27]

27. *Annals of Congress*, 1st Cong., 2nd Sess., 1200; Staughton Lynd, *Class Conflict,
Slavery, and the United States Constitution* (Indianapolis, 1967), 153–54.

Apprehension that an antislavery majority eventually would control the new government and turn its power against the South explained some of the widespread reluctance among southerners to ratify the Constitution. Their fears were not without foundation. That slavery violated human rights was no longer a novel or eccentric opinion, even in the South. In a national government, such antislavery sentiment would find a larger and more effective sphere of influence than ever would have been available under the decentralized Confederation. Creation of a national forum promised to intensify the clash of sectional interests and give opponents of slavery enhanced opportunity for expression. There, in a strong Congress, antislavery sentiment and sectional interest might someday combine to ruin the slaveholding class.

In northern states, some Federalists assured voters that in forming the new government the Founding Fathers had arranged for the eventual end of slavery. Or, as William Dawes explained to the Massachusetts ratifying convention, "We may say, that although slavery is not smitten by an apoplexy, yet it has received a mortal wound, and will die of a consumption." James Wilson of Pennsylvania tried to be less figurative. By making possible the end of the slave trade in 1808, he told voters, the Constitution had laid "the foundation for banishing slavery out of the country." It was not simply, as some believed, that by halting slave importation Congress would unleash ill-defined forces that eventually would destroy slavery; instead, Wilson promised direct antislavery action: "Yet the lapse of a few years, and Congress will have power to exterminate slavery from within our borders."[28]

Suspicion that this was exactly what some northern interests intended gave southern delegates pause as they prepared to hold the ratifying conventions that would determine whether they joined the new union or went their separate ways. Southern proponents of ratification found it necessary to overcome grave misgivings. Charles Cotesworth Pinckney acknowledged that the "religious and political prejudices of the Eastern and Middle States" turned the people of those sections against southern institutions; but, he assured South Carolinians, the disagreeable northern antipathies could have little practical significance. The powers of Congress were strictly limited to those enumerated in the Constitution. Congress could not intervene in southern local affairs or interfere

28. Elliot (ed.), *Debates*, II, 41, 452, 484.

with local institutions. Further, observed Pinckney, the new government offered slaveholders a most desirable advantage. The Constitution guaranteed the return of fugitive slaves, an obligation the
Confederation had neglected to place on its members. With that provision, a grievance suffered for a century and a half—the escape of
blacks to areas beyond their owners' reach—now promised to be
remedied.[29]

But not all were convinced. Patrick Henry, steadfast against
ratification, felt nearly as confident as did antislavery northerners
that Congress someday, somehow, would find in the new document
power to end slavery. It would be led to such action, Henry predicted, by "urbanity" and, he added—perhaps recalling the difficulties slavery caused the South during the Revolution—by "the necessity of national defence."[30]

James Madison, a leading participant in the Philadelphia convention, discounted Henry's forecast. Just as Pinckney argued in South
Carolina, Madison assured doubters in Virginia that the powers of
Congress were confined solely to those specified in the document.
Thus, he promised, Congress never could trespass on slavery. Despite reassurance from such prestigious figures, skeptics still found
grounds for questioning the efficacy of a mere document to forestall
the will of a politically and religiously aroused North. "I apprehend
it means to bring forward manumission," insisted James Galloway
of North Carolina. Though his colleague James Iredell worked hard
to persuade him of his mistake, Galloway still could not bring himself to vote for ratification.[31]

Such persistent doubters failed to dissuade the southern pro-
union majority. Southern apprehensions, though strong, were counteracted by the still more compelling reasons for accepting the new
government. While most of the proratification arguments bore no
direct relation to slavery, one of the most persuasive clearly did. The
new, stronger union, southern advocates argued, provided an invaluable assurance—it would help suppress slave rebellions. "Our
negroes are numerous, and are daily becoming more so," observed
Governor Edmund Randolph at the ratifying convention in Virginia. "When I reflect on their comparative number, and comparative condition, I am the more persuaded of the great fitness of becoming more formidable than ever."[32]

29. *Ibid.*, IV, 285, 286. See also James Madison's comments, *ibid.*, III, 453.
30. *Ibid.*, III, 590. See also p. 623. George Mason argued similarly, *ibid.*, III, 270.
31. *Ibid.*, III, 621–22; IV, 101–102.
32. *Ibid.*, III, 192.

Madison agreed with Randolph's assessment of both the danger and the means of security: "The Southern States are, from their situation and circumstances, most interested in giving the national government the power of protecting its members." George Nicholas, who had little patience with indirection, spelled out for Virginians the exact meaning of Madison's observation: The new Constitution provided "an additional securing" against slave insurrections, "for, besides the power in the state governments to use their militia; it will be the duty of the general government to aid them with the strength of the Union when called for." The Confederation, as Nicholas knew, had been charged with no such obligation, and during the Revolution, southern states had been forced somewhat ignominiously to appeal to the North for military aid. Slaveowners long would value the Union, despite its irritating aspects, partly because they believed it provided them with an essential safeguard. The national government would preserve the peace in South Carolina, a Charleston newspaper assured its readers following revelation of Denmark Vesey's conspiracy in 1822: "It was established expressly to ensure domestic tranquility and suppress insurrection."[33]

The southerners' deeply rooted misgivings about the new government were effectively countered in the 1790s, if not quite eliminated, by the unmistakable advantages a stronger union offered. Southerners also believed that they would dominate the new government.[34] Slavery as a local institution presumably lay forever beyond national jurisdiction. Yielding to that benign interpretation, the slaveholding states joined in ratifying the Constitution. In so doing, however, southern leaders committed themselves to constant vigilance lest the new government, at the bidding of antisouthern or antislavery groups, overstep its bounds, usurp power, and interfere in matters properly outside its province. From the day the new government became operative, slaveholders assumed the role of perpetual guardians of state sovereignty.

Though fearful of centralized power, slaveholders could take comfort in the knowledge that however menacing to some southern interests the newly operative government potentially might be, it still offered protection against slave insurrection. Almost any sacrifice would be worth making in order to guard against that horror.

Such an emergency soon loomed. When the French Revolution of 1789 threw Europe into tumult, the United States possessed no coin

33. *Ibid.*, 415, 427; Charleston *City Gazette and Daily Advertiser*, September 27, 1822.
34. Lynd, *Class Conflict*, 202–203.

with which to purchase certain exemption. Revolutions, it became clear, were not to be relegated to the heroic past, nor would future upheavals always be as limited in social impact as the war for American independence had been. No sooner did evidence for these disquieting generalizations appear in Europe than events in the French colony of Saint-Domingue taught a third shattering truth: Revolution could not be held as a monopoly in the hands of whites. The expanding revolutionary impulse had led to race war on an island near the United States, and there was no assurance that the upheaval could be stopped at the American shore. Thus, in the 1790s, southerners faced special strains as the possibility grew that slavery would be subverted either by blacks themselves or by white dissidents mobilizing nonslaveholders against it.

3

Another Kind of Revolution

In 1788, in a mood of enthusiastic patriotism, Charles Cotesworth Pinckney contrasted for his fellow South Carolinians the fortunate condition of postrevolutionary America with the Old World's decadence. "To the liberal and enlightened mind," said Pinckney, most of Europe afforded "a melancholy picture of the depravity of human nature, and of the total subversion of . . . rights." But happier days lay ahead, because young America had put ancient Europe to school. According to Pinckney, the people of Ireland, the Netherlands, and France recently had added to their freedoms under America's tutelage, and he hoped the process would continue: "Let it be our prayer that the effects of the revolution may never cease until they have unshackled all the nations that have firmness to resist the fetters of despotism."[1]

But how, from what, and by whom would nations be freed? Pinckney, a member of South Carolina's planter class, could not have foreseen the consequences of his answered prayer. His self-congratulatory words were spoken before mobs in Paris stormed the Bastille, before the rise of the Jacobins, before the Terror, and—to him most disconcerting of all—before blacks in the French colony of Saint-Domingue, echoing slogans of revolutionary Europe, overthrew and slaughtered their white masters.

1. Elliot (ed.), *Debates*, IV, 319–20.

In 1791, revolution convulsed Saint-Domingue. There, in the Atlantic Ocean southeast of the United States, free mulattoes, black
slaves, white settlers, and French, English, and Spanish armies fell
into a desperate, confused struggle that drenched the island with
blood. Led first by Toussaint L'Ouverture and then by Jean-Jacques
Dessalines, the once-captive blacks gained the upper hand. They defeated all European efforts to subdue them and eventually established their own dominion. The creation of the Republic of Haiti in
1804 as the second independent nation in the Western Hemisphere
was a triumph of revolutionary theory and of black military prowess. As such, few white Americans and almost no white southerners
could welcome the event. President Jefferson observed to the French
chargé d'affaires in Washington that the example of Haiti threatened white rule in every slaveholding state.[2]

Once again, as in the days of the Spanish menace a half century
earlier, the large American slave population (approximately one out
of every five Americans in 1800 was black) sharpened southerners'
awareness of their vulnerability to external threats. Slavery thus far
had managed to survive war and the challenge of liberating ideology, but those stresses had left the institution temporarily weakened in parts of the South and had even brought emancipation to
much of the North. Now the interests of American slaveholders were
threatened as never before by a manifestation of the French Revolution occurring in the West Indies dangerously close to American
shores.

The close trade relations Americans enjoyed with Saint-Domingue
allowed them easily to follow its turbulent affairs, and when, in the
summer of 1793, a French fleet brought thousands of refugees to
southern coastal cities, their tales of horror gave immediacy to the
awful impact of black revolt. With some of them came ostensibly
still-loyal household slaves whom white southerners suspected of
being contaminated with revolutionary intent.[3]

The uprising appalled South Carolinians in particular. The situation of planters in the low country and those in Saint-Domingue
were too similar for Carolinians to regard revolt in the island with
anything but alarm. White officials there, recognizing the bonds of

2. Alexander De Conde, *This Affair of Louisiana* (New York, 1976), 101. Detailed
accounts of the revolt are in T. Lothrop Stoddard, *The French Revolution in San Domingo* (Boston, 1914), and C. L. R. James, *The Black Jacobins: Toussaint L'Ouverture
and the San Domingo Revolution* (Rev. ed.; New York, 1963).
3. Frances S. Childs, *French Refugee Life in the United States, 1790–1800: An
American Chapter of the French Revolution* (Baltimore, 1940), *passim*.

sympathy that united the two societies, dispatched anguished appeals for aid: "This rich country will soon be nothing more than a heap of ashes" was the message sent Governor Charles Pinckney by the island assembly in its plea for troops, ammunition, and provisions. Soon afterward, an emissary appeared before the South Carolina legislature to plead the slaveowners' cause. The lawmakers, readily conceding their interest in suppressing the rebellious blacks, eventually authorized up to three thousand pounds to aid the French.[4]

The slaveowners' concern was not the preoccupation of a moment. The shock of successful black rebellion never ceased reverberating through the antebellum South. For decades it called forth racial fears and insecurities. As long as slavery existed, the island's name symbolized how extensive racial disorder might be and served to rally whites to defense of their race and institutions.[5]

The United States government early displayed official concern for the insurrection, with George Washington's administration advancing money to aid whites fleeing the island. As partial payment of the revolutionary war debt owed France, the French minister, Jean Baptiste de Ternant, also received American funds to help supply French military forces in Saint-Domingue. However, these tokens did little to deflect the course of the insurrection. The United States for the most part refrained from interfering in the confused internal affairs of the French colony.[6]

A more aggressive antirevolutionary policy might have won public support, but it could have done so only by overriding opposition from those white Americans who, to the distress of slaveowners, continued to defend the right of the oppressed, whatever their color, to resist tyranny. Echoes of the American Revolution sounded through public discussion of the issue. "Is not their cause as just as ours?" asked Abraham Bishop of Connecticut, a question certain

4. Colonial Assembly of Saint-Domingue to Governor of South Carolina, August 26, 1791, in Enclosures, Governor's Message to the House, December 5, 1791, in Governors' Messages, 1791–1800, South Carolina Department of Archives and History; George Terry, "A Study of the Impact of the French Revolution and the Insurrection in Saint-Domingue upon South Carolina, 1790–1805" (M.A. thesis, University of South Carolina, 1975), 42–43.

5. Monroe Fordham, "Nineteenth-Century Black Thought in the United States: Some Influences of the Santo Domingan Revolution," *Journal of Black Studies*, VI (1975), 115–26; Alfred N. Hunt, *Haiti's Influence on Antebellum America. Slumbering Volcano in the Caribbean* (Baton Rouge, 1988).

6. Harry Ammon, *The Gênet Mission* (New York, 1973), 21; Rayford W. Logan, *The Diplomatic Relations of the United States with Haiti, 1776–1891* (Chapel Hill, N.C., 1941), 100–107, 179, 301–303.

to disconcert any planter who heard it. In 1791, when the Pennsylvania legislature debated supplying aid to the besieged whites, a member pointed out the inconsistency "on the part of a free nation to take measures against a people who had availed themselves of the only means they had to throw off the yoke of the most atrocious slavery."[7]

To the consternation of southerners, exploits of the black rebels found still more outspoken admirers. The Connecticut Federalist Theodore Dwight saw in the fate that had overtaken the island planters "a dispensation of Providence which Humanity must applaud." Jabez Bowen, Jr., a Rhode Island native then living in Georgia, risked a public declaration of sympathy for "the brave sons of nature," and in Kentucky, David Rice, a Presbyterian preacher and politician, defied the values of the slave society developing around him by praising the black rebels as "brave sons of Africa . . . sacrificing their lives on the altar of liberty." The cleavage in American opinion and the deep hostility to slavery revealed by such statements could only compound southern insecurities.[8]

Antislavery radicals, sharing southern apprehension that American slaves might at any moment follow the Saint-Dominguan example, speculated on their own course of action should this happen. When slaveholders faced servile rebellion, predicted Thomas Branagan of Philadelphia, God would not come to the aid of the oppressors, nor, he suggested, should God-fearing men. Dwight, too, thought no help would be forthcoming from earthly sources: "Surely, no friend to freedom and justice will dare to lend them his aid." The Reverend Charles Nisbet, British-born principal of Dickinson College in Pennsylvania, welcomed the prospect of an American slave insurrection for its political value. "A Negro war, which may probably break out soon," he wrote, was just what was needed to further the antislavery cause. A rebellion would convince Americans that their own survival required emancipation. In 1796, in an early statement of the Higher Law doctrine, a northern abolitionist

7. [Abraham Bishop], "Rights of Black Men," *American Museum*, XII (1792), 299; Jean de Ternant to Armand de Montmorin, September 30, 1791, in Frederick Jackson Turner (ed.), *Correspondence of the French Ministers to the United States, 1791–1797*, Vol. II of American Historical Association, *Annual Report . . . for the Year 1903* (Washington, D.C., 1904), 53.

8. Timothy Dwight, *An Oration Spoken Before the Connecticut Society for the Promotion of Freedom and the Relief of Persons Unlawfully Holden in Bondage* (Hartford, 1794), 19; Walter G. Charlton, "A Judge and a Grand Jury," in *Papers of the 31st Annual Session of the Georgia Bar Association . . . 1914* (Macon, Ga., 1914), 210; David Rice, *Slavery Inconsistent with Justice and Good Policy . . .* (Philadelphia, 1792), 9.

declared that if slaves rose against their masters, the "political claims" slaveholders had upon the North would "be opposed by the claims and the remonstrances of conscience."[9]

Such sentiments understandably both offended and alarmed white southerners. Only a few years earlier, they had been persuaded to support the new Union, in part because of its promise to assist in suppressing slave revolts. Now they had reason to doubt that the promise would be fulfilled. If they felt themselves misled, even cheated, who could be surprised?

Northern expressions of sympathy for the black Saint-Dominguans—they were actually taunts addressed to slaveholders—supplied an additional source of anxiety for the safety of southern institutions. These scattered antislavery, antisouthern statements made by private citizens in unofficial capacities were rendered still more alarming by attacks mounted during the same years in the United States Congress. As southern opponents of the Constitution had warned might happen, antislavery voices made themselves heard in the national government almost from its inception. Persons hostile to the interests of slaveholders attempted to use federal power against them. In particular, those veterans of antislavery thought and action, the Quakers, repeatedly petitioned Congress to end the slave trade. The resulting debates produced strong antislavery statements from northern legislators and correspondingly strong defenses from southerners.[10]

Congressmen from Virginia, where doubts about slavery were common, remained for the most part silent while they listened to northern colleagues assail their institutions. Not so the Georgians and South Carolinians. Untroubled by conscience, representatives from the Deep South had determined to acknowledge their interests without apology and to defend them. They responded in angry debate by condemning all antislavery petitions and by entering motions aimed at silencing any discussion of slavery. Many reasons were offered to justify such policy, but preeminent was the charge that public controversy would reach the ears of slaves. Knowledge that they had white partisans and potential allies would undermine the slave-master relationship; it might even incite insurrection.

9. Thomas Branagan, *The Penitential Tyrant; or, Slave Trader Reformed* . . . (2nd ed.; New York, 1807), 147–48; Dwight, *Oration*, 19–20; Charles Nisbet to William Rogers, August 17, 1792, in Pennsylvania Abolition Society Papers, Historical Society of Pennsylvania, Philadelphia; *Connecticut Courant* (Hartford), December 12, 1796.

10. Thomas E. Drake, *Quakers and Slavery in America* (New Haven, Conn., 1950), 102–107.

Slave resistance easily could be linked to politics. Although uprisings would be put down, they explained, the necessary result would be increasingly severe repression of the slaves rather than the amelioration the petitioners claimed to seek.

Congressmen from Georgia and South Carolina refused to tolerate even petitions that called only for ending the slave trade, a measure supported by a broad spectrum of humanitarians, not by antislavery advocates alone. However philanthropic the measure might seem, southern congressmen explained, it would serve as the first step toward destroying slavery itself, and that was unacceptable. They first made their views explicit in February, 1790, when the House of Representatives heard a petition from the Pennsylvania Abolition Society, signed by Benjamin Franklin, calling upon Congress to "step to the very verge of [its] power" to act against slavery. Southern statesmen did not underestimate the significance of the document. Did the Pennsylvanians "expect a general emancipation of slaves by law?" asked Representative Thomas Tucker of South Carolina. If so, they were much deluded: "This would never be submitted to by the Southern States without a civil war." James Jackson of Georgia concurred. A federal effort to end slavery, he warned, would "light up the flame of civil discord; for the people of the Southern States will resist one tyranny as soon as another." Slavery never would end peacefully, he predicted. Southerners already had taken their stand on the issue. "The other parts of the Continent may bear them down by force of arms, but they will never suffer themselves to be divested of their property without a struggle."[11]

Later, in response to yet another antislavery petition from free blacks, John Rutledge, Jr., of South Carolina, put forward a peaceful but ominous defense of slaveholders' interests. There need be neither abolition nor civil war. Many northerners and even a few persons in the South, Rutledge conceded, thought abolition "reasonable and unavoidable," but they were mistaken. "Sir, it never will take place. There is one alternative which will save us from it; . . . that is, that we are able to take care of ourselves, and if driven to it, we will take care of ourselves." Secession and the creation of a separate southern nation was the defense Rutledge proposed against the menace of abolitionism. Further speculation about so drastic a recourse proved unnecessary, at least for the moment, for Congress already had adopted the report of a special committee headed by

11. *Annals of Congress*, lst Cong., 2nd Sess., 1197–98, 1200.

Abiel Foster of New Hampshire, which accepted the southern position that Congress had no authority over slavery within a state.[12]

Although the Foster report was a substantial and long-lasting southern victory, it could not altogether remove concern. Antislavery sentiment was not likely to wither away, and there was no reason to believe that a mere committee report would cause its advocates to cease agitation or abandon their efforts to gain political power. The flurry of antislavery petitions that reached Congress in the 1790s might make a slaveholder uncertain whether the more immediate threat to property and social order arose from antislavery groups and their potential influence in the national government or from the black revolutionary forces in Saint-Domingue. There was one important difference, however. The slave rebellion in the French colony posed danger to southern interests against which rhetoric and parliamentary maneuver offered no defense.

If American slaves did not spontaneously rise against their masters in imitation of the island revolt, blacks on the island, enthusiastic and doctrinaire, might themselves take the initiative and try to transport their revolution to the mainland. In 1793, Secretary of State Thomas Jefferson relayed to the governor of South Carolina reports (though he said he himself did not believe them) that Saint-Dominguan agents had been dispatched to the southern states to incite insurrection. Some years later, when relations with France had drastically deteriorated, the South was swept by rumors of a projected French invasion to be launched from the island. In April, 1797, Alexander Hamilton, assuming that American slaves would be "probable auxiliaries of France," recommended increasing the artillery and providing two thousand cavalrymen as "guards against insurrection." Shortly afterward, on the eve of the undeclared naval war with France, former Secretary of War Henry Knox urged President John Adams to prepare for an attack by ten thousand French-recruited blacks. If this force should land in a "defenceless part" of the Carolinas or Virginia, he warned, the slaves would "instantly join them." At about the same time, Robert Goodloe Harper of South Carolina disclosed his belief that the French expected the invasion to be followed by an insurrection whose groundwork already had been laid by "missionaries previously sent." Suspicion persisted that foreign agents had infiltrated the South. In March, 1799,

12. *Ibid.*, 6th Cong., 1st Sess., 242; Howard A. Ohline, "Slavery, Economics, and Congressional Politics, 1790," *Journal of Southern History*, XLVI (1980), 335–60.

South Carolina's Senator Jacob Read warned that the danger of subversion did not lie in a distant future: "Emissaries are now actually
in the Southern States at *their pious work*. They may be of all com-
plexions & not known to each other." Representative John Rutledge,
Jr., also of South Carolina, shared Read's belief in the reality of subversion. In his opinion South Carolina slaves were no longer the
ideological innocents masters hoped for. French agents had been
sent to America to incite slaves, he charged, "to feel the pulse of this
country, to know whether these are the proper engines to make use
of: these people have been talked to; they have been tampered
with." Similar apprehension also was voiced in the North. Saint-
Domingue could be expected to serve as a springboard for invasion,
warned the antislavery Pennsylvanian David Bard in 1804. "European powers have armed the Indians against us, and why may they
not arm the negroes?" was Bard's nervous question.[13]

Invasion, of course, did not materialize, but this good fortune did
not allay suspicion that American slaves had taken courage from the
success of the black revolt. White southerners did not suppose their
slaves were immune to the libertarian ideas that aroused the hopes
of oppressed people everywhere. They recognized that slaves, as in-
tently as whites, sought to be masters of their own lives and would
seize on any model that proved freedom could be attained. Thus it
may not have been nervousness alone that led white southerners in
the 1790s to interpret overheard slave conversations as evidence of
slave plots. Masters in Richmond, Norfolk, Charleston, Savannah,
and other cities where French refugees had settled suspected their
slaves of conspiring to follow the Saint-Dominguan example. "We
dread the future & are fearful that our feelings for the unfortunate
inhabitants of the wretched island . . . may be our own destruction,"
wrote a self-pitying resident of Charleston. "How hard upon our
poor citizens to be always patrolling and guarding."[14]

Deteriorating foreign relations contributed to domestic alarm. In

13. Andrew A. Lipscomb (ed.), *The Writings of Thomas Jefferson* (Washington, D.C.,
1903–1904), IX, 275; Alexander De Conde, *The Quasi-War: The Politics and Diplomacy
of the Undeclared War with France, 1797–1801* (New York, 1966), 84; Elizabeth Donnan (ed.), *Papers of James A. Bayard, 1796–1815*, Vol. II of American Historical Association, *Annual Report . . . for the Year 1913* (Washington, D.C., 1915), 90; Jacob Read
to James P. Jackson, March 23, 1799, in Jacob Read Papers, South Caroliniana Library, University of South Carolina, Columbia; *Annals of Congress*, 6th Cong., 1st
Sess., 242; 8th Cong., 1st Sess., 996.
14. Aptheker, *American Negro Slave Revolts*, 96–97; Mrs. Pinckney to Mrs. Manigault, February 5, 1798, in Manigault Family Papers, South Caroliniana Library, University of South Carolina, Columbia.

June, 1798, when war with France was expected hourly, word reached Georgia that a shipload of blacks from the West Indies was about to land at Savannah. The governor immediately ordered "all the horse companies in the state . . . held in readiness to march" and appealed for federal aid. "The President," he explained, "will no doubt see the propriety of preventing those people from being landed . . . where so many thousands of persons of color might be ignited to insurrection by their seditious tenets." The Georgia governor provided South Carolina officials with an explanation of French intent: "The political prospect is dark & the enemies of the U.S. may think to profit from the different classes of people among us, previous to a possibility of support from, or even a knowledge of attack by the general government." In July the governor saw danger looming from yet another quarter. Fugitive slaves on Amelia Island might "attempt to force their way . . . into this state which must be prevented by all possible means, for war now appears inevitable & to have that description of persons sowing sedition among our slaves whilst we are facing an invading army might be attended with almost fatal consequences."[15]

As in earlier years, white southerners viewed the blacks as potentially dangerous enemies in time of war—but not in wartime only. In March, 1800, the British brig *Maria* sailed into Charleston harbor from Kingston, Jamaica, with black troops aboard. The ship had been engaged in helping suppress the Second Maroon War in the British colony. Under other circumstances, South Carolinians might have considered the ship's black crew "loyal," but so insistent was the concern produced by the arrival of armed blacks from the revolt-ridden Caribbean that the ship's arrival, reported South Carolina's governor, caused "some anxiety to the citizens." He shared the feeling, for he suspected "that some of the Black troops, have been, and probably now are notorious villains; and, that as French negroes they have been concerned in some of the mischiefs in the West Indies." The governor took every conceivable precaution to allay both public fear and his own. No South Carolina black, free or slave, was to be allowed to board the ship. He ordered the vessel to position itself "under the guns of Fort Johnson" in order to guard "against the injurious consequences which . . . might come from the

15. James Jackson to Mayor John Glen, June 11, 1798, James Jackson to the Secretary of War, June 17, 1798, James Jackson to the Governor of South Carolina, June 14, 1798, Jackson to James Seagram, July 23, 1798, all in Executive Papers, Georgia State Archives, Atlanta.

landing of those negroes, and their consequent communication with
our Slaves." He requested the British consul in Charleston to order
the crew to use "no arms whatever while in this port."[16]

Two years later, the South Carolina governor dispatched alarming news to officials in neighboring states and to President Jefferson:
A frigate carrying "french negro incendiary prisoners" was about
to land somewhere along the southern coast and the prisoners
"turned loose upon us." So determined was the governor to prevent
contamination of South Carolina slaves that he issued sanguinary
instructions to the state's military commanders—"*none,* of such *incendiaries,* are to be *taken prisoners.*" This fear, bordering on para-
noia, would lead South Carolina and several other southern states
in the 1820s to pass Negro seamen's acts. These laws provided that
black crewmen either could not land at all or must be confined to
jail while their ships were in port. Although the United States Supreme Court declared South Carolina's law unconstitutional, the
state defied federal authority and enforced it anyway.[17]

Recurring perils from abroad during the Federalist period made
the divisive effects of domestic political disputes appear dangerous
in the extreme. The white population must present a solid front
against both slaves and foreign foes. They must set aside sectional
and ideological differences and seek consensus. In particular, urged
southern leaders, no more antislavery petitions should be debated
in Congress. Representative James McDowell of North Carolina, the
specter of Saint-Domingue still before him, entered a plaintive appeal for silence: "When thousands of people have been massacred,
and thousands have fled for refuge to this country, when the proprietors of slaves . . . could only keep them in peace with the utmost
difficulty, was this a time for such inflammatory motions?"[18]

Still, the motions did not cease. In January, 1800, an especially
exasperating antislavery petition originating in Philadelphia
reached the House of Representatives. Its signers—Absalom Jones

16. John Drayton to Timothy Pinckney, March 26, 1800, Drayton to British Consul,
March 8, 1800, Drayton to Constant Freem, March 22, 1800, all in Executive Journals,
John Drayton, 1800, in Governors' Papers, South Carolina Department of Archives
and History, Columbia.
17. General Orders to Brigadier Generals Horry, Vanderhorst, and McPherson,
September 9, 1802, and Drayton to Jefferson, September 12, 1802, both in Governors'
Papers, South Carolina Department of Archives and History; Phillip M. Hamer,
"Great Britain, the United States, and the Negro Seamen Acts, 1822–1848," *Journal
of Southern History,* I (1935), 3–28.
18. *Annals of Congress,* 3rd Cong., 2nd Sess., 2043.

and others—were free blacks, leaders of their race in Philadelphia who engaged in antislavery activity before many whites outside the Religious Society of Friends were prepared to do so. The petition particularly annoyed supporters of slavery because it demonstrated that some blacks already occupied a position that theories of racial subordination denied was possible. Harrison Gray Otis found the document nearly as offensive as did his southern colleagues. Political activity of the sort Philadelphia blacks engaged in "must be mischievous to America very soon," said the Massachusetts representative. "It would teach them the art of assembling together, debating, and the like, and would soon, if encouraged, extend from one end of the Union to the other." [19]

Blacks throughout the country, Otis understood, were about to assume an active political role. Perhaps even in the Deep South a few already held such aspirations. Representative Rutledge of South Carolina observed that the Philadelphia petitioners were doing in the North what slaves aspired to do in the South. "Already had too much of this new-fangled French philosophy of liberty and equality found its way and was too apparent among these *gentlemen* [slaves] in the Southern States, by which nothing would do but their liberty." [20]

Evidence of black striving and fear of contamination from abroad led to official measures aimed at security. Nearly all slave states in the 1790s enacted laws to prevent admission of slaves from the West Indies, and state officials redoubled vigilance to detect spies and hurl back invaders. Domestic carelessness needed remedy as well. "After the scenes which St. Domingo has exhibited to the world, we cannot be too cautious," observed Postmaster General Gideon Granger, himself a native of Connecticut. Granger warned southerners of a danger arising from within the postal service. "The most active and intelligent" slaves, he observed, "are employed as post riders. These are the most *ready* to *learn*, and the most *able* to *execute*. By travelling from day to day, and hourly mixing with people, they must, they will acquire information. They will learn that a man's rights do not depend on his color. They will, in time, become teachers to their brethren." [21] The objectionable practice, it goes without saying, soon was ended.

19. *Ibid.*, 6th Cong., lst Sess., 231.
20. *Ibid.*, 230.
21. *American State Papers, Class VII: Post Office Department* (1834), 27.

That some southern whites were genuinely fearful can hardly be doubted; yet circumstances required them to continue to live and work in intimate contact with slaves even while professing to dread their fury. Crops had to be planted, tended, and harvested; household chores had to be done. Such necessity set practical limits on repression. The number of slave patrols in most states was increased in the 1790s and supervision became more vigilant. Yet in day-to-day practice, considerable freedom of action still was allowed, and black-white relationships continued to be conducted, if with something less than complete trust, then as if trust were possible.

The relaxed state of affairs was particularly evident in Virginia and Maryland, the part of the South where antislavery sentiment was strongest and most freely expressed. The numbers of free blacks in the upper South increased considerably in the 1780s and 1790s as many owners manumitted part or all of their slave property, either out of pangs of conscience or because slaves had greatly declined in value. There, too, the severe criticism of slavery that accompanied the revolutionary movement and the lingering humanitarianism it fostered had helped temper some of the harshest aspects of the institution.[22]

Both in towns and throughout the countryside, a class of artisan slaves had appeared—carpenters, blacksmiths, masons—whose skills assured them a measure of autonomy inconsistent with an ideal of total control. Some accumulated small amounts of money, thus adding to their sense of independence while also gaining access to a measure of the world's material pleasures. In carrying out their duties practically free from supervision, skilled slaves moved about and consulted with other people besides their owners. Slaves who operated river boats, for instance, traveled many miles through the interior of the states, talking and dealing with whomever they wished. Even plantation slaves commonly enjoyed considerable freedom of movement beyond their home places. They patronized grog shops and with no consistent interference held sizable social gatherings and religious meetings. On occasion repression

22. Such was the opinion of contemporaries: James Monroe to Speakers of the General Assembly, December 5, 1800, in Stanislaus Hamilton (ed.), *The Writings of James Monroe* (New York, 1893–1903), III, 240–41; [St. George Tucker], *A Letter to a Member of the General Assembly of Virginia on the Subject of the Late Conspiracy . . .* (Baltimore, 1801), 5–6, 8–9; George Drinker to Joseph Bringhurst, December 10, 1804, in Pennsylvania Abolition Society Papers.

could be severe and reprisal for offenses could be savage; yet slave patrols operated only sporadically, and authorities often winked at violations.[23]

When this relative freedom was brought to their attention, white southerners had trouble justifying their laxity. Instead they were likely to profess alarm at what had taken place and to predict its ultimately harmful effect. As it turned out, they were not mistaken in their apprehension.

In the summer of 1800 it became clear that some of the most privileged slaves in Virginia had become intensely embittered as a result of their bondage and hostile to the whites responsible for perpetuating it. The opportunities afforded them by a diversifying economy and a republican society taught them that even more might be theirs. Not surprisingly, some of the "freest" of the slaves sought through concerted action and violence to shake off all restrictions.

In counties around Richmond, enterprising slave artisans and preachers moved through the countryside organizing the discontent that festered within the black population. Some who were not legitimately supplied with passes by their owners wrote their own. They traveled to slave barbecues and religious meetings to seek out fellow conspirators; they met like-minded slaves in taverns and blacksmith shops and at secret rendezvous. Their plan was to develop a military organization and then capture Richmond, kill many of the whites, and establish black control. They believed the mass of disaffected but less acculturated and less committed slaves would eventually come to their support.[24]

Leadership of the conspiracy, uncertain at first, eventually fell to twenty-four-year-old Gabriel, who with his brothers Solomon and Martin (a preacher) ran a blacksmith shop for their young master Thomas Henry Prosser, one of the wealthiest men in Henrico County. Able and dependable though Gabriel was, he also had a fierce temper. In 1799, before his revolutionary activity made him notorious, he had been convicted of maiming his white neighbor Abraham Johnson by biting off part of his ear. Although this was a capital offense, Gabriel had been sentenced only to be branded on the hand and confined for a month in Rose's brig, Henrico County's

23. On the relaxed conditions in Virginia, see Gerald W. Mullin, *Flight and Rebellion*, 127–30, and Robert McColley, *Slavery and Jeffersonian Virginia* (Urbana, Ill., 1964), 57–75.

24. The following account of the conspiracy generally follows Gerald W. Mullin, *Flight and Rebellion*, 140–63.

noisome jail.[25] Within a few months of his release, he was planning rebellion.

As became a skilled craftsman, Gabriel developed his plan and selected his lieutenants with studied care. He was, above all, a practical man. He dismissed enthusiasm alone as insufficient grounds for service in his corps. A candidate's ability to command and to fight was the prime qualification. Gilbert wanted to be a captain, but Gabriel refused him—"He stuttered too much." Toby held rank as captain for a time, "but was turned out being undersize." Martin was too old to be a soldier, Gabriel decided. Instead, he would "run bullets and keep them in bullets."[26]

The leaders did not count on the inspiration of the moment to carry them to victory. They made careful assessments of their strategic situation, using the best information they could get. In the summer of 1800 no armed forces were available for Virginia authorities to use against a rebel force. Since for two years the United States had been engaged in undeclared naval war with France, a French army, the rebels believed, might land to support the revolt. The Catawba Indians also might come to their aid. Recognizing their military limitations, the conspirators sought expert advice. One Charles Quersey, a French veteran of the Battle of Yorktown and supposedly sympathetic to the slaves' cause, would help direct the first phase of military operations.

Under Gabriel's leadership, the conspiracy took secular and rational form. In spite of preacher Martin's large role the plan showed few features of a religious or messianic movement. It could hardly have been otherwise, for notwithstanding heavy gains recently made in Virginia by evangelical churches, this was still a secular age. Although both Baptists and Methodists were making many converts, especially among blacks and nonslaveholding whites, the new revivalism had not yet altogether displaced the rationalistic outlook of the dominant white element; neither had it quite beaten back the influence of the Enlightenment on the blacks, especially among such privileged craftsmen as Gabriel. But insofar as it had done so,

25. Philip J. Schwarz, "Gabriel's Challenge: Slaves and Crime in Late Eighteenth-Century Virginia," *Virginia Magazine of History and Biography*, XC (1982), 283–309; Bert M. Mutersbaugh, "The Background of Gabriel's Conspiracy," *Journal of Negro History*, LXVIII (1983), 209–11.
26. Palmer, McRae, and Flournoy (eds.), *Calendar of Virginia State Papers*, IX, 145, 153; Trial of Samuel Prosser, September 11, 1800, in Negro Insurrection File, in Executive Papers, Virginia State Library. The latter source contains important details omitted from the record printed in *Calendar of Virginia State Papers*.

the doctrine of spiritual freedom as preached by the revivalistic clergy powerfully reinforced the secular justification for throwing off bondage. Nevertheless, the conspirators proceeded to develop their plans with little overt recourse to religious inspiration. On the battle flag the leaders planned to display, they would inscribe the words "death or Liberty," a slogan transmitted to them from the revolutionary era.[27]

The conspirators had large, though limited, political goals. Their aim, said Gabriel, was "to subdue the whole of the country where slavery was permitted, but no further." The slave John testified that Gabriel asked him "to join him to fight for his country." Although the slaughter required to attain their goals undoubtedly would be vast, the leaders did not intend it to be indiscriminate. According to the slave Ben Woolfolk, "All the whites were to be massacred, except the Quakers, the Methodists, and the Frenchmen, and they were to be spared on account . . . of their being friendly to liberty." They intended also to spare all the "poor white women who had no slaves."[28] Far from providing reassurance, such discrimination could only add to slaveholders' alarm, for it suggested that the conspirators recognized a community of interest between themselves and antislavery advocates and, still more ominous, that they saw members of certain religious groups and the nonslaveholding whites as their friends.

By August 30, Gabriel's plan had matured. It would be set in operation at midnight. But on the afternoon of that day, Tom and Pharaoh, two slaves privy to the conspiracy but not committed to it, decided to end their silence. They revealed the plot to Mosley Sheppard, their master. Since the uprising was scheduled to begin within a few hours, authorities had no time to prepare to meet the danger. But preparation proved unnecessary. A torrential rain storm began at noon and continued into the night. Bridges were washed out, and roads became impassable. Slaves could not assemble; the revolt could not take place.

With Governor James Monroe in charge, a massive roundup of suspects began immediately. Authorities took scores of depositions, trials were held, and eventually the courts condemned more than twenty slaves. The judges acquitted some twelve of the accused. Another seven received pardons. One of the last of the conspirators to

27. Palmer, McRae, and Flournoy (eds.), *Calendar of Virginia State Papers*, IX, 147, 151, 152.
28. *Ibid.*, 152.

be captured was Gabriel himself, who evidently had been harbored for an extended period by whites—exactly by whom never was determined. When authorities conducted him from jail to the governor's house for a private—and unrevealing—interview, "a great cloud [crowd?] of blacks as well as whites gathered around him." Whether it was hostility, admiration, or only curiosity that drew them there, we cannot know.[29]

Revelation of Gabriel's conspiracy occurred before any part of it became operative and even before evidence of unusual slave unrest appeared. Extensive in organization and devastating in potential though it was, the conspiracy remained only a plan. Although some whites were terror-struck when they realized the fate Gabriel and his men had designed for them, public officials went about the investigation and the trials that followed with not even momentary surrender to hysteria. Under Governor Monroe's direction, officials made every effort to avoid exploiting the sensational aspects of the affair, and the jurists who gathered the evidence gave their discoveries minimal publicity. It is evident that Monroe and his advisers hoped in this way to avoid arousing panic, but they also may have had political reasons for wishing to make as little as possible of the incident. As Jeffersonians, they were vulnerable to accusation of having spread the radical principles that evidently encouraged the conspirators.

Elsewhere, too, officials made sure the projected uprising was not sensationalized. In South Carolina, where danger of imitation was thought to be extreme, Governor John Drayton, who already had advised editors to refrain from discussing Jefferson's antislavery views, now urged them to ignore recent events in Virginia. Charleston newspapers thus printed only sketchy accounts of a "rebellion" with no hint that slaves had been involved. But such self-censorship did not mean that white southerners remained uninformed about what had happened. Even in remote Mississippi Territory, the event aroused concern.[30] Gabriel's conspiracy never acquired the charged aura that would surround Nat Turner's revolt a generation later; yet its implications could not be evaded, and for years afterward, rumors of new plots and impending rebellion troubled the South.

29. *Ibid.*, 156.
30. Charleston *City Gazette and Daily Advertiser*, October 22, 1800; Winthrop Sargent to "Sir," November 16, 1800, printed broadside (N.p., n.d.), in Ohio Historical Society.

In keeping with the spirit of moderation set by Governor Monroe, the courts exercised more forbearance toward the accused than might have been expected; nevertheless, the number of death sentences was large enough to trouble Monroe. He appealed to Jefferson for advice on how the state could punish the convicted slaves without resorting to execution. Although he provided no clear-cut answer, Jefferson replied that even in his neighborhood, "where familiarity with slavery and a possibility of danger from that quarter prepares the general mind for some severities," sentiment was strong "that there has been hanging enough." As usual, Jefferson was conscious of acting on a stage open to universal observation. "The other states & the world at large will ever condemn us," he advised, "if we indulge a principle of revenge, or go one step beyond absolute necessity." And then he proceeded to express again those familiar doubts that for so long had plagued members of Virginia's ruling class. Critics outside the South, wrote Jefferson, "cannot lose sight of the rights of the two parties, & the objects of the unsuccessful one."[31] Even slaves, Jefferson implied, possessed the right to fight for their liberty, and those who oppressed them were in the wrong.

Jefferson's was an attitude that if widely held could only encourage more attempts at rebellion. Self-doubt also would be likely to hinder efforts to suppress antislavery dissent. But slavery could not long be maintained unless apology were banished, rational defense—a proslavery argument—took its place, and all whites accepted it. Division among the white population simply could not be tolerated. Ample material for such defense already existed, as statements by South Carolina congressmen recently had proved, but for the moment its formulation in Virginia was delayed.

In the wake of the conspiracy a northern newspaper published a bit of topical verse on the subject:

> . . . remember ere too late,
> The tale of St. Domingo's fate.
> Tho *Gabriel* dies, a host remain
> Oppress'd with slavery's galling chain.

---

31. James Monroe to Thomas Jefferson, September 14, 1800, in Stanislaus Hamilton (ed.), *Writings of James Monroe*, III, 208–209; Jefferson to Monroe, September 20, 1800, in Paul Leicester Ford (ed.), *The Writings of Thomas Jefferson* (New York, 1892–99), VII, 457–58.

> And soon or late the hour will come
> Mark'd with Virginia's dreadful doom.[32]

The taunting prophecy—written by a New England Federalist—grasped a reality that slaveholders in Virginia found hard to evade. Whites in South Carolina and Georgia, too, felt apprehensions similar to those that haunted Virginians and, perhaps, experienced them even more keenly. But in those states, unlike Virginia, fear was for the most part uncomplicated by the doubts of rectitude that, at least for the moment, so clearly plagued slaveholders in the upper South.

32. Quoted in Linda Kerber, *Federalists in Dissent: Imagery and Ideology in Jeffersonian America* (Ithaca, N.Y., 1970), 46.

4

🙵🙵🙵🙵🙵🙵🙵🙵🙵🙵🙵🙵🙵🙵🙵🙵🙵🙵🙵🙵🙵🙵🙵

Domestic Conspiracy and New Foreign Threats 1800–1819

Slaveholders in the upper South found themselves poorly prepared to meet the challenge that Gabriel's plot forecast. While acknowledging the gravity of their situation, they dealt with it only halfheartedly and with no clear sense of direction. While Governor James Monroe and his advisers remained composed, others throughout the state acted in a confused, aimless, almost distracted manner. Fears of insurrection, no doubt reinforced by the revolt in Saint-Domingue, were so deep and of such long standing that official efforts to promote calm could not entirely succeed. Terror-stricken whites fled neighborhoods where danger seemed imminent.[1] Some of the more stolid, while remaining outwardly calm, still revealed a sense of helplessness before the prospect of an entire people rising in rebellion. Even the wisest among them could conceive of no sure way to resolve the crisis.

It was not simply that the white population lacked military resources adequate to put down servile rebellion, though some of the many patrols and military units hastily formed to intimidate the blacks indeed do seem to have been deficient in both equipment and leadership. Yet the irresolution and apparent lack of clear direction did not arise just from matters subject to computation and rational

1. *Hints for the Consideration of the Friends of Slavery, and Friends of Emancipation* (Lexington, Ky., 1803), 11–12; speech of Representative Daniel Sheffey, January 11, 1813, *Annals of Congress*, 12th Cong., 2nd Sess., 701.

assessment. Something of its intangible, emotional aspect was suggested when even proposals aimed at more effective defense were criticized on the ground that these plans contained their own fatal element of risk. For example, objections were raised when state officials distributed arms to strengthen local regiments: Slaves, with their superior and insurmountable power, might capture the arsenals and seize the weapons for their own use.[2]

Further, some suspected the conspiratorial slaves of benefiting from strategically placed white friends who supported their aim of destroying the Virginia planters—perfect unity of the white population never had been achieved. Plantation disorder, in some minds, was linked to larger social and political conflicts. The planters' enemies were thought to lurk everywhere. The opposition of antislavery religious groups—Quakers, Methodists, Emancipating Baptists—and of some envious poor white people might be presumed, but persons of high degree fell among the suspect as well. Thomas Jefferson reported that his neighbors believed John Adams' administration deliberately encouraged slave attack by leaving federal arsenals poorly guarded. And advice reached Governor Monroe, as he was preparing to prosecute Gabriel and his coconspirators, that the state's deputy attorney could not be trusted to uphold the slaveholders' interests—he was by birth an Englishman, he associated with suspected abolitionists, he supported "all the measures of the Executive of the United States."[3] White Virginians, fearing they were facing a coalition of blacks, Englishmen, Federalists, and abolitionists, and already only too aware of the Saint-Dominguan upheaval, saw themselves threatened on many fronts, with no adequate defense at hand.

These unsubstantiated notions reflected the profound self-doubt that by 1800 plagued members of the ruling classes in Virginia as well as ordinary citizens. They were dependent upon an institution that ideologically was fast becoming an anachronism. Of course, it was common knowledge that slave labor formed the base of the

2. Benjamin Oliver to James Monroe, September 23, 1800, in Executive Papers, Virginia State Library; Thomas Newton to James Monroe, December 29, 1800, in Palmer, McRae, and Flournoy (eds.), *Calendar of Virginia State Papers*, IX, 173; T. M. Randolph to James Monroe, February 14, 1801, in James Monroe Papers (microfilm), Manuscripts Division, Library of Congress; W. Bentley to James Monroe, September 8, 1800, in Palmer, McRae, and Flournoy (eds.), *Calendar of Virginia State Papers*, IX, 138.
3. Thomas Jefferson to James Monroe, November 8, 1800, in James Monroe Papers; Richard E. Lee to James Monroe, September 25, 1800, in Executive Papers, Virginia State Library.

thriving economy of the sugar-rich Caribbean islands and of the rice-indigo culture of South Carolina and Georgia. Slavery remained a vital economic interest in Virginia as well. Yet Enlightenment ideas and changed religious sensibilities had become so pervasive that never again could slavery be accepted unquestioningly as part of an unchanging social order. Only if blacks were defined as being outside the rest of humanity, hopelessly incompetent and innately savage, could their permanent subjugation be defended. Planters increasingly resorted to this solution for the contradiction within their society. But even if racist ideas prevailed, however earnestly voiced, a troublesome possibility intruded to contradict them: Some of the clearest-minded Virginians at the turn of the century conceded that in America's evolving republican society, blacks could not be kept in that state of ignorance and servility that alone might assure their continued subjugation. Yet no alternative to slavery appeared feasible. A few years later, Monroe would inform Jefferson of his support for gradual emancipation—if it could be accomplished "on principles consistent with humanity, without expense or inconvenience to ourselves."[4] A proviso of such magnitude, of course, assured the perpetuation of slavery despite widespread acknowledgment of its inequity and despite the insecurities it bred. Virginians were caught in a dilemma from which there was no escape.

A society thus perplexed might be expected to shore up its foundations. The Virginians tried to do this, but their efforts appeared fretful and halfhearted. Some whites believed they faced an absolutely overwhelming challenge against which no preparation could avail. Here and there, vigilante groups took the offensive by waging warfare against unarmed blacks.[5] But the success of such campaigns brought little assurance, for Virginians did not foresee themselves threatened by sporadic, localized outbreaks of a few dissident slaves whom available military units could quell. Instead, they expected large-scale, coordinated warfare. Fierce black armies shouting "the negro-war song" would materialize in the countryside and fall upon helpless towns and plantations. White civilians, defended only by improvised, inept military forces, would be crushed by fe-

4. [Tucker], *Letter to a Member of the General Assembly of Virginia*, 5–6; Stanislaus Hamilton (ed.), *Writings of James Monroe*, III, 353.

5. An account of one such foray is in Charles William Janson, *The Stranger in America, Containing Observations Made During a Long Residence in That Country . . .* (London, 1807), 395–98. See also James Fletcher to James Monroe, January 1, 1801, in Executive Papers, Virginia State Library.

rocious slave assault. Whatever the explanation, it is apparent that the mood in parts of Virginia from 1800 to 1802 strikingly resembled the Great Fear that swept rural France only a dozen years earlier, terrorizing the populace with the delusion that "the brigands" were coming.[6]

A manifestation of the anxiety felt in that troubled time was the white Virginians' belief that the generally peaceable black people who were their daily associates could be transformed in a day or a night into ferocious warriors. A contemporary noted "the treacherous submission of their demeanor"—the air of harmlessness that they affected, the better to confound the whites.[7]

Slaveowners had learned long ago to take for granted a troublesome, irreducible amount of resistance on the part of their bondsmen and a degree of resentment toward the master's authority, but recent events in Saint-Domingue had revealed hatred extending beyond the experience of any Virginian. Devastation of the French colony suggested that the blacks' thirst for vengeance was unlimited, that ordinary slaves could become terrible and warlike. Apparently they possessed both will and ability to combine to destroy their oppressors. An anonymous writer contrasted the whites of Virginia, panic-stricken after Gabriel's conspiracy, with the deceitful blacks who, "tho' watched by the jealous eyes, and threatened by the united opposition of thousands, maintain an unaccountable cheerfulness of mind, that renders them terrible as an army with banners."[8] No ordinary preparation would be adequate to meet so fearsome a confrontation. Perhaps, in fact, the challenge could not be met successfully at all. It was the contrast between what *was* and what at any moment *might be* that helped create nearly intolerable apprehension in certain slaveholding areas.

State officials tried with little success to account for the slaves' conspiratorial behavior and to prepare a policy for resisting it. The many trials of slaves accused of plotting insurrection "and the applications growing out of them for pardon or transporation ... of those condemned" led Governor Monroe in 1802 to forgo his usual spring visit to his plantation. He stayed at his desk in Richmond and pondered recent events. "The spirit of revolt has taken deep hold of the minds of the slaves," he wrote at that time, "or the symp-

6. Janson, *Stranger in America*, 398. The standard work is Georges Lefebvre, *The Great Fear of 1789: Rural Panic in Revolutionary France* (New York, 1973).
7. Janson, *Stranger in America*, 360.
8. *Hints for the Consideration of the Friends of Slavery*, 11–12.

toms which we see are attributable to some other cause." He confessed puzzlement at the widespread disaffection: "After all the attention which I have paid to the subject my mind still rests in suspense on it."[9]

But what other explanation than a desire for freedom could there be? Monroe found the evidence disagreeable and hard to accept; nevertheless, the proof lay in the official records—dozens of slaves charged with plotting rebellion had confessed guilt. Their goal, according to their own testimony, was freedom for themselves and death for the slaveholding whites.

Association of the conspiracies with the whites' own concepts of liberty made the unrest especially disquieting and hard to deal with. The state might hang the leading conspirators, but ideas, as Virginians had reason to know, were not likely to be extinguished by the snuffing out of lives. The only just solution and the only sure means of restoring order was emancipation. Yet any attempt to end slavery would encounter so many obstacles and so much opposition as to make the goal all but impossible to achieve. Even if, by some means, slavery could be done away with, slaveholders believed the result—the creation of a greatly enlarged population of free blacks—would produce terrible problems, perhaps even the racial conflict emancipation proposed to avert.[10] What course, then, was left to follow? Nothing but repression, which almost certainly would be accompanied by continuing anxiety among whites while bringing no assurance of slave tranquillity.

In the absence of acceptable policy for dealing with slave unrest, it was tempting to search for scapegoats. Blame might take the place of remedy. Upon the first revelation of Gabriel's plot, a Virginia newspaper confidently located its source: "This dreadful conspiracy originates with some vile French Jacobins. . . . Liberty and equality have brought that evil upon us." The explanation was thought valid in other slaveholding regions as well. Although William R. Davie of North Carolina found scant evidence of conspiracy in that state, he noted abundant signs of slave discontent, arising, he believed, from the same source as in Virginia. "It is plain," he

9. James Monroe to Thomas Jefferson, May 17, 1802, in Stanislaus Hamilton (ed.), *Writings of James Monroe*, III, 348–49.

10. Robert Sutcliff, *Travels in Some Parts of North America in the Years, 1804, 1805, and 1806* (Philadelphia, 1812), 50; Jack P. Greene (ed.), *Diary of Colonel Landon Carter*, II, 1055; John Taylor, *Arator; Being a Series of Agricultural Essays, Practical and Political* (2nd ed.; Georgetown, 1814), 114–16.

wrote, "that the much abused terms of '*Liberty and equality*' have misled these wretched people as well as many others; under these every crime is sanctified; and all feeling and reflection banished."[11]

Governor Monroe, himself an exponent of republican ideology, could not endorse the easy explanation, for it placed primary blame on men and principles identified with his own political associates. Yet he did not reject the charge out of hand either. After long reflection he offered a slightly more complex reason for the slaves' treachery than his political opponents had set forth, a theory brave enough to locate its origin not in France but in Virginia itself.

Monroe attributed "the public danger" to the "contrast in the condition of the free negroes and slaves, the growing sentiment of liberty existing in the minds of the latter, and the inadequacy of the existing patrol laws." But even this interpretation, for all its suggestion of sober, informed thought, offered no remedy. The presence throughout Virginia of free blacks was a social fact not easily altered; neither could the slaves' ideas of liberty—ideas they shared with the white population—be eradicated. Only more restrictive laws could be passed. But Monroe saw no benefit in subjecting black people to stricter controls. There was no answer to the problem of revolts short of eliminating slavery. "Unhappily while this class of people exists among us," Monroe concluded, "we can never count with certainty on its tranquil submission."[12]

With this statement Monroe joined critics of his own time and earlier who also took for granted that slavery itself generated rebellion. However, such a verdict pointed to a fatal flaw in southern society and thus could not generally be accepted. Few indeed were willing to acknowledge that so fundamental a source of wealth and position carried with it the probability of disaster. Easier, more comfortable explanations were sought—and found.

Despite lack of evidence that anyone except slaves themselves were involved in the conspiracies, the search went on for culprits. Suspicions of that sort were hardly new. Well before the Revolution, Landon Carter charged "new light" religion with making slaves insubordinate. The continued growth of evangelicalism throughout

11. Fredericksburg *Herald*, September 23, 1800, quoted in Jordan, *White over Black*, 396; William R. Davie to Benjamin Williams, February 19, 1802, in Benjamin Williams Letter Books, Vol. III, in Governors' Papers, North Carolina Division of Archives and History.

12. James Monroe to the Speakers, January 16, 1802, in Stanislaus Hamilton (ed.), *Writings of James Monroe*, III, 238–39; *ibid.*, December 5, 1800, p. 243.

the South—and among both races—appeared to promote discontent. Further, it threatened to unite blacks and whites in an egalitarianism that was utterly at odds with slavery. Now even certain slaves designated themselves preachers and brought still more blacks under the sway of subversive religious fervor. Some persons who discounted the disruptive influence of religion nonetheless located the source of discontent in ideas that incited the slave population. A few years after the rash of conspiracies had subsided, the Virginia statesman John Randolph credited slave unrest to "the silent but powerful change wrought by time and chance upon the composition and temper" of society. To this imprecise analysis Randolph added a specific impetus to disorder: "The French Revolution had polluted even them." Then he identified a particular category of villains: "Peddlers from New England and elsewhere" disseminated egalitarian ideas "throughout the Southern Country." The South's problem originated, then, in the idea of universal liberty. "From the spreading of this infernal doctrine," Randolph concluded, "the whole Southern country has been thrown into a state of insecurity."[13]

John C. Calhoun, usually more optimistic in those years than was the saturnine Randolph, never disputed the truth of Randolph's charge. Calhoun took second seat to no one in suspicion of New Englanders and of French libertarianism, but he found that slave unrest was a problem peculiar to Virginia and not one characteristic of the entire South. Slaves in the rice-growing regions of South Carolina lived in greater isolation than those in the upper South. Thus a smug Calhoun reported that none of the fears that daily plagued white Virginians were felt in his own state. Slaves in South Carolina, he declared, remained untouched by radical thought: "I dare say more than half of them never heard of the French Revolution."[14] What might be expected from the other half, Calhoun did not say.

13. Jack P. Greene (ed.), *Diary of Colonel Landon Carter*, I, 378; Jacob Read to Charles Pinckney, June 10, 1807, in Charles Pinckney Papers, South Caroliniana Library, University of South Carolina, Columbia; Elisha Dick to James Monroe, September 26, 1800, in Palmer, McRae, and Flournoy (eds.), *Calendar of Virginia State Papers*, IX, 178; John Scott Strickland, "The Great Revival and Insurrectionary Fears in North Carolina: An Examination of Antebellum Society and Slave Revolt Panics," in Orville Vernon Burton and Robert C. McMath, Jr. (eds.), *Class, Conflict, and Consensus: Antebellum Southern Community Studies* (Westport, Conn., 1982), 57–95; *Annals of Congress*, 12th Cong., 1st Sess., 450–51.

14. *Annals of Congress*, 12th Cong., 1st Sess., 480.

Unlike either Calhoun or Randolph, Governor Monroe held that the progress of liberty could neither be resisted successfully nor turned back. The liberal ideas of the age, he assumed, created slave disaffection. One need not search for peddlers of sedition to account for unrest, although it was natural, he admitted, to suspect "others who were invisible."[15]

Minds less spacious than Monroe's found blame easy to assess and remedy close at hand. Since exponents of liberty and the rights of man—Jacobins, Jeffersonians, abolitionists, evangelicals, Quakers—as well as free blacks were held responsible for inciting slave discontent, it followed that order could be restored and the South made secure by adopting two drastic measures: The libertarians should be silenced, and the free blacks should be got rid of by colonizing them elsewhere.

The strongest of motives—self-preservation—suggested to slaveholders the wisdom of tempering their long-standing enthusiasm for universal liberty and human rights. An era of reaction and increased repression was about to begin throughout the slave country. It would be marked by fear and suspicion of all influences judged subversive of slavery. Unfortunately for the composure of white southerners, such hostile influences materialized at once from several directions and in unmanageable forms.

At just the moment when slaveholders located in radical thought the source of threats to domestic security, news arrived that France, the reputed seat of worldwide subversion, planned to reestablish its power in North America. By the secret Treaty of San Ildefonso negotiated in 1800, Spain had transferred its vast territory of Louisiana to France. Observers in New England did not hesitate to explain what this move might mean. "If the French once get an establishment upon the Spanish territory, in the vicinity of the southern states, it will behoove the planter to look well to his own household," commented a Connecticut editor.[16] "Much evil is apprehended . . . from the spirit of insurrection which will inevitably be infused into the slaves by their *Gallic brethren*," wrote another. A year later, the *Port Folio*, a Federalist magazine, reported with little sign of regret that the French were expected "(. . . soon after their arrival in Louisiana), to deprive our southern democratic citizens of their property, by exciting their negroes to run away from them."[17]

15. Stanislaus Hamilton (ed.), *Writings of James Monroe*, III, 241.
16. Quoted in Aptheker, *American Negro Slave Revolts*, 28.
17. Quoted in Kerber, *Federalists in Dissent*, 40.

These prospective dangers were not, as might be supposed, taunts set forth only by self-satisfied New Englanders bent on antagonizing interests they opposed. The British chargé d'affaires found that nearly all politicians he met in Washington dreaded the consequences the transfer of Louisiana would bring to the South. From their new outpost, the French would contaminate American slaves with a "spirit of insurrection." A Virginia planter relayed to Governor Monroe his own speculations on the disturbing news that, since the cession of Louisiana to France, importation of slaves into the western territory had been prohibited.[18] What would that exclusion mean to the American South? A free area to which slaves would escape? The loss of a potential market for excess slaves? Whatever the answers, the transfer of Louisiana undoubtedly signified ominous change. A hostile power on the border of the southern states, friend and foe of slavery agreed, would constantly endanger southern institutions.

The United States, one reasonably might believe, faced a diminished and troubled future if Louisiana remained in French control. The concern immediately was felt in diplomacy. Secretary of State James Madison authorized Robert Livingston to convey to French officials the United States' "momentous concern" over France's acquisition of Louisiana. Among other baneful aspects of the transfer, he was instructed to emphasize the unsettling effect the French presence would have on American slaves, who, in Madison's words, had been "taught to regard the French as patrons of their cause."[19]

As it turned out, Livingston found no need to dwell on dire predictions. Contrary to all expectation, Napoleon abandoned plans to create a new American empire. His financial problems and the inability of his armies to subdue the blacks in Saint-Domingue stripped glitter from the scheme. He would sell Louisiana. The surprised American agents seized the opportunity, and in 1803 President Jefferson cast aside every constitutional scruple in order to accept the offer.

Several powerful arguments could be advanced for buying the

18. De Conde, *This Affair of Louisiana*, 112; Richard King to Secretary of State, February 5, 1802, in U.S. Department of State, *State Papers and Correspondence Bearing upon the Purchase of the Territory of Louisiana* (Washington, D.C., 1903), 13; George Goosely to James Monroe, June 5, 1802, in Executive Papers, Virginia State Library.

19. Department of State, *State Papers and Correspondence*, 7. For a discussion of Jefferson's views on Louisiana and Saint-Domingue, see John C. Miller, *The Wolf by the Ears* (New York, 1977), 130–41.

territory, most of them quite unrelated to slavery or exclusively to planter interest, but hardly any consideration was more compelling than the chance to eliminate a source of slave unrest. For years after Louisiana became American territory, planters still found the rich lands of Mississippi and Alabama of doubtful value because of hostile Indians and their Spanish allies in East and West Florida. If Louisiana had remained in French hands, it seems unlikely that the Black Belt could have been developed as a slave region at all.

The security and opportunity promised by Jefferson's diplomatic achievement would be fully enjoyed only in later years. For the present, the United States continued its constricted existence in a world made hazardous by the war-to-the-death in which England and France engaged. As the war entered a desperate phase, issues growing out of neutral rights on the seas threatened to engulf the nation in conflict with first one and then the other of the great combatants. Once again southerners had special reason for concern.

With war imminent, from both North and South came appraisals of the slave population as a source of military weakness as well as a menace in its own right: "They may be considered as a piece of artillery . . . which the most unskilled of our enemies may play off against us," wrote George Tucker of Virginia. The Federalist Timothy Pickering's assessment was little different. "In case of foreign war," he predicted, "Virginia must keep at home half her force to prevent an insurrection of her negroes; and if attacked in her own dominions her danger and imbecility would be still more manifest." The existence of an internal enemy, both Tucker and Pickering implied, must be considered in shaping the nation's foreign and domestic policy.[20]

Concerns such as these helped make possible abolition of the foreign slave trade by Congress in 1807, near the height of the diplomatic controversy with England over neutral rights. Perhaps the measure would have been enacted even had fears of the blacks not assumed new dimensions during those years. Since the slave population grew steadily by natural means, importations were found less necessary than before. Further, the trade faced steady moral onslaught, and British moves toward ending it within their empire exerted powerful influence on Americans. Nevertheless the sense of emergency generated by recent slave conspiracies and the growing

---

20. [Tucker], *Letter to a Member of the General Assembly of Virginia,* 14; Kerber, *Federalists in Dissent,* 40.

likelihood of war helped remove whatever reluctance congressmen felt toward supporting the measure. In the air of apprehension prevailing in 1807, even defenders of slavery were likely to agree with the Quaker abolitionist Thomas Branagan's comment that "every slave ship that arrived at Charleston, is to our nation what the Grecian's wooden horse was to Troy."[21] On that issue a majority of congressmen from all sections could concur. Momentarily ignoring sectional differences, northern and southern congressmen joined in putting an end to slave importations.

Motives in this, as in most political decisions, were mixed. Some representatives from slave districts perhaps saw in the act means of reducing the supply of slaves and thus of increasing prices. At the other extreme, antislavery congressmen, more sanguine than they had cause to be, welcomed the prohibition as promising an early end to slavery itself. For others with humane intentions, a philanthropic desire to end the notorious horrors of the slave trade was critical in determining votes. But threading through all these considerations was fear of the blacks, a sentiment outsiders were more likely to feel free to express than were slaveholders themselves. "To import slaves is to import enemies," was the blunt assessment of David Bard, antislavery congressman from Pennsylvania. "It is this trade," wrote a visiting Englishman, "that has multiplied the lurking assassins, till they swarm wherever the planter turns his eyes."[22]

Abolition of the slave trade did little in the short run to lessen the danger whites saw in a rapidly growing black population, and the looming war with England appeared to magnify the menace. The wave of reputed conspiracies that had swept the upper South following Gabriel's conspiracy subsided after 1804, but awareness of the potential for catastrophe by no means disappeared.

A massive slave rebellion—not merely a conspiracy—in Louisiana impressed this truth on all who learned of it. On the evening of January 8, 1811, slaves on the German Coast, the sugar-producing area some forty miles northwest of New Orleans, rose in rebellion

21. Thomas Branagan, *The Penitential Tyrant: A Juvenile Poem* . . . (Philadelphia, 1805), 51. A group of South Carolinians complained that their state's reopening of the trade in 1803 was a measure "fraught with evils which may threaten our country with ruin and destruction . . . from beyond the seas—or elsewhere." Petition from Fairfield District, in Slavery Petitions, 1800–30, Legislative Papers, South Carolina Department of Archives and History, Columbia.

22. Betty L. Fladeland, *Men and Brothers: Anglo-American Antislavery Cooperation* (Urbana, Ill., 1972), 79, 80; *Annals of Congress*, 8th Cong., 1st Sess., 995; Janson, *Stranger in America*, 360.

under the leadership of the mulatto Charles, who probably was from Saint-Domingue. Starting from the plantation of Manuel Andre, the insurgents gathered recruits from neighboring plantations until somewhere between 150 and 500 slaves, including maroons, were in the field. Armed with cane knives, axes, hoes, and a few small arms and led by mounted chiefs with their "colors displayed and full of arrogance," they plundered plantation houses, burning two of them, and killed two white men as they advanced some fifteen miles to the southeast. The next day, however, two companies of voluntary militiamen and thirty regulars arrived and, under the command of General Wade Hampton, defeated the rebellious slaves in battle. The rebels were no match for these well-armed and well-trained forces. Sixty-two blacks, apparently including the leaders, were killed in the encounter. Eighteen of those remaining were convicted of rebellion, assassination, arson, and pillage and were sentenced to be shot on their owners' plantations. Their heads then were cut off and placed on poles as a warning to others.[23]

Nothing so extreme was soon to happen along the Atlantic coast; yet there, too, evidence of discontent remained plentiful enough to suggest that slaves eventually might combine in actual rebellion. Meanwhile reports of massive devastation by West Indian slaves continued to reach the United States and, probably, the ears of slaves. Against that background a reputed conspiracy in Camden, South Carolina, in 1816 caused great alarm, and slaves everywhere continued in unmistakable ways to manifest resistance and make clear their urge for freedom.[24]

Although many blacks apparently reconciled themselves to slavery, even forged bonds of loyalty and affection with their owners and, so far as records show, displayed little overt resentment toward whites in general, it is equally true that unmasked hatred for their oppressors smoldered in others. This emotion might be expressed in isolated acts of violence or in the decision to run away, but it also

23. James H. Dorman, "The Persistent Specter: Slave Rebellion in Territorial Louisiana," *Louisiana History*, XVIII (1977), 393–404; New York *Evening Post*, February 19 and 20, 1811; Clarence E. Carter (ed.), *Territory of Orleans, 1803–1812* (Washington, D.C., 1940), 915–19. Vol. IX of *The Territorial Papers of the United States*, 28 vols.; "Summary of Trial Proceedings of Those Accused of Participating in the Slave Uprising of January, 1811," *Louisiana History*, XVIII (1977), 472–73; Harriet DeLonge to John Peters, February 16 and May 14, 1811, in Peters Family Letters, New York Public Library; Isaac L. Baker to Stephen F. Austin, February 15, 1811, in Eugene C. Barker (ed.), *The Austin Papers*, Vol. II, Pt. 1 of American Historical Association, *Annual Report . . . for the Years 1919 and 1922* (Washington, D.C., 1924–28), 184.
24. Aptheker, *American Negro Slave Revolts*, 257.

could take the form of quiet satisfaction at misfortunes suffered by whites, the adversity seen as evidence that slavery violated divine order. This is what happened in Virginia on the eve of the second war with England.

On December 26, 1811, fire consumed the Richmond Theater. Among the seventy-two who died was an array of notables including George W. Smith, governor of the state, and Abraham B. Venable, president of the state bank. Blacks attending the performance were more fortunate. By lucky circumstance the location of exits leading from their part of the theater allowed most of them to escape. Waves of sympathy for the unprecedented loss of life swept the nation, reaching as far north as Boston, where the city council passed a resolution of condolence. But among blacks in Virginia, the fiery scene was lifted from the mundane to the providential. To them, it took on overtones of religious significance involving retribution and judgment. Thus their response to the disaster was satisfaction and hope rather than sorrow. Slaves in Henry County were heard to say "they were glad that the people were burnt in Richmond, and wished that all the white people had been burnt with them. That God Almighty had sent them a little Hell for the white people, and that in a little time they would get a greater."[25]

If such feelings became at all widespread among the black population, southern whites would have much to dread from the war with England that by early 1812 seemed impossible to avert. Memories of British depredations and slave reaction during the American Revolution offered no ground for confidence in the forthcoming conflict. All evidence suggested that the new generation of slaves, still better educated in the principles of freedom than their forebears, would be even more responsive to political appeals from opportunistic liberators than were their parents and grandparents in the 1770s and 1780s. Few could doubt that slaves in 1812 would welcome American involvement in war as a means of attaining their freedom.

Slaveholders were correct in suspecting that slaves followed the developing quarrel with England, understood war was near, and planned to take advantage of hostilities when they began. War created opportunities for slaves unknown in times of peace. Few of the

25. *Niles' Weekly Register* (Baltimore), I (January 4, 1812), 329–30; William Henry Foote, *Sketches of Virginia, Historical and Biographical, 2nd Series* (2nd ed.; Philadelphia, 1856), 321; Palmer, McRae, and Flournoy (eds.), *Calendar of Virginia State Papers*, X, 121.

recurring rumors of conspiracies in peacetime ever issued in open rebellion, for slaves realistically assessed their chances in an armed encounter with white Americans as poor and not worth the risk.[26] But war would change everything. It was at times when white society faced external challenge or was beset by internal dissension that slaves were most likely to try to fulfill their desire for freedom.

Tom, a slave whom two justices of the peace in Montgomery County, Virginia, described—perhaps hopefully—as "young and artless," disclosed his own expectations. As soon as war began, he intended to join the other slaves in his neighborhood in revolt. A point of added significance not likely to be lost on authorities was that Tom learned about public affairs not from his master or other members of the slaveholding class, but "from the poor people in the neighborhood" with whom he familiarly associated, and "by hearing the newspapers read."[27]

Tom lived in a predominantly rural county, but urban slaves, too, looked at the nation's foreign problems as offering a way to become free. While "Poor Black Sam" proved his own loyalty to the whites in 1812, he revealed the hostility of others when he informed the governor and council of Virginia that "all the niggres" planned to rise up, seize the arms stored in the capitol, and destroy Richmond. English agents had been active in Richmond and Petersburg, Sam continued, "[dis]rupting the niggres and tells them that as soon as this pact is made the Inglish will land and then they will be free."[28]

The dread possibilities described by Tom and Black Sam made an impression on southern whites, who warned of the peculiar risks the South incurred in fighting England. The likelihood of slave hostility entered into congressional debate over war. John Randolph assumed his practiced anti–War Hawk stance to advise Congress in December, 1811, that "while talking of taking Canada, some of us were shuddering for our own safety at home." He had witnessed "the alarms in the capitol of Virginia" and knew that "the nightbell never tolled for fire in Richmond that the mother did not hug her infant more closely to her bosom." An English invasion promised disaster. "God forbid, sir, that the Southern States should ever see

26. Slave interview in Nottaway Jail, May 5, 1802, in Executive Papers, Virginia State Library.
27. Palmer, McRae, and Flournoy (eds.), *Calendar of Virginia State Papers*, X, 121–22.
28. Robert S. Starobin (ed.), *Blacks in Bondage: Letters of American Slaves* (New York, 1974), 139–40. For activities of a purported British spy in Richmond, see Palmer, McRae, and Flournoy (eds.), *Calendar of Virginia State Papers*, X, 264–65.

an enemy on their shores, with these infernal principles of French fraternity in the van."[29]

Although Congress overruled such forebodings and declared war in April, 1812, apprehensions of the sort Randolph voiced did not evaporate. While the country steeled itself for English attack, southerners continued their gloomy prophecies: "Unfortunately we have two enemies," said the mayor of Richmond, "the one open and declared; the other nurtured in our very bosoms!" Slaves "want nothing but means and opportunity to break their shackles," warned Representative Daniel Sheffey of Virginia in January, 1813. Assurances of the slaves' incompetence to coordinate plans for freedom struck him as unconvincing: "Man is strong, resolute, and ingenious when liberty is concerned." Sheffey sharpened his familiar allusion to "the fate of Santo Domingo" by warning of the havoc that would follow if "ten thousand men landed on the Southern shores . . . [with] fifty thousand stand of arms" for the slaves. "Every man would find in his own family an enemy ready to cut the throats of his wife and children."[30]

Calhoun took note of such unbecoming predictions. He saw them not only as signs of unmanly resolution in white leadership but also as confessions of weakness certain to embolden slaves. In South Carolina, he was proud to say, "no such fears in any part" were felt. (The great Camden conspiracy had not yet occurred.) Calhoun insisted that hostilities with England posed no threat to southern institutions. On the contrary, war strengthened slavery, for in wartime "the public force and vigilance are of necessity the greatest."[31]

Calhoun was only partly correct. Thoroughly equipped, well-trained white armies undoubtedly would experience great success in awing unarmed blacks. But their advantage would last only so long as enemy forces remained far from slaveholding areas, and this they could not be counted upon to do.

Southerners were more apprehensive about the war's possible effect on their property than Calhoun cared to admit. Even masters confident of the harmlessness of their slaves nonetheless expected the appearance of a British army in their neighborhood to disrupt the slave-master relationship, exactly as it had done a generation earlier during the Revolution. They did not see how slave disci-

29. *Annals of Congress*, 12th Cong., 1st Sess., 451.
30. Quoted in Johnston, *Race Relations*, 118; *Annals of Congress*, 12th Cong., 2nd Sess., 401.
31. *Annals of Congress*, 12th Cong., 2nd Sess., 819, and 12th Cong., 1st Sess., 48.

pline—which was essential to coerced labor—could be maintained in the face of invasion. At her estate near Washington, D. C., Mrs. Margaret B. Smith was resigned to the loss of her slave property. She awaited the arrival of the British armies, when "our enemy at *home*," as she described the slaves, would abandon their owners and flee to British lines. Local officials took every precaution to prevent this from happening. When military necessity removed militia from areas of large slave population, special patrols sometimes took their place in order to keep the bondsmen at work. In Washington in the summer of 1813, Elbridge Gerry, Jr., expected to be called upon to patrol more frequently now that the British approached, "and this is very necessary, for the blacks in some places refuse to work, and say they shall soon be free, and then the white people must look out." [32]

Such efforts at control proved only partly successful. It is true that in 1812, as in 1776, many slaves and free blacks so closely identified with the views of their white countrymen as to serve loyally in American land and naval forces. It also is true that in both wars many slaves (and white Americans, too), especially those distant from the seacoast, evidenced little political awareness and thus continued their regular routine almost as though war were not being waged. Yet the War of 1812, like the Revolution, found some slaves alert to the opportunity it offered to profit from their masters' military peril by gaining advantage within the slave system or by escaping from it altogether. Again, just as they did during the Revolution, slaves took advantage of their masters' weakness by deserting the plantations to take refuge on British ships and within British lines, a course that in effect allied them with the enemy. The "Black population of these Countries," wrote a British admiral, "evince upon every occasion, the strongest predilection for the cause of Great Britain, and a most ardent desire to join any Troops or Seamen active in the Country." [33] The mayor of Richmond told a similar story. "The standard of revolt is unfurled," he reported. "Wherever practicable these deluded creatures, regardless of consequences have flocked to it." In an effort to be completely evenhanded, some British commanders allowed the slaves' owners to come within their lines

32. Margaret Bayard Smith, *The First Forty Years of Washington Society* (New York, 1906), 90; Claude G. Bowers (ed.), *The Diary of Elbridge Gerry, Jr.* (New York, 1927), 198–99.

33. Quoted in Sarah McCulloh Lemmon, *Frustrated Patriots: North Carolina and the War of 1812* (Chapel Hill, N.C., 1973), 197.

and try to persuade the fugitives to return to their old allegiance. How often these persuasions succeeded is not known.[34]

British Vice Admiral Sir Alexander Cochrane on April 2, 1814, issued a proclamation inviting slaves to flee to British ships or military posts and designated a base for them on Tangier Island, near the mouth of the Potomac River. Having placed themselves under British protection, the blacks enhanced British offensive capacity by performing an active military role. Eventually two hundred escaped slaves joined with three hundred royal marines to form an integrated battalion. A black marine corps took part in the major Chesapeake campaigns of 1814, and black marines aided in assaults on Virginia. To the distress of white Americans, runaway slaves served as willing soldiers in military campaigns against their former masters. "Our negroes are flocking to the enemy from all quarters, which they convert into troops, vindictive and rapacious," complained Brigadier General John P. Hungerford as he observed this form of slave rebellion taking place in Virginia. "They leave us as spies upon our posts and our strength, and they return upon us as guides and soldiers and incendiaries."[35]

In an effort to check such behavior, Virginia authorities kept some militia units close to home rather than sending them to more distant points to oppose the British advance. Partly this policy resulted from fear of violence at the hands of unruly slaves; partly it was designed to deprive the British of black manpower; partly it was dictated by reluctance to lose a valuable economic resource. "The Northumberland [Virginia] slaves are every day effecting their escape," ran one plea for military reinforcement, "and I am confident that unless some vigorous measures are adopted and a sufficient force allowed us, this whole penninsula will be stripped of its most valuable personal property."[36]

In July, 1813, John Randolph, noting that the militia in his part of Virginia had been dispatched to fight the British, warned of "the danger from *an internal foe* augmented by the removal of so large a portion of our force." The same danger in North Carolina brought

34. Palmer, McRae, and Flournoy (eds.), *Calendar of Virginia State Papers*, X, 368. See also *Annals of Congress*, 14th Cong., 2nd Sess., 1105, 1117.

35. Frank A. Cassell, "Slaves of the Chesapeake Bay Area and the War of 1812," *Journal of Negro History*, LVII (1972), 144–55; Palmer, McRae, and Flournoy (eds.), *Calendar of Virginia State Papers*, X, 368. For an instance of spying by a slave, see Lieutenant Colonel R. E. Parker's report, Palmer, McRae, and Flournoy (eds.), *Calendar of Virginia State Papers*, 338.

36. Palmer, McRae, and Flournoy (eds.), *Calendar of Virginia State Papers*, 338–39.

the militia company of Wilmington special treatment. "The peculiar situation of the town as respects the enemy and the negroes," an official explained, "induced me to exclude them from a draft." In 1814 the Wilkinson County Court in Mississippi Territory established a draft—not to bring men into the army, but to keep them out. It was instituted, Jefferson Davis later explained, to make sure a sufficient number of men stayed at home to guard the slaves rather than enlisting for the defense of New Orleans.[37]

In some instances domestic unrest required American commanders to dispatch troops to troubled areas in order to awe slaves. Charleston received a regiment of militia sent from the interior in the summer of 1812 for that purpose. On another occasion members of the White Oak militia of North Carolina were sent home when rumors of an imminent slave uprising reached their encampment at Beaufort. At another point in the war, forces were dispatched to the Northern Neck in Virginia to guard slaves on the home front after most of the local troops had been sent to the defense of Norfolk. An officer in the North Carolina militia stationed at Fort Johnson appealed to the governor for "a few cavalry" to prevent a slave rebellion "so probably and so much to be dreaded in this section of the state."[38]

On at least one occasion, American forces operated directly against slaves rather than against the British invaders. In the fall of 1814, upon learning that British arms had fallen into the hands of blacks in Georgetown and Washington, General Tobias E. Stansbury ordered troops to move against them for fear they would "insult the females, and complete the work of destruction commenced by the enemy."[39]

Slavery in the Chesapeake area and the Carolinas experienced severe disruption as a consequence of war, but the southern frontier presented American forces with equally challenging problems. Hostile Indians, blacks, and Spanish offered a major test of United

37. John Randolph to Josiah Quincy, July 4, 1803, in William Cabell Bruce, *John Randolph of Roanoke, 1773–1833* (New York, 1922), I, 394; William Watts Jones to William Hawkins, July 13, 1812, in Governors' Papers, North Carolina Division of Archives and History; Haskell M. Monroe, Jr., and James T. McIntosh (eds.), *The Papers of Jefferson Davis* (Baton Rouge, 1971–), I, lxix.

38. Aptheker, *American Negro Slave Revolts*, 23; Thomas Brown to William Hawkins, July 14, 1812, and Mathew Morris, "Report," July 18, 1813, both in Governors' Papers, North Carolina Division of Archives and History; Richard Brent to the Governor, February 10, 1814, in Palmer, McRae, and Flournoy (eds.), *Calendar of Virginia State Papers*, X, 300.

39. Tobias E. Stansbury to Richard M. Johnson, November 14, 1814, in *Annals of Congress*, 13th Cong., 3rd Sess., 1633.

States power on the long frontier extending westward from the Atlantic Ocean to the Mississippi River. Two years earlier, in October, 1810, the United States had begun the process of annexing West Florida, but East Florida remained in Spanish hands, a haven for fugitive slaves and a site for the launching of guerrilla attacks against Georgia as well as against the new American territory of West Florida. So hateful to the planters' interests was the maroon settlement in Florida that in the late summer of 1812 Georgia officials, on their own initiative, sent the state militia across the border only to have it driven back by combined Indian and black forces.[40]

Soon after Congress declared war against England, the Spanish allowed British officers to assemble a force of black Cuban troops at Pensacola. The Tennessee *Herald* spelled out the fearsome implications of this development: "The same band which has initiated against us the scalping knife and the tomahawk of the Indians will not stop to renew upon the Mobile and Lower Mississippi the tragedy of St. Domingo." The area's nearest neighbors, Georgia and South Carolina, were not "in a situation to afford them assistance," the newspaper pointed out, for the danger of slave revolt distracted planters in those states just as it did in the Southwest.[41]

Despite these early warnings, the Americans did not have to face up to their vulnerability in that quarter until the summer of 1814, when the British extended their operations to the Gulf of Mexico. Vice Admiral Cochrane, British commander of the North American Station, earlier pointed out the advantage of invading the United States from the south. The operation would require only a few British troops, he supposed, for they would be joined by the Spanish and by the Creeks and Choctaws. This massive force then would drive up the Mississippi Valley to Canada, thereby overwhelming the Americans and ending the war.

There was every reason to expect slaves to respond to the projected British campaign in ways destructive to American interests. In May, 1814, a report from the Gulf claimed that 2,800 Creeks, an equal number of Choctaws, plus another thousand Indians near Pensacola stood ready to support a British invasion. They would be joined, some predicted, by the slaves in Georgia.[42] Indians incited

40. *Niles' Weekly Register*, III (December 3, 1812), 235–37; Rembert Wallace Patrick, *Florida Fiasco: Rampant Rebels on the Georgia-Florida Border, 1810–1815* (Athens, Ga., 1954), Chap. XIV.

41. Quoted in *Niles' Weekly Register*, III (October 17, 1812), 107.

42. Robert V. Remini, *Andrew Jackson and the Course of American Empire, 1763–1821* (New York, 1977), 235, 301.

against the whites could exert awful vengeance, as Americans learned in the massacre at Fort Mimms in 1814, but the fury of blacks was to be dreaded still more, if for no other reason than because, unlike Indians, the blacks were scattered throughout the white settlements.

"We must be prepared to act with promptness," General Andrew Jackson wrote in the summer of 1814, "or Mobile and New Orleans by a sudden attack may be placed in the hands of our enemies, and the negroes stimulated to insurrection and massacre, may delluge [*sic*] our frontier in blood." By September, Governor William C. C. Claiborne of Louisiana was warning Jackson of local fears of "Domestic Insurrection; We have every reason to believe that the Enemy has been intriguing with our *slaves*." New black arrivals had been seen in New Orleans, he added, including Saint-Dominguans "of the most desperate characters."[43]

As Jackson prepared his defense against the British advance, an eight-man committee of safety representing New Orleans and the sugar-plantation district told him to expect no help from those places: "The maintenance of domestic tranquility in this part of the state obviously forbids a call on any of the White Inhabitants to the defense of the frontier, and even requires a strong additional force." While a British force prepared to drive inland, the sugar planters of Louisiana—no doubt remembering the great rebellion that overwhelmed the region only four years earlier—appealed for a hundred cavalrymen to be stationed along the Mississippi to suppress slave insurrection.[44] The plea of the New Orleans citizens was supported by Secretary of War James Monroe, who advised Jackson in September that "the militia of Louisiana will be less effective for general purposes from the dread of domestic insurrection, so that on the militia of Tennessee your principal reliance must be."[45] Thus Jackson's army at the Battle of New Orleans in January, 1815, was made up mostly of militia from Tennessee and Kentucky—states having relatively few slaves—together with smaller groups of regulars, free blacks, pirates, Indians, and Louisiana militia.

43. Andrew Jackson to David Holmes, July 21, 1814, in John Spencer Bassett (ed.), *Correspondence of Andrew Jackson* (Washington, D.C., 1926–35), II, 19; William C. C. Claiborne to Jackson, September 20, 1814, *ibid.*, 55–56. See also E. Fromentin to Jacques Philippe Villeré, October 19, 1814, in Jacques Philippe Villeré Papers, Historic New Orleans Collection, New Orleans.

44. Committee of Safety to Jackson, September 18, 1814, in Bassett (ed.), *Correspondence of Andrew Jackson*, II, 51–53.

45. Quoted in Tommy R. Young II, "The United States Army and the Institution of Slavery in Louisiana, 1803–1815," *Louisiana Studies*, XIII (1974), 212.

With the approach of a British army, the large and competent free-black population of New Orleans presented American military planners with a problem faced nowhere else. "They will not remain quiet spec[ta]tors of the interesting contest," Jackson decided. "They must be for, or against us." He proposed to assure their allegiance and defuse a potentially explosive force by raising a regiment from among them, which he then would deploy outside the state. The plan aroused objections. Some "respectable citizens" opposed "putting arms into the hands of men of Colour," for doing so would "only add to the force of the Enemy." Members of the council of defense—"men well-informed and well-disposed"—refused to endorse the enlistment of blacks unless "there could be a guaranty, against the return of the Regiment." If at the close of war, city leaders explained, "the Individuals were to settle in Louisiana, with a Knowledge of the use of Arms, and that *pride of distinction*, which soldiers pursuits so naturally inspires, they would prove dangerous."[46]

This reasoning did not persuade Jackson to withdraw his plan. He enjoyed total confidence in his ability to dominate common soldiers, either black or white. But more important, he viewed enlistment of free blacks as an essential safety measure, a device for maintaining white control. "If they can be enrolled," he explained, "they may when danger appears be moved in the rear to some point where they will be kept from doing us an injury. If their pride and merit entitle them to confidence, they can be employed against the Enemy. If not they can be kept from uniting with him."[47]

Jackson soundly defeated the British at the Battle of New Orleans, and the war ended with the slaveowners' worst fears unrealized. Open rebellion had not occurred in Louisiana or anywhere else. Nonetheless, numerous individuals had lost property, as an undetermined number of slaves took advantage of the British military presence to establish their freedom and followed the example set by their forebears during the Revolution by seeking to accompany the British as they withdrew from the United States. In the fall of 1814, some three hundred former slaves from the Chesapeake area arrived at Halifax under British auspices; nine hundred more were expected to follow. In January, 1815, a British major general at New Orleans informed Jackson that a "considerable number" of

46. Andrew Jackson to William C. C. Claiborne, September 21, 1814, in Bassett (ed.), *Correspondence of Andrew Jackson*, II, 57; Claiborne to Jackson, October 17, 1814, *ibid.*, 77.
47. Andrew Jackson to William C. C. Claiborne, October 31, 1814, *ibid.*, 88.

slaves had gathered at his headquarters with the intention of embarking with the British army. Others already were aboard British ships in Mobile Bay.[48]

Experience during the War of 1812, just as during the Revolution, demonstrated the fragility of the slave-master relationship and its vulnerability to military challenge. Once more, southerners saw the loyalty of slaves evaporate in the presence of an invading force. But these painfully learned lessons had little immediate relevance because the end of the second war with England inaugurated a long period of peace for the United States. Secure on the continent as never before and facing no serious challenges from abroad, Americans could confidently turn all their energies toward internal development. With the southeastern Indians defeated and their English allies repulsed, a considerable part—but not all—of the southern frontier had been made secure. The most conspicuous exception was Spanish East Florida, which remained occupied by hostile Indians and vengeful blacks organized as a maroon settlement. Along the Apalachicola River only sixty miles from the United States border, some 250 fugitive slave men and women held the "negro fort," an abandoned British post, from which they issued invitations for others to join them and launched guerrilla attacks against the property of their former owners in Georgia.

Secretary of War William Crawford, formerly a senator from Georgia, complained to Jackson that the Florida maroons joined the Creeks in efforts "to inveigle" slaves from Georgia. Crawford's report was hardly news to Jackson, who, partly in order to subdue the maroons, had conducted earlier raids into Florida. Now Jackson instructed Brigadier General Edmund P. Gaines that "this fort must be destroyed" if it harbored fugitive slaves or held out "inducements to the Slaves of our citizens to desert."[49]

In August, 1816, under orders from Gaines, Lieutenant Colonel Duncan A. Clinch "invested" the fort. When the blacks answered his demand for surrender by firing a cannon and hoisting a red flag with the English Union Jack above it, Clinch proceeded to blow up the fort's magazine. Among the few to survive the explosion were a black man and a Choctaw chief whom Clinch considered leaders of

48. *Niles' Weekly Register*, VII (October 6, 1814), 54; Major General Lambert to Jackson, January 20, 1815, and Maunsel White to Jackson, February 20, 1815, both in Bassett (ed.), *Correspondence of Andrew Jackson*, II, 151, 176–77.

49. William Crawford to Jackson, March 14, 1816, in Bassett (ed.), *Correspondence of Andrew Jackson*, 236–37; Andrew Jackson to Gaines, April 8, 1816, *ibid.*, 238–39.

the resistance. He ordered these men turned over to the Seminoles for torture and execution.[50]

Destruction of the Negro fort did not secure the southern frontier. Indians in Florida continued for many years to conduct raids into Georgia, and Florida long remained a refuge for runaway slaves. But the aggression went both ways. "It is quite common for the crackers . . . to make incursions into Florida & steal or take off by force the negroes," wrote James Bankhead from his vantage point just south of the Georgia border.[51]

In 1818, under orders from President James Monroe to clear United States soil of marauding Seminoles, Andrew Jackson led an army composed chiefly of Georgia militiamen into Florida with the intention, his actions suggest, of making the Spanish province an American possession. When in the course of the campaign Jackson captured and executed two British subjects, the entire incident became a matter of international dispute and, especially, of controversy within the United States government. There Jackson had more defenders than he had critics. Representative Henry Baldwin of Pennsylvania put the matter bluntly and in a manner certain to win commendation in the South. The Georgia militia under Jackson, he explained, "were, in fact suppressing an insurrection of slaves, aided by an Indian force, all assembled and armed for purposes hostile to the country."[52] Thus Jackson's aggression could be forgiven because it had been conducted for the purpose of safeguarding slavery and in what was thought to be the national interest.

The next year Spain ceded East Florida to the United States, an event Georgians, even in the colonial period, had regarded as essential to the maintenance of slave discipline. Although for decades after 1819 the Seminoles and blacks in the Florida swamps continued to resist American authority, requiring a long and costly military campaign before they were subdued, the southern frontier at last could be considered secure.

By 1819, with all European powers gone from territory east of the Mississippi, slaves had lost a century-old source of external support.

50. John Bach McMaster, *A History of the People of the United States from the Revolution to the Civil War* (New York, 1915), IV, 432–33; John D. Milligan, "Slave Rebelliousness and the Florida Maroon," *Prologue*, VI (1974), 4–18.
51. James Bankhead to Christopher Van Deventer, January 15, 1818, in Christopher Van Deventer Papers, William L. Clements Library, University of Michigan, Ann Arbor.
52. *Annals of Congress*, 15th Cong., 2nd Sess., 1040. See also *ibid.*, 16th Cong., 1st Sess., 1194.

No longer could black fugitives readily find a haven outside the United States, although some in Louisiana managed to flee to Texas. The eventual destruction of the maroon society in Florida deprived slaves in Georgia and South Carolina of an external stimulus to freedom present since early in the eighteenth century. Slaves now sank more completely into bondage. They became more thoroughly a part of American society because no alternative to it existed.

The diplomacy and military achievements of Jefferson's, Madison's, and Monroe's administrations went far toward providing security for the nation. A momentous part of those achievements was the elimination of long-standing threats to slavery. By acquiring French and Spanish possessions lying on the path of American westward advance, the three Virginia presidents made possible the opening of a vast new region to a slave-based plantation system. It is of at least equal importance to note that the same achievements also made slavery a more stable institution than it ever had been before. Planters would have found it futile to try to develop the lands of Alabama and Mississippi with slave labor if an unfriendly government on the border encouraged slaves to escape or to rebel.

The removal of French and Spanish power also had the effect of strongly reinforcing the southern spirit of independence. Much as British defeat of French power in 1763, by removing a threat to American security, lessened the need for close colonial ties with Britain and thereby made possible the colonial protests that led to revolution, so the confidence inspired by the accomplishments of the Virgina Dynasty allowed the South to resist national authority.

Southern leaders could risk defiance only because they felt little need for national protection against foreign threats. It was not the fault of southern statesmen that, despite their imperial achievements, slavery continued to be eroded by developments beyond their control and menaced by interests they could not touch.

5

☗☗☗☗☗☗☗☗☗☗☗☗☗☗☗☗☗☗☗☗☗☗☗☗☗☗☗☗☗

Confronting Internal Dangers

Invasion and revolt—the threats to slavery that so vexed eighteenth-century Americans—were joined after the Revolution by a challenge of a different order. Slavery, it now appeared, also could be ruined by the quiet, eroding force of hostile public opinion even before many owners realized what was happening.

If the nearly absolute authority masters sought to exercise over slaves ever was questioned by white members of the community and its legitimacy destroyed, then owners—having lost their white allies—might be compelled to make large concessions to their black labor force as the price of continued service. Should that happen, the controls that kept blacks in a subservient caste would be loosened, and slavery in its familiar, profitable form would disappear. The plantation system then would change in unpredictable and devastating ways, transforming all social relationships in the process. This prospect proved nearly as disquieting as did the threat of insurrection itself. "We have among us in the very Bosom of our Country and Families, a property who although valuable as the means of our Cultivation can only continue so by being kept completely subordinate," explained the governor of South Carolina in November, 1798.[1] If slaves grew insolent and proud and unwilling to submit to

---

1. Governor's message to the Senate, November 29, 1798, in Governors' Messages, 1791–1800, South Carolina Department of Archives and History.

their masters' will, and if that dissidence gained outside support, the economy and society of the South would break down because the core of the system, the slave-cultivated plantation, would be made inoperable. Such might be the outcome if critics of slavery grew in numbers and influence.

Slaveowners never constituted more than a minority in the total southern white population. They could not by themselves, alone and unaided, preserve the institution upon which the plantation system depended. The labor force could be kept subordinate only so long as masters enjoyed community support, not only for the institution itself, but also for the devices required to maintain discipline—strict rules enforced by the whip. The means necessary to control must never be allowed to come under outside scrutiny and supervision. "If they take away the power of discriminatory punishment altogether, they are no longer slaves," a South Carolinian wrote. "They will soon set the master's power at defiance, and be transformed into insurgents and out-laws."[2]

Servile behavior among blacks depended almost entirely on the attitudes and conduct of whites, whose determination to exercise coercive power defined slavery and maintained it. The institution had no other basis. Yet the apparent simplicity of this fact may be misleading. Whites never had everything their own way in relations with slaves. By its very nature, slavery involved a contest of wills. The will of the owners, who were intent on commanding respect, subservience, and labor from their slaves, was constantly pitted against that of the bondsmen, who were struggling to retain control of their own persons and to establish bearable conditions for survival.

The outcome of the battle—and *battle* is the word that best describes master-slave relationships—almost always was inconclusive. Neither contestant found it easy to impose unconditional surrender on the other. Accommodation and concession ordinarily were required of each. Advantage in the power struggle typically fell to the owners, for they had much besides their own strength and wit to rely on, while the slaves had little. All the instruments of the state, including the courts and militia, supported the owners' claims. Behind these lay the potent force of majority approval for

2. Review of *The Tenth Annual Report of the American Society for Colonizing the Free People of Colour . . .* , in *Southern Review*, I (1828), 231.

the institution of slavery itself, as well as for the practices necessary to maintain it.[3]

But despite this mighty array of resources, well-informed masters could not approach these challenges with complete self-confidence, for none of the auxiliaries to power enjoyed absolute immunity to subversion. Permanent majority support could not be taken for granted. In February, 1794, Miles Parker of Gates County, North Carolina, made this point when he appealed his conviction on the charge of assaulting a black man: "Some members of the jury were friendly to the emancipation of negroes and their equality with the whites."[4] If Parker was right, slavery in Gates County faced an uncertain future, for there, the verdict suggests, slaves had allies. Hard to explain away was the fact that a white man had been brought to trial for an offense against a black and that he had been found guilty. In future plantation contests in that neighborhood, slaves could be expected to make full use of that strategic advantage.

Only a few years earlier, events of the revolutionary era had proved that public opinion, the ultimate source of the master's authority, was subject to manipulation by skilled propagandists. If clever men could organize support for a break with England, they also could mobilize an antislavery crusade. This is exactly what began to happen. Under that influence, majority endorsement for slavery became dubious. In the years immediately following the Revolution, numerous antislavery critiques were published in both North and South, and slavery ended in the northern states—by 1804 the last holdout, New Jersey, had passed a gradual-emancipation act. No one having an interest in preserving slavery could quite ignore these developments. An area of freedom on the border of the slaveholders' dominion would prove as unsettling in the nineteenth century as it had been in earlier times.

By 1800 a number of subversive influences worked to undermine slavery. The South became a stronghold of republican thought, an ideology that southern partisans employed in defense of their right

3. On paternalism and struggle and accommodation, see Eugene D. Genovese, *Roll, Jordan, Roll: The World the Slaves Made* (New York, 1974), 5–7; Leslie Howard Owens, *This Species of Property: Slave Life and Culture in the Old South* (New York, 1976), 70–105; Bobby Frank Jones, "A Cultural Middle Passage: Slave Marriage and Family in the Ante-Bellum South" (Ph.D. dissertation, University of North Carolina, Chapel Hill, 1965), 45–47.

4. Miles Parker's Affidavit, February court term, 1794, in Gates County Slave Records, 1783–1867, North Carolina Division of Archives and History, Raleigh.

to be free from outside interference. Yet republicanism, with its hostility toward inequities in privilege, wealth, and status and to the exercise of arbitrary power, could be turned against planter interest. This was so because the single most important element promotive of aristocracy within the South was slavery, and slavery, more starkly than any other institution, demonstrated the misuse of power. But republicanism was only one of several influences with potential for weakening the basis of the planters' life. A contemporary set forth the complexity of the threat: "Rewards and punishments, the sanctions of the best government, and the origin of love and fear, are rendered useless by the ideas excited by the French Revolution; by the example of St. Domingo; by the lure of free negroes mingled with slaves; and by the reproaches to masters and sympathies for slaves, breathed forth from the Northern States."[5]

The writer was the republican idealogue John Taylor of Caroline. Although it is tempting to discount the lament as expressing only middle-aged regret for the passing of better days, Taylor's crotchety analysis was by no means uniquely his. By the first years of the nineteenth century, common wisdom held that slaves had become less humble, less easily disciplined than in earlier times. "Certain events which have taken place in the West Indies . . . with some internal causes, have concurred to change considerably the habits of subordination among the Slaves," observed a resident of Northampton County, North Carolina, in 1802. Northerners discerned a like transformation in the blacks who lived among them. By "wise regulations," Pennsylvania had been "kept undisturbed by negro conspiracies, for more than half a century," wrote a Philadelphia editor; "carnal intercourse between whites and blacks, now scandalously common, was extremely rare . . . and the blacks were more industrious, sober, contented, and useful . . . than they have ever been at any period, since their heads have been turned by the modern jargon of liberty, and the rights of man."[6]

Whether observations in this vein reflected a truly new spirit among blacks or only changed perception by whites matters less for our purpose than the course of action the perception dictated. According to one North Carolinian, "Firm and steady policies are in-

5. Taylor, *Arator*, 118. Taylor characterized slaves as "docile, useful and happy," unless interfered with. *Ibid.*, 119.

6. Petition, September 1, 1802, in Petitions 1800–59, Legislative Papers, North Carolina Division of Archives and History, Raleigh; "People of Colour," *Port Folio*, I (May 23, 1801), 164.

dispensably necessary to keep them in their present condition."[7] Almost no measure designed to stabilize slavery and to halt subversion could be dismissed as too extreme for so vital an end.

Firm policies might not suffice, however, for among the internal developments thought to imperil slavery in the Early National Era was a major cultural change occurring in blacks themselves, a process beyond the power of individuals to direct or to check. In the years following their arrival in America, Africans had been transformed into African-Americans, thereby acquiring essential aspects of the culture they were helping to create. Blacks everywhere, especially those in the North, in the Chesapeake Bay area, and in urban centers, soon shared the language and religion as well as many of the values characteristic of American society. Furthermore, in the process of turning New World wilderness into civilization, slaves in all regions demonstrated skills and accomplishments comparable with those of their white countrymen. For example, Peter Deadfoot, twenty-two years old, was described by his owner as "a tall, slim, clean limbed, active, genteel, handsome fellow, with broad shoulders." He was "very sensible and smooth tongued." He was an indifferent shoemaker, a good butler, ploughman, and carter, an excellent sawyer and waterman. He understood breaking oxen very well and was "one of the best scythemen, either with or without a cradle, in America." In summary, said his master, "He is so ingenious a fellow, that he can turn his hand to anything; he has a great show of pride, though he is very obliging." Peter Deadfoot's accomplishments may not have included reading and writing, but thirty-year-old Elleck, who called himself Alexander Brown and whose master described him as "very artful," could read "pretty well." He was a bricklayer, mason, and plasterer. "There is hardly any thing in a common way but what he understands, can behave very well," his master reported.[8] Such men as these were obvious threats to slavery, for they shattered one of the strongest justifications that could be advanced for maintaining it—the argument that Africans were savages suited only for routine, menial labor and were unqualified to live in America as free persons.

The appearance of skilled, talented, acculturated blacks called for reassessment of slavery by the white population, a reassessment

7. Petition, September 1, 1802, in Petitions 1800–59, Legislative Papers, North Carolina Division of Archives and History.

8. Windley (comp.), *Runaway Slave Advertisements*, I, 289–90; II, 357.

it generally did not get. Rethinking also was demanded by the rising voices of antislavery protest that in the wake of the Revolution appeared in the South itself, sometimes even within plantation communities.

Antislavery agitation threatened to spread disruptive ideas throughout society. Such concepts might even become an element in localized plantation hostilities. Reformers' claims that slaves possessed "inalienable rights," that punishments were excessive and unjust, or, most damaging of all, that slavery itself was wrong and ought to be ended might infiltrate the plantations to add further tension to already strained master-slave relations.[9]

But that was only part of the problem. Masters themselves might succumb to the antislavery argument and defect from slaveholding ranks. When in 1799 "Othello," ostensibly a free-black resident of Maryland, alluded to "that corrosive anguish of persevering in anything improper, which now embitters the enjoyment of life," he identified a persistent problem. Some slaveowners believed themselves in the wrong and suffered in consequence. Some went so far as to free their slaves.[10]

Troubled consciences offered the antislavery cause potential for spectacular gains. On one of his early tours through Maryland, the Methodist evangelist Francis Asbury found that the slaveowner John Willson "acknowledged the wrong done the blacks by taking them from their country, but defended the right of holding them." Abolitionists managed to exploit this obvious weakness in the slaveholders' armor. Their success in encouraging manumissions perhaps was related to the decline in agriculture that made slaveholding in parts of Virginia and Maryland temporarily less profitable than it once had been. But however that may be, thousands of owners in the 1780s and afterward freed their slaves, offering moral and religious justification for doing so. Even in regions where explicitly antislavery argument was never tolerated, masters nevertheless sometimes were inclined at least to relax discipline and grant concessions to their bondsmen. "In many parts of this dis-

9. On this point, see an 1838 comment by Charles B. Shepard, quoted in Guion Griffis Johnson, *Ante-Bellum North Carolina: A Social History* (Chapel Hill, N.C., 1937), 565.

10. James O'Kelley, *Essay on Negro Slavery* (Philadelphia, 1789), 42. On the disputed issue of the southerners' sense of guilt, see Charles Grier Sellers, Jr., (ed.), *The Southerner as American* (Chapel Hill, N.C., 1960), 40–71, and James Oakes, *The Ruling Race: A History of American Slaveholders* (New York, 1982), 117–22.

trict," ran a report from South Carolina, "negroes have every other Saturday, keep horses, raise hogs, cultivate for themselves everything for home consumption, & for market, that their masters do." In this manner, generous and humane owners no doubt satisfied their sense of duty and salved their conscience; yet such laxity was not without drawbacks for the rest of the community. Planters who loosened control made the lives of less indulgent masters more difficult, while they also introduced a disruptive element into the lives of ordinary white folk who were trying to establish communities based on caste and patterns of "respectable" behavior. "Every measure that may lessen the dependence of a Slave on his master ought to be opposed, as tending to dangerous consequences," advised a group of South Carolinians in 1816. "The more privileges a Slave obtains, the less depending he is on his master, & the greater nuisance he is likely to be to the public."[11]

When the master's philanthropy extended to manumitting his slaves, the menace became extreme. The growing numbers of freed blacks acted as a particularly unsettling influence on those who remained slaves, a troublesome effect pondered even by antislavery advocates. "From this increase of free Negroes, their bondage will become intolerable to the Slaves, & their Efforts to escape from it will probably produce a catastrophe not to be contemplated without horror and dismay," predicted a committee of antislavery activists in 1796.[12] Such prophecy seemed well based, for despite the restrictions that hedged them, free blacks still enjoyed freedoms and initiative beyond those accorded any slave. The emotions experienced by slaves when they saw friends and relatives leaving as free persons may be imagined, although no writer seems ever to have explored them.

One such incident that did enter the historical record suggests the disruptive potential of the manumission vogue. In 1785 when the will of Joseph Mayo of Powhatan, Virginia, was opened, his heirs learned that he had freed his large slaveholdings. The Mayo slaves doubtless blessed their late master, but white neighbors found reason to regret his generosity. News of the manumissions destroyed

11. Elmer T. Clark et al. (eds.), The Journal and Letters of Francis Asbury (London, 1958), I, 442; petition, Orangeburgh, Amelia Township, December 4, 1816, Slavery Petitions, 1800–30, Legislative Papers, South Carolina Department of Archives and History.
12. Report of the Committee for Improving the Condition of the Free Blacks [1796], in Pennsylvania Abolition Society Papers.

discipline on nearby plantations and, according to one of Thomas Jefferson's correspondents, "caused 2 or 3 combats between slaves and their owners, now struggling for the liberty to which they conceive themselves entitled."[13]

Experiences of that sort taught lessons in caution and social responsibility. However strong the antislavery appeal, property interest and concern for order kept all but the most pious or philanthropic slaveowners firmly in line. But with nonslaveholders it was a different matter. When Hercules, a worker at the Nottingham Forge near Baltimore, was returned to his owner in 1782, he explained that he had "been back among the Dutch [Germans?], and they use him kindly, and pay him good wages." In 1790 the slave brothers Caesar and Jack escaped "into the frontier country" where, their master supposed, they were harbored by free Negroes or "by white persons who are enemies to slavery, and may think such a conduct warrantable." Perhaps most small farmers by the early nineteenth century identified their interests with those of the slaveholders and looked forward to owning slaves themselves. At very least, the majority of them apparently accepted the institution as necessary for social control. Yet working against their support of the masters' interests were counterclaims among which human sympathies ranked as the most compelling. The miseries and hardships to which slaves were subject caused even an aristocratic South Carolinian to muse that "if the Quakers travelled this road, I should not wonder at their wishes to end slavery. The abuse is glaring and wicked." In particular, the domestic slave trade, an essential feature of the institution, came under attack by lower- and middle-class persons who saw its cruelty and did not profit from it. It was this aspect of slavery that first awakened the conscience of Benjamin Lundy, the Quaker abolitionist, when he observed the slave trade in western Virginia. At about the same time, a traveler in that state noted that "the people on the road loaded the inhuman drivers with curses and execrations."[14] The loyalty of nonslaveholders to the system was essential; yet their loyalty was suspect and never could be

13. James Currie to Thomas Jefferson, August 5, 1785, in Boyd (ed.), *Papers of Thomas Jefferson*, VIII, 342–43. For the legal problems encountered in carrying out Mayo's will, see Hutchinson and Rachal (eds.), *Papers of James Madison*, IX, 150–51.

14. Windley (comp.), *Runaway Slave Advertisements*, II, 258–59, 382; Alize Izard to Ralph Izard, November 21, 1794, in Ralph Izard Papers, South Caroliniana Library, University of South Carolina, Columbia; [Thomas Earle], *Life, Travels, and Opinions of Benjamin Lundy* (Philadelphia, 1847), 15; Ulrich B. Phillips (ed.), *Plantation and Frontier, 1649–1863* (Cleveland, 1909), II, 55.

taken for granted. The support even of small slaveholders seemed to hang in the balance. At the turn of the century it was common for them to free their slaves in their wills and to use that solemn occasion to record for the benefit of survivors fervent antislavery testimony. Would a younger generation succumb to similar influence and follow the emancipating example of their elders?

The fact that southern whites voiced antislavery opinion at all proved that slaves possessed at least tentative allies in their incessant struggle against bondage. For the present, these advocates remained few and eccentric, but if antislavery ideas someday ceased being the monopoly of prophets and passed to the multitude, slaveowners would face a threat all but impossible to contain. One could foresee a three-way contest in which slaveowners—always a minority—would find themselves pitted against the combined forces of blacks and a white majority sympathetic to abolition. If that alliance materialized, the balance of power on the plantations almost certainly would shift, the master's authority would evaporate, and slavery would end. Much of the planters' effort from the Revolution to the Civil War was designed to prevent the alliance from being forged.

The endeavor achieved a large measure of success, yet the danger never entirely disappeared. Throughout the antebellum years, persons of uneasy mind detected subversive influences everywhere. A North Carolinian in 1840 thought he could see campaigns at work "both at home & abroad, which will render negro property very unsafe & insecure. I really fear more for our own citizens than I do from Northern influence."[15] The best defense was never to yield the slightest ground to antislavery critics or their argument. Even well-meaning owners, by excessive kindness toward their slaves, might promote the very disorder they sought to avoid.

An impression prevailed that philanthropic influences in the late eighteenth century and afterward had removed some of the most extreme impositions against slaves and had led to marked improvement in their circumstance. Fewer barbarities than in colonial days and more consistent attention to physical well being, it was thought, now characterized their lot. Thus, in 1794 on their travels through North Carolina, members of the great Izard family happily contrasted the plenty enjoyed by their own slaves back home in

15. Quoted in Johnson, *Antebellum North Carolina*, 506; David Brion Davis, *The Slave Power Conspiracy and the Paranoid Style* (Baton Rouge, 1970), 32–61; Steven A. Channing, *Crisis of Fear: Secession in South Carolina* (New York, 1970), 255–56.

South Carolina with the misery and squalor of the unfortunates belonging to their backward neighbors.[16] A degree of self-congratula-
tion showed through observations in that vein, obscuring the danger of indulgence. Other persons no less concerned for the public
good found the change alarming. They did not welcome relaxations
as progress but, rather, they viewed them as signs of white weakness
in the relentless struggle that characterized race relations in the
plantation South. While convention held that kindness and generosity brought greater benefits—that is, more productive labor—
than did severity, it also was believed that the kindness must be
freely granted and not extorted either by slaves or by white critics.
Unthinking relaxation of the bonds of slavery, these persons argued,
menaced the social order by inviting still further costly discord.[17]

Slaveowners everywhere would have found a complaint from
Orangeburgh District, South Carolina, in 1812 illustrative of one
of the dread results to be expected from diminished rigor. In that
plantation region, male slaves, "forgetting they were such"—that
is, having been *allowed* to forget their status—attempted "to exercise among some of the lower classes of white people freedoms and
familiarities which are dangerous to society." The petitioners complained especially about "the attempts which are made and some of
them with success at sexual intercourse with white females." The
lesson was easily drawn. Such boldness was "one of the consequences of softening their condition as slaves," a product of the
"general disposition . . . to ameliorate" the treatment traditionally
accorded blacks. In the absence of state law prohibiting this sexual
license (the offense was not rape), citizens of the "incensed and indignant neighborhood" thought it necessary "to erect a tribunal of
their own and to measure out justice to the offender with their own
hand."[18] The white community as a whole—slaveholder and non-
slaveholder alike—had come to the support of slavery by compen-
sating for certain masters' negligence or philanthropy. By no means
incidentally, they also had helped maintain essential social distance
between slaves and "the lower classes of white people." By prompt,
extralegal action, the community had reinforced the subordination

16. Jordan, *White over Black*, 367–68; Alize Izard to Ralph Izard, November 21,
1794, and Ralph Izard to Alize Izard, December 7, 1794, both in Ralph Izard Papers.
17. The debate continued. See the Minutes of the ABC Farmers' Club, 1846–48,
pp. 104–13, in Aiken County Records, South Caroliniana Library, University of South
Carolina, Columbia.
18. Petition, December 12, 1812, in Slavery Petitions, 1800–1830, Legislative Papers, South Carolina Department of Archives and History.

essential to the maintenance of slavery and a caste system. They had demonstrated further that in Orangeburgh slaves were to find no allies.

Such persuasive display of community backing strengthened the hands of masters in their day-to-day dealing with slaves. In the atmosphere that evidently prevailed in Orangeburgh District, even the most severe plantation discipline was unlikely to call forth rebuke from the tenderhearted. The slaves now had no place to turn. They were overwhelmed by white unity. Plantation resistance had lost its political import. As long as the majority sanctioned slavery and the means necessary to maintain it, the master held the upper hand on his own plantation and careless owners would be forced into line. Any subversion by slaves would be temporary and its effects localized. But if the situation should be reversed, and non-slaveholding whites sided with blacks in the continuing struggle, the owners certainly would go down to defeat. As the Democratic senator Stephen A. Douglas of Illinois liked to point out in the 1850s, slavery could not exist "for a day or an hour" in jurisdictions where the masters' claims failed to secure public sanction.[19] That condition never prevailed in the South, but unlikely as it now may seem, it appeared for a moment to be on the verge of developing.

Religion supplied the principal subversive force. Beginning near the middle of the eighteenth century, a succesion of evangelists— "new light" Presbyterians, Baptists, Methodists—moved through the South gaining converts as they went, especially from lower- and middle-class whites and slaves. Whatever the literal content of the revivalists' message, its effect was to blur social distinctions. Those who came under its sway were likely to magnify their own consequence while shedding some of their former deference by calling into question the values and behavior of their social betters, many of whom owned slaves.[20]

Slaves readily subscribed to the new gospel, finding in its teaching and method more vivid promise of salvation than was offered by the Anglicanism that previously had been virtually the sole source of their spiritual fare. For some of them, as for their white neighbors, evangelicalism bespoke equality and even the prospect

19. Edwin Earle Sparks (ed.), *The Lincoln Douglas Debates of 1858* (Springfield, Ill., 1908), 160.
20. Donald G. Mathews, *Religion in the Old South* (Chicago, 1977), 28–38, 40–41, 68–71; Rhys Isaac, "Evangelical Revolt: The Nature of the Baptists' Challenge to the Traditional Order in Virginia, 1765–1775," *William and Mary Quarterly*, 3rd ser., XXXI (1974), 345–68.

of temporal freedom. It also set forth a persuasive scriptural critique of slavery. Under the new dispensation, some slaves themselves became preachers—unordained and unauthorized, but preachers nonetheless—who exerted great influence within the black community.

Slaveowners were given much reason to look upon the new religious developments with disapproval, even anxiety, for they were associated with discontent and rebelliousness and a general loosening of the bonds of slavery. At Essex County courthouse in Virginia in 1767, Jupiter was tried and convicted "for stirring up the Negroes to an insurrection, being a great Newlight preacher." Three years later, the Virginia planter Landon Carter mused on what he regarded as the decline in trustworthiness of his slave Toney: "His first religion that broke out upon him was new light and I believe it is from some inculcated notions of those rascals that the slaves in this Colony are grown so much worse."[21]

Though blacks appear to have had special affinity for the gospel as preached by Baptists, it was Methodists in particular who late in the century occupied the vanguard of the small army of preachers intent upon evangelizing the South. All but inseparable from Methodist gospel was an antislavery message paralleling the liberal view of human rights associated with the Revolution. Like other evangelists, Methodists preached to free and slave alike. If overt condemnations of slavery generally were absent from their services for blacks, a gospel of personal worth and spiritual liberation assuredly was not. Further, it is unlikely that the antislavery views that many evangelists held could be altogether hidden from black worshipers.

Itinerant Methodist ministers did not hold back from attempting to proselytize whites to the antislavery cause. They were noted for their attempts to influence the behavior of new church members by insisting upon emancipation as a corollary to salvation. The Reverend Samuel Mitchell remembered the years when he rode circuit in Virginia and "was in the constant habit of advising all such as attached themselves to the Methodist church to emancipate their slaves."[22] Preachers urged nonslaveholding converts to become advocates of emancipation. Not surprisingly, Methodist efforts provoked hostility from those who foresaw in their successes shifts in

21. Windley (comp.), *Runaway Slave Advertisements*, I, 56; Jack P. Greene (ed.), *Diary of Landon Carter*, I, 378.
22. Catterall (ed.), *Judicial Cases*, I, 183–84.

opinion that, if allowed to grow unchecked, promised social discord and the consequent doom of slavery.[23]

At their Baltimore conference in 1784, Methodist bishops challenged the existing social order by adopting emancipation as an official goal. Few could doubt the sincerity of their pronouncements, for preachers and their converts displayed no hesitancy in moving beyond antislavery rhetoric to direct action. Not only did they spread an antislavery gospel; they sometimes defended slaves from the impositions of patrols, helped fugitives elude their pursuers, and acted in other less overt ways to undermine slaveholding society.

From the sheriff of King William County, Virginia, in 1789 came a report certain to give pause to those fearful of the rising white sympathy for slaves. At a rural schoolhouse east of Richmond, Methodists and Baptists "two or three times a week" held nighttime religious meetings for whites, slaves, and free blacks. These interracial gatherings disrupted plantation discipline, complained the sheriff: "Our Negroes are not to be found when we are in want of them, but are at such meetings." Under evangelical influence, blacks apparently considered themselves almost emancipated. They moved freely about the countryside and stole "everything they can lay there hands on." Fully as outrageous was the disdain pious whites displayed for the authority of patrols charged with maintaining order among slaves and confining them to plantations. When on one occasion the patrol tried to break up the Methodists' meeting, "Mr. Charles Neale through one of them out of the doore & said that they should not take up any negro that was there." If Methodist influence were not checked, warned the sheriff, "Our negroes wood next under the same pretence disobey the orders of there Masters under the pretence of Religion." Only one conclusion was possible: "If there is nothing done with those people we shall not have a negro to command."[24]

Doubtless the situation the sheriff described was extraordinary; yet sympathy for blacks and antagonism toward the instruments of racial control, if manifested at all, signified danger. The burgeoning religious enthusiasm fostered by Baptist and Methodist preachers

23. For two such instances, see Wesley M. Gewehr, *The Great Awakening in Virginia, 1740–1790* (Durham, N.C., 1930), 247, and Clark *et al.* (eds.), *Journal and Letters of Francis Asbury*, I, 355, 442, 488.

24. Johnston, *Race Relations*, 97–98. For a former slave's understanding of the masters' dread of Methodist egalitarianism, see [John Thompson], *Life of John Thompson, a Fugitive Slave . . .* (Worcester, Mass., 1856), 19.

brought blacks and whites together in situations that ignored, even defied, the social and political order. At the end of such a path lay the fall of slavery. Religiously inspired opposition to slavery in the Early National Era constituted a grave internal threat to the plantation order.

It was not that slaveowners opposed the spread of religion among lesser whites or even among slaves. Indeed, beginning in the mid-1830s, a "mission to the slaves" became central to southern Protestant activity. But masters expected their slaves to be inculcated with a faith that reinforced slavery rather than undermined it. A Presbyterian missionary assigned to North Carolina found that slaveowners welcomed "intelligent" ministers, but were "opposed to those ignorant preachers who endeavor to work more upon the Passions & Sympathies of the negro by loud unmeaning bawling, instead of truth."[25] They expected the result of preaching to be pacification and spiritual ease, not enthusiasm and unrest.

Although some believed religion contributed to slave docility, others found the newly converted to be less humble, less slavelike than before. The Louisiana planter Bennet Barrow thought he knew why sixteen of his neighbor's slaves ran away: "All this grows out of his having them preached to for 4 or 5 years past—greatest piece of foolishness any one every [sic] guilty of." As born-again Christians, some slaves preferred to devote themselves to religious exercises rather than to the owner's tasks. If daytime routine left them no room for their new concerns, they would pursue them at night, the time custom conceded to be their own. Night meetings ruin "the servants," a North Carolina owner complained. Not even the most pious master was likely to count the spiritual welfare of bondsmen as worth the sacrifice of discipline and labor. Religious activity among slaves could be tolerated only within limits: "We all seem to live in peace & quietness," wrote a South Carolina planter, "& by putting a stop to all this pretended Religion the Negros gits their Rest of nights."[26]

25. Donald G. Mathews, "The Methodist Mission to the Slaves, 1829–1844," *Journal of American History,* LI (1965), 615–31; D. A. Campbell to Absalom Peters, September 15, 1834, in American Home Missionary Society Papers, Amistad Research Center, Tulane University, New Orleans.

26. Edwin A. Davis (ed.), *Plantation Life in the Florida Parishes of Louisiana, 1836–1846, as Reflected in the Diary of Bennet H. Barrow* (New York, 1943), 323–24; N. H. Harding to Absalom Peters, August 16, 1829, in American Home Missionary Society Papers; Hugh McCauley to Isaac Ball, June 2, 1814, in Ball Family Papers, South Caroliniana Library, University of South Carolina, Columbia.

Most objectionable to the slaveowners was the evangelists' mingling of religious zeal with secular policy. The practice was opposed because it so nearly proved successful. For a few years during the 1780s there was reason to expect liberal ideas eventually to dominate the white population of Virginia and Maryland and thus bring about the collapse of slavery in the upper South. No such prospect seemed at all likely in either South Carolina or Georgia, where religion and philosophy offered only feeble and easily handled challenges. Only a few antislavery voices were heard in Georgia—at the academy at Augusta, for example, and on one brief but notable occasion from the judicial bench. The protest in South Carolina was just as ineffective.[27]

There, a combination of great planters, the near equivalent of an oligarchy, controlled affairs. Among South Carolina gentry there existed no group parallel to Virginia's aristocratic critics of slavery. Long before abolitionism had caused much stir elsewhere, political candidates whose background suggested weakness in support of slavery found they had little chance of winning elections in South Carolina. With the conspicuous exceptions of Henry Laurens and his son John (whose great wealth derived in part from the slave trade), virtually all leading South Carolinians in the revolutionary and Early National eras stood foursquare behind slavery. Efforts to circulate contrary views, even within the confines of the upper class, were scarcely tolerated, as Henry Laurens himself discovered. In 1785 he ventured to give a copy of Richard Price's much-read pamphlet in defense of the American Revolution to John F. Grimké, one of the state's wealthiest planters. Grimké shared the pamphlet's amazing antislavery message with his still richer friend Ralph Izard. The two magnates were predictably indignant. Grimké "thought himself almost affronted by having the pamphlet presented," because it advocated "measures for preventing too great an inequality of property and for gradually abolishing the Negro trade and Slavery." They "reprobate" your work, Laurens informed the author.[28]

27. Adam Boyd to Committee of Correspondence, November 25, 1797, and Isaac Briggs to President of the Society, September 10, 1790, both in Pennsylvania Abolition Society Papers; Charlton, "Judge and a Grand Jury," 206–15.

28. Robert L. Brunhouse (ed.), "David Ramsay, 1749–1815: Selections from His Writings," *Transactions of the American Philosophical Society*, n.s., LV, Pt. 4, (1965), 123; Richard Price to Thomas Jefferson, July 2, 1785, in Boyd (ed.), *Papers of Thomas Jefferson*, VIII, 258.

Before the westward spread of cotton culture, up-country farmers, having few obvious economic ties to slavery and not much sympathy for it, might have acted as a countervailing influence to low-country planters, but that potential could not be realized because earlier generations had apportioned representation in the General Assembly so as to deprive the up-country of effective political voice. Such opposition to slavery as did appear secured no permanent toehold in any part of South Carolina society. Even the resistance to its spread, which early in the century surfaced in up-country counties, withered by 1820 in the face of the westward-moving cotton culture and rising land prices.[29]

The clergy were not immune to such influence. The fate of antislavery religious protest in South Carolina, as eventually through most of the South, was foreshadowed by a clerical gathering at Charleston. There, in January, 1795, twenty-three Methodist ministers from the South Carolina low-country drew up a statement affirming the "impropriety" and "baneful consequences" of slavery. They then took note of the trend that soon was to overwhelm their southern efforts. Falling under their censure were those Methodist ministers who had "become the patrons of Slavery as well as the holders of Slaves themselves; to the Scandal of the ministry, and the strengthening of the hands of Oppression."[30] Not even antislavery clergymen could easily resist conforming to social norms.

In Virginia, antislavery ideas spread more widely than in most other parts of the South. By 1782 humanitarians in the state legislature had acquired enough influence to enact a law permitting individuals to manumit their slaves without first securing special permission from state authorities. The new measure led to rapid increase of the state's free-black population. Their numbers grew from three thousand in 1780 to thirty thousand in 1810.[31] Those who distrusted blacks found this a deplorable development. In Accomac

29. Examples of up-country antislavery thought—all expressed in the aftermath of a slave-conspiracy scare in Camden, South Carolina—appear in Grand Jury Presentments from Chester, November, 1816, Fairfield, November 19, 1816, Kershaw, November 19, 1816, Lexington, October, 1816, Richland, October, 1816, and York, October 29, 1816, all in Grand Jury Presentments, South Carolina Department of Archives and History.

30. Quoted in George C. Rogers, Jr., *Charleston in the Age of the Pinckneys* (Norman, Okla., 1969), 143.

31. William Waller Hening (comp.), *The Statutes at Large, Being a Compilation of All the Laws of Virginia . . .* (Richmond, 1810–23), XI, 39–40. For statistics on growth, see Jordan, *White over Black*, 406–407, and Ira Berlin, *Slaves Without Masters: The Free Negro in the Antebellum South* (New York, 1974), 46–47.

County in the 1780s, free blacks were popularly thought to be unreconstructed Tories, covertly maintaining British sympathies and sheltering runaway slaves. But even when they did nothing illegal or overtly subversive, their mere presence—"a race or nation of people between the masters and slaves"—made slaves discontented and hard to control.[32] Slavery, one could believe, would be more difficult to maintain now that humanitarians had persuaded the legislature to ease the avenue of escape from it.

Under religious tutelage in the mid-1780s, antislavery sentiment grew confident enough for its advocates to seek enactment of a gradual-emancipation law. The Virginia law of 1782 had *allowed* manumissions; under terms of the new proposal the state would *require* them. But antislavery advocates were not to have their way. By 1785, when petitions supporting their measure reached the General Assembly, defenders of slavery had mobilized to resist their critics. While antislavery partisans had been circulating petitions among small farmers and church members, their opponents were traveling through the state gathering signatures urging defeat of a measure that would multiply the free-black population and revolutionize the state's social structure.

The pro-slavery petitions, signed by 1,244 Virginians, reveal the attitude and interests of those early defenders of slavery. They cited scripture to counter the evangelists' claim that slavery conflicted with religious principles. Further, they argued, victory in the Revolution confirmed the right to private property. Abolition would violate that natural right and thus surrender a patriotic accomplishment. They dwelt at length on the dangers posed by free blacks, whom they termed "banditti." These objections no doubt carried much weight, but so, too, did another point. Slavery, the petitioners implied, was a distinctively American institution essential to continued growth. Persons who tried to destroy it were, at best, sentimental and impractical reformers. At worst, they were disorganizers, opponents of progress, enemies seeking to tear down the country.[33]

Confronted by such a formidable argument, the gradual-emancipation plan failed to win a hearing in the state legislature. The lawmakers' decision was made easier by the abolitionists' inability to

32. Johnston, *Race Relations*, 42; McColley, *Slavery and Jeffersonian Virginia*, 151; Hutchinson and Rachal (eds.), *Papers of James Madison*, VIII, 403–404, 442, 477.

33. Fredrika Teute Schmidt and Barbara Ripel Wilhelm, "Early Proslavery Petitions in Virginia," *William and Mary Quarterly*, 3rd ser., XXX (1973), 133–46.

gain overt support from the older, traditional source of antislavery thought in Virginia, the great liberal spokesmen who during the recent struggle for independence had identified themselves with the cause of human rights. While antislavery groups were preparing their petition campaign, Methodist leaders traveled to Mount Vernon in hope of enlisting the aid of George Washington. The general disappointed them. He gave the visitors "his opinion against slavery" but declined to sign their petition, although he promised that if the legislature took up the measure, he would write a letter of support.[34]

Thomas Jefferson did not go even that far. At the height of the revolutionary era, Jefferson showed signs of becoming an active proponent of antislavery measures, but his enthusiasm soon was checked and then as rapidly declined. Eventually he assessed the problems involved in antislavery programs as beyond the wisdom of his generation. In neither large ways nor small ones would he follow a course designed to weaken slavery. He even declined appointment as executor of Thaddeus Kosciuszko's will, which authorized use of the revolutionary hero's estate to acquire slaves for the purpose of freeing and educating them.[35]

It had become clear that despite the resounding words of the revolutionary era, the self-interest of slaveowners would not permit general emancipation. Though finely honed consciences found evils and inconsistencies in slavery, it nonetheless had been an accepted part of life in Virginia during nearly all the commonwealth's existence. Its removal would require major readjustments from everyone in the state, black and white alike. If slavery ended, the old familiar problems and anxieties associated with it would be replaced by new ones fully as difficult and painful as the old.

Perhaps the strongest objection raised to any emancipation plan was the obvious fact that it would remove from the black population the controls that now kept most of them profitably employed at their masters' work and in a well-defined servile position. The behavior of those already freed did not seem reassuring. Although many newly manumitted blacks lived the kind of sober, industrious lives that commended them to substantial white citizens, a number of them conspicuously did not. Even abolitionists sometimes de-

34. Clark *et al.* (eds.), *Journal and Letters of Francis Asbury*, I, 489. With respect to slavery, George Washington wrote to Alexander Spotswood on November 23, 1794, that "I shall frankly declare to you that I do not like even to think, much less talk of it." Phillips (ed.), *Plantation and Frontier*, I, 56.
35. Catterall (ed.), *Judicial Cases*, IV, 178–79.

plored the idleness and intemperance in which some free blacks indulged, and found their wayward conduct a strong obstacle against popular commitment to emancipation. The presence of a landless, civilly irresponsible class was an object of dread nearly everywhere in early America, perhaps in no place more strongly than in Virginia, where in the seventeenth century unruly poor whites had been a source of political and social unrest and a menace to law and property.[36] If landless whites, bound to the ruling class by ties of race and culture, once had flirted with rebellion, how much greater the danger to be expected now from landless and alien blacks!

Abolitionists in the upper South also encountered strong opposition in efforts to aid blacks already free. They had concentrated their activities in the city of Alexandria. There, as in the South's other urban centers, the black population rapidly increased in the 1780s. The discrimination and poverty that commonly afflicted the newly freed aroused compassion in some whites but suspicion in others. As oppressed and relatively unassimilated people—outsiders—the blacks' loyalty to existing social and political arrangements could not be taken for granted. Would they become sober, productive workers? Would they be reconciled to the permanent bondage of their fellow blacks? Free blacks in the North already had taken an active antislavery stance. Would they themselves be content to remain a caste at the bottom of society? What terrible social convulsions might they precipitate?

Virginia and Maryland abolitionists attempted to remove the anxiety such questions generated by providing free blacks with schools. This was a less oblique assault on poverty and unrest than it may at first appear. As a device for instilling conventional values, education might serve as a tranquilizing influence. Looked at more generously, education also could help outsiders become participating members of society. The schools taught skills that might be expected to promote economic and social mobility. The educational experiments in Alexandria and elsewhere thus demonstrated abolitionist assumptions that blacks formed part of the social order and should be encouraged to rise within it. But these assumptions clashed with the intentions of persons pledged to the opposite: Blacks must forever remain outsiders—subordinate to whites, pref-

36. Alexander Addison to the Society, December 6, 1790, Report of the Virginia Abolition Society, May 5, 1797, George Drinker to Joseph Bringhurst, December 10, 1804, Report of the Choptank, Maryland, Abolition Society, April 26, 1797, all in Pennsylvania Abolition Society Papers; Edmund S. Morgan, *American Slavery*, 215–270.

erably as slaves—and the existing social order must be perpetuated. Not easily eliminated was the suspicion that free blacks retained sympathy with slaves and, in conjunction with them, would act as fatal counterbalance to white power.

Not surprisingly, the educational activities of the antislavery societies came under attack even before revelations of major slave plots magnified racial antipathies. Their most effective critic was the distinguished young physician and planter Elisha Cullen Dick (he served as consulting physician during George Washington's last illness). His early objection could be dismissed as prophecy, but Gabriel's conspiracy four years later made his views appear realistic and unanswerable.

Abolition societies, he warned, tended to produce "the most serious calamities" in the South. Abolitionist schoolteachers "constantly" inculcated "natural equality among the blacks of every description. They are teaching them with great assiduity the only means by which they can at any time be enabled to concert and execute a general insurrection." Literate free blacks would teach their skills to slaves and thus make coordinated resistance easy. Prudent citizens, it followed, must unite to suppress antislavery activity.[37]

By the time Dick penned his warning, the wave of fear that followed Gabriel's conspiracy had swept across the state. Blacks did not wait for whites to tell them how to respond. Education and emancipation became less important to them than survival. They now made themselves as inconspicuous as possible, avoiding abolitionists and no longer attending the societies' schools. White abolitionists, too, gave in to the constraints of popular disapproval. So low did the fortunes and prospects of Virginia abolitionists fall that a year later the reporter for the society at Alexandria declared, "We are in fact dead, and I may say, I have no hope of reanimation."[38] The conclusion was inescapable: No effective measures promoting the demise of slavery and the elevation of free blacks were at all likely to be put forth in Virginia or anywhere else in the South.

Thoroughly foreshadowed though it was, such pessimism emerged suddenly. Even as late as the spring of 1800, Methodists

37. Berlin, *Slaves Without Masters*, 82–83; Archer McLean to William Rogers, February 15, 1796, and Report of the Alexandria Society, May 28, 1801, both in Pennsylvania Abolition Society Papers; Elisha Dick to James Monroe, September 26, 1800, in Palmer, McRae, and Flournoy (eds.), *Calendar of Virginia Papers*, IX, 178.
38. James Wood, Address of the Virginia Abolition Society, May 22, 1801, in Pennsylvania Abolition Society Papers.

apparently hardly felt it at all. On May 2, only three months before revelation of Gabriel's conspiracy, the Methodist bishops set forth a reinvigorated campaign to promote emancipation. Their recent failure to move Virginia legislators to enact a gradual-emancipation law had not proved disspiriting, for the momentum of continued church growth appeared to belie the permanence of such reversals. In a printed address, the bishops directed each annual conference to instruct special committees of elders, deacons, and traveling preachers to gather signatures from all their "acquaintances and all the friends of liberty" calling upon the southern state legislatures to provide for gradual emancipation.

The bishops did not intend to confine their campaign to the South nor to make it solely a denominational effort. They urged persons in the North to join the crusade by exerting their influence on acquaintances in the slave states, "whether those friends be Methodists or not." This activity was not designed as an experiment or a one-time enterprise. The bishops directed that pressure on the southern state legislatures "be continued from year to year, 'till the desired end be fully accomplished.'" In effect, the rapidly growing Methodist church announced its transformation into an aggressive antislavery society. Its goal, declared the bishops, was "equal liberty."[39]

News of the Methodists' plan and reports of Gabriel's conspiracy reached South Carolina at nearly the same time, a coincidence no doubt adding to the alarm expressed by state officials over both. Senator Jacob Read sent a copy of the bishops' printed address to the governor with a warning. If South Carolinians allowed Methodists to proceed with their petition drive, they would "bring down the firebrands to our houses and daggers to our throats. . . . Quakers and Methodists have long been sapping the existence of the Southern States," Read charged. "The former are however harmless when compared to the latter." The governor placed a copy of the Methodist document before the state legislature along with his own observation of "its improper tendency, as highly incompatible, with the rights of all the Southern States; and extremely interesting to this State in particular."[40]

39. [Methodist Episcopal Church], *The Address of the General Conference of the Methodist Episcopal Church, to All Their Brethren and Friends in the United States, Baltimore, May 23, 1800* (N.p., n.d.).
40. Jacob Read to John Drayton, July 18, 1800, in Governor's Message to the Senate, November 25, 1800, in Governors' Messages, 1791–1800, South Carolina Department of Archives and History.

Citizens in Charleston did not wait for the legislature to act. A mob confronted the city's leading Methodist preachers, burned their petitions, and escorted the Reverend George Daugherty to the town pump. There they held his head under the spout until he nearly drowned. Not only did public opinion in South Carolina thus check the petition campaign at its beginning, but the Methodist clergy's work among slaves was made more difficult as owners all over the state became leery of allowing them to preach on their plantations. At the same time, the legislature controlled religious services for blacks by forbidding them to be held at night or behind closed doors.[41]

Popular opposition and legislative action halted antislavery activity in South Carolina, as it had elsewhere in the South, before it had a chance to become politically effective. Yet one of its troublesome side effects, the free-black population, remained. The problem of the free blacks, a group likely to oppose slavery and by its mere existence to weaken it, grew more urgent as their numbers continued to rise. Southern determination to perpetuate slavery strengthened the motive to eliminate free blacks.

No doubt many white persons were sufficiently informed of the course of the Saint-Domingue revolt to know that it originated in an uprising by the colony's free mulatto population. If that class could initiate insurrection in one slave society, presumably it could do so in another. Accordingly, a group of slaveholders in the upper South joined with northern philanthropists to develop a plan to remove the troublesome element from the country. A number of early antislavery writers, recognizing "the race problem" as being an obstacle to any plan to end slavery, earlier had ventured proposals to make emancipation more palatable by exporting freed blacks. Some blacks appeared to welcome the idea. In Boston in 1788, a group requested the city council to help them emigrate to Africa.[42] But it was prejudice and fear of insurrection rather than hopes for abolition that infused the scheme with whatever appeal it had in the South. In 1800, as a response to Gabriel's conspiracy, the subject first gained official consideration in Virginia.

First discussed in secret by the House of Burgesses, the proposal

41. Albert Deems Betts, *History of South Carolina Methodism* (Charleston, S.C., 1952), 92, 169, 170.

42. St. George Tucker to John Page, March 29, 1790, and John Pemberton to Committee of the London Society, November, 1788, in Pennsylvania Abolition Society Papers.

soon received endorsement from an array of persons regarded as leaders in the upper South. John Marshall, chief justice of the United States; Bushrod Washington, the first president's nephew; and Henry Clay, a rising young political star—all soon ranked in the leadership of the colonization movement. At the same time, philanthropists and clergymen in the northern and southern states favored the project as both a humanitarian measure benefiting oppressed people and a missionary enterprise likely to promote the conversion of Africa. Diplomatic conflict leading to war with England in 1812 prevented implementation in the first years of the century. But with peace restored, the plan emerged as an enterprise to be conducted on a nationwide scale.

In 1816 the American Colonization Society was formed in Washington, D.C., in part for humanitarian motives, in part to lessen the likelihood of slave unrest by removing the slaves' most obvious allies. The society's efforts came to little. The number of persons to be transported was too great and the society's resources were too small to make the project feasible, even had slaveowners generally resolved to support it. Approval for the society's program—never very extensive—rapidly declined, especially in the lower South. The activity of its agents and the spread of its publications, some warned, would incite slaves just as other antislavery propaganda did. A writer in the *Southern Review* set forth the society's probable effect on slaves: "Conceiving that there is some power at work for their relief, the nature of which they do not accurately understand—constantly reminded that there are those in the world who think them the victim of injustice, and who have the power to protect and relieve them—they contract of course, the anxious restlessness which is the natural effect of anticipated good deferred."[43] In short, colonizationists would encourage slaves in waging their plantation struggles for autonomy.

White southerners soon concluded, although with much hesitancy, that free blacks could be tolerated, that they were a lesser danger to plantation order than was colonizationist propaganda. Free blacks continued to be seen as a social problem and a source of aid and encouragement to disruptive slaves, but their concentration in cities and towns reduced their irritating effect. Few free blacks lived in rural, agricultural regions where they might contaminate

43. Review of *The Tenth Annual Report of the American Society for Colonizing the Free People of Colour. . .* , 228–29.

the large numbers of plantation slaves. Further, in the 1820s and 1830s the continued westward spread of plantation slavery reduced the proportion of slaves likely to be in contact with them. At the same time, state legislatures restricted the possibility of further manumissions and placed the free-black population under increasingly rigid controls designed to minimize its subversive potential.

Meanwhile, internal sources of dissent lessened. The churches that had so boldly challenged southern society before 1800 modified their critical stance. For the most part they abandoned their effort to undermine the worldly order in which they functioned. No more harsh condemnations emerged from church councils. Abolitionist clergymen left the South voluntarily or were expelled. Silence, of course, never was total. Here and there, mostly in the upper South, Quakers, Baptist Friends of Humanity, and resolute evangelicals continued to expound the ideals of an earlier day and throughout the 1820s supported tiny antislavery societies. But however much these homegrown dissidents annoyed slaveowners, they functioned so far from the centers of power and so clearly diverged from the mainstream of sectional development as to seem merely embarrassing rather than dangerous.

Nonslaveholders, too, ceased being the imminent threat they had seemed at the start of the century, when antislavery preachers appeared to be mobilizing them in the slaves' favor. Many of the small farmers who aspired to become planters themselves or who lived among them in close economic and social association wholly accepted the planters' views and leadership, while others, unwilling to join the consensus, chose to leave the South rather than stay on to fight dubious battles.[44]

However, remaining and scattered throughout the region was an unabsorbed nonslaveholding element—upland farmers not bound economically to the planters, and, especially in the cities, artisans, teachers, tradesmen, and laborers of every sort—whose ties with slavery were loose or nonexistent. Their allegiance to the planters' values and leadership could not be assumed. Chiefly on their account, the specter of crumbling support for slavery and thus of a changed balance of power within the South never could be completely dispelled.

44. *Annals of Congress*, 16th Cong., lst Sess., 292, 1354; William T. Allan in *Liberator*, August 25, 1843; John Rankin, *Letters on American Slavery Addressed to Mr. Thomas Rankin* . . . (Newburyport, Mass., 1837), 72; Avery O. Craven, *The Coming of the Civil War* (New York, 1942), 95; John D. Barnhart, "Sources of Southern Migration into the Old Northwest," *Mississippi Valley Historical Review*, XXII (1935), 49–62.

The challenge to planter dominance offered by liberal theorists and evangelicals had been met successfully. The spread of cotton culture had secured for slavery a tight hold on the South, making it possible for the many who would defend it to overcome the few inside the section who would end it. No organized group remained to question slavery or to contest the planters' control. Nonetheless, the potential for challenge by nonslaveholders remained. And always contributing to insecurity was knowledge that disruptive abolitionist influences still might come from outside the South, influences that slaves—and nonslaveholders—might find seductive and that slaveholders would have no tested means to forestall.

6

Growing Antislavery
Pressures

In the first years of the new century antislavery sentiment studded northern public discourse and newspapers, particularly those of Federalist persuasion. Although these criticisms of southern institutions could be read as reflections of pure philanthropy, they carried obvious political implications as well. Federalist authors could not hide their delight in exposing the hypocrisy of Jeffersonian Democrats who celebrated liberty and republicanism while living from the labor of slaves.

Even if partisan politics sometimes appeared to furnish both occasion and motive for northern strictures against slavery, that explanation by no means detracted from their subversive impact on the South. Neither did it lessen their influence on northern opinion. Antislavery and antisouthern ideas appeared so often in northern print, sermons, and conversation as to become commonplace. In that way they acquired the authority of any other conventional belief. In 1821 Representative Henry Meigs of New York could speak, with little likelihood of contradiction, of northerners' and southerners' twenty-year-long "series of sarcasms upon each others customs, modes of living, and manners."[1] In the North antislavery early became a cultural given.

New Englanders in particular came to see themselves as morally

1. *Annals of Congress*, 16th Cong., lst Sess., 943.

superior to residents of the slave states, a conviction some of them made little effort to conceal. Thus, as early as 1806 a South Carolinian, evidently feeling no need for elaboration, referred to "the inhabitants of New England, some of whom look upon their Southern Brethren as an inferior race of men." Such northern self-pride could cause even persons who moved from New England intending to make the South their home to experience a sense of loss rather than hope and anticipation. "I can assure you I am not very well pleased with South Carolina," wrote Susan Blanding in 1808, shortly after she arrived in Camden. "I think a person to quit the Northern states to spend their life in the South, must make a great sacrifice, yes, sacrificing a land of Liberty for a land of slavery . . . a land of luxury, acquired by the hearts blood of the poor ignorant Africans—such indeed is the difference."[2]

Moral self-satisfaction came to seem inseparable from northern birth, and its development did not need to await the arrival of aggressive abolitionism in the 1830s. In 1816 James K. Paulding wrote of northern men who floundered "into Virginia . . . loaded with a pack of prejudices as large as a pedlar's [sic]." And in 1820 residents of Laurens District in South Carolina complained of the supercilious air assumed by northern-based "Hawkers and Peddlers" who "have generally a great aversion to the southern and western or Slaveholding States." Little happened afterward to lessen Yankee prejudice. "Texas and Arkansas are to me more truly foreign than Canada or the West Indies or even Van Diemensland," wrote a Connecticut clergyman in 1848.[3]

Such private aversion was easily transmitted to public and official bodies. Although Congress long remained immune to antislavery pressures, state legislatures more readily succumbed. Thus in February, 1805, Pennsylvania dispatched an intemperate resolution to its southern counterparts: "The House of Representatives unhesitatingly, declare, that Slavery in any shape, within the United States, is a blot on the American character; and that they will, with

2. William James Ball to Isaac Ball, November 24, 1806, in Ball Family Papers; Susan Blanding to the Blanding Family, December 2, 1808, in William Blanding Papers, South Caroliniana Library, University of South Carolina, Columbia.
3. [James K. Paulding], *Letters from the South, Written During an Excursion in the Summer of 1816* (New York, 1817), I, 31; Grand Jury Presentment from Laurens District, November, 1820, in Grand Jury Presentments, South Carolina Department of Archives and History; James T. Dickinson to George Whipple, March 6, 1848, in American Missionary Association Archives, Amistad Research Center, Tulane University, New Orleans.

ardour, seize any occasion, to lend their aid, to wipe off and prevent the extension of the foul stain."[4]

Slaveowners deplored the mounting northern criticism of southern institutions as menacing, insulting, unconstitutional interference with local affairs. Its effect, complained the astute southern partisan John Taylor of Caroline, was exactly as intended—it undermined slavery by encouraging slave resistance.[5] Northern antislavery critics, as expected, yielded nothing to the objection, but early developed a response derived in part from their impression that widespread discontent already prevailed among slaves. They construed the well-publicized slave plots of 1800–1803 as events justifying opposition to slavery rather than as reason to abandon it. Only by freeing the slaves, they argued, could catastrophe be avoided. In this way northern antislavery activity early became associated with fears for the physical safety of American society. By rebelling and plotting to rebel, slaves contributed to the growth of a northern antislavery movement.

The threat of insurrection gave calls for emancipation an urgency they might otherwise have lacked and provided antislavery programs an attraction that religious and moral argument alone could never have supplied. White southerners warned that antislavery agitation would promote slave rebellion, but early abolitionists were just as insistent that their program offered a means of averting disaster rather than of encouraging it. As long as slavery existed, the American Convention for Promoting the Abolition of Slavery warned in 1801, the danger of race war would persist.[6]

Northerners had to explain to themselves and to others why they were so troubled about an institution that already had been ended in their own section. Slavery, abolitionists insisted, was a national problem; the Constitution, with its package of sectional compromises, had made it so. Each part of the Constitution pertaining to slavery had its northern critic, but the most objectionable clause (second only to the three-fifths compromise) concerned military affairs. The Constitution's provision for federal military aid to suppress insurrection made the South's volatile labor system a national concern. If rebellion broke out, abolitionists explained, northern

4. Commonwealth of Pennsylvania, Resolution Addressed to the Legislature of North Carolina, February 20, 1805, in James Turner Papers, Vol. III, in Governors' Papers, North Carolina Division of Archives and History.

5. Taylor, *Arator*, 115, 118–19.

6. American Convention for Promoting the Abolition of Slavery, *Minutes of the Proceedings of the Convention of Delegates . . . 1801* (Philadelphia, 1801), 38–39.

soldiers would be called upon to march against the South's blacks, and northern taxpayers would share the burden of financing the campaign. Even if by some miracle slaves remained quiet in peacetime, involvement in foreign war—and that seemed likely as long as the Napoleonic Wars continued—would make them an immediate danger, or so events of the preceding century taught. In any future conflict northern soldiers would be saddled with a disproportionate share of the military burden because white southerners would have to stay at home to control dissident slaves. "Take away those [southern] whites who must remain to watch over the Slaves, and how many will there be, to act against the enemy? . . . Who fought the Battles of Independence?" These embarrassing questions—some of them soon to be given added pertinence by the War of 1812—appeared in the Boston *Repertory* on April 24, 1804.[7]

Discussions of slavery in this way assumed the pragmatic quality that characterized them for some years after 1800. Still it was all but impossible to bar abstract questions of right and wrong from discussion of an institution that so glaringly clashed with the frequently celebrated national ideals of liberty and equality. The waves of religious revivals that periodically swept America, reaching a height in the 1740s and continuing into the new century, encouraged a moralistic approach to all public issues. At the same time, the revivals brought about a reordering of values in those who came under their sway. Emerging from the experience with sharpened awareness of their own individuality and worth, new converts were likely to seek equal social station and recognition for themselves. Some extended to others, even to slaves, the concern they felt for their own personal dignity. Moved by heightened religious sensibility, some of them called for the end of slavery, less because they had calculated its damage to society and the economy than because they now counted it a great wrong perpetrated against fellow human beings.

Contributing to the strength of the religious argument, as evangelicals shaped it, was their overpowering sense of doom. Although for some persons, as the historian Linda Kerber once observed, every age is an Age of Anxiety, the early years of the Republic were exceptionally so.[8] Optimists might find in those troubled times re-

7. Quoted in Kerber, *Federalists in Dissent*, 40. See also *Annals of Congress*, 9th Cong., lst Sess., 370–71.
8. Kerber, *Federalists in Dissent*, 158. See also Page Smith, "Anxiety and Despair in American History," *William and Mary Quarterly*, 3rd ser., XXVI (1969), 416–24.

juvenation and hope, but others detected in the same events only decline. Evangelicals in particular viewed sin and self-indulgence and growing secularism (which they believed characterized the age) as an invitation to God's wrath.

Some of the evangelicals considered slavery the most flagrant of the many sins in which Americans, individually and collectively, indulged. Retribution must be expected. Persons who supposed themselves wise enough to fathom God's ways speculated that the divine punishment would precisely fit the crime. Already the righteous discerned signs supporting prophecy that a slaveholding nation would be destroyed in a holocaust of slave rebellion and race war. They could not easily ignore the portent of Saint-Domingue and the warnings supplied by Gabriel and the unnumbered, mostly anonymous black conspirators who succeeded him.

Through such ominous associations the antislavery argument early acquired the evangelical quality that in the 1830s became its hallmark and helped supply its proponents with their abundant, remorseless energy. Abolition, argued its religious advocates, was not primarily a matter of secular policy and rational choice; it was, above all else, a religious duty. American Home Missionary Society agents who worked in the southern states in the late 1820s and 1830s sent back to society headquarters complaints that slavery was a threat to virtue and pure religion and was an obstacle to evangelizing the South. They decided that slavery impeded the carrying out of God's will and at the same time menaced the nation's security.[9]

These solemn convictions help explain why abolitionists in the 1830s, unlike their more secularly oriented predecessors of a generation earlier, seldom heeded even the most urgent warnings of the perils of antislavery agitation. Religiously motivated abolitionists were unlikely to be deterred by difficulties met in carrying out their program or by warnings of the risks involved in emancipation, for they were demanding what they believed ought and must be done, not what was popular or comfortable to do. Judgment would come, whether the nation was ready to accept it or not. History could be cited as proof: "The strong arm of omnipotence bro't deliverance to the oppressed, without paying the least respect to the courtly poli-

9. Daniel Gould to Absalom Peters, July 31, 1826, and November 10, 1828, Hugh Carlisle to Peters, July 28, 1830, James H. Fowler to Peters, June 19, 1834, all in American Home Missionary Society Papers.

ticians of Egypt," wrote the secretary of an obscure southern anti-slavery society as early as 1820.[10]

Until well into the 1820s, the tie between evangelicalism and antislavery was closer in the South than in most parts of the North. Slavery long remained a legal institution in Pennsylvania, New York, and New Jersey; yet untraveled farmers and villagers in those states, when they thought of slavery at all, must have viewed it as a totally exotic practice of no concern to them, in spite of the census returns that showed New York City having as many blacks as Charleston. In postrevolutionary years northern preachers infrequently dwelt on their parishioners' responsibility for slavery and racial injustice within their own states, an omission that struck the English-born Methodist missionary Francis Asbury, who in 1795 remarked the inequity of New York masters having for the most part escaped the verbal lashings to which Methodist preachers regularly subjected slaveholding Virginians.[11]

Northern states were not quite so barren of religiously inspired antislavery activity as Asbury evidently thought; nevertheless, he was correct in believing that some of the most prominent northern emancipationists, organized as the American Convention for Promoting the Abolition of Slavery, asked for less drastic action against slavery than evangelical faith required. Unlike later antislavery advocates, they seldom demanded immediate emancipation. Even so, they could not avoid arousing opposition. They found at an early date that even their moderate approach provoked misgivings. Antislavery activity, their opponents warned, eventually would lead to civil war.[12]

The rather moderate members of the American Convention, however, were not the only early critics of slavery. There were other abolitionists near the beginning of the century, particularly those remaining in the South, who, unlike the more distinguished members of the American Convention, had no close ties with dominant elements in society. They saw themselves, instead, as outsiders hurling challenges at powers and principalities. They seldom adjusted their rhetoric or program in order to secure favor and influence or to

10. *The Emancipator (Complete), Published by Elihu Embree, Jonesborough, Tennessee, 1820* (Rpr.; Nashville, 1932), May 31, 1820, p. 22. All further citations to the *Emancipator* are to this reprint of the original.
11. Clark *et al.* (eds.), *Journal and Letters of Francis Asbury,* II, 62.
12. George Benson to William Rogers, February 19, 1791, in Pennsylvania Abolition Society Papers.

avoid recrimination. In their situation the effort would have failed in any event, for they could do little to hide the fact that they were bent on elevating the humble and bringing the mighty low.

After official bodies of the leading evangelical churches that operated in the South relaxed their early antislavery zeal, southern antislavery groups would be confined mostly to the hill country of western North Carolina and Virginia and to east Tennessee. In that relative isolation, Quakers and members of evangelical churches remained unreconciled to slave-plantation society. Their small, tightly knit antislavery societies issued condemnations and supplied jeremiads to abolitionist editors, who in turn circulated their writings throughout the country. In that way these otherwise obscure and isolated persons spread their antislavery message far and wide. But they were powerless in their own region to slow the economic and social developments that throughout antebellum years tied slavery to progress. The further these obscure people traveled from the seats of power, the more alienated they became, the less restrained grew their program, and the more remorseless was their message. Not surprisingly, some of the most impassioned antislavery protest ever written came from those little-known southerners.[13]

In essays published in the 1820s, these backwoods abolitionists reiterated their belief in the likelihood of retributive judgment coming upon the nation through slave insurrection and their conviction of Christian duty to work to avert it. But in those years one did not have to fret about "judgment" and "duty" and "retribution" in order to be concerned about the prospect of slave revolt. Even unbelievers and rationalists, who scoffed at such abstractions as "national sins" and "imputed guilt" and who were unperturbed by the prospect of divine punishment, admitted to worry about slave revolts, for these events, unlike God's prospective judgment, actually had taken place both in the United States and the West Indies. Facing such dangers, one need not decide whether they were punishments dealt by the hand of God or by the will of the incensed and outraged blacks acting by and for themselves.

It was possible to dread the prospect of slave insurrection and to seek ways of averting it while at the same time accepting it as

13. James Brewer Stewart, "Evangelicalism and the Radical Strain in Southern Antislavery Thought During the 1820s," *Journal of Southern History*, XXXIX (1973), 379–96; Merton L. Dillon, *Benjamin Lundy and the Struggle for Negro Freedom* (Urbana, Ill., 1966), 52–54; Merton L. Dillon, "Three Southern Antislavery Editors: The Myth of the Southern Antislavery Movement," *East Tennessee Historical Society's Publications*, XLII (1970), 47–56.

being just. A Quaker abolitionist newspaper on one page could warn southern readers of the "unwise and impolitic" practice of maintaining "inveterate and desperate" black enemies "in our homes, and about our farms, and in our towns and cities," and print on the next page a poem calling down God's vengeance against white oppressors. To help "avert the impending storm" forecast by such passages, Elihu Embree, a Quaker ironmaker, in 1820 founded the *Emancipator* in Jonesborough, Tennessee. "The Slavery of the Africans in the United States," he wrote, "if continued a few generations longer, will produce such scenes of misery and destruction for our posterity . . . as have not been exceeded in the history of man."[14]

Comprehending—as few others in those days did—the conflict between master and bondsman that was inherent in slavery, Embree directed against the institution the distaste for war and violence that was inseparable from his Quaker faith. Embree's firsthand observations in Tennessee led him to emphasize the harshest aspects of slavery and to interpret the institution much as did Senator James Burrill of Rhode Island, who viewed slavery only from afar. Burrill, too, found no place for sentimentality and illusion when describing slavery. If it could be called a patriarchal system in Virginia and the Carolinas, it was not so in the West: "The greater number of slaves, in new countries," he told the Senate, "will be connected with their master by no other tie than that heartless one of bargain and sale."[15]

Embree likewise found few elements of paternalism in the master-slave relationship as he saw it function in the new West. Instead, violence lay at its core. Embree characterized the slave population in America as a nation held in unwilling bondage by exploitative oppressors. "I view the slaves as prisoners of war," he wrote, who "according to the laws of nations have the right to seize any opportunity to free themselves—nor have we doubt that they will embrace every opportunity that promises success."[16]

Viewing master and slave as locked in an adversary relationship, Embree portrayed abolitionists as "mediators, between the oppressor and the oppressed," arbitrators attempting to end a protracted war. Their purpose, wrote Embree, was not to encourage insurrection, as slaveholders charged, but to avert violence by promoting emancipation. Their efforts, Embree thought, would be regarded by

14. *Emancipator*, April 30, 1820, pp. 12, 13; October 31, 1820, p. 112.
15. *Annals of Congress*, 16th Cong., 1st Sess., 218.
16. *Emancipator*, September 30, 1820, p. 85.

slaves as conciliatory and thus would "appease" their "restless and dissatisfied disposition." [17]

Although predictions of slave violence of the sort that filled Embree's newspaper were almost as old as American slavery itself, they conspicuously surfaced in public prints for the first time only in 1819 and 1820 during congressional debates over the admission of Missouri. The Missouri issue brought slavery to public attention and injected it into national politics as never before. Not even the long agitation preceding abolition of the slave trade in 1808 created anything like the widespread public concern that accompanied the Missouri issue. All across the North, while Congress debated the fate of slavery in the new state, local meetings and antislavery societies—and in some instances state legislatures—passed anti-Missouri resolutions designed to register grass-roots disapproval of the further spread of slavery into the Louisiana Purchase. [18]

The political ambitions of out-of-favor New Englanders no doubt helped precipitate the opposition and perhaps shaped congressional debates on the issue, as southern critics then insisted. But whatever their own views on slavery may have been and whatever their motives, congressmen representing certain districts in the Northeast would have found it imprudent to ignore the diffused antisouthern and antislavery opinions that even then formed part of the thought of many northern voters.

A slow, steady flow of antislavery tracts had appeared in recent years, most of them written by Quakers or evangelicals who had lived in or at least had visited slave states. These writings, filled with supposedly accurate information about slavery, had reached sympathetic clergymen and politicians as well as laymen and in that way achieved a pyramidal effect on public opinion. Although their influence cannot be measured, it seems likely that to them in large part must be credited the generalized sense that slavery was wrong, that it was an outworn remnant of the barbaric past, a system contrary to the genius of the new nation. However that may be, it is evident that abolitionists had faith in the power of their writings to influence political decisions. Before antislavery petitions reached the Senate in March, 1818, someone placed a copy of John Kenrick's *Horrors of Slavery* on every senator's desk. [19] But explicitly

17. *Ibid.*, 87; October 31, 1820, p. 100.
18. The entire episode is treated in Glover Moore, *The Missouri Controversy, 1819–1821* (Lexington, Ky., 1953).
19. *Annals of Congress*, 15th Cong., 1st Sess., 237.

abolitionist arguments such as Kenrick's—which unsympathetic readers found easy to dismiss as fanatical—were not the only persuasive force moving congressmen to question the wisdom of allowing slavery to spread into the West.

Statistics, themselves value-free and untouched by either politics or moralism, further supported the view that in the national interest slavery ought to be ended. By constitutional mandate, the United States government every ten years conducted a census and in due time made the results available as official public documents. Thus in 1791, 1801, 1811, and again in 1821, the government published the facts of population change. Federalists in particular, with their interest in the tangible—in banks and currency, in taxation, in tariff policy, in growth itself—found the information disclosed by the census both fascinating and frightening, for the columns of numbers that filled its pages confirmed the racial imbalance to which alarmists had called attention, even in colonial days. Blacks increased in the South at a rate considered highly dangerous to national safety. Slave population grew by 33 percent from 1800 to 1810, the census showed, and by a further 29 percent in the next decade.[20]

As early as 1806 Samuel Blodgett prepared a manual in which he drew from comparative statistics an antislavery lesson. Free states increased in population and wealth more rapidly than slave states; free labor was more productive than slave labor. The author provided explicit antislavery instruction for persons interested in national well-being. The United States should encourage commerce and "useful emigration," wrote Blodgett. "*This we ought to do*, to place our country immediately in a state unvulnerable to foreign invaders."[21] But such a policy, his northern readers must have known, the slave states were in no position to implement. Blodgett's publication confirmed northern self-satisfaction and self-pride. To northern eyes, the South, doggedly tied to slavery, held back national progress, even endangered national security.

A few years later, after the 1810 census rendered Blodgett's work out-of-date, Adam Seybert prepared yet another statistical abstract. This also presented, but in still more striking form, the enumerable indicators of national growth. Seybert showed that in all indices of

20. U.S. Bureau of the Census, *Negro Population, 1790–1915* (Washington, D.C., 1918), 26, 28, 29.
21. Samuel Blodgett, *Economica: A Statistical Manual for the United States of America* (Washington, D.C., 1806), 80–82.

progress but one, slave states lagged behind every other section of the country. Only in the increase of slave population did the South outstrip the North.[22]

The alarming fact, made evident by publications such as these, was the large part of the total population made up of slaves and the speed with which that part grew. When critics placed this information alongside the then commonly held notions about blacks—their propensity to violence, the danger they posed in wartime, their unassimilability—the reader could hardly fail to conclude that in the South's slave population the nation faced a severe and intensifying problem.

Not surprisingly, statistics delineating the expansion of slavery were turned to the support of antislavery arguments and programs. As early as 1804, Congress heard alarms over census revelations. One-fifth of the nation's total population—one-half the population of some states—was enslaved, said Representative David Bard. "Their circumstances, their barbarism, their reflections, their hopes and fears, render them an enemy of the worst description." Bard expanded upon his dread of the enslaved blacks. "If they are ignorant, they are, however, susceptible of instruction, and capable of becoming proficient in the art of war." Not racial prejudice, as it is commonly understood, but fear was reflected in Bard's antislavery position.[23]

By the time the Missouri issue reached Congress in 1819, the statistics of population growth had become a staple in antislavery argument. Abolitionists recognized the census data as a resource of peculiar power. Such facts were unanswerable. Numbers possessed an objectivity that could not be dismissed as easily as could the more familiar but disputed charges of the cruelty and sinfulness of slavery. However, antislavery reliance on the census carried with it a troublesome corollary. The force of these statistics depended for the most part on the assumption that blacks were unassimilable, that they constituted, as Embree wrote in the *Emancipator*, an enemy nation within America, whose presence meant constant struggle and peril.

Much in the recent experience of white Americans encouraged such conclusions. Memories of Saint-Domingue, Gabriel's conspir-

22. Adam Seybert, *Statistical Annals: Embracing Views of the Population, Commerce, Navigation, Fisheries . . . of the United States of America . . .* (Philadelphia, 1818), 24, 38, 53.

23. *Annals of Congress*, 8th Cong., lst Sess., 995–96.

acy, and subsequent plots were not easily erased. The statistical arguments, based as they often were on a particular analysis of slave temperament and inclination, served better to support the program of the American Colonization Society, which aimed to transport blacks to Africa, than that of persons who advocated their incorporation into American society. But despite the varied uses to which they might be put, statistics long continued to bolster the antislavery argument. The Presbyterian O. P. Hoyt predicted in 1827 that by 1880 the nation would contain four million more blacks than whites. Throughout the 1820s Benjamin Lundy made use of similar population projections in his *Genius of Universal Emancipation*, as did abolitionists in the 1830s and afterward, to support the call to eliminate a problem that seemed to threaten the national future.[24]

Related to the disquiet produced by population data was a fact of momentous political import, especially in the eyes of northern Federalists. Constitutional mandate linked both congressional representation and membership in the Electoral College to the size of the slave population, thereby adding to southern influence in setting national policy. The three-fifths compromise, which made this possible, was a festering grievance, particularly to New England politicians, who found in slavery the key to southern political power.[25]

All this could only strengthen the determination of restrictionists to block the extension of slavery into Missouri. When Representative James Tallmadge of New York introduced his proposal to make Missouri a free state and to ban slavery from the rest of the Louisiana Purchase, southerners understandably fought back—to save their political lives, if for no other reason. They detected in efforts to close the West to slavery a grave challenge to their position in the Union. Restrictionists, it appeared, aimed to erect a western wall beyond which southern institutions could not go. Southern leaders found the probable effects of such containment intolerable—perpetual minority political status for the South and eventual racial conflict arising from confinement within narrow geographical bounds of a rapidly growing black population. Less often mentioned

24. *Freedom's Journal*, May 11, 1827; *Genius of Universal Emancipation*, IV (November, 1824), 17; Amos A. Phelps, *Lectures on Slavery and Its Remedy* (Boston, 1834), 209; John Greenleaf Whittier, *The Works of John Greenleaf Whittier* (New York, 1892), VII, 71.

25. Kerber, *Federalists in Dissent*, 36–39; James M. Banner, Jr., *To the Hartford Convention: The Federalists and the Origins of Party Politics in Massachusetts, 1798–1818* (New York, 1970), 101–104.

was the further likelihood that a ban on the South's territorial expansion would lead to decline in the price of slaves with consequent
financial loss to all who held such property.[26]

Southern spokesmen also found in the Missouri controversy an
immediate danger. The much-publicized congressional debate over
slavery, they charged, would encourage slave resistance and promote insurrection, for slaves could not be prevented from learning
that powerful men outside the South—their friends and potential
allies—had called their servile status into question. The prospect of
unmanageable slave restiveness led southerners to reassert their opposition to public discussion of slavery. Southern political power
and manipulative skill, of the sort John C. Calhoun eventually mas-
tered, might be sufficient to block national antislavery legislation,
but pacification of slaves made hopeful by congressional debates
would prove a more formidable task.

In addressing the Missouri issue, southern congressmen confined
their attention almost exclusively to the effect restriction would
have on them, their slaves, their section. In the most precise sense
of the term, they reacted to the issue as provincials. Charles Pinckney of South Carolina stood alone among southern statesmen in
placing the matter in spacious context. The senator looked beyond
the bounds of his own state and section to count the worth of slavery
to the entire nation. America's prosperity and world position, Pinckney asserted, derived from the forced labor of blacks. Destroy slavery, and the financial and commercial structure of the United States
together with its international eminence, such as it was, also would
be destroyed.[27]

Such a remarkable but wholly eccentric analysis of the American
economic system could not be accepted by northern congressmen,
who, in their own fashion, doubtless were as culture-bound as were
their southern colleagues. They ignored Pinckney's insights as well
as his conclusion. They refused to acknowledge the constructive role
of slavery in American foreign and domestic trade and in northern
capital accumulation and their own section's involvement with it.
Instead they charged slavery with being a source of national weak-

26. The discussion of slavery, which raised doubts about its future, was thought
to lower slave prices. See Johnson, *Ante-Bellum North Carolina*, 564–65. In parallel
concern, John Quincy Adams believed that criticism of the United States Bank
caused decline in the price of bank stock. John Quincy Adams and Lewis Condit,
*Report of the Minority of the Committee on Manufactures, Submitted to the House of
Representatives of the United States, February 28, 1833* (Boston, 1833), 6.
27. *Annals of Congress*, 16th Cong., lst sess., 1313–15.

ness, an obstacle to continued progress, even a threat to the nation's existence.

In this way northern opponents of the admission of Missouri succeeded in identifying the restrictionist position with the national interest, while nearly all advocates of slavery continued to focus on purely sectional concerns. In the Missouri debates, nationalism and antislavery became one. From that time forward, persons ambitious for the continued growth of American power and having a large vision of the nation's future indicted slavery as an obstacle frustrating national achievement. For the idealistic, slavery was a moral blot canceling out the virtues upon which greatness supposedly depends; for others, who imagined themselves realistic and practical, it was a source of political and military weakness that eventually would prevent the United States from playing its destined large role in world affairs.

During the Missouri debates, Representative Tallmadge pictured for his colleagues the alternatives offered for their choice: a strong, prosperous, influential nation without slavery or a weak, distracted nation if slavery continued its growth. According to his premise, slavery divided and weakened society; social unity brought strength. Daniel P. Cook, the youthful antislavery congressman from Illinois, provided a still more graphic critique. Slavery, said Cook, "is calculated to invite invasion, and no one will deny that it exposes the State to domestic violence." His reminder of the Indian wars that accompanied the recent conflict with England carried an appropriate warning: England "arrayed the savages against us" during the War of 1812, and some future enemy also might arm the slaves.[28]

Cook's reference to the military menace inherent to a servile population embodied a theme restrictionists succeeded in tying explicitly to the Missouri issue. They dwelt upon the opportunities for intrigue slaves offered to external enemies. At first glance, the argument, though appropriate to an earlier time, now seemed out-of-date. Recent diplomatic triumphs brought slaveholders a greater degree of security than they ever had enjoyed before. As we have seen, the purchase of Louisiana in 1803 pushed American boundaries well to the west of slave population. Shortly afterward, a series of military adventures and diplomatic negotiations culminating in the Adams-Onis Treaty of 1819 dislodged the Spanish from all their ancient positions east of the Mississippi. By these means Americans

28. *Ibid.*, 15th Cong., 2nd Sess., 1206; 16th Cong., 1st Sess., 1111.

acquired undisputed control of the southern frontier, except for the nagging presence of a number of Indian tribes, and these soon would be removed west of the Mississippi. Thus a prime incitement to slave violence and an encouragement to would-be runaways at last was eliminated. By 1820, for the first time since slavery was introduced in the English colonies two centuries earlier, slaveholders need feel no concern that foreign powers were in a position to endanger master-slave relations. But almost before southern whites adjusted to their new freedom and prepared to exploit it, restrictionists came forward to shake the complacency the new situation invited. Expansion of slavery into the trans-Mississippi West, antislavery congressmen warned, would renew the danger that southerners supposed diplomacy had eliminated forever.

Harrison Gray Otis, representative from Massachusetts, explained why this was so. He looked farther west than Missouri and to a distant future, when the vast Louisiana Purchase would be peopled with slaves, its population at last reaching the western frontier. There in the far Southwest and on the Pacific coast, American settlement would collide with Spanish, English, and Russian interests. All the old rivalries that plagued Americans in the past would be renewed, and with them, Otis warned, would come fresh dangers of "intrigue and revolution." Although the entire nation might suffer from the resulting collisions, slaveholders would bear the chief burden, for once again, slaves would serve as willing instruments of European hostility to the United States.[29]

But it was not European rivals alone who would threaten slavery as it followed its westward course. So volatile were slaves thought to be under every circumstance that the likelihood of a free-black population within the United States inciting slaves gave pause even to persons of antislavery reputation. It led Tallmadge, who was no advocate of servile rebellion, to express strange inconsistencies in policy. Although he was the author of slavery restriction, Tallmadge announced his opposition to proposals to exclude slavery from Alabama Territory, because "surrounded as it was by slaveholding states, and with only imaginary lines of division, the intercourse between slaves and free blacks would not be prevented and a *servile* war might be the result."[30]

Slave rebellion was a specter neither friend nor foe of extending slavery to Missouri easily dismissed. Its stubborn presence became

29. *Ibid.*, 16th Cong., 1st Sess., 254.
30. *Ibid.*, 15th Cong., 2nd Sess., 1203.

evident when congressmen of both persuasions addressed themselves to the "diffusion" argument, a defense of the right to extend
slavery that owed its sole claim for consideration to fears of insurrection. In order to justify their expansionist program on other
grounds than self-interest, southerners urged its necessity as a
safety measure. Confinement of a growing slave population would
produce pressures that at last would explode into violence. Southern spokesmen thus accepted the restrictionists' prophecy of ultimate slave revolt, but by advocating "diffusion," they turned the
prospect to their own advantage. Slaves might indeed rebel, they
agreed, but only if restrictionists succeeded in their campaign to
confine the black population behind artificial, politically designed
barriers.[31]

Let slavery be spread through new regions, and all predicted
dangers would disappear. Slavery then would remain the institution its defenders claimed it now was—gentle and humane and
characterized by paternalistic relationships. Enjoying these advantages, slaves would have no reason to become dissatisfied. Such dis-
gruntled slaves as there were would find collusion difficult, for they
would be scattered so thinly that revolt would be hard to arrange
and, if attempted, would easily be put down. Only if Congress confined slavery to its present range and the black population grew increasingly dense, as census statistics indicated was its tendency,
would severity and rigor out of necessity come to characterize it.

Restriction would have other, equally disastrous results. Failure
to spread slavery would make life for nonslaveholding southern
whites difficult and unpleasant. Many would decide to leave in order to escape the region's ever-growing black population. Thus
would the older South be further depleted of white population and
the section's already ominous racial imbalance be made still more
menacing. The Tallmadge Amendment, some warned, would result
in the "negro-izing" of the South.[32]

Although neither party to the contest had everything its own way,
the South achieved a significant victory in the Missouri Compromise. Congress in 1820 agreed to admit Missouri as a slave state and
to open the southern portion of the Louisiana Purchase to slavery.
While the Missouri settlement plunged abolitionists into despair,
southern leaders could take satisfaction from the result.[33] Yet their

31. *Ibid.*, 1276; 16th Cong., lst Sess., 1012, 1085.
32. *Ibid.*, 16th Cong., lst Sess., 315, 1532.
33. "Hell is about to enlarge her borders; and tyranny her domain," wrote Elihu
Embree in *Emancipator*, September 30, 1820, p. 89.

optimism was tempered by recognition of the dangers that the debates revealed, not only to the South's continued political influence
in the Union, but to the survival of the Union itself. The apprehension felt in the wake of the compromise brought forth Jefferson's
famous, oft-quoted admission that the controversy "like a fire bell
in the night, awakened me and filled me with terror. I considered it
at once the knell of the Union," a sentiment that we may suppose
was shared by others less given to eloquent statement.[34]

The issues raised in the debates did not soon disappear. In particular, the specter of black violence, made vivid by the congressmen's bold depictions, left sharp imprints on the consciousness even
of persons who lived far from the probable scenes of terror. Perhaps
the controversy was responsible for staging apocalyptic visions even
in a mind customarily so controlled as that of John Adams, who
wrote in 1821: "Slavery in the Country I have seen hanging over it
like a black cloud for half a century. If I were as drunk with enthusiasm as Swedenborg or Wesley, I might probably say I had seen
Armies of Negroes marching and countermarching in the air, shin-
ing in Armor. I have been so terrified with this phenomenon that I
constantly said in former times to the Southern Gentlemen, I cannot
comprehend this object: I must leave it to you."[35]

If thoughts of slavery could thus agitate an aged resident of
Quincy, Massachusetts, who surely knew he was not likely ever to
be confronted by angry black hordes, how much more severely must
the composure of slave-state residents have been shaken by the concentrated attention abolitionists and the United States Congress
had turned to the subject!

Insurrection was the abolitionists' aim, declared Senator William
Smith of South Carolina, even while he joined his colleague Phillip
Barbour of Virginia in expressing confidence in the loyalty and docility of slaves. Not "one among twenty" slaves in South Carolina
could at that moment be incited to rebellion, said Smith, a calculation perhaps not wholly reassuring to persons aware of the small
and often obscure beginnings of revolution. But even loyal slaves,
the senator believed, could be contaminated by antislavery sentiments of the sort so freely expressed in Congress during the Missouri

34. Thomas Jefferson to John Holmes, April 22, 1820, in Paul Leicester Ford (ed.),
Writings of Thomas Jefferson, X, 157–58.

35. John Adams to Thomas Jefferson, February 3, 1821, in Lester J. Cappon (ed.),
*The Adams-Jefferson Letters: The Complete Correspondence Between Thomas Jefferson
and Abigail and John Adams* (Chapel Hill, 1959), II, 571.

debates. Those ideas could not be depended upon to remain confined within the halls of the capitol. Representative Edward Colston of Virginia was much upset when he spied a black face among listeners in the gallery. How far might the subversive ideas expressed in congressional debate be spread by such agents? No doubt it was this consideration that led Colston to accuse a New England congressman of endeavoring through antislavery speeches to "excite a servile war" and of being "no better than Arbuthnot or Arbruster [the British citizens executed in Spanish Florida in 1818 by General Andrew Jackson], and deserves no better fate." [36]

The fears expressed by southern congressmen were to be realized perhaps earlier than they had imagined. Slaves commonly were thought to grow more restive in the 1820s under influences emanating from the North and, especially, from Washington. This perception, recorded by white observers, depended upon connections that may in truth not have existed. The balkiness of slaves, if it did in fact increase, perhaps arose from some source other than external stimulus. Yet southern alarm appeared not altogether unfounded, for in South Carolina evidence soon appeared to suggest a tie between resistant blacks and northern antislavery activity. The great slave conspiracy that rocked Charleston in the summer of 1822 apparently owed part of its inspiration to the well-publicized congressional debates over slavery in Missouri.

36. *Annals of Congress*, 16th Cong., 1st Sess., 267; 15th Cong., 2nd Sess., 1205.

7

From Denmark Vesey to Nat Turner

Up and down the southern coast in 1820, slaves struck the white population as being exceptionally hard to control. Reports from Virginia, South Carolina, and Georgia told of mounting discontent. So menacing did blacks appear that officials of all three states warned Secretary of War John C. Calhoun to prepare for desperate slave attacks on federal military installations. In Virginia discontented and belligerent slaves might be deluded enough, thought Governor Thomas M. Randolph, to try to seize the federal arsenal near Richmond. A moment's relaxation would encourage "that necessary consequence of a system of slavery, occasional Rebellion." The governor doubted that full-scale revolt was near, yet he was unwilling "by any omission . . . to provoke audacity, or even to excite hopes, which at the least must produce insubordination."[1]

Randolph agreed with conventional wisdom—hopes for freedom made slaves harder to control and exaggerated the perpetual problem of keeping them at work on the masters' terms. Recently, some whites believed, the slaves' expectations had received encouragement from events beyond southern control. The Missouri debates and abolitionist activity had led them to speculate, as at no time

1. John C. Calhoun to James Bankhead, July 27, 1818, in Robert L. Meriwether *et al.* (eds.), *The Papers of John C. Calhoun* (Columbia, S.C., 1959–), II, 427; Decius Walworth to John C. Calhoun, January 15, 1820, *ibid.*, IV, 580; Thomas M. Randolph to John C. Calhoun, April 18, 1821, *ibid.*, VI, 57.

since the Revolution, about the possibility of changing their condition. Now these outside influences must be counteracted in order to stabilize slavery and forestall insurrection. Blacks must be taught again that their hopes were illusory and their would-be allies ineffectual. Slave resistance must lose its political import.

To promote security, Randolph suggested removing locks and bayonets from the weapons stored near Richmond, thereby making them useless to mutinous slaves who might manage to storm the arsenal. Calhoun complained that on account of a recent congressional cut in military appropriations the War Department could ill afford the expense. Nevertheless he promised to find the money somewhere, for "in a point so important nothing ought, if possible, to be left to hazard."[2]

If slaves appeared menacing in Virginia, their discontent in South Carolina seemed still more dangerous. As early as the summer of 1818, reports reached Calhoun of "indications lately of turbulence" in Charleston. When, a few months later, anxieties among whites increased, Calhoun ordered the federal arms and ammunition that were stored in the city removed to the harbor and the greater protection of Fort Moultrie.[3]

The tightening of security in Charleston and elsewhere in the seaboard South helped relieve at least one source of apprehension. With skill and a bit of luck, rebellious blacks might have captured some lightly defended federal arsenal. Thus armed, they could have converted a local uprising into a formidable regional threat. It was this possibility that prompted Calhoun, after taking emergency measures, to establish policy designed to make sure nothing of the sort ever happened. Following reorganization of the army on June 1, 1821, he ordered one company of artillery deployed to each arsenal in the slave states as surety that any attack by blacks would be repulsed.[4] This became standard practice, thus rendering successful slave revolt all but impossible, however widespread unrest might be. With the arsenals virtually impregnable, no source of arms in significant quantity was anywhere available to rebels. Firearms would remain a monopoly in the hands of whites.

Southern governments always had tried to make sure that only the white population had access to weapons. There had been sur-

2. John C. Calhoun to Thomas M. Randolph, April 30, 1821, *ibid.*, VI, 84.
3. John C. Calhoun to James Bankhead, July 27, 1818, *ibid.*, II, 427; Calhoun to John Geddes, December 31, 1819, *ibid.*, 529.
4. John C. Calhoun to Thomas M. Randolph, April 24, 1821, *ibid.*, VI, 72.

prising exceptions, as in the days of free-and-easy relations in early South Carolina, when blacks served as armed militiamen.[5] But this was a temporary aberration not to be repeated in later years. Colonial and state governments required white militia members to supply themselves with arms, and every household was expected to be so equipped. In practice, however, purchase of weapons sometimes exceeded the means of ordinary persons. Far more disconcerting was the thought that in regions where white population was sparse, even possession of a gun promised to be of little help in standing off an embodied mass of angry blacks.

A report from North Carolina in 1813 claimed that "the seaboard in general has a scattered population of Whites—they poor & generally without arms & ammunition," and as late as 1831, Benjamin Cabell wrote from Danville, Virginia, to express his doubts "whether upon an emergency we could turn out 20 efficient pieces."[6] Such deficiencies may have been exceptional, yet it remains true that the disparity in strength between whites and blacks during the first two or three decades after 1800 was less than it came to be in later years. In parts of the South early in the century, initial advantage in a test of power conceivably would lie with blacks on account of their superior numbers, a possibility both critics and defenders of slavery went to great lengths to point out. Yet in any such racial clash the blacks' numerical advantage would disappear as soon as the white militia could be mobilized. Accordingly, in the first years of the new century, every slave state made special exertions to supply itself with efficient, well-equipped militia units, and individuals able to afford the cost armed themselves and cultivated marksmanship.[7]

After American independence the states and national government established armories, where weapons and ammunition were stored

5. Clarence L. Ver Steeg, *Origins of a Southern Mosaic: Studies of Early Carolina and Georgia* (Athens, Ga., 1975), 105–106.

6. Christopher Dooley *et al.* to Governor William Hawkins, January 23, 1813, in Governors' Papers, North Carolina Division of Archives and History; Benjamin Cabell to John Floyd, September 20, 1831, in Executive Papers, Virginia State Library. See also Benjamin Oliver to James Monroe, September 23, 1800, and Thomas Newton to James Monroe, December 29, 1800, both in Executive Papers, Virginia State Library.

7. [Joseph Blunt], *An Examination of the Expediency and Constitutionality of Prohibiting Slavery in the State of Missouri* (New York, 1819), 11–12; Jacob Read to Charles Pinckney, June 10, 1807, in Charles Pinckney Papers; [Paulding], *Letters from the South*, II, 247; James Semple to Lieutenant Alexander McRae, May 6, 1808, in Executive Papers, Virginia State Library.

ready for use against foes, either foreign or domestic. The arsenal at Fayetteville, North Carolina, appears to have been established specifically as a resource against insurrection. By this means, the contest between slaves and masters became a most unequal one. However, this fact did not altogether reassure the white population, who sometimes became unnerved by the prospect that these vital government stores, meant for their own defense, might fall into the hands of slaves, as indeed Gabriel in 1800 was said to have intended.[8]

In Charleston in 1822, the free black Denmark Vesey, plotting rebellion, showed himself fully aware of the whites' superior firepower as he developed plans for arming his coconspirators. The participants in Vesey's scheme were enterprising and industrious, but were as unsuccessful as Gabriel in overcoming their lack of weapons. Vesey's men, witnesses reported, made or secured 300 daggers and some 250 picks and bayonets (authorities never located any of these, a striking fact that has encouraged some historians to doubt their existence and, consequently, to doubt the reality of the plot itself). They also systematically noted the location of firearms in stores and houses. These they planned to seize at the start of the revolt. But the advantage thus gained was certain to be only temporary. Vesey's preparations, resourceful though they were, could have counted for little against the white militia and the large store of firearms cached by the United States government—as Calhoun recently had directed—at Fort Moultrie.[9]

There were still other reasons, if more were needed, for doubting the possibility of successful rebellion in antebellum years. The prevalence of strong slave families created attachments that must have led to second thoughts on the part of many would-be rebels. Foreign enemies, once a source of encouragement and potential aid for slave revolt, had practically disappeared. Although Saint-Domingue still provided inspiration to slaves—major inspiration

8. Lemmon, *Frustrated Patriots*, 196; Gerald W. Mullin, *Flight and Rebellion*, 202–203.

9. Richard C. Wade, "The Vesey Plot: A Reconsideration," *Journal of Southern History*, XXX (1964), 154–55. Some slaves understood their disadvantage: Report of Interview with Slaves in Nottoway Jail, May 15, 1802, Lewis' statement, 1802, Bob's deposition in trial of Frank and Sancho in Halifax County, April 23, 1802, all in "Slave Insurrection Folder," Executive Papers, Virginia State Library; slave testimony in "Criminal Action Concerning the 1831 Insurrection of Slaves," in Onslow County Miscellaneous Records, North Carolina Division of Archives and History, Raleigh. For similar views in a much earlier time, see Horsmanden, *New York Conspiracy*, 244–45.

for Vesey and his followers—its distance from the American coast and its own distracted condition made intervention unlikely. After 1815, the year that saw the generation-long European wars end, the United States seemed unlikely to be drawn into foreign conflict or to face invasion. Slaves could no longer hope for aid from that quarter. By 1819, except for the sparsely settled Spanish state of Texas, all foreign territories touching upon the slave states had come under the United States flag. The United States Army had inflicted costly defeats on the Indians during the War of 1812, and most of the remaining southern tribes, which once might have offered support to slave resistance, were moved west of the Mississippi River in the 1830s. Beginning shortly afterward, the Seminoles in Florida, whose troublesome habit it was to harbor fugitives, were subjected by the United States Army to a long and bloody war of attrition.

The only remaining sources of encouragement and aid to slave resistance were whites and free blacks living within the United States itself. This was a danger nineteenth-century slaveowners could not dismiss or take lightly. Abolitionists and antisouthern congressmen already exerted a disruptive effect on master-slave relations, and their activities were unlikely to diminish. Evidence appeared to suggest in the Vesey plot, as it had on earlier occasions, that blacks knew their status was at issue in northern-based political maneuvers and reform movements and that they might be tempted to act in response to them. To white southerners the possibility of their doing so, instead of subsiding, appeared to grow ever more menacing, as abolitionists intensified their merciless condemnations of the slaveholding South.

Southern whites dwelt upon the dangers that confronted them rather than on their own armed strength and the blacks' relative weakness and isolation. Their failure to view events in perspective helps account for the thunderbolt effects of the exposure in May, 1822, of Denmark Vesey's plot to seize Charleston. Although such an event would have brought distress at any time, its impact doubtless was magnified because it so nearly coincided with the marshaling of antislavery, antisouthern political forces during the Missouri controversy.

Vesey's scheme did not take Charleston residents altogether by surprise. For many months before the day the slave Devany Prioleau revealed the first inkling of a planned uprising, abundant signs pointed to the blacks' discontent. Much of the unrest resulted from recent official suppression of the African Methodist church, a measure adopted after city authorities decided that religious meetings had become seedbeds of sedition. In June, 1818, legal action was taken against the black ministers. Four were given the choice of leaving the state or being imprisoned. These measures left blacks in the city, including Vesey, much aggrieved, for the church had served as a treasured center of spiritual and social life and provided a rare source of esteem for the class leaders, the men responsible for church activities.[10] The ensuing resentment grew so ominous that, as we have seen, authorities advised the War Department to take emergency precautions.

These measures did not prevent Charleston blacks—slave and free—from continuing to discuss among themselves means for remedying their grievances. For a number of reasons, they thought their chances of doing so were good. Like other persons in South Carolina, Vesey was familiar with the tumultuous history of Saint-Domingue, a colony he had visited as a youth, and imagined its government would support black revolt on the mainland. Further, public discussions of slavery were common enough by the 1820s for their general import to reach those from whom such information ideally would be kept hidden. Even rural areas far more isolated than Charleston did not remain untouched by subversive notions. In Edgecombe County, North Carolina, for example, black preachers were reported to have convinced their congregations that "the national government had set them free . . . and that they were being unjustly held in servitude."[11] Wherever that kind of misinformation circulated, whether in rural North Carolina or in Charleston, the result was likely to be unrest and reluctance to fulfill the role of slave. Knowledge that the masters' authority had been called into question and that the white population was divided in its support of slavery encouraged the impression that bondage was temporary and early deliverance a possibility.

Vesey had read some of the Missouri debates, especially the anti-

10. Marina Wikramanayake, *A World in Shadow: The Free Black in Antebellum South Carolina* (Columbia, S.C., 1973), 125–28. For general accounts of the Vesey conspiracy, see *ibid.*, 133–53; John Lofton, *Insurrection in South Carolina: The Turbulent World of Denmark Vesey* (Yellow Springs, Ohio, 1964); and William W. Freehling, "Denmark Vesey's Peculiar Reality," in Robert H. Abzug and Stephen E. Maizlish (eds.), *New Perspectives on Race and Slavery in America: Essays in Honor of Kenneth M. Stampp* (Lexington, Ky., 1986), 25–47.

11. Johnson, *Ante-Bellum North Carolina*, 525; Aptheker, *American Negro Slave Revolts*, 81.

slavery speech delivered by Rufus King, and was said also to have owned, even earlier, an antislavery pamphlet—exactly which one never was ascertained. Joel R. Poinsett may not have been altogether mistaken when he wrote from Charleston in the wake of Vesey's conspiracy that the "discussion of the Missouri question at Washington, among other evils, produced this plot. It was considered by this unfortunate and half instructed people as one of emancipation."[12]

Unfolding events in Charleston in the summer of 1822 appeared to confirm some of the white South's deepest suspicions—Saint-Domingue continued to inspire American blacks, and discussion of slavery, either by Congress or by abolitionists, encouraged expectations of freedom. Evangelical religion, it appeared, also operated as a powerful influence among Charleston blacks. Vesey himself was an avid reader of the Bible. For years he had served as an informal religious teacher, pointing out to others scriptural passages that he interpreted as condemning slavery and promising deliverance. He thus harnessed to his cause the religious spirit that missionaries of the evangelical churches had fostered among blacks. Vesey's plans also gained the support of Gullah Jack, a sorcerer in whose grotesque and misshapen person lingered remnants of African religious belief that appealed to those plantation slaves who had assimilated fewer elements of Christianity than had blacks in Charleston.[13]

Among the myriad influences that were suspected of emboldening slaves were the many outsiders—northerners, foreigners, transients—whose business or whim happened to bring them to the city. During the trials of the Vesey conspirators, a witness testified that though a Scottish sailor "had a white face he was a negro in heart." A German peddler reputedly sympathized with blacks, and a stranger named Andrew S. Rhodes had been heard to defend the right of slaves "to fight for their liberty." The court suspected that this short list did not come close to identifying all the pro-blacks who had infiltrated Charleston.[14] The voicing of such suspicions revealed once again the slaveholders' awareness that they lived in a world full of elements uncommitted, even hostile, to their system and that these might someday coalesce and overwhelm them.

12. Joel R. Poinsett to James Monroe, August 13, 1822, in James Monroe Papers.
13. Gerald W. Mullin, "Religion, Acculturation, and American Negro Slave Rebellions: Gabriel's Insurrection," in John H. Bracey, Jr., August Meier, and Elliott Rudwick (eds.), *American Slavery: The Question of Resistance* (Belmont, Calif., 1971), 160; John Oliver Killens (ed.), *The Trial Record of Denmark Vesey* (Boston, 1970), 61, 64.
14. Killens (ed.), *Trial Record*, 148–49, 152–53.

But that day had not yet come. The conspirators' zeal and motivation did not exceed the whites' determination to crush them. After Vesey's plan was exposed by a slave informer, much as Gabriel's had been a generation earlier, Charleston authorities set about to prove to blacks as well as to anxious whites that the white population remained solidly in control of the city and were united in resolve. A court investigated the conspiracy in all its ramifications and traced it to its furthest origins. Authorities arrested 131 blacks and finally convicted 49. Thirty-seven of these, including Vesey and Gullah Jack, were hanged. The court spared the remaining 12 on condition their owners send them out of the state. The state legislature freed Devany Prioleau for having exposed the conspiracy and granted him a lifetime pension.

By such means, blacks learned again, as white Charlestonians intended, that every participant in a plan for revolt, every person remotely implicated with discussion of the right to freedom signed his own death warrant. Misguided masters might be indulgent and forgiving, but the state would be ruthless in dealing with black rebels. This was powerful deterrent indeed, but not even this lesson could absolutely assure that slaves elsewhere would refrain from developing similar plans, nor could it guarantee their quiet acceptance of slavery. Resistance was certain to continue, and its tie to political developments and to social change always remained a possibility.

Slave society, like every other, contained its portion of desperate persons willing to act in disregard of personal risk. Further, and perhaps in the long run equally troublesome to slaveowners, nothing could altogether stamp out the slaves' inclination to resist authority in ways short of coordinated rebellion. External influences continued to reinforce slave recalcitrance. One of the strongest forces operating against slave docility was the persistent agitation of white critics. In the 1820s, as politicians and abolitionists continued to debate the legitimacy of slavery, resistance might be expected to become still more difficult to contain.

While slaveowners could do little to eliminate this irritant at its northern source, they could undertake to lessen its impact on slaves. One means of achieving at least the outward appearance of servility (and realistically this was the most that could be hoped for) was to keep slaves under constant surveillance and to punish deviance whenever it appeared. Following Vesey's conspiracy, patrols, an old device designed to control and intimidate blacks, were made more efficient. Harsh laws strictly enforced were intended to prevent unauthorized slave assembly and slave movement off the plantations, the instruction of slaves to read, their unsupervised instruction in religion, slave contacts with northern subversives, and the circulation of seditious literature. Some twenty years earlier, a northerner had provided the rationale for such restrictive measures: "Every thing which tends to increase their knowledge of natural rights, of men and things, or that affords them an opportunity of associating, acquiring, and communicating sentiments, and of establishing a chain or line of intelligence, must increase your hazard, because it increases their means of effecting their object."[15] Constant vigilance, supplemented by ruthless suppression of the slightest sign of black unrest, discouraged even minor forms of resistance, though it could not prevent them.

Although the goal of perfect tranquillity was impossible to attain, repression became thorough enough to bring perceptible change in slave life. Unrestricted movement through the countryside became more difficult than it once had been. Increasingly rare were the easy social gatherings that had been a relieving feature of slavery in the eighteenth century and that had so clearly facilitated Gabriel in developing his conspiracy. The slaves' religious meetings—a source of racial cohesiveness and inspiration—came under the scrutiny of whites and, as we have seen, for a time virtually were abolished in Charleston. Thereby an important element of independence was lost to the city's slaves, and the continued development of autonomous black culture was impeded.

Relations between blacks and whites were altered in the 1820s as well. Nonslaveholding whites in earlier days sometimes formed easy, friendly relationships with blacks. These never entirely ceased, but as slavery faced new domestic threats, such associations increasingly became furtive and exceptional, for those who formed them risked being viewed with suspicion and being treated contemptuously.[16]

But despite these valiant efforts in the 1820s to protect slavery, its subtle undermining continued, and white southerners found themselves nearly powerless to halt the process. Subversive influences continued to work upon the black population in spite of all countervailing efforts. Ordinarily slaves learned of antislavery political developments at Washington or in the North only through chance re-

15. *American State Papers, Class VII: Post Office Department*, 27.
16. Catterall (ed.), *Judicial Cases*, I, 319; II, 319–30, 362, 419; *State v. Jacob Boyce*, Superior Court of Law, Spring Term, 1847, in Perquimans County Slave Papers, 1759–1864, North Carolina Division of Archives and History, Raleigh.

marks by whites. But on rare occasions, especially in the upper South, they were exposed directly to antislavery teachings. In August, 1818, the Reverend Jacob Gruber, presiding Methodist elder from Carlisle, Pennsylvania, preached at a camp meeting in Maryland. Some three thousand whites and four hundred blacks, many of them slaves, attended the service. For most preachers the presence of blacks would have signaled discretion, but not for Gruber, who only a short time earlier had been pastor of a black church in Baltimore. To the outrage of whites, Gruber presented the camp meeting with an antislavery sermon. Slavery, he told the biracial congregation, contradicted the Declaration of Independence and unless modified would lead to insurrection and racial war. The way slaves interpreted Gruber's remarks is nowhere recorded, but his message and the text from which he preached, "Righteousness exalteth a nation; but sin is a reproach to any people" (Prov. 14.34), could hardly have been lost even on untutored listeners.[17]

Gruber's camp meeting sermon was a highly exceptional event. Probably few southern blacks ever experienced such frank antislavery indoctrination. But its repercussion surely did not end with the four hundred who attended his service. It was not fanciful to suppose that Gruber's preaching had geometrical effect extending well beyond the locality where it took place, for the blacks who heard him could not be counted on to keep the experience to themselves. The sentiments Gruber expressed that day could be expected to spread among the slave population in ever-widening circles.

Whites generally succeeded in shielding slaves from direct exposure to antislavery sentiments of the sort voiced by indiscreet Methodist preachers, but they failed to do the same for free blacks. Especially in Maryland and Virginia, such persons enjoyed ready access to abolitionist thought. Throughout the 1820s, Benjamin Lundy's journal, the *Genius of Universal Emancipation*, with its harsh condemnation of slavery and slaveholding society, was patronized by free blacks in the upper South as well as those in the North. While they lived in Baltimore in the late 1820s, both Lundy and his coeditor William Lloyd Garrison associated with members of the free-black community, whom they counted among the most

---

17. William P. Strickland, *The Life of Jacob Gruber* (New York, 1860), 105–109, 130–41; Donald G. Mathews, *The Methodists and Slavery: A Chapter in American Morality, 1780–1845* (Princeton, N.J., 1965), 35–36; John B. Boles, "Tension in a Slave Society: The Trial of the Reverend Jacob Gruber," *Southern Studies*, XVIII (1979), 179–97.

loyal of their supporters. *Freedom's Journal*, the short-lived newspaper edited in New York in the late 1820s by Samuel Cornish and
John Russworm, also circulated among blacks in Virginia and
Maryland, thereby carrying into slave country its message urging
black uplift and resistance to slavery.[18] It is impossible to suppose
that the information contained in these journals and the hopes and
expectations they inspired among blacks who were free remained
unshared with blacks still enslaved.

An event of particular interest to the southern free-black community in the 1820s occurred in New York, when the state legislature completed the emancipation process it had started at the end
of the preceding century. On July 4, 1827, all remaining slaves in
the state were set free. The occasion assumed significance extending well beyond New York, for it came at a time of sectional tension
and growing awareness of racial issues by whites and of heightened
anticipations by slaves. Southern free blacks welcomed the New
York emancipation as a prophetic event. On the auspicious day, the
Friendship Society of Baltimore, a black fraternity, held a dinner to
celebrate the occasion. The members drank toasts to John Jay, the
New York advocate of emancipation; to Elisha Tyson, a renowned
Quaker abolitionist in Maryland; and to *Freedom's Journal* and the
Genius of Universal Emancipation. On the same day, blacks in Fredericksburg, Virginia, assembled to toast *Freedom's Journal* and their
own state: "May Virginia, and her sister slave states, show to the
people of Colour on the 4th of July 1828, that they have approved of
the example set them by the legislature of New York." In July, 1829,
blacks in Richmond commemorated the New York accomplishment
once more.[19]

These occasions allowed blacks in the upper South, responding to
abolitionist influence from the North, to take antislavery stands.
The influence was not likely to end with them, for free blacks could
not be prevented altogether from associating with slaves. On this
account, southern whites dreaded free blacks as a threat to slavery,
a subversive force that must be closely watched. Nevertheless, it
was slaves, not free blacks, who had the opportunity to carry antislavery impressions throughout the South. Maryland and Virginia,
the southern states where antislavery influences were strongest,

    18. Dillon, *Benjamin Lundy*, 89, 99, 145; *Freedom's Journal*, July 13 and 20, 1827.
    19. *Freedom's Journal*, July 13 and 20, 1827; "At a Public Dinner Held by the Free
Colored People of Richmond, July 4, 1829," in American Colonization Society Papers,
Manuscripts Division, Library of Congress.

also were the states that in the 1820s supplied many of the slaves who cultivated the new cotton plantations of the Gulf states. Thus were widely sowed among the South's black population the abolitionist and evangelical convictions that whites exercised usurped power, that slavery was wrong, and that someday the wrong would be made right. These same slaves had the greatest opportunity to learn that the white population was far from united in support of slavery.

Antislavery influences conveyed a message of hope rather than of despair. They counseled slaves to be patient for a while longer until the combination of circumstances that already had brought deliverance to blacks in the North worked the same release for them. A continued pacific reading of the abolitionist message would depend finally, however, on evidence of liberal trends within the South that would indicate movement toward freedom. Such evidence, always scant, became increasingly hard to detect.

Persons of authority in the South in the 1820s seldom expressed doubts about the legitimacy of slavery. By that time, slaveholders had progressed far toward establishing dominance over the region. Although acquiescence in their control never was total and did not extend to equal degree through all geographic areas, the slaveholders' position was enhanced early in the new century when a portion of the disaffected and potentially disaffected whites migrated to new frontiers, often to those north of the Ohio River. Most of the dissidents who chose to remain either harbored their opinions in silence or expressed them where few in the South could hear.[20] Seldom in antebellum years did any come forward publicly to disclose resentments. But in Virginia, especially, there were notable exceptions.

Part of the basis for discord became apparent in the late 1820s. At that time nonslaveholders in Virginia's western counties opened a new chapter in their long political struggle for enlarged representation in the General Assembly. Insofar as slavery entered the dispute, it was from considerations of politics rather than philanthropy. Disaffected westerners saw slaves more as symbols of the unequal power wielded by eastern planters than as objects of humanitarianism. In July, 1829, a petition from residents of Augusta

20. *Annals of Congress*, 16th Cong., lst Sess., 1354; John Spencer Bassett, *Slavery in the State of North Carolina* (Baltimore, 1899), 98; *Niles' Weekly Register*, XXXVI (July 25, 1829), 345, 357; Dillon, *Benjamin Lundy*, 108–109; William T. Allan in *Liberator*, August 25, 1843; Avery O. Craven, *Coming of the Civil War*, 95; Barnhart, "Sources of Southern Migration," 49–62.

County called for emancipation, less because slavery was unjust than because they found it harmful to white society. But even though few western Virginians manifested much sympathy for the rights and aspirations of blacks, the bitterness that characterized the intersectional contest within the state gave slaveowners pause, for by skilled manipulation sectional antagonisms might turn western farmers toward support of emancipation projects.[21]

Discord within Virginia took forms other than sectional rivalry. While Virginians west of the Blue Ridge Mountains were calling for legislative reapportionment, small farmers and mechanics in eastern counties demanded extension of the suffrage. Neither these antagonisms nor their antislavery implications were new. Some fifteen years earlier, "Mr. Richardson" had promised "something warmly" that if English armies invaded Virginia, as then seemed likely, "he would volunteer his services . . . at the hazard of all he possessed, but if the Negroes were to rise in an insurrection and destroy their masters, he would not turn out and risk his life for any set of men that would deprive him of his just right." Likewise, the presence of blacks—the property of well-to-do men—and the crimes they sometimes committed awakened in poorer whites a sense of alienation and powerlessness that might nourish resentment toward slaveowners as well as toward slaves. A petition opposing leniency for a slave accused of molesting a poor white woman in Loudon County illustrates the process. The document called attention to the dangers to be expected from slaves—a familiar point—but it also revealed a further threat to slaveholders' dominance: the disaffection of the lowly. If the court let the accused slave off easily, said the petitioners, "there is no telling where crime is to end among that class. . . . The community will not be safe from their outrages; and especially females in the humble walks of life, who have not thrown around them the protection of wealth and of influential friends—we claim to be as human as the mass of folks."[22]

The petitioners' unintended revelation of festering social rancor in eastern Virginia may well have given state authorities pause, for they could not fail to know that wherever slaves lived, white solidarity was essential to maintain their subjugation. Slaveowners incurred risks when they neglected to give adequate attention to the concerns of lesser members of society. Despite its brutality, slavery was a fragile institution depending for its continuance on commu-

21. *Niles' Weekly Register*, XXXVI (July 25, 1829), 356–57.
22. Johnston, *Race Relations*, 99–100; J. N. Rose *et al.* to the Governor, July 11, 1831, in Executive Papers, Virginia State Library.

nity support. Inducements to unity among whites undoubtedly were strong. Perhaps racial interests could bridge all schisms, but no one yet had measured the cohesive power of race or found the point at which white solidarity would break.

Eastern planters were foolhardy when they delayed granting all white males equal participation in political affairs. The new southwestern states, in contrast, moved quickly to establish full white manhood suffrage and equal representation. These measures harmonized with democratic trends in the country at large, but they also served the peculiar interests of slaveholders. Fully incorporating all white males into the body politic reduced the potential for dangerous social cleavage. Planters of eastern Virginia begrudged the necessity to make political concessions to disfranchised and underrepresented whites in their state, but they, too, found it necessary to set aside their objections in the interest of welding the white population into a solid whole.

A delegate to the Virginia constitutional convention in 1829 explained why this was so: "The time is not far distant when not only Virginia, but all the southern states, must be essentially military, and will have military governments. . . . We are going to such a state as fast as time can move. The youth will be taught not only in the arts and sciences, but they will be trained in arms." That policy would be required, he explained, in order to meet forthcoming challenges, either internally from slaves or externally from the North. In the looming emergency, the state would need to call forth "every free white human being and to unite them in the same common interest and government."[23] When all are needed for military service, all must be admitted to political privilege. The ancient Athenians had known as much.

Aside from such prophecy, some read into the convention's deliberation grand designs that, if present at all, were not to be achieved. The mildly antislavery editor Hezekiah Niles of Baltimore believed the convention's effects would reverberate throughout the South and lead to the eventual end of slavery in the entire section. "The greatest question before the Virginia convention," he wrote, "is the perpetual duration of slavery or the increase of a generous and free white population."[24] As Virginia went, so would go the South. At stake was the future of slavery itself.

Niles exaggerated. The momentous implications he saw in the

23. Charles Henry Ambler, *Sectionalism in Virginia from 1776 to 1861* (Chicago, 1910), 161.
24. *Niles' Weekly Register*, XXXVII (October 31, 1829), 145.

debates were not there, for slavery itself was not openly at issue. Instead, deliberation centered on the basis of representation and suffrage in Virginia. Should property remain the significant determinant for both? But since "property" included slaves, slavery became a legitimate topic for discussion both in the convention and outside it, provoking alarm similar to that aroused a decade earlier during the Missouri debates. To voice any doubt at all about southern institutions, some believed, was to take the first step toward destroying them. The editor of the Charleston *Mercury* pointed out the danger of Virginia's public examination of slavery. Such scrutiny gave false encouragement to slaves; it also prompted northern meddlers to enlarge their efforts. "Already do the advocates of abolition rejoice even at the agitation of the subject and confidently predict the day of triumph," wrote the editor.[25]

Slaves became more restive, whites believed, as the date for the convention drew near. "We have lately been seriously alarmed," reported Oliver Cross. But then he added, as though resigned to the fact, "We are always more or less alarmed." As owners feared, slaves themselves followed the developing controversy, gathering from it hope where little hope was warranted. In Mathews County, slaves supposed that the election for the convention had liberated them, though their masters tried to conceal this fact, and that all would receive "free papers" on August l. Some, it was said, had made up their minds to revolt if the papers were withheld.[26] Evidence of growing antiplanter sentiment among portions of the white population gave to slave unrest—a persistent feature of plantation life—greater than usual purposiveness. Resistance now signified more than merely individualized opposition to the slave's own condition; it had found an apparently attainable goal that in the immediate past neither master nor slave could have formulated. Cleavage within white society had strengthened the slaves' position. Convening of the constitutional convention suggested for the first time since the 1780s that emancipation in Virginia was a distinct possibility rather than a utopian goal.

Much evidence in the summer and fall of 1829 pointed to both increasing slave unrest and corresponding concern among whites that the unrest could not be contained. At the end of the year, the

25. Ambler, *Sectionalism*, 146.
26. Oliver Cross to Garrett M. Quarles, September 3, 1829, in Executive Papers, Virginia State Library; Aptheker, *American Negro Slave Revolts*, 82; Colonel Tompkins to William Giles, July 18, 1829, in Executive Papers, Virginia State Library.

governor of Virginia noted in his annual message that a "spirit of dissatisfaction and insubordination was manifested by the slaves in different parts of the country from . . . [Richmond] to the seaboard."[27] From Accomac County came a particularly startling report. Slaves there had undertaken a mass exodus to New York and Pennsylvania. Some went "off in gangs and armed, bidding defiance to the citizens," while others—maroons—took refuge on islands in Chesapeake Bay and fought off would-be captors.[28]

New incitement from the North deepened anxiety. On September 29, 1828, in Boston, David Walker finished composing a pamphlet addressed to his fellow blacks and sent it to the printer. *Walker's Appeal, in Four Articles Together with a Preamble to the Coloured Citizens of the World, but in Particular, and Very Expressly to Those of the United States of America* was no ordinary antislavery tract nor was its author a typical abolitionist. Walker, a North Carolina–born free black, had lived in Charleston at the time the city's black population seethed with the discontent that Denmark Vesey would mobilize for revolt. Sometime in the mid-1820s, sharing the anger of other black southerners and acquainted with the arguments and aspirations of such revolutionaries as Vesey, he arrived in Boston.[29] There, while making his living by dealing in used clothes, he devoted himself to writing for *Freedom's Journal* and furthering organization of the city's blacks. But as the title of his pamphlet suggests, his concerns extended well beyond the limits of Boston. *Walker's Appeal* spoke to a race rather than to a class or community. It called on colored people everywhere to unite in action to end their subjugation. Blacks should rely on themselves to restore their rights and not wait for whites to extend rights to them. Instead of cringing in humility, blacks should radiate pride; instead of submission, they should defy all who would oppress and exploit them.

Walker understood that in strict sense no people could be kept

27. Theodore M. Whitfield, *Slavery Agitation in Virginia, 1829–1832* (Baltimore, 1930), 54; Benjamin Brand to R. R. Gurley, August 18, 1829, in American Colonization Society Papers. For insurrectionary alarms in North and South Carolina and Georgia, see Thomas P. Hunt to R. R. Gurley, September 3, 1829, Francis Kinlock to R. R. Gurley, January 19, 1830, and Samuel K. Talmadge to R. R. Gurley, May 29, 1829, all *ibid.*

28. Colonel Joyner *et al.* to the Governor, August 13, 1829, in Executive Papers, Virginia State Library.

29. Donald M. Jacobs, "David Walker, Boston Race Leader, 1825–1830," *Essex Institute Historical Collections*, CVII (January, 1971), 94–107. Peter Hinks generously allowed me to read chapters of his manuscript study of David Walker, in which he sets forth important new evidence for the Walker-Vesey connection.

enslaved without their own consent. That consent, he insisted, must be withdrawn. Walker did not overtly counsel race war, though the militant posture he advised blacks to assume seemed calculated to invite retaliatory violence. Blacks, he implied, would be justified in destroying their tormentors, and they were quite competent to the task. "I do declare," he wrote, "that one good black can put to death six white men."[30]

The boast had a long tradition in Walker's home state. During an insurrectionary alarm in Bertie County, North Carolina, in 1802, Mrs. Dwyer's Plato was heard to declare that "the negroes were so much stronger than the white people that one black would be a match for two or three whites." Plato's notion persisted. In 1831 a planter in Hertford County, just to the north of Bertie, complained that he had lost control of his labor force. Nothing he did could persuade them of their weakness. They had repudiated the idea that was essential to servility: "By reason or calculation, their minds cannot be convinced of the great disparity between them and the whites."[31] David Walker's sentiments were those of Plato and the Hertford County slaves. His pamphlet was designed to persuade blacks to believe in an idea essential to successful resistance—that in no respect, martial capacity not excepted, need they feel in any way inferior to their white oppressors. But on account of the growing armed strength of the whites, Walker's advice would have been more realistic had it been given in 1800 rather than in 1828.

Before the year ended, *Walker's Appeal* came into the hands of free blacks in Savannah. Shortly afterward, authorities discovered copies in other cities up and down the coast and even as far from Boston as New Orleans. To distribute his pamphlet, Walker had employed his intimate knowledge of the communication network commanded by black southerners and northern seamen, black and white, who penetrated southern harbors. The pamphlet soon went into a second edition and then a third, as it circulated among northern blacks and in slave country.[32]

Such widespread distribution could not have been unorganized. Evidently Walker, or someone acting for him, had set into operation

30. Herbert Aptheker, *"One Continual Cry": David Walker's "Appeal to the Colored Citizens of the World," 1829–1830, Its Setting, and Its Meaning* (New York, 1965), 89.
31. Bertie County Slave Papers, 1800–1805, North Carolina Division of Archives and History, Raleigh; Solon Borland to Roscius C. Borland, August 31, 1831, in Governors' Papers, North Carolina Division of Archives and History.
32. Clement Eaton, "A Dangerous Pamphlet in the Old South," *Journal of Southern History*, II (1936), 1–12.

a plan to put his *Appeal* into the hands of southern blacks. The pamphlet soon turned up in Wilmington, North Carolina, Walker's former home, and there the slave Jacob Cowan confessed. He had been Walker's designated agent through whom some two hundred copies shipped from New York were to be funneled to blacks in other towns throughout the state. Cowan's master soon sold him to an unsuspecting purchaser in Mobile, Alabama.[33]

The unsettling effect on whites of *Walker's Appeal* is understandable. The writings of white abolitionists were regarded as an outrage, yet they possessed the comparative virtue of being directed ostensibly only toward members of their author's own race. Now slaveholders confronted a black revolutionary bent upon inciting other blacks to throw off bondage. No wonder southern whites found the pamphlet a cause for alarm. They saw it as a threat to their physical safety as well as a challenge to their labor system and to white supremacy.

Wilmington's police chief read the pamphlet and took time to summarize its message for the governor of North Carolina. The *Appeal* contained passages, wrote James F. McRae, "treating in most inflammatory terms of the condition of the slaves . . . exaggerating their sufferings, magnifying their physical strength and underrating the power of the whites; containing also an open appeal to their natural love of liberty; and throughout expressing sentiments totally subversive of all subordination in our slaves; and inculcating principles wholly at variance with existing relations between the two colours of our southern population."

McRae appended to his perceptive summary a worrisome observation designed to put the governor on guard. Already the *Appeal*—or the whites' reaction to it—had accomplished part of its mission. "A very general and extensive impression," he believed, "has been made on the minds of the negroes in this vicinity that measures have been taken toward their emancipation on a certain & not distant day."[34]

With such authoritative evidence of sedition before him, the North Carolina governor dispatched urgent messages to police offi-

33. Marshall Rachleff, "David Walker's Southern Agent," *Journal of Negro History*, LXII (1977), 100–103; William H. Pease and Jane H. Pease (eds.), "Walker's *Appeal* Comes to Charleston: A Note and Documents," *Journal of Negro History*, LIX (1974), 289–92.

34. James F. McRae to John Owen, August 7, 1830, in Governor John Owen's Letter Books, 1828–30, Governors' Papers, North Carolina Division of Archives and History.

cers throughout the state and to the state senators. They must alert their neighborhoods to intercept subversive writings and to detect signs of insurrection. But along with these instructions went the governor's strange confession. He himself considered all efforts at suppression futile. Little could be done to correct the state's perilous situation. Not even doubled vigilance would guarantee security. "It is mortifying to know," he concluded, "that we are suffering an evil without the possibility of a remedy."[35]

Others, even if sharing Governor John Owen's sense of doom, were inspired to adopt defensive measures. Throughout much of the South, the alarm led to passage of new legislation designed further to suppress and humble blacks and thereby to safeguard slavery. In the emergency, lawmakers gave renewed attention to the problem of the free blacks. The *Appeal* had reminded whites of a fact they would have preferred to forget: Bonds of unity between free blacks and slaves remained strong. *Walker's Appeal* contributed to antagonism toward free blacks and encouraged proposals to restrict their activity, even to expel them from the South. At the same time, as agents of the American Colonization Society discovered, the pamphlet steeled the blacks' determination to remain where they were.[36]

Despite the flurry of lawmaking and the widespread air of emergency generated by Walker's pamphlet, only persons with short memory found either the occasion or the reaction altogether new. Walker told southern whites only what they always had known. Slaves wanted freedom; they remained in bondage only because superior force and white unity compelled them to do so; and when opportunity appeared, they would rebel in an attempt to change their condition. Walker had tried to impress upon blacks his idea that they themselves were responsible for their continued enslavement. Slavery was not only something done to them; it was something they did to themselves. What restrained slaves from rising up and destroying the whites at this very moment? asked one white Virginian. "Nothing but an universal horror of so diabolical an act."[37] Only the blacks' compassion saved the whites from destruction. The writer had grasped the insight Walker sought to convey to blacks. They *allowed* whites to oppress them, and it was in their

35. John Owen, Circular Letter, August 19, 1830, *ibid.*
36. Josiah F. Polk to R. R. Gurley, August 13 and September 20, 1830, in American Colonization Society Papers.
37. Oliver Cross to Garrett M. Quarles, September 3, 1829, in Executive Papers, Virginia State Library.

power *now* to end their degradation. Southern whites lived at the sufferance of their slaves. The *Appeal* was designed to remove the slaves' reticence and hesitation, much as Thomas Paine in *Common Sense* aimed in 1776 at destroying vestiges of American loyalty to the king.

Despite the obvious grounds for deepening southern concern after 1829, some whites failed to support the repressive measures that most whites evidently believed essential. In some places, philanthropy warred with prudence and a noticeable lag occurred between the stimulus Walker provided and the appropriate response. In North Carolina, free blacks were allowed to vote as late as 1835, when a constitutional amendment finally excluded them from the polls, and some white persons, especially in Virginia and North Carolina, persisted in urging humanitarian programs to benefit slaves. Tyron McFarland, for one, could not understand such folly. In 1831 the North Carolina legislator, famed for his advocacy of state-financed schools for the poor, requested the governor to send him a copy of *Walker's Appeal*. He had heard frightening things about the pamphlet and often referred to it in his political speeches, but for all its notoriety, he had never had a chance to read it, had never even seen a copy. Neither had his constituents. Now he must have the pamphlet in order "to prove to some individuals that their ideas as to slaves are founded on 'faulse philanthropy.' " Some infatuated voters in Richmond County, he regretted to say, criticized his stand against allowing the instruction of slaves. He needed something as persuasive as Walker's pamphlet to convince doubters, and perhaps himself, too, that he was right to advocate keeping slaves in ignorance and, as he explained, that "I have no selfish or inhuman wish to gratify, all I wish is the good of my Country and Posterity."[38] Repression of blacks, insisted McFarland, was not motivated by prejudice or cruelty, but only by the stern necessity of self-preservation.

At the time McFarland sent his request to Governor Montfort Stokes, the legislator apparently did not yet know that only a few days earlier in Southampton County, Virginia, an episode of overt racial war had occurred. No pamphlet would be needed now to convince southern whites of their peril. For the first time in twenty years, a considerable body of North American slaves had rebelled,

38. Johnson, *Ante-Bellum North Carolina*, 601; Tyron McFarland to Montfort Stokes, September 3, 1831, in Governors' Papers, North Carolina Division of Archives and History.

and for the first and only time in United States history, slaves had indiscriminately slaughtered scores of white citizens. Nat Turner's slave revolt provided sufficient evidence to convince remaining skeptics that slaves did indeed pose a grave threat to the lives and security of white southerners.

On Sunday evening, August 21, 1831—the fortieth anniversary of the start of slave participation in the revolt in Saint-Domingue—Nat Turner and five other slaves launched a violent crusade against whites in their neighborhood, beginning with the family of Turner's master. Other slaves, perhaps as many as seventy in all joined the attack, which finally left at least fifty-seven whites—men, women, and children—dead.[39]

There is no proof whatever that Turner or any of his recruits had read *Walker's Appeal* or even knew it existed. There is no proof either that they ever saw copies of William Lloyd Garrison's *Liberator*—another Boston production—or any other abolitionist writing, although many took for granted that Turner, at least, surely must have done so. In fact, no one at the trials and investigations that followed the revolt produced evidence to associate Turner or members of his band with any of the alien influences to which southern whites customarily attributed slave disaffection. This negative evidence, far from providing reassurance, was in itself unnerving, for it demonstrated that slaves required no prodding from outside agitators to cause them to rise up in fury against whites.

The only influence ever shown to have operated on Turner, besides the all-important condition of slavery itself, was the religious teaching offered by the Bible and spread by evangelical preachers. Both the Bible and preachers were everywhere. They could neither be hidden from slaves nor restricted to those who could be trusted to interpret their message "correctly" and use it "wisely." Nothing could be done to alter the fact that the black population long ago had acquired the essentials of Christianity. By now Biblical lessons of justice and retribution had blended with the grievances of slavery to generate violence in Southampton County.

Surviving sources of information about the Turner revolt lead unmistakably to that conclusion, and it was the lesson some drew

39. The most thorough account, with accompanying documents, is Henry Irving Tragle, *The Southampton Slave Revolt of 1831* (Amherst, Mass., 1971). This volume contains Nat Turner's invaluable confession as recorded by Thomas Gray (pp. 300–21). For the perspective of a white participant, see F. N. Boney, *Southerners All* (Macon, Ga., 1984), 108–12.

at the time. But for most white southerners, that was not its most appealing lesson or, in the end, the most influential one. Few relinquished belief that outside influences in some way inspired the outbreak. Hostile ideas filtering in from the North, conventional wisdom charged, set Turner on his murderous course.

Benjamin Cabell, member of the aristocratic Virginia family, thought he understood the force that drove Turner and his followers. "The damnable spirit of fanaticism," Cabell declared, "engendered by northern publications and perhaps disseminated by missionaries as well as through the P. office, seems to pervade the country at distant and remote points." Mrs. Lawrence Lewis of Alexandria could be still more specific: "To the Editor of the 'Liberator'. . . . we owe in *greatest measure* the calamity," she told her Boston cousin Harrison Gray Otis. N. D. Sutton of Bowling Green in Caroline County offered his own explanation. He was perfectly satisfied that "these traveling preachers and peddlers have been instrumental to a great degree in producing the present state of things." From this premise Sutton drew an obvious, popular moral. Slaves "should not be permitted to have preaching at anytime nor should they be permitted to go about contracting for themselves." In North Carolina, too, where evidence of slave discontent appeared almost as flagrantly as in Virginia, observers agreed that religion and northern fanaticism must be charged with creating the slaveowners' problems.[40]

When Governor John Floyd of Virginia finally offered the governor of South Carolina his own reasoned theory of its cause, he had had nearly three months to ponder the meaning of the Southampton revolt. But for all its ripening, his analysis hardly improved upon those offered earlier. Much thought had left him "fully persuaded" that the "spirit of insubordination" that inflamed Turner and threatened to ignite similar revolts "had its origin among . . . the Yankee population, upon their *first* arrival amongst us."[41] It was

40. Benjamin Cabell to John Floyd, September 20, 1831, and N. D. Sutton to John Floyd, September 21, 1831, both in Executive Papers, Virginia State Library; Mrs. Lawrence Lewis to Otis, October 17, 1831, in Samuel Eliot Morison, *Life and Letters of Harrison Gray Otis, Federalist 1765–1848* (Boston, 1913), II, 260; Calvin Jones to Montfort Stokes, December 28, 1830, in Governors' Papers, North Carolina Division of Archives and History. Inconclusive evidence suggesting a wider conspiracy involving northern free blacks and abolitionists and poor white southerners appears in Aptheker, *American Negro Slave Revolts*, 303–304, and Ira Berlin (ed.), "After Nat Turner: A Letter from the North," *Journal of Negro History*, LV (1970), 144–51.

41. Tragle, *Southampton Slave Revolt*, 275–76.

an explanation the South Carolina governor—whose state then approached the Nullification Crisis—was prepared to accept.

"They began first, by making them religious," Floyd wrote, ". . . telling the blacks God was no respecter of persons—the black man was as good as the white—that all men were born free and equal— that the white people rebelled against England to obtain freedom, so have the blacks a right to do." Finally, continued Floyd, "our females and of the most respectable were persuaded that it was piety to teach negroes to read and write . . . that they might read the Scriptures." Government shared blame with misguided, pious women. Officials had grown lax. Under a permissive regime, laws designed to restrict slaves "became more inactive." While authorities looked the other way, black preachers found in northern-produced religious tracts and "incendiary publications" the subversive ideas that they communicated to slaves in unsupervised church services. Through the agency of black preachers, Floyd believed, a widespread conspiracy had taken shape to destroy white control in Virginia. "In sum," he wrote, "the Northern incendiaries, tracts, Sunday Schools, religion and reading and writing" produced Turner's revolt.[42]

Floyd omitted only one important element from his wide-ranging indictment. He did not take into account the crucial part played by grievances inseparable from slavery in explaining the Southampton fury. It was a pardonable oversight, for conventional wisdom held that the lot of slaves in the Old Dominion was enviable. Only the ungrateful, the infatuated, or the misled would reject so fortunate a condition. But that benign view neglected aspects of slave life that had little to do with its incidents of work, food, clothing, and shelter. No more clearly than most of his white contemporaries did the Virginia governor see the fierce wounds produced even in well-treated slaves by the reality of bondage and forced submission. No spokesman for the state could be expected to acknowledge as legitimate the aggrieved slaves' sense of injustice.

The deep-seated grievances and the motives of earlier slave rebels had long been on record, revealed by witnesses in the numerous trials resulting from the Gabriel and Vesey conspiracies and from others less well-known. Curiously, only a few statements made by the Southampton rebels survive; yet even this sparse evidence establishes the circumstance that led slaves to support Turner's desperate venture. Just as Turner himself—as recorded in the state-

42. *Ibid.*, 430–32.

ments he made to Thomas Grey—was moved not by uncommonly harsh treatment but by the demands of retributive justice, so his followers struck out against unmerited bondage and the impositions of despotic masters. When the first reports of violence reached nearby neighborhoods on the morning of August 22, 1831, some ill-informed persons assumed that the traditional enemy, the British, must have invaded Virginia once again. Among slaves the assumption did not produce alarm, however, for blacks—slave and free alike—generally looked upon the British with much favor. The slave Hardy felt no regret at being told that British armies marched through Virginia. "He said that 'If they really were in the County killing white people . . . it was nothing and ought to have been done long ago—that the negroes had been punished long enough.' "[43]

On the morning of the revolt, before many outside the immediate area grasped exactly what was happening, Nancy Parsons, a young white woman, came upon a slave lying along the road "kicking up his heels" in his own unique posture of ecstasy. The prospect of the British presence accounted for his immoderate joy. Wasn't he afraid of the British? Isaac answered no and "that if they came by he would join them & assist in killing all the white people—that if they succeeded he would have as much money as his master." Ever since 1829, when his hopes for emancipation aroused by the constitutional convention of that year were dashed, Isaac had felt the impositions of his bondage more keenly. "If he had been set free two Courts ago," he explained, "this would not have happened."[44]

In Onslow County, North Carolina, many miles from Southampton, slaves responded much as did slaves in Virginia to the excitement Turner's revolt produced and to the prospect of freedom. Jacob talked about his own plans. "He said that 'If they rose he had a pretty good sword, that he would be amongst them . . . and since that time at Mr. Hawkins he . . . wished that the camp meeting was nearer than it was, so that he might aid in destroying the whites.' " Sometimes, it appeared, slaves moved toward revolt from a generalized sense of injustice, as did Turner, but they might also be prompted by specific, personal grievance, as was Jacob, who still smarted from the unspecified incident "at Mr. Hawkins."[45]

Similarly, in Virginia near the site of the revolt, the master's immoderate exercise of power led Frank to support the rebels: "His

43. Aptheker, "One Continual Cry," 106; Tragle, Southampton Slave Revolt, 202.
44. Tragle, Southampton Slave Revolt, 189.
45. Criminal Action Concerning the 1831 Insurrection of Slaves, September 20, 1831, in Onslow County Miscellaneous Records.

master had crop[p]ed him [cut off his ears]," he explained, "and *he* would be crop[p]ed before the end of the year."[46] Turner's most intimate coconspirators were confident that their initiative would arouse the other slaves' deep-seated hatred and would rally them to revolution. When Jack first learned of the plan "to rise and kill all the white people," he objected, reasoning that Turner's band was far too small to accomplish so large a scheme. But Hark, one of Turner's few confidants, discounted the objection. He predicted that "as they went on and killed the whites the blacks would join them." Most slaves, Hark believed, shared his own hatred and would join the revolt.[47]

There was little time at the end of August and start of September, 1831, for white citizens to undertake extensive efforts to locate the wellsprings of revolt. Mobilization to subdue the rebels seemed to be the sole necessity. Alarm was widespread. Officials across the state border ordered out the North Carolina militia, some units to guard the immediate border area, others to rush to the aid of their embattled neighbors. Word of the revolt reached both Mayor J. E. Holt at Norfolk and Governor John Floyd at Richmond at almost the same early hour on August 23. Lacking means to coordinate military plans, each official acted independently of the other to meet the emergency. Both men interpreted the news from Southampton as evidence that a state of war existed. Accordingly, both mobilized massive military force. Within a few hours, Floyd dispatched troops and cavalry, drawing forces especially from Richmond, Norfolk, and Brunswick. The mayor likewise ordered the volunteer and militia units under his command to move to Southampton. But the Norfolk authorities went still further. At their own initiative and without consulting Governor Floyd, the mayor and his advisers requested help from federal forces. Colonel James House, commandant of Fortress Monroe, responded at once by dispatching three companies from the First Artillery Regiment and marines and sailors from the USS *Natchez* and the USS *Warren*, two warships then stationed in Hampton Roads. At the same time, the commander of the United States naval yard depot agreed to furnish equipment for the volunteer company hastily formed at Norfolk and Portsmouth.[48]

46. Tragle, *Southampton Slave Revolt*, 214–15. Emphasis added.

47. *Ibid.*, 196.

48. *Ibid.*, 16–19, 42, 264–65, 269–70, 424–25; George C. Dromgoole to Nathaniel Mason, August 23, 1831, in Nathaniel Mason Papers, Southern Historical Collection, University of North Carolina, Chapel Hill.

Concern that use of federal troops without the governor's request disregarded constitutional nicety was allayed by a letter from the United States adjutant general to Colonel House expressing "the entire satisfaction of the President and Secretary of War, at the promptitude with which you dispatched three companies of Artillery . . . at the request of the civil authority, on this lamentable and unforeseen occasion." Federal military authorities cooperated still further. Before the summer ended, five companies of troops had been moved from the northern seaboard to Fortress Monroe to meet the additional outbreaks that hourly were expected. As an additional precaution, the navy announced plans to discharge the black mechanics who had been employed at naval installations at Portsmouth, "which will increase the number of white men in that town about four hundred."[49]

Although Governor Floyd did not at all minimize the gravity of the emergency, he could not conceal his displeasure that Norfolk officials had appealed for federal troops. No doubt it was comforting to know that the United States had made good on its constitutional obligation to help put down rebellion—a fact perhaps not lost on those slave states that soon afterward refrained from supporting South Carolina in its nullification adventure. Nevertheless the mayor had erred, the governor believed, in requesting federal aid. Sending troops to the interior left the seacoast, with its large black population, dangerously depleted of military force. But more to the point, resort to federal troops may have suggested to blacks that the people of Virginia were too weak to cope with their own racial problems, that the maintenance of slavery depended on federal force. Such an impression could only make slaves contemptuous of their white masters. Widespread insubordination—refusal to be disciplined, reluctance to work—must be the result. And what would happen, asked Floyd, if someday foreign war required withdrawal of federal troops, leaving Virginia to defend herself? How would slaves respond then? It was something to think about.[50]

Important though such considerations were, it is doubtful that they entered the minds of many persons in the last days of August, 1831. At that moment, they could think of little else than how to save themselves from the ferocious blacks. Women and children especially were afflicted with terror as word of Turner's onslaught

49. Tragle, *Southampton Slave Revolt*, 58, 19–20; William Murdaugh to John Floyd, September 24, 1831, in Executive Papers, Virginia State Library.
50. Tragle, *Southampton Slave Revolt*, 271–72.

spread. Many fled to woods and swamps and remained there for an extended period. If it were possible, even greater panic appears to have been experienced in North Carolina than in Virginia. Rumors swept the state that Wilmington had been burned and its white citizens massacred. A black army two thousand strong was said to be advancing on Raleigh. Nearly a thousand women were reported to have gathered for protection at Halifax, a similar number at Murfreesboro, and still others at defensible points in Gates and Northampton counties.[51]

Alarm was slow to subside. On September 29, more than a month after Turner's band was destroyed, twelve hundred men, women, and children fled their homes in the northern part of Pittsylvania County, Virginia, and collected at "Col. Estes's" on report that six hundred slaves had attacked a camp meeting. When similar rumors continued to spread with like effect and no factual base, some citizens began to calculate their impact on blacks. James Peirce thought that "the rumours afloat, and the alarms with which the people have been so unfortunately harassed . . . and the fact which cannot and does not escape the notice of the Slaves, that many persons are under great apprehensions, must of necessity, bring the Slaves to think on the subject, and are unfortunately too much calculated to encourage them to make such attempts."[52]

At last some concluded, no doubt correctly, that the continuing rumors of impending violence lacked any foundation whatever, and that immoderate response to them made whites appear ridiculous. "I believe indeed," wrote Benjamin Cabell, "that the blacks themselves have in some instances, had the address to put reports into circulation in order to enjoy the spectacle resulting from the unaccountable panic of the whites."[53] If so, this was indeed grim humor and reckless in the extreme, for when whites mobilized to suppress

51. *Ibid.*, 85; [Samuel Warner], *Authentic and Impartial Narrative of the Tragical Scene Which Was Witnessed in Southampton County (Virginia) on Monday the 22nd of August Last* . . . [New York, 1831], 19–25; Pattie Mordecai to Ellen Mordecai, September 16, 1831, and R. Lazarus to George W. Mordecai, October 6, 1831, both in Pattie Mordecai Collection, North Carolina Division of Archives and History, Raleigh.

52. Benjamin Cabell to John Floyd, [October 6, 1831], and James Peirce to John Floyd, October 10, 1831, both in Executive Papers, Virginia State Library; Deborah Shea (ed.), "Spreading Terror and Devastation Wherever They Have Been: A Norfolk Woman's Account of the Southampton Slave Insurrection," *Virginia Magazine of History and Biography*, XCV (1987), 65–74.

53. Benjamin Cabell to John Floyd, October 19, 1831, in Executive Papers, Virginia State Library.

revolt, real or imaginary, they did not scruple from inflicting reprisals. The massacre of whites in Southampton County was followed immediately by a massacre of blacks. Although no one kept tally sheets, almost surely far more blacks than whites were murdered.

"Last Tuesday and Wednesday [August 23 and 24] there was something like 40 negroes kill'd by the Murfreesboro Company, the Governor Guards, and the *ballance* of the enemy was kill'd and taken by the Virginians on Thursday. . . . Negroes are taken in . . . and executed every day," reported Robert S. Parker, who had been at the seat of war. On August 25, he continued, "there was a negro from Ahosky Ridge bending his course toward Southampton, and undertook to pass through the Boro' and when he had got as far through town as Mr. Manny's office, there were about 8 or 10 guns fired at him by the Guard, they then cut off his head, stuck it on a pole, and planted the pole at the cross streets."[54]

Indiscriminate murder and torture characterized efforts to suppress revolt and uncover conspiracy. At Enfield, North Carolina, a skeptic about the reality of the purported conspiracies reported that "the good people about town have taken a free negro to the Vice & screwed him up to extort confessions & failing in their object threaten to shoot him forthwith."[55]

It was hard for whites anticipating destruction to separate the guilty from the innocent. "We have testimony that will implicate most of the negroes in the county," wrote a resident of Sampson County, North Carolina. The frightened whites in neighboring Duplin County responded to an alleged conspiracy by putting "10 or 15" to death. At the height of the panic at Murfreesboro, a black man was shot and beheaded for having predicted "there would be a war between the black and white people."[56]

Although no one recorded the effects of the insurrection on the blacks who survived the reprisals, Charity Bowery, who was a slave in North Carolina near the Virginia border, remembered some sixteen years afterward that "the brightest and best men were killed in

54. Robert S. Parker to Rebecca Manney, August 29, 1831, in John Kimberly Papers, Southern Historical Collection, University of North Carolina, Chapel Hill.
55. S. Whitaker to the Governor, August 26, 1831, in Governors' Papers, North Carolina Division of Archives and History. See also William Kauffman Scarborough (ed.), *The Diary of Edmund Ruffin* (Baton Rouge, 1972–89), II, 207–209.
56. William Blanks to the Governor, September 13, 1831, and T. Borland to the Governor, September 18, 1831, both in Governors' Papers, North Carolina Division of Archives and History.

Nat's time. Such ones are always suspected. All the colored folks were afraid to pray in the time of the old prophet Nat. There was no law about it; but the whites reported it round among themselves, that if a note was heard, we should have some dreadful punishment; and after that, the low whites would fall upon any slaves they heard praying or singing a hymn, and often killed them before their masters or mistress could get to them."[57]

In Southampton County a reign of terror against free blacks as well as slaves followed the revolt. "Many white people of low character take advantage of the prejudice excited against them to maltreat and abuse them so that they are obliged to flee from their homes to save their lives." Their only recourse, the report continued, was to take refuge "in the houses of those benevolent white men that will afford them protection. Mr. [Joseph] Lewis and [Carr] Bowers have a number of them at their plantations."[58]

Whites in North Carolina subjected free blacks to similar reprisals. At Elizabeth City in September, 1831, two white men broke into the home of a free black and killed him. One of the murderers was apprehended, but, wrote an agent of the American Colonization Society, "I feel satisfied should our Grand Jury find a true bill against the murderer he will be acquitted. . . . The mere imprisonment of this man has already caused considerable excitement among our nonslaveholding population." In such an atmosphere, a number of blacks who previously had been unresponsive to proposals to send them to Africa now welcomed the chance to leave. Others fled to the North.[59]

Whites caught up in the hysteria suffered in their way as well. "In almost every section of our county," wrote a resident of Southampton, "conversation instead of being as it was a month since, light and cheerful, is now clothed in dismal forebodings.—Some of our citizens will leave us—and all agree, that they never again can feel safe, never again be happy." A well-to-do resident of Wilmington regretted "holding so much property here, and if not actually tied down to this place, would gladly remove to the north." Suppression of revolt, the writer believed, had left the fundamental problem con-

57. John W. Blassingame (ed.), *Slave Testimony: Two Centuries of Letters, Speeches, Interviews, and Autobiographies* (Baton Rouge, 1977), 267.
58. Jonathan McPhail to R. R. Gurley, September 22, 1831, in American Colonization Society Papers.
59. Miles White to R. R. Gurley, October 1, 1831, and John C. Ehringhaus to R. R. Gurley, September 29, 1831, both *ibid*.

fronting southern whites unresolved: "In the bosom of almost every family the enemy still exists."[60]

The perception of continuing, unavoidable danger fed the militarism that for years had characterized southern culture. State and local governments endeavored to bring militia units to a high state of preparedness. Volunteer groups were formed to help defend the social order. Eighty-eight students at the University of Virginia formed an association to study military tactics under an instructor appointed by the faculty and asked the governor to supply them with arms. At the University of North Carolina, students organized a volunteer company and requested sixty stand of arms.[61]

Not surprisingly, the emergency led citizens to call upon government to solve a problem that seemed beyond the capacity of individuals. Some demanded expulsion of the free blacks. Some thought slavery should be ended gradually and the freed slaves removed. Some called for more severe laws regulating all blacks. Others offered no specific remedy, but merely pointed out the state's perilous condition and pled for legislative action—any action—that might bring security.

Such evidence of widespread concern led to an unprecedented debate in the Virginia General Assembly. For the first and last time, a southern legislature subjected slavery to public examination. Yet the scrutiny produced no evident gains, for as discussion proceeded, it became clear that no action could be taken. Compensated emancipation at state expense appeared too costly, even if a plan could be agreed upon. Emancipation without compensation would destroy property rights and in any event was politically impossible. There simply was no politically feasible solution.

No legislator placed a bill calling for emancipation before the General Assembly. Instead, the entire matter of slavery and free blacks was referred to a select committee, which failed to agree on a recommendation. When the committee chairman moved to discharge the body on the ground that legislation on slavery was "inexpedient," Thomas J. Randolph offered a substitute resolution favoring gradual emancipation of slaves born after July 4, 1840, to be

60. *Liberator*, January 28, 1832; Rachel Lazarus to G. W. Mordecai, October 6, 1831, in Pattie Mordecai Collection.

61. Joseph Caldwell to the Governor, September 17, 1831, and Joseph B. Southell and 67 others to the Governor, September 17, 1831, in Governors' Papers, North Carolina Division of Archives and History; Robert M. Patterson to John Floyd, October 24, 1831, in Executive Papers, Virginia State Library.

followed by their colonization. His motion to submit the proposal to popular referendum encountered strenuous objection on the ground that public discussion would have dangerous consequences. Controversy would sharpen the long-evident divisions between rich and poor and between slaveowners and nonslaveowners. It would aggravate the slaves' discontent, making them still harder to control. Willoughby Newton painted the scene: "The hustings—the muster ground—nay, sir, every crossroad and grog-shop, will be made the scene of angry debate, and noisy declamation, upon this agitating subject. What must be the inevitable consequence? . . . Revolt and insurrection among our slaves."[62]

Newton's misgivings already had been foreshadowed during the debate, when several legislators voiced resentment not only toward free blacks and slaves but toward slaveowners as well. "At all times the non-slave-holders of Virginia are subjected to the most outrageous imposition by the presence of this population," said George W. Summers of Kanawha County. Small farmers performed patrol duty "to protect the slave-holder in the enjoyment of that which it is the interest of non-slave-holders, should not exist." These were ominous sentiments indeed, for they revealed social divisions that imperiled the consensus upon which slavery depended. Although he was a man of substance and the owner of land and slaves, Thomas J. Randolph put himself forward on this occasion as champion of the small farmers. He accepted the validity of their grievance: "It has been the practice, if not the policy of the large slaveholder," he said, "to make the poor man the instrument of their police and their punishments to their slaves; which has begotten hostility between the slave and the less wealthy."[63] But to acknowledge the grievance, as Randolph did, was not to relieve it.

The General Assembly succeeded in solving no part of the racial problem. When it adjourned, the petitions that had called for emancipation and for expulsion of free blacks remained unanswered. Rather than finding solutions, the legislators had opened forbidden subjects to examination and had revealed seldom-exposed tensions. It was partly to counteract the divisive result such action was expected to have that Thomas R. Dew, professor at the College of Wil-

62. Joseph C. Robert, *The Road from Monticello: A Study of the Virginia Slavery Debate of 1832* (Durham, N.C., 1941), 19, 98.
63. *Ibid.*, 86; Alison Goodyear Freehling, *Drift Toward Dissolution: The Virginia Slavery Debate of 1831–1832* (Baton Rouge, 1982), 122–69; Robert, *Road from Monticello*, 96.

liam and Mary, prepared a major defense of slavery in the form of a review of the General Assembly's debates. Slavery could not—and should not—be ended, Dew argued; and the free blacks could not be removed. Freedom or moves toward freedom would produce discord and violence. Only forthright defense of slavery could guarantee tranquillity.[64]

Dew came forward with his ingeniously structured proslavery argument at an opportune moment. Recent events in Virginia suggested the need to bolster the slaveholders' position in the face of internal dissension among whites and discontent among slaves. At the same time, vigorous abolitionist agitation was under way in the North. Southern institutions, it appeared, were about to be subjected to a pincerslike attack against which defense and justification would be needed as never before.

64. Dew's argument appeared as Thomas R. Dew, *Review of the Debate in the Virginia Legislature of 1831 and 1832* (Richmond, 1832).

8

A Pacific Crusade

By the time Nat Turner's rebels tore through Southampton County, William Lloyd Garrison had published the *Liberator* for nearly eight months in Boston, and copies of the newspaper had carried his shrill abolitionist message to the slave states. The conjunction of events made certain that some Virginians would blame Turner's violence on Garrison's rhetoric. Soon officials throughout the South were demanding suppression of the *Liberator* in the name of public safety, and state legislators were calling for Garrison's extradition from Massachusetts to be tried for the crime of inciting slaves to revolt.[1]

There was some irony in all of this, for already in 1831 Garrison had progressed far toward the nonresistant position that later would make him notorious. Although early opponents of slavery commonly believed slaves would be justified in rising against their oppressors, neither Garrison nor the many abolitionists who preceded him urged slaves to revolt. Garrison often advised the opposite. His views decrying slave violence had been on record for many months—ever since the alarm produced throughout the South by *Walker's Appeal*.

Garrison lived in Baltimore in 1829 and was just beginning his

1. Wendell Phillips Garrison and Francis Jackson Garrison, *William Lloyd Garrison, 1805–1879* (Boston, 1885–89), I, 239–42, 247–48.

spectacular career when copies of the *Appeal* came to light in several southern cities. With characteristic flouting of the expedient, he had added to his published statement deploring the pamphlet an admiring comment on "the bravery and intelligence of its author." But later, in answer to charges that he endorsed Walker's militancy, Garrison declared the contrary to be true: "We do not preach rebellion—no, but submission and peace."[2] Slaveholders might doubt the sincerity of Garrison's disclaimer, yet he had voiced what remained standard abolitionist policy throughout the 1830s. While freely asserting the slaves' theoretical right to rebel, abolitionists customarily shrank from the prospect of their doing so. It was partly to avert such a disaster, Garrison insisted, that he founded the *Liberator* at Boston in January, 1831. He would try to persuade whites to end slavery before they became the victims of their vengeful bondsmen.

He insisted that he had no connection with Turner's revolt, but appended to the disclaimer was an assertion that must have infuriated southern readers. Slaves, he wrote, "would be justified in using retaliatory measures more than any people on the face of the earth." Their use of violence in the cause of liberty was as fitting as that of the American revolutionary patriots.[3] Garrison's distinction between the right to revolt and the wisdom of doing so was not particularly subtle, yet it is easy to understand why in the emotional atmosphere of 1831 southerners ignored Garrison's clear distinction and read his words as a message urging blood and destruction. To slaveowners, assertion of the injustice of slavery seemed equivalent to inviting insurrection. Even if the worst did not happen—even if by good fortune antislavery propaganda did not lead to overt rebellion—at very least such criticism would undermine plantation discipline, with consequent decline in labor productivity and in the value of slaves.

Garrison found in the blacks' status as slaves sufficient cause for revolt, but he also agreed with his southern critics who held that outside influences might stimulate disorder. The Southampton rebels, he wrote, had found inspiration in a worldwide movement toward freedom, of which the antislavery campaign and his own career formed only a part. According to Garrison, ideological currents

2. *Genius of Universal Emancipation*, X (January 15, 1830), 147; *Liberator*, January 8, 1831.
3. *Liberator*, September 3, 1831.

impinging upon the South from many directions prompted slaves to rebel—"voices in the air, sounds from across the ocean, invitations to resistance above, below, around them!"[4] Southerners would have found this an especially alarming observation, for Garrison implied that the impulse to throw off bondage was irresistible and that it might not be within anyone's power to prevent slaves on their own initiative from striking for freedom.

Slaveowners unhesitatingly rejected advocates of emancipation as "fanatics," but they could not be so sure that the northern majority would similarly repudiate them and their program. To the contrary, evidence suggested growing northern affinity for antislavery thought. Even though in 1831 abolitionists comprised only a tiny, obscure element in the northern population, the disquieting fact could not be evaded that a generalized antislavery, antisouthern sentiment had long pervaded much of the North and apparently intensified. The course followed by a number of northern congressmen and publicists during the Misssouri controversy, together with a myriad of lesser events, amply supported that conclusion.

Abolitionism's seditious effect in undermining slavery, southerners believed, could be detected among softhearted white men and women even within the South. How else could be explained their insistence on teaching slaves to read and their winking at violation of regulatory laws? Further, a large body of potentional abolitionist recruits existed among the South's many nonslaveholders. What, for example, would a slaveholder make of this lament written by a farmer in Iredell County, North Carolina, in 1825: "The great men of our county seem determined to engross all the best land of the country—and then how are the poor to live amongst their slaves and overseers?"[5] Slaveowners must seize every available means to limit the abolitionists' opportunity to subvert members of their own race as well as the black population. But suppose the effort failed. Suppose that, under the promptings of northern-based fanatics and the encouragement of corrupted southern whites, slaves made a desperate bid for freedom through a revolt too widespread and intense for southern resources to subdue. In that extremity, it was true, the Constitution offered recourse. Yet its provision for federal military

4. *Ibid.*, October 15, 1831.
5. John Floyd to James Hamilton, Jr., November, 1831, in Tragle, *Southampton Slave Revolt*, 175; Christopher Houston to Placebo Houston, April 23, 1825, in Gertrude Dixon Enfield (ed.), "Life and Letters of Christopher Houston" (Typescript in Perkins Library, Duke University, Durham, N.C.).

aid would count for little if an abolitionized northern public sympathized with the insurgents instead of with their masters.

If present trends continued, southern spokesmen believed, slaveholders eventually would find themselves isolated and friendless when calamity struck. The day might even come when a hostile North openly promoted insurrection. A northern black editor early formulated the possibility. "The nation cannot bear everything," wrote John Russwurm in 1827, "and if the indignation of the people should compel our government to withdraw her protection, and give notice that the slave states shall be left to themselves, I tremble for the consequence." In the same year, one of Benjamin Lundy's southern correspondents, anticipating imminent revolt, expressed similar dread. North-South political disputes and cultural differences, he suggested, already had grown so intense as to destroy comity between the sections. Thus, predicted the Kentuckian, when the slaves unleashed their fury, besieged southern whites would stand alone, and the hostile North would "laugh at their calamity and mock when their fear cometh."[6]

Here and there in the 1820s, northerners voiced sentiments suggesting that such predictions already had acquired a factual base, that a common front uniting whites in support of slavery no longer could be taken for granted. In 1826, Judge Benjamin Tappan, a native of Massachusetts then living in Ohio, startled an agent of the American Colonization Society with his remark that he hoped the slaves would rise up and cut the throats of their masters. In the same year, a writer in the *Genius of Universal Emancipation*, pondering his responsibility toward slavery, arrived at a conclusion likewise hostile to southern white interest: "I would inquire whether the slave has not a resort to the most violent measures, if necessary, in order to maintain his liberty? And if he has the least chance of success, are we not, as rational and consistent men, bound to justify him?" The writer stopped short of advocating encouragement and aid to black rebels, but not very far short. Conversation with Quakers in Pennsylvania and Ohio in 1829 led Josiah F. Polk, an agent of the American Colonization Society, to conclude that "some of them would grieve to see the Southern States freed from this curse *without the severest chastisement.*" Polk shared the opinion already held

6. *Freedom's Journal,* April 13, 1827; *Genius of Universal Emancipation and Baltimore Courier,* II (May 19, 1827), 218. See also Thomas Law to John C. Calhoun, August 10, 1821, in Meriwether *et al.* (eds.), *Papers of John C. Calhoun,* VI, 328, and *Annals of Congress,* 9th Cong., 2nd Sess., 626–27.

by some slaveholders, "that in the event of a formidable insurrection in the South scarcely a man would cross the line to aid in its suppression, even *at the hazard of the dissolution of the Union.*"[7]

It was in the uneasy atmosphere generated by such sentiments that both southerners and abolitionists assessed the slave violence of 1831. Abolitionists could not escape their reputation as accessories to the Southampton revolt, though the accusation fell hardest on Garrison, whose newspaper more outspokenly than any other condemned slavery and slaveholders. Southern white leaders might take comfort, however, in knowing that even in the North, where slavery fell under general disapproval, persons concerned for social order and intersectional harmony denounced the abolitionists' policy and the rhetoric in which their arguments often were presented. Following Turner's revolt, Francis Wayland, president of Brown University, requested Garrison to stop sending him the *Liberator.* Its attitude toward slaveowners, he complained, was "menacing and vindictive," prejudicing them against "cool discussion" of slavery. Still worse, the newspaper's presentation of "the miseries of the slaves" was "calculated to arouse their most destructive passions [and to urge] them on to resistance at all hazards."[8]

Garrison and his associates continued to insist that such critics misunderstood the abolitionists' purpose. Their program, wholly pacific in intent, was designed to prevent repetition of the catastrophe that had struck Virginia. In thus responding to his opponents, Garrison utilized one of the oldest themes in antislavery argument. A powerful objection advanced against slavery since at least the early eighteenth century was the near certainty that an enraged slave population someday would rise up and destroy its oppressors. This familiar expectation as motive for urging emancipation had been joined more recently by the potent but still relatively novel force of moral and religious duty. Thus the antislavery crusade of the late eighteenth and early nineteenth centuries represented an amalgam of old prudential and newer idealistic elements. The two strands of antislavery thought were never again separated and persisted until slavery finally was destroyed, though sometimes one, sometimes the other was emphasized.

7. Benjamin C. Peers to R. R. Gurley, October 13, 1826, in American Colonization Society Papers; *Genius of Universal Emancipation and Baltimore Courier,* I (August 26, 1826), 403; Josiah F. Polk to R. R. Gurley, December 17, 1829, in American Colonization Society Papers.
8. Francis Wayland to Garrison, November 1, 1831, in Antislavery Collection, Boston Public Library.

While religious revivals in the 1820s supplied new dynamism to antislavery argument, sharpening political rivalries between North and South joined events in Europe and South America to augment fears of revolt. The result by 1830 was the marked urgency with which abolitionists faced the slavery issue.

Freedom was in the air. In 1827 Nathaniel Paul, black pastor of the First African Baptist Society in Albany, New York, identified some of the diverse forces that he thought would impel slaves to try to cast off their bonds: "the catastrophe and exchange of power in the Isle of Hayti, the restless disposition of both master and slave in the southern states, the constitution of our government, the effects of literacy and moral instruction, the influence and spread of the holy religion of the cross of Christ, and the irrevocable decree of Almighty God."[9] Paul's catalog barely hinted at an additional stimulus to antislavery thought. Principles of liberty inseparable from the Age of Revolution still generated expectations that supported liberal political movements throughout Europe as well as in America. While oppressed peoples on the Continent battled for liberty in the 1820s, white Americans applauded their efforts and prayed for their success.

In particular, the struggle of the Greeks to win independence from Turkey aroused admiration. "Greece & the Greek cause are the reigning topic," reported a South Carolinian from Boston in 1824. By the end of the decade, the Polish revolt against Russian despotism supplemented the Greek struggle as an object of American esteem, and in 1830 the triumph of liberal forces in France was cheered in Washington. Humanitarian urges could shift focus as need required, and when the shift occurred, black people, slave or free, might well be beneficiaries. "Three little girls a few weeks since expressed the wish to form a society for the benefit of the Greek children," reported E. M. Balch from Maryland in 1830, "but since they have learned that they are no longer in need of their mite they have interested their youthful zeal and tender feelings in behalf of the unfortunate people of colour." Such flexibility was not likely to be confined to children. Although rebellions by white Europeans had no immediate relation to slavery, the example of a people rising in behalf of freedom—an example that so many Americans clearly admired—bore transferable implications for a country pledged to retaining a large part of its population in bondage. Some slavehold-

9. Nathaniel Paul, *An Address, Delivered on the Celebration of the Abolition of Slavery in the State of New York, July 5, 1827* (Albany, N.Y., 1827), 16.

ers frankly acknowledged the prospect. Upon hearing a Virginia ma-
tron express extravagant sympathy for the rebellious Greeks, John
Randolph, with reference to nearby blacks, retorted, "The Greeks,
madam, are at your door."[10]

Revolutionary movements acquired an unmistakable antislavery
cast when in the wake of the Napoleonic Wars Spain's possessions
in the Western Hemisphere threw off colonial ties and also provided
for emancipation. The significance for the American South could
not be missed. The slave states faced new isolation as the free territory surrounding them grew. No sooner had the Missouri Compromise opened a door through which slaves and plantation agriculture could enter the West than the South American revolutions
diminished the boon by creating a free neighbor on the southern
and western border. Who in the 1820s could doubt that an antislavery Mexico sooner or later would encourage slave unrest in the
United States and offer refuge to black fugitives from the South, as
all earlier neighbors had done? Indeed, the entire Latin American
revolutionary example could be expected to unsettle North American slavery. "A secret influence is imperceptably conveyed from the
land of Bolivar to the miserable slaves," said a northern Presbyterian preacher. "It invites them to freedom. You cannot intercept
that influence."[11]

Of mounting concern, too, was the aggressive antislavery movement under way in England, with its proclaimed goal of abolition
throughout the British Empire. In the late 1820s, an array of notable
English reformers gained parliamentary support for emancipation
in the British West Indies. Antislavery Americans followed the progress of British abolitionism admiringly but also with apprehension, for the measure promised to revolutionize race relations in
areas well outside British territory. Success of the parliamentary
reformers, it appeared, would force Americans to act against slavery
sooner than they might find convenient. Slavery in the United
States, some believed, could not long survive emancipation in the
West Indies. Such prophets counted partly on the prestige and encouragement the British example would supply to American antislavery reformers. But more than that, they measured the effect

10. M. C. Darby to Mrs. Manigault, June 22, 1824, in Manigault Family Papers;
E. M. Balch to R. R. Gurley, July 4, 1830, in American Colonization Society Papers;
Robert Dawidoff, *The Education of John Randolph* (New York, 1979), 63–64.
11. O. P. Hoyt at Potsdam, N.Y., in *Freedom's Journal*, May 11, 1827.

British abolition would have on American slaves. Abolition in the British Empire, wrote John Quincy Adams, "may prove an earthquake upon this continent."[12]

A northern periodical accounted for the unsettling effect commonly expected to flow from success of the British antislavery movement: "Their slave population is in the immediate neighborhood of our own. They speak the same language. The intercourse is easy, constant, and unavoidable."[13] Despite all efforts to keep them isolated and ignorant, slaves still would manage to learn about events that affected their status, even when those events occurred far from regions where they lived. It was in South Carolina and Georgia, states long having close economic and social relations with the Caribbean islands, that the impact of British emancipation was expected to be the most severe. "Let those resolutions be carried into effect in the West Indies," remarked a Georgia planter, "and in six months I shall see the effect on my slaves."[14] The *Christian Spectator* addressed to American celebrators of foreign revolution a menacing question about the ultimate consequence of British antislavery. When the British West Indian slaves become free, "who will say that a war of extermination [in the American South] will not ensue, in which the African cause may excite as much sympathy and as liberal contributions in England and in the West Indies, as the Greek cause has done in this country?"[15]

Such speculation, with its mingling of painful memories of Saint-Domingue and prospects of renewed foreign intrigue, could only add to the planters' concern. It was tempting for anglophobes to suspect the traditional enemy of evil intent and impossible to doubt the evil intent of northern abolitionists. The northern-based antislavery movement was a front, some concluded, for hostile English interest bent on spoiling the American experiment in republicanism and economic freedom. Conspiracy was in the air. "It is somewhat singular that the passion of humanity should, at the same instant of time, have seized so strongly upon New England and Old England,"

12. Charles Francis Adams (ed.), *Memoirs of John Quincy Adams Comprising Portions of His Diary from 1795 to 1848* (Philadelphia, 1874–77), VIII, 269. See also [Elliott Cresson] to R. R. Gurley, November 10, 1831, in American Colonization Society Papers.
13. *Christian Spectator* as quoted in *Freedom's Journal*, March 23, 1827.
14. Quoted in American Anti-Slavery Society, *First Annual Report . . . 1834* (New York, 1834), 22.
15. Quoted in *Freedom's Journal*, March 23, 1827.

observed a Virginia congressman, "that this passion would have been so strongly and so singularly enlisted in favor of the black slaves."[16]

Aspersions such as these may have confirmed some persons in already established resistance to antislavery argument, but they did little to lessen reformers' admiration for the steady British advance toward emancipation and nothing to allay apprehension that ending slavery in the British West Indies would increase discontent among slaves in the United States. Abolitionists remained convinced that antislavery measures in America must parallel English accomplishment. The alternative, they insisted, would be race war. As the British moved toward emancipation in the 1820s and early 1830s, hardly any element in antislavery argument loomed larger than warnings of eventual slave uprisings. These would come soon, abolitionists repeatedly warned, unless Americans agreed to make drastic changes in race relations. To those who reply "that the danger *may be distant*," said Yale College professor Benjamin Silliman, "I answer, it *may* also be near."[17]

The many new influences awakening northern reformers to the menace of slavery led some of them by 1831 to seek to coordinate their efforts through national organization. Free blacks were at the forefront of the project. After they and a few white reformers discussed the subject at the First Annual Convention of People of Color held at Philadelphia in June, 1831, hopes rose for early agreement on "an enlarged and extensive plan" of antislavery action. But the project had not proceeded far when the Southampton revolt intervened, bringing with it general reassessment of reform policy. Some were led to caution, others to greater initiative by Nat Turner's exploits.

It was a troublesome and confusing time. Reformers, watching the turbulent national scene, tried to assess not so much their own chances for success as the probable effect their actions would have, either to lessen or increase turmoil. Some abolitionists found in the tensions of sectional politics a compelling reason to delay organized activity. In the early 1830s, the bonds of national union were being tested as never before by South Carolina's threatened nullification

16. *Annals of Congress*, 15th Cong., 2nd Sess., 1370.
17. *Abolition Intelligencer*, I (May 7, 1822), 7, 9, 10; *Genius of Universal Emancipation*, VI (November, 1824), 17; Phelps, *Lectures on Slavery*, 109, 210; Whittier, *Works of John Greenleaf Whittier*, VII, 33–34; American Anti-Slavery Society, *First Annual Report*, 19–20; Benjamin Silliman, "Some of the Causes of National Anxiety," *African Repository*, VIII (August, 1832), 170.

of the Tariff of 1832. National authority faced unprecedented challenge at the hands of slaveowners. Understanding of this fact reinforced antislavery and antisouthern impressions among nationalistic New Englanders; it also produced caution. Even northern members of the American Colonization Society feared their relatively conservative program would contribute to southern political disaffection. Accordingly, they proceeded with still greater wariness than usual.[18] In that tense atmosphere, a number of antislavery advocates concluded, any action promising still further intersectional discord ought to be shunned.

Among some antislavery reformers in New York and New England, however, considerations of duty managed to overrule caution even in that troubled time, and voices calling for expanded antislavery action continued to be raised. In particular, free blacks, whose interest in emancipation bore an immediacy no white reformer could match, viewed Turner's revolt as opportunity for antislavery accomplishment rather than as cause for retreat: "This insurrection in the south," wrote the Philadelphia black reformer James Forten, "will be the means of bringing the evils of slavery, more prominently before the public, and the urgent sense of danger . . . will lead to something more than mere hopes and wishes." But early optimism of the sort Forten displayed was tempered when reformers gauged the deep anxiety resulting from Nat Turner's revolt. "The Southampton affair has paralyzed our Philadelphia friends," explained Arthur Tappan of New York, "and nothing has been done or can be done there now, towards organizing a National Society."[19]

Nearly two years were to pass before the three antislavery groups—New Yorkers, New Englanders, and Pennsylvanians—could bring themselves to assume the risks involved in forming the American Anti-Slavery Society. During that extended interval, Garrison and others who were bent upon intensifying antislavery effort clarified their attitude toward violence. They also scrupulously defined their relationship to the slaves. In these undertakings, Quakers exercised influence beyond their numbers.

18. Charles Tappan to R. R. Gurley, March 13, 1830, in American Colonization Society Papers. Of Garrison, Tappan later would write, "I sometimes wish Arthur Tappan had let him lay in Baltimore jail—." Charles Tappan to R. R. Gurley, August 8, 1831, *ibid.*

19. James Forten to William Lloyd Garrison, October 12, 1831, in Antislavery Collection, Boston Public Library; Lewis Tappan to Garrison, January 21, 1832, *ibid.*; Bertram Wyatt-Brown, *Lewis Tappan and the Evangelical War Against Slavery* (Cleveland, 1969), 107.

The hesitancy Quakers displayed toward national organization did not obscure the fact that no religious group could claim a longer, more firmly established antislavery commitment. So closely identified were they with the cause that others regarded their support as essential. Any new abolitionist campaign must build on the base Quakers had created. Their commitment to nonviolence was similarly venerable. No antislavery program that seemed at all likely to result in bloodshed could win their endorsement.

Apprehension about the possibly violent effect of abolitionism was felt in other quarters of the reform community as well. Indeed, the entire "benevolent empire," the informal coalition of New York- and Boston-based reform societies, would follow Quakers and the American Peace Society in shying from programs that seemed productive of violence and confusion rather than of peace and order.

It was against this background that the founders of the American Anti-Slavery Society drafted their platform and decided upon a mode of operation. They found in Quaker belief and practice means to allay the fears produced by the specter of slave revolt. The men and women who convened at Philadelphia in December, 1833, to form the new society specifically renounced violence in the antislavery cause. And they also pointedly rejected cooperative effort with slaves. The society's Declaration of Sentiments, drafted by Garrison, set forth the new organization's principles and intended plan of operation.[20] These were altogether pacific and on the Quaker model. There is every reason to suppose, however, that this feature of the document accurately reflected views then held not just by Quakers but by the great majority of northern opponents of slavery, with the possible exception of the free blacks.

Garrison's Declaration of Sentiments forthrightly condemned slavery. Slavery was a sin that ought not to be tolerated for another instant, but despite its enormities, wrote Garrison, slavery should be combated solely by means of moral suasion. Abolitionists renounced all use of "carnal weapons." They would argue the wrong done the slaves, the danger of keeping them longer in bondage, and the duty of immediately setting them free. While they would place no limit on verbal assaults, they would not take up arms against slaveholders. More important, in view of prevalent insurrectionary fears, they would instruct slaves to follow their peaceful example.

20. Garrison's "Declaration of Sentiments of the American Anti-Slavery Society" is most conveniently found in Louis Ruchames (ed.), *The Abolitionists: A Collection of Their Writings* (New York, 1963), 78–83.

That the words abolitionists employed to alter opinion among whites might also reach slaves was an incidental and unsought probability. Such an outcome was neither calculated nor desired. Abolitionists would direct their condemnations to free persons alone—to the white electorate, whose opinions on slavery presumably could be changed and mobilized. They would not address their arguments to slaves, who in any event could be assumed already to have made up their minds on the subject. Slaves needed no "moral suasion" concerning slavery—except for what was regarded as the all-important counsel to remain at peace.

Garrison took care, nonetheless, to note that white Americans in the revolutionary era finally grew impatient with petitions and protest, the unavailing tactics of moral suasion. When the colonists no longer could endure oppression, they took up arms against English despots. Garrison did not face up to all the implications of that historic fact, nor did he expand upon the analogy. Instead, he advised slaves, whose grievances he acknowledged to be greater than those of the colonists, to be more noble and self-restrained than white Americans had been. Slaves should continue uncomplainedly to suffer oppression until deliverance came—at the hands of others.

Despite its simplistic quality and detachment from reality, Garrison's counsel was politic, the only advice possible at a time when abolitionism was suspect in the North and feared in the South, and when slaves nearly everywhere were thought to stand at the brink of rebellion. Any other program than the one adopted at Philadelphia probably would have aroused such widespread revulsion against antislavery activity as to bring the movement to an abrupt end.[21]

But these policies were not adopted solely out of expediency; they reflected the abolitionists' own convictions. Few of them in the 1830s were bloody-minded enough to wish to provoke slave revolt and race war. Further, they did not yet envision themselves acting in concert with blacks to end slavery. The widespread support for the position taken at Philadelphia is indicated by the fact that antislavery groups throughout the North incorporated it in the platforms and constitutions of all other antislavery societies founded in the 1830s. The only important dissenters were free blacks. Although several black people took part in forming the American Anti-Slavery Society and endorsed its program, probably members of that group

21. See Bertram Wyatt-Brown, "William Lloyd Garrison and Antislavery Unity: A Reappraisal," *Civil War History*, XIII (1967), 5–24.

felt less drawn toward pacifism than did white reformers. Some at an early date apparently even thought of direct military support for slave rebellion. Thus in 1832, George Carey of Cincinnati, an early black follower of Garrison, opposed an abolitionist project to found a college for blacks at New Haven. He favored instead a site outside the United States. If it were located in Canada, he explained, "we could have a military department attached to the college."[22]

The decision not to enlist slaves in the antislavery campaign accorded with abolitionists' principles and their perception of political necessity and was adopted chiefly for those reasons. But it also harmonized with the paternalistic attitude humanitarians commonly held toward the objects of their philanthropy and probably seemed even more acceptable to them on those grounds. Abolitionists seldom articulated paternalism. They never stated that they thought themselves superior to slaves. They did not hint that they regarded blacks as moral or intellectual defectives who required their aid. Indeed, the important role played in the movement by such persons as Frederick Douglass and Charles and Sarah Remond suggests the opposite assumption. Yet, in the long run, their pacific advice to slaves and their unilateral conduct of the abolitionist campaign encouraged a sentimental attitude toward slaves, an attitude that had remained for the most part recessive before the 1830s.

Although racial prejudice had not been absent even among reformers in earlier years, it acquired new bases as the antislavery movement proceeded. This outcome certainly was not intended, and it ran counter to the abolitionists' persistent and sincere efforts to combat prejudice as a chief bulwark of slavery. White abolitionists eloquently defended black equality and black capacity. Yet elements of their campaign worked against the outcome they desired. Slaves, who once had been romantically pictured as fierce, wronged warriors about to break their bonds and devastate the South, gradually were transformed in abolitionist writings into pathetic, helpless victims, trembling to accept the benevolence of wise and competent white reformers. This view of slaves harmonized with reformist attitudes toward other "defectives"—the poor, the blind, the insane, the deaf and dumb—who also required aid from their more fortunate betters.[23] Such attitudes, first reflected in action, soon were

22. Carey to Garrison, May 15, 1832, in Antislavery Collection, Boston Public Library.
23. See David Rothman, *The Discovery of the Asylum: Social Order and Disorder in the New Republic* (Boston, 1971).

crystallized in language and print, and finally were perpetuated as truth. The image of blacks as incompetents accompanied, perhaps strengthened, notions of its opposite—the moral, even genetic, superiority of whites.

Despite its nobility of purpose, philanthropic activity fostered such beliefs, for however unselfishly aid might be extended, the giver unavoidably assumed a position of superiority before the recipient. Such posture had been inseparable from the philanthropic work of the constituent societies of the antislavery American Convention and of the various "humane societies" whose object in the 1820s and earlier was to aid blacks and protect them from kidnappers and other would-be exploiters. Although totally unintended, both paternalism and prejudice received heavy reinforcement from the program abolitionists adopted in response to the political situation they found themselves in during the early 1830s. Their decision to make the antislavery movement a pacific enterprise confined solely to free persons cast slaves in a subordinate, inferior role, while also denying them the right to participate in their own liberation.

Despite these unfortunate ultimate effects, the pacific tactics and unilateral action decided upon by the founders of the American Anti-Slavery Society reflected shrewd appraisal of prevailing fears and power relationships. Although the abolitionists' Quaker-like program may to a later age seem inevitable, persons at the time did not find it so.[24] Instead of the self-denying policies adopted at Philadelphia in 1833, abolitionists might have decided to employ the slaves' evident desire to be free as a major weapon in their crusade. They could have advised slaves to abandon their masters and flee to the North. They could have mobilized northern free blacks and militant whites into invading guerrilla bands. They could have announced an alliance with slaves and proclaimed a war for liberation. These tactics seem unthinkable (though white southerners at the time would not have been surprised to find them implemented), but only because they are so at variance with the peaceable tactics actually adopted and so unlike the mode of operation almost universally adopted by other nineteenth-century protest groups. In short, they seem "un-American."

Yet as abolitionists surely knew, the means they rejected had

24. Bertram Wyatt-Brown makes this point and explores the possible range of tactics in his "William Lloyd Garrison and Antislavery Unity," 5–24.

found ample precedent in the American past. They were modes of hostility eighteenth-century enemies freely employed against American colonists. The Spanish, French, and English at various times had undertaken tacit alliances with slaves and had urged them to escape and to rebel, though always for political and nationalistic purposes, not primarily for philanthropic ones.

In contrast, the goals as well as the methods of the nineteenth-century American antislavery movement reflected its origin in religious and humanitarian principles and in prudential concern. But as slaveholders generally understood, abolitionism also possessed unmistakable political overtones. It was related to, and was in some sense a product of, fundamental social and economic changes that by the 1820s were moving the northern states toward open rivalry with the South for the right to control the nation and to set its future course. If the time should arrive when its political aspects became dominant and took command, then abolitionists might cast aside moral suasion and at last resort to modes of rivalry made familiar to earlier Americans by Spanish, French, and English enemies. In the eighteenth century, hostile powers had not shrunk from exploiting slave discontent, inviting slaves to flee their masters and encouraging them to violent resistance—all in order to achieve political and imperialistic ends. The same things might be done again.

9

A Disruptive Influence

Not for a moment did white southerners believe the abolitionists' repeated denials of insurrectionary intent. From the slaveholders' point of view, nothing in their record inspired trust. If abolitionists sincerely wanted to avoid provoking rebellion—so southerners thought—they would not persist in issuing the kind of propaganda that might persuade nonslaveholders to withdraw support from the planter class, thereby making revolt more likely. Neither would they conduct their campaign in such a way as to encourage slaves to believe they had partisans in the North. But antislavery activity, under any circumstance and in any shape, was not something toward which slaveholders could afford forbearance. It struck at the source of their livelihood and the foundation of their status, power, and self-esteem. "It is my property they seek to take," complained James Barbour of Virginia; "it is my person, my safety, my happiness, that are put to hazard."[1]

By the 1830s, slaveholders' growing awareness of the abolitionist threat eclipsed every impulse toward tolerance. The most aggressive vehicles of antislavery propaganda, the Boston *Liberator* and the New York *Emancipator*, lay so far to the north as to be physically unassailable. But offending editors close to the border lived in peril. The violence that border-state mobs directed against anti-

1. *Annals of Congress*, 16th Cong., 1st Sess., 330.

slavery editors in the mid-1830s—James G. Birney in Cincinnati, Elijah P. Lovejoy first in St. Louis and then in Alton, Illinois— represented release of long-standing tension.[2] Slaveholders and their partisans had been incited almost beyond endurance by a recent, well-organized and well-financed abolitionist propaganda campaign. In May, 1835, the American Anti-Slavery Society resolved to flood the nation with antislavery publications. Newspapers, pamphlets, and tracts would be sent everywhere, especially into the slave states, where antislavery agents themselves dared not go. While the mails carried abolitionist ideas to the South, a small army of lecturers would march across the North voicing the abolitionist gospel.

All went as planned. The lecturers kept their appointments, and abolitionist presses in New York turned out thousands of pages of print, many bearing well-executed woodcuts illustrating the sufferings of slaves. Slaveholders regarded the literature as insulting to themselves, but worse, it might fall into the hands of slaves, who, even if not literate, could understand the vivid pictures. And nearly as troublesome, it might persuade impressionable southern whites to question the peculiar institution.

Although abolitionists already had learned that the way of the antislavery advocate was hard, few could have foreseen the wave of hostility aroused by their propaganda campaign of 1835. Mobs greeted abolitionist lecturers almost everywhere they went in the North, and in the South, arrival of the antislavery publications provoked hysterical responses. Reports of increased slave unrest accompanied the furor. In the summer and fall of 1835 at widely separated points, alleged servile conspiracies were uncovered. Abolitionists, southern whites charged, instigated these new plots just as they bore responsibility for the Nat Turner atrocity.[3]

In the ensuing panic, southern whites directed violence against slaves and free blacks, against whites suspected of being abolition-

2. Betty L. Fladeland, *James G. Birney: Slaveholder to Abolitionist* (Ithaca, N.Y., 1955), 130–43; Merton L. Dillon, *Elijah P. Lovejoy, Abolitionist Editor* (Urbana, Ill., 1961), Chaps. VII-XIII.

3. Russell B. Nye, *Fettered Freedom: Civil Liberties and the Slavery Controversy, 1830–1860* (East Lansing, Mich., 1949), 41–85. A conspiracy allegedly involving white men is described in Edwin A. Miles, "The Mississippi Slave Insurrection Scare of 1835," *Journal of Negro History*, XLII (1957), 48–60, and Laurence Shore, "Making Mississippi Safe for Slavery: The Insurrectionary Panic of 1835," in Orville Vernon Burton and Robert C. McMath, Jr. (eds.), *Class, Conflict, and Consensus: Antebellum Southern Community Studies* (Westport, Conn., 1981), 96–127.

ists, and against antislavery publications. A mob at Charleston burned the mail as it arrived by ship from New York. Southern state legislatures demanded from their northern counterparts laws suppressing antislavery societies and throttling the abolitionist press. Citizens' meetings posted rewards for delivery into their hands of the best-known antislavery advocates—"dead or alive." Similar reaction was not unknown in the North. At about the same time that Charlestonians burned abolitionist pamphlets, a mob in Philadelphia destroyed boxes of such literature while the city's mayor looked on.[4]

President Andrew Jackson grew apprehensive as he saw mobs in both North and South take law into their own hands. "The spirit of mob-law is becoming too common and must be checked, or ere long it will become as great an evil as servile war," he told the postmaster general. Yet as a slaveholder and Tennessean, Jackson, too, was repelled by the abolitionists' "attempt to stir up amongst the South the horrors of a servile war." Although the stern disciplinarian knew the remedy, he also knew the federal system prevented its being imposed. "Could they be reached," wrote the president, "they ought to be made to atone for this wicked attempt, with their lives." But if abolitionists could not legally be hanged, they might at least be made ineffective. Thus in his annual message of 1835, Jackson asked the northern states to enact laws suppressing abolitionist activity and called upon Congress to close the mails to "incendiary publications intended to instigate . . . insurrection."[5]

Congress passed no such law, in part because southern members, increasingly conscious of "state rights," refused to concede the national government's authority in such matters. Neither did any northern state legislature grant either Jackson's request or the southern demand to outlaw abolitionist agitation.

Although some northern state governors—especially Edward Everett of Massachusetts and William Marcy of New York—expressed sympathy for the South's plight, no legislature went further than censuring abolitionists for their "incendiary" actions. The legisla-

4. Wyatt-Brown, *Lewis Tappan*, 149–63; Frank Otto Gatell, "Postmaster Huger and the Incendiary Publications," *South Carolina Historical Magazine*, LXIV (1963), 193–201; Gary B. Nash, *Forging Freedom: The Formation of Philadelphia's Black Community, 1720–1840* (Cambridge, Mass., 1988), 277.

5. Andrew Jackson to Amos Kendall, August 9, 1835, in Bassett (ed.), *Correspondence of Andrew Jackson*, V, 360; James D. Richardson (ed.), *A Compilation of the Messages and Papers of the Presidents* (Washington, D.C., 1896), IV, 1394.

tures of only three states—Maine, New York, and Ohio—bothered to reply at all to southern requests for repressive legislation, and none of these responses came near to satisfying slaveholders' demands. From the viewpoint of southerners, this was an ominous refusal, for it led to an inescapable conclusion: The South must stand on its own resources in defense of slavery. John C. Calhoun read the situation gloomily: "Not a step has been taken [by northern states], not a law has been passed, or even proposed; and I venture to assert that none will be."[6]

Disheartening though these failures were, the South for the present was not quite so friendless as Calhoun's statement implied. Every northern state contained its share of influential persons eager to demonstrate to their slaveholding countrymen that abolitionists were as objectionable north of the Ohio River as south of it. Instead of truly representing spontaneous rank-and-file sentiment, the mobs that plagued abolitionist lecturers often resulted from encouragement and support—sometimes instigation—by such prominent citizens. Throughout the 1830s, dozens of violent antiabolitionist episodes across the North testified to the influence of persons bent upon maintaining cordial relations with the South and leaving slavery undisturbed. Some northerners found nearly as unwelcome as did southerners the prospect that antislavery activity would add to already threatening intersectional discord and perhaps even incite race war.[7]

Antislavery partisans themselves, it appeared, were no longer united in attitude toward slave revolt. John Farmer drew a historical analogy from the disagreement. The flinty New Hampshire abolitionist marveled at the stand taken by those who shrank from the thought of slave insurrection: "How near they are approximating to the old tory doctrines of the Revolution." But more typical was William Oakes, an eminent botanist with unimpeachable abolitionist credentials, who expressed relief to find so many of his associates again going on record against violence. "Let it be fully understood," he wrote, "that 3/4 of the abolitionists do not believe even in defensive war, much less in the 'sacred right' of insurrection." Oakes

6. Garrison and Garrison, *William Lloyd Garrison*, II, 73–76; William L. Marcy to John Gayle, [1835], in Miscellaneous Manuscripts, New-York Historical Society; Richard K. Cralle (ed.), *Speeches of John C. Calhoun . . .* (New York, 1853), II, 531.

7. Leonard L. Richards, *"Gentlemen of Property and Standing:" Anti-Abolitionist Mobs in Jacksonian America* (New York, 1970); Lorman Ratner, *Powder Keg: Northern Opposition to the Antislavery Movement, 1831–1840* (New York, 1968).

noted, too, the reassuring fact that "they all rejoice to use any opportunity to speak to slaves & entreat to them to wait in patience ever so long rather than recourse to insurrection." To those who viewed repetition of such points as more ritualistic than convincing, Oakes offered evidence designed to calm: After a half-dozen years of intensified antislavery effort, slave insurrections were no more common than before the campaign began.[8]

Oakes's observation could not be disputed. Despite repeated alarms, Nat Turner as yet had no imitator. Suspicion nonetheless ran deep, and the South's having been spared further overt rebellion did little to remove objections to antislavery agitation, for as planters understood, the undermining of slave discipline in forms short of outright revolt could ruin the plantation South.

Slaveowners never underestimated the threat to their welfare posed by the rising antislavery movement. Few and scorned as were the declared adherents of abolitionism, southerners suspected that the values they represented were not so generally despised as mob action against them might suggest. They could not forget that, despite plentiful evidence of northern antiabolitionist sentiment, no northern state government had acted to halt abolitionist activity. This omission constituted a troublesome paradox that southerners found hard to ignore and northerners could not explain away. On one hand, governmental nonaction could be excused as reflecting nothing more than traditional commitment to freedom of expression; on the other hand, it could be understood as proceeding from profound and as yet unacknowledged changes in the North that eventually would challenge planter influence in national affairs. The latter explanation seemed the more credible, for despite the conspicuous presence throughout the free states of southern sympathizers, the section as a whole appeared to be changing from a region simply adhering to values and institutions somewhat different from those of the South into a rival, perhaps even an overt enemy, with abolitionists helping supply motive power for the transformation. Those individuals in the North who were committed to a free-labor system and who advocated governmental policies designed to foster commercial and industrial growth found in the antislavery movement an auxiliary to their purpose. The abolitionists' morally derived hostility to the plantation South complemented their own am-

8. William Oakes to Samuel E. Sewall, August 20, 1835, in Antislavery Collection, Boston Public Library.

bition and helped elevate their drive to power from expediency to high ethical ground.[9]

The ambition of some opponents of slavery evidently extended into the South itself to embrace more aims than only persuading owners to substitute free labor for the labor of slaves. Abolitionists, some suspected, schemed both to subvert the nonslaveholding whites' allegiance to the planters and to forge an alliance with blacks. The ultimate success of their efforts seemed possible, for the natural affinity of the three groups might someday effect such a union, with dire consequence to plantation society. Blacks then would be transformed from being merely a neutral element around which moral controversy raged into a positive force in an intersectional struggle for power.

The understanding that slaves played a political role in the nation reached far into the past. It was a role recognized and made operative by the three-fifths compromise of the Constitution. To that extent, slaves were made adjuncts of southern power within the nation and became inseparable from it. But slaveholders long had regarded slaves also as potential enemies, recruits for hostile use against the white South. When a generation earlier Jefferson and Monroe conferred about a site for settling blacks found "guilty of insurgency," Jefferson set forth an all-important condition: "We should prefer placing them with whatsoever power is least likely to become an enemy, and to use the knolege [*sic*] of these exiles in predatory expeditions against us."[10]

Misgivings that an enemy might turn to its own advantage the blacks' desire for freedom became still more pressing with the rise of aggressive, organized antislavery activity after 1830. In the geometry of external relationships, the North then assumed the hostile position earlier occupied by Spain, France, and England. Free blacks at that point entered into the racial configuration almost as ominously as did slaves, for whether located in North or South and whether free or slave, black people were counted as being natural allies of northern antislavery forces. Southern free blacks, existing only at the sufferance of whites, rarely made common cause with slaves in any overt way and practically never challenged white

9. Julian P. Bretz, "The Economic Background of the Liberty Party," *American Historical Review*, XXXIV (1929), 250–64; Margaret Shortreed, "The Antislavery Radicals: From Crusade to Revolution, 1840–1868," *Past and Present*, XVI (November, 1959), 65–87.

10. Jefferson to Monroe, June 3, 1802, in Executive Papers, Virginia State Library.

dominance. The relative autonomy enjoyed by their northern counterparts allowed them to act far differently. Uncertainty as to how northern free blacks would respond to their independence troubled their white neighbors. Shortly after the Southampton revolt, a resident of Parkersburg, Virginia, worried that just across the river in Ohio lay a free-black settlement whose residents enjoyed "the same privileges nearly as free men." On that account, he added, "we have a great deal to fear." Even northern whites sometimes doubted the loyalty of free blacks. "There is much uneasiness," reported a Stark County, Ohio, resident in 1830, "in consequence of a colony that is now forming in upper Canada, which no doubt will be a source of trouble some day to these western states."[11]

Worrisome though these people were, especially to white southerners, no plan for removing them could be agreed upon. The chief difficulty in finding an alternative to their immigration to Africa— a project that early proved chimerical—was their supposed affinity with antislavery northerners. In 1836 the Maryland legislature considered a plan to expel them from the state on the familiar ground that they constituted both a nuisance and a danger. But the proposal never came out of committee, not because the lawmakers rated them less objectionable than was alleged, but because the suggested remedy promised still greater danger. Expulsion of free blacks, said the committee, "would be to send them to the free States, to make easier the path for runaway slaves, and to league with fanatic abolitionists." It was better to keep these troublesome people in the South, where they could be watched and controlled, than to send them to the North, where they would swell enemy ranks. "Especially do I object to the colonization of our Negroes upon our northern frontier," said a Georgian in 1858. "They facilitate the escape of our fugitive slaves. In case of civil war, they would become an element of strength to the enemy."[12]

Although southern whites spent much time discussing the free-black problem, their greater concern naturally lay with abolitionist influence on slaves. Suspicion of abolitionist-induced disaffection

11. J. B. Creele to John Floyd, November 26, 1831, *ibid.*; William D. Barrett to R. R. Gurley, March 3, 1830, in American Colonization Society Papers. The specter persisted: In 1846 an abolitionist predicted that 20,000 blacks from Canada would aid Mexico by attacking the United States, and in 1857 an antislavery preacher in Kentucky advised that "40,000 Negroes in Canada are training and plan to come down and slit the throats of the slaveholders." *Liberator*, May 22, 1846; John Fee to Executive Committee, July 15, 1857, in American Missionary Association Archives.

12. Brackett, *Negro in Maryland*, 24; Catterall (ed.), *Judicial Cases*, III, 61.

focused on the upper South, where, white southerners suspected, slaves had been contaminated by antislavery doctrine filtering across the border as well as by their close knowledge of the precedent set by Nat Turner. Outside influences, some observed, made border-state slaves ambitious for freedom and hard to discipline. No longer were they tractable workers. Their unsavory reputation spread well beyond the region. Thus citizens of South Carolina in the 1830s protested importation of slaves from Virginia and Maryland on grounds that those "Villains of the North" would demoralize their own more isolated and therefore uncorrupted slaves.[13]

Abolitionists relished as evidence of progress the attitudes among slaves that their owners viewed with alarm. They, too, took for granted that slaves transported from the upper South to the developing plantations of the Gulf states carried liberating ideas with them, ideas for which abolitionists gladly took credit. Through transfer of slaves from the upper to lower South, predicted the Reverend Amos A. Phelps, the "whole mass will be leavened; and the spirit of insurrection—the creature of oppression . . . will not then be dead. . . . On the contrary, it will be instinct with life."[14] Phelps, a founder of the American Anti-Slavery Society, did not recoil from the prospect of rebellion, even though it was totally at variance with the professed pacifism of the society he had helped establish.

In contrast, the abolitionist Beriah Green, president of the convention that organized the American Anti-Slavery Society, continued to hold the more conventional belief that antislavery activity protected southern whites against vengeful blacks. Only the fact that slaves were pacified by northern reformers' efforts in their behalf, Green claimed, prevented rebellion. In Kentucky, where antislavery ideas circulated rather freely in the early 1830s, Robert S. Finley, an agent of the American Colonization Society, likewise credited his own activity with giving slaves hope of eventual freedom and thereby tempering their hostility. A North Carolina planter in 1835 believed he detected among slaves in his neighborhood some of the influences antislavery reformers spoke of: "It seems that the abolition question so much talked of latterly has gotten to their [ears] and they have taken up the idea that the northerners will free

13. Catterall (ed.), *Judicial Cases*, III, 61; Grand Jury Presentment from Beaufort, April 17, 1832, in Grand Jury Presentments, South Carolina Department of Archives and History.
14. Phelps, *Lectures on Slavery*, 211.

them which has [led] some of them to exult in anticipation of freedom."[15]

Although the extent of slaves' accurate knowledge of antislavery activity remains unmeasured, their frequent escapes from border areas testify to their understanding that in one part of the country blacks were free, and there refuge could be found. No other response to the deepening sectional conflict should have been expected. Precedent could be found in the past, when members of their grandparents' generation had acted in much the same way upon learning that foreign powers across the border offered sanctuary from colonial masters.

The understanding led to unsettling consequences after 1830 as the tempo of attempted escapes increased. By 1834, as a device for intercepting runaways, authorities regularly assigned guards to packet boats sailing between Baltimore and Philadelphia. Although most escapes to the North appear to have been acts of individual desperation, sometimes they approached the magnitude of mass movement, as in 1829 in Virginia, when slaves "in gangs" left Accomac County, and again in September, 1832, when a band of some eighteen slave men in Northampton County sailed in a stolen boat from Chesapeake Bay to a wharf in New York City. Shortly afterward, thirty more Northampton slaves unsuccessfully tried to duplicate the feat. These events, wrote Abel P. Upshur, "proving the utter insecurity of this property among us, have rendered it of very little value. . . . The impoverishment and ruin of the people will be the necessary consequence."[16]

Even as far south as the lower coast of North Carolina, slaves dreamed of similar exploits. In Onslow County in 1831, the slave

15. American Anti-Slavery Society, *First Annual Report*, 12; Robert S. Finley to R. R. Gurley, April 12, 1831, in American Colonization Society Papers; John Blount to Charles W. Jacocks, October 3, 1835, in Charles W. Jacocks Papers, North Carolina Division of Archives and History, Raleigh. Slave testimony about the extent of knowledge of abolition activity is hard to come by, but see remarks by Frederick Douglass in *Liberator*, May 19, 1843, and by Booker T. Washington in Louis R. Harlan (ed.), *The Booker T. Washington Papers* (Urbana, Ill., 1972–84), I, 218. See also Stanley Feldstein, *Once a Slave: The Slaves' View of Slavery* (New York, 1971), 185–87, 273–75.

16. Catterall (ed.), *Judicial Cases*, IV, 81; Colonel Joynes to William Giles, August 13, 1829, in Executive Papers, Virginia State Library; Upshur to the Governor, October 4, 1832, in Palmer, McRae, and Flournoy (eds.), *Calendar of Virginia State Papers*, X, 278; American Anti-Slavery Society, *First Annual Report*, 54. For other, similar incidents, see John W. Blassingame, *The Slave Community: Plantation Life in the Antebellum South* (Rev. ed., New York, 1979), 206–208.

Peter revealed that "there is about thirty head about here that is for going to the free states, that they were going in the vessel belonging to Col. Dudley."[17] From such bold undertakings, southerners learned that antislavery activity threatened economic disaster even if it did not lead to violence. Mass escapes demonstrated that through its recently expanded antislavery reputation, the North exerted a seriously disruptive influence on the South's society and economy. Slave response to the lure of the North could be taken as evidence that an abolitionist-slave political alliance might be in the making. Further, it revealed to slaveowners unpleasant truths that eventually would prove to be their nemesis: Total control of their labor force was impossible, and preventing slave contact with forces hostile to the planters was impossible.

In the lower South and in interior regions, the slaves' knowledge of the antislavery North probably was less detailed than in states along the border, but even in isolated areas it may not have been wholly lacking. Slaves bought from the upper South—and such trade was constant—were likely to bring with them contaminating information that they could pass to others, a result owners understood but found no way to avoid.

Border-state slaves were not the only source of subversive information available to slaves of the lower South. Occasional travelers and the ubiquitous Yankee peddler offered them as well as their owners glimpses of a different world. Rafts and steamboats on the Mississippi arrived from the free states, with sometimes seductive effect on slaves along the river. Situations unique to a particular locality might be responsible for disruption, as in southern Georgia, where lumbermen from Maine spent winters working in the region's great live oak forests. There they labored alongside slaves to prepare timbers for New England shipyards and, according to a suspicious neighbor, tried to incite them to rebel.[18] Neither these northern woodsmen nor many members of the small army of travelers who regularly made their way through the South were likely to be avowed abolitionists. Slaves nonetheless could learn from them that work-

17. Criminal Action Concerning the 1831 Insurrection of Slaves, in Onslow County Miscellaneous Records.
18. Willie Lee Rose (ed.), *A Documentary History of Slavery in North America* (New York, 1976), 416. On the whites' suspicion of peddlers and the slaves' response to them, see *Annals of Congress*, 16th Cong., 1st Sess., 1024. An account of a slave who ran away with a peddler is in George P. Rawick (ed.), *The American Slave: A Composite Autobiography* (Westport, Conn., 1972), XIX, 121.

ers elsewhere—including blacks—led lives very unlike their own, and some would find the difference inviting.

Such enlightening contacts, necessarily infrequent and limited to relatively few persons, did not go far toward counteracting the isolating effect that movement into the undeveloped Southwest had on slaves as well as on their owners. But isolation, which might have helped stabilize slavery, was made less stultifying by advances in technology, especially in the 1840s and afterward, and by the growing popular enthusiasm for politics. With multiplication of newspapers and ever-improved means of travel, white southerners—and slaves too—enjoyed expanded opportunity to learn about faraway events and to be influenced by them. The inland South then lost some of its isolation, with unsettling consequences. Absorption in the heated electoral campaigns of the 1830s and 1840s brought backcountry whites into periodic contact with national affairs. Politics opened curtains for slaves as well. Not even black people were altogether deprived of the diversion and enlightenment offered by political activity. Slaves, along with their masters, heard political discussions, watched parades and rallies, listened to rumors. As early as 1830, a complaint about this reached the governor of North Carolina. Slaves, said the writer, were permitted to assemble "at musters, elections and other places where they acquire insolence and audacity." In North Carolina in 1836, a slave remembered, "there came a report from a neighboring plantation that, if Van Buren was elected, he was going to give all the slaves their freedom. It spread rapidly among all the slaves in the neighborhood, and great, very great was the rejoicing." The "negroes in Georgia are already saying to each other that great men are trying to set them free and will succeed, and many other expressions of similar import," the Georgia politician Howell Cobb was told in 1844. In South Carolina on the eve of the Civil War, when special precautions respecting slaves commonly were thought essential, ten percent of the audience at political rallies, James H. Hammond estimated, were black.[19]

The topics commonly discussed in electoral campaigns—tariffs, banks, land policy—must have been incomprehensible and of ab-

19. Calvin Jones to Montfort Stokes, December 28, 1830, in Governors' Papers, North Carolina Division of Archives and History; Blassingame (ed.), *Slave Testimony*, 136; John W. H. Underwood to Howell Cobb, February 2, 1844, in Ulrich B. Phillips (ed.), *Correspondence of Robert Toombs, Alexander H. Stephens, and Howell Cobb*, Vol. II of American Historical Association, *Annual Report . . . for the Year 1911* (Washington, D.C., 1913), 55; Steven A. Channing, *Crisis of Fear*, 39.

solutely no interest to most blacks. But occasionally it was otherwise. Slavery itself became an issue in some elections. Thus in 1840,
when Democrats accused the Whig presidential candidate of abolitionist leanings, slaves in Georgia, Emily P. Burke remembered,
"were all bold enough to assert publically that 'when William
Henry Harrison became President of the United States, they should
have their freedom.'" Doubtless, not "all" Georgia slaves said any
such thing, but the fact that a similar independent report came from
Alabama at about the same time suggests at least some substance
for both accounts.[20]

Political use of the slavery issue continued through the 1850s,
with predictable effect on slaves. In 1856 when John C. Fremont ran
as candidate of the new, antislavery Republican party, and again in
1860 when opponents branded Abraham Lincoln the abolitionist
choice of an abolitionist party, southern white voters' frankly expressed concern could not be confined to themselves. At such times,
slaves learned from local politicians that their status was a point of
contention, that somewhere white men and women advocated freedom for blacks. In his fourth annual message, delivered December
2, 1856, President Franklin Pierce referred to abolition as "a foreign
object" that could be accomplished only "through burning cities,
and ravaged fields, and slaughtered populations, and all there is
most terrible in foreign complicated with civil and servile war."[21]
Pierce's sentiments achieved printed form, circulated through the
South, and, like other written material, may have been compre-
hended by slaves.

Much rarer opportunities for abolitionist indoctrination appeared, one from so distinguished a source as William Tecumseh
Sherman, the later scourge of the South. Despite his well-earned
Civil War reputation, Sherman was never an abolitionist sympa-
thizer, and his supplying slaves with antislavery literature in 1844
while stationed at Fort Moultrie signifies neither subversive nor insurrectionary intent. Rather it suggests his contempt for abolitionists and his confidence in the docility of slaves. It also supplies the
incidental information that apparently some of the slaves he associated with could read. Sherman found ridiculous an abolitionist
pamphlet written "by that crazy fool Bob Levering," but the slaves

20. Rose (ed.), *Documentary History*, 412; *Liberator*, January 22, 1841.
21. Richardson (ed.), *Messages and Papers*, VII, 2931–32.

to whom he gave Levering's essay "for their amusement," as he said, may well have regarded it differently and perhaps put it to unintended use.[22]

So far as is known, publications of the sort Sherman treated with such abandon seldom reached slaves in the Deep South, but much as in the 1820s, antislavery literature continued to circulate among free blacks in Baltimore and Washington and to a lesser extent in towns in Virginia.[23] The news and ideas such material conveyed to free-black readers could not easily be concealed from slaves there and, eventually, from slaves in more remote southern regions as well.

It is, of course, unnecessary to demonstrate external influence in order to account for the high value blacks placed on freedom. The slaves on President James K. Polk's Mississippi plantations, for example, who made life miserable for the overseers by persistently demanding better treatment and running away, may not even have known there was a North, to say nothing of being informed about the antislavery movement. When they fled beyond the immediate neighborhood, their goal apparently was not to reach a free state but to go to Tennessee. So far as the records show, Polk's slaves did not even enjoy access to religious teachings, which, for many, powerfully reinforced aspirations for freedom. Yet for all their apparent ignorance, his slaves—like countless others—repeatedly proved, to the pain of overseers, that they wanted to be free.[24]

In the case of the slaves on Polk's plantation, "evil" poor-white neighbors were blamed for encouraging and aiding resistance. The charge well may have been true, for although slavery and the racial attitudes that supported it now received massive endorsement at all social levels, some southern whites still remained outside the consensus, and much as in colonial days, behaved toward slaves in a manner subversive of the institution. Especially in those rural areas where small farmers and still-poorer whites were numerous, and in cities, where social barriers of every sort were frail, slaves came into

22. Sherman to Ellen B. Ewing, February 8, 1844, in William Tecumseh Sherman Papers, Ohio Historical Society, Columbus. The pamphlet was Robert E. H. Levering, *The Kingdom of Slavery . . .* (Circleville, Ohio, 1844).

23. Ethan Allen Andrews, *Slavery and the Domestic Slave Trade in the United States* (Boston, 1836), 36–37, 57.

24. John Spencer Bassett (ed.), *The Southern Plantation Overseer as Revealed in His Letters* (Northampton, Mass., 1925), 54, 63, 146–47, 263.

contact with lower-class whites in ways that violated some notions of racial etiquette.[25] The loyalty of urban dwellers to slavery, some assumed, could not be depended on. H. W. Connor in 1849 believed that though most of Georgia still solidly supported slavery, Savannah and Augusta could not be counted on: "The cities all of them are becoming more and more unsound and uncertain and all for the same reason"—their northern and foreign-born population. But there were native apostates as well. Nearly anywhere, though especially in cities, one could find persons willing to engage in unauthorized trade with slaves, exchanging whiskey, finery, even necessities for farm products, possibly stolen from masters or white neighbors. By thus establishing an independent economic connection with slaves, these merchants challenged the exclusiveness of the slave-master relationship. Further, by such commerce they identified their interests with those of the slave rather than with the slave's master, thereby creating the possibility of an additional political threat to the institution. In 1831 in Virginia, N. E. Sutton complained of the scene at "every village" of blacks and whites "vending and trad[ing] in various ways. . . . The exhibition of white and black mingling together beggars description. . . . What I ask is to be expected but disorder and consequences of the most dangerous and alarming results[?]"[26]

If even in those propriety-assailing situations certain barriers between the races seldom were breached, such interracial familiarity nevertheless nurtured attitudes incompatible with the submission that plantation discipline required. Partly on account of that influence, urban slaves, it was thought, significantly differed from slaves in rural areas. In towns, blacks developed a sense of independence, copied the manners and attitudes of their white associates, and became resentful of close supervision. Not surprisingly, planters commonly tried to prevent their field slaves from associating with town slaves, who enjoyed varied sources of information and range of social contact. Blacks displaying unslavelike traits and urban whites

25. For examples, see Bassett (ed.), *Southern Plantation Overseer*, 66; State v. Jacob Boyce, Superior Court, Spring Term, 1846, in Perquimans County Slave Papers, 1759–1864, Case of Amos Ellis, in Criminal Actions Concerning Slaves, 1817–19, in Wayne County Records, North Carolina Division of Archives and History, Raleigh; Catterall (ed.), *Judicial Cases*, II, 329, 355; Phillips (ed.), *Plantation and Frontier*, II, 84.

26. H. W. Connor to John C. Calhoun, June 12, 1849, in J. Franklin Jameson (ed.), *Correspondence of John C. Calhoun*, Vol. II, Pt. 2 of American Historical Association, *Annual Report . . . for the Year 1899* (Washington, D.C., 1900), 1188–89; N. E. Sutton to John Floyd, September 21, 1831, in Executive Papers, Virginia State Library.

careless of racial barriers should be given no chance to sow in rural slaves the seeds of discontent that unfitted them for steady labor. Nonetheless, despite taboo and precaution, slaves and white people continued to mingle in social situations, drinking and playing cards together, on terms that approached equality. An occasional white person still flouted every expectation by helping slaves escape, as the fugitive John Brown discovered when he found a poor man willing to provide him with a forged pass in exchange for an old hen. And sexual barriers still were broken, sometimes in forms threatening to the social order. "Do not many of our pretty white girls even now, permit illicit negro embraces at the South?" was the unsettling question addressed to the rice magnate Robert F. W. Allston in 1858.[27] Transgressions such as these, originating within the South, had no discernible ties to northern antislavery, yet their effects on the social order were similar, and the eventual coalescence of the two was not unlikely.

The slaveholders' distrust of white dissidents in their midst had a long history, as we have seen. Early in the century, slaves in Virginia apparently took for granted the sympathy and good will of neighboring lower-class white people, even for violent schemes. Thus Gabriel, plotting his rebellion in 1800, intended to spare Quakers, Methodists, Frenchmen, and poor women who owned no slaves. Two years later, Virginia slaves, questioned about newly revealed plots, testified that "the poorer kind of white people in and about Richmond" offered to aid their projected insurrection.[28] Whether the slaves' expectation was well-founded or not, such testimony probably would not have been offered had not both slaves and slaveholders judged it entirely credible. When in 1815 a white Virginian named George Boxley developed an elaborate plan to free the slaves by means of insurrection, these suspicions gained substance. But by at least the 1820s, relations between the races clearly were deteriorating, while white solidarity strengthened. Although the economic opportunity that slavery and cotton offered the ambitious white southerner doubtless contributed to the change, solidarity also was furthered by the steady flow of small farmers and antislav-

27. James Harold Easterby (ed.), *The South Carolina Rice Plantation, as Revealed in the Papers of Robert F. M. Allston* (Chicago, 1945), 146; [Brown], *Slave Life in Georgia*, 72.

28. Peter Randolph's Interview with Slaves Accused of Insurrection, May 5, 1802, in Executive Papers, Virginia State Library. See also Enoch Sawyer to "Dear Sir," May 10, 1802, in Perquimans County Slave Papers.

ery dissidents out of the South, thereby removing rather than converting a source of opposition. Thus, by the time of Turner's revolt, slaves contemplating violent plans no longer realistically could hope to receive significant aid from white southerners, though there were rare exceptions, as in North Carolina, where in 1831 a slave preacher accused of organizing a conspiracy was "proved" to have gone to "Mr. Gibbs and asked him if he would join them for they were about to rise," and in Mississippi, where in 1835 white men— not all of them "respectable"—were implicated in an alleged slave conspiracy.[29]

Evidence of stress within southern white society reappeared in the 1850s, however, generating new doubts about the permanency of racial solidarity. Only this unease makes comprehensible the untempered hostility southern whites directed against Hinton Rowan Helper's *Impending Crisis* (1857), with its antislavery arguments addressed to southern nonslaveholders. "All attempts . . . to widen the breach between classes of citizens are just as dangerous as efforts to excite slaves to insurrection," observed Calvin Willey in the 1860 report on public education in North Carolina.[30] Occasionally white disloyalty surfaced as apparent fact rather than mere suspicion or potential. Thus, on the eve of the Civil War, a woman wrote from South Carolina that in the Abbeville District "five negroes are to be hung, twenty white men implicated all southern born, the poor white *trash* who have associated with negroes and are jealous of the higher classes and think insurection [*sic*] will place all on a footing, and they get some plunder in the bargain."[31]

Although white leaders sometimes doubted the constancy of nonslaveholders and fretted over signs of class division, such discontent as poorer whites felt in antebellum years by no means necessarily manifested itself in sympathy for blacks. One can hardly claim, for

29. *Annals of Congress*, 16th Cong., 1st Sess., 292, 1354; William T. Allan in *Liberator*, August 25, 1843; John Rankin, *Letters on American Slavery*, 72; Avery O. Craven, *Coming of the Civil War*, 95; Barnhart, "Sources of Southern Migration," 49–62; Isaiah H. Spencer to the Governor, September 20, 1831, in Governors' Papers, North Carolina Division of Archives and History.

30. Johnson, *Ante-Bellum North Carolina*, 79.

31. Quoted in Steven A. Channing, *Crisis of Fear*, 272–73. For other comments on the nonslaveholders' disaffection, see John H. McHenry to R. M. T. Hunter, February 21, 1850, in Charles Henry Ambler (ed.), *Correspondence of Robert M. T. Hunter, 1826–1876*, Vol. II of American Historical Association, *Annual Report . . . for the Year 1916*, (Washington, D.C., 1918), 105–106; Conway P. Wing to Milton Badger, August 3, 1848, John McMillan to Milton Badger, March 25, 1853, and Joseph McKee to Milton Badger, July 28, 1845, all in American Home Missionary Society Papers.

example, that the small farmers in Virginia who in the late 1820s and early 1830s agitated for constitutional change at the slaveholders' expense were motivated by racial philanthropy, or that the movement in North Carolina in the 1850s to change the basis of taxation, again at slaveholders' expense, intended benefits to slaves. Nonslaveholders in plantation areas commonly were integrated into the planter-dominated society and economy and seldom manifested disapproval of slavery. Economic and social grievances might lead yeoman farmers outside such areas to resent, even oppose, planters and the institution that sustained them, but even so, they were not often disposed to take up the slaves' cause.[32] Nevertheless, the effect of class division, even if not so calculated, was to destabilize slavery.

Relations between whites of low degree and blacks became less friendly in the immediate antebellum decades than they once had been, thus diminishing the likelihood that slaves could find dependable nearby allies in their freedom struggles. Two different forces contributed to the estrangement. Mounting fears of abolitionism and sedition, carefully fostered by the molders of southern opinion, made intimate relationships of the kind that sometimes prevailed in the seventeenth and eighteenth centuries suspect and dangerous. Whites who in an earlier day might have followed their inclinations toward friendship with blacks now were likely to be deterred by the embarrassment and risk that accompanied charges of "abolitionism." At the same time, an antagonism born of distrust and fear of blacks became increasingly evident among nonslaveholders.

The prolonged series of alarms, marked especially by Gabriel's and Vesey's conspiracies and culminating in Turner's revolt, took its toll on interracial sympathies. Among the consequences of these events was confirmation of the distrust whites long ago had begun to feel toward blacks. Some nonslaveholders, now regarding them as enemies beyond reconciliation, vowed to wage a war of annihilation should another Turner-like episode occur. In such event, blacks must be shown no mercy; all should be held responsible for the deeds of a few. "They must be convinced that they must and will be soon destroyed if their conduct makes it the least necessary," wrote a North Carolinian. Yet not even such ruthlessness quite guaranteed slaveholders blind support for their interests. That lower-

32. Eugene D. Genovese, "Yeoman Farmers in a Slaveholding Democracy," *Agricultural History*, XLIX (1975), 331–42.

class antipathy toward blacks carried with it resentment toward slaveholders is suggested by the North Carolinian who vowed in 1832 that "we will not be harassed to protect ourselves from injury by other peoples negroes but if one blow is struck we will murder them indiscriminately."[33]

And of course that is exactly what they did. Whenever blacks manifested a disposition toward violence, a spirit of untempered vengeance was raised against them. The ferocious reprisals that followed Turner's rebellion were not unprecedented. In 1811, at the time of the great insurrection in Louisiana, a visitor to New Orleans reported that "about 150 negroes have been killed in various ways— Only two white men killed and three good dwelling houses burnt." In the aftermath of Gabriel's conspiracy, Governor James Monroe received draconian advice: "Where there is any reason to believe that any person is concerned, they ought immediately to be hanged, quartered and hung up on trees on every road as a terror to the rest.... It will not do to be too scrupulous now," Joseph Jones had gone on to warn, "but to slay them all where there is any reason to believe they are concerned."[34]

In Monroe's day, officials could check application of such sentiments, but in an era characterized by democracy, they would have difficulty doing so, even if so inclined. Ruthless though Monroe's correspondent was in 1800, he nonetheless confined his advocacy of slaughter to persons suspected of conspiracy. In the 1830s, a mood of far greater severity captured the population. White southerners then warned slaves and abolitionists of the merciless retribution that awaited all blacks in the event of revolt by a few. Even extermination was considered.[35] Warm relationships between slaves and nonslaveholders could not be expected to flourish in that kind of atmosphere.

If white southerners had come to distrust blacks, blacks with as much cause feared whites, slaveholders and nonslaveholders alike.

33. Solon Borland to Roscius C. Borland, August 31, 1831, in Governors' Papers, North Carolina Division of Archives and History; Johnson, *Ante-Bellum North Carolina*, 519. See also Eric Foner, *Nat Turner* (Englewood Cliffs, N.J., 1971), 24, 67, 69–70.

34. Isaac L. Baker to Stephen F. Austin, February 25, 1811, in Barker (ed.), *Austin Papers*, Vol. II, Pt. 1, p. 184; Joseph Jones to Monroe, September 9, 1800, in Executive Papers, Virginia State Library.

35. Joseph Speed to Gerrit Smith, December 17, 1835, in Gerrit Smith Papers, Syracuse University Library, Syracuse, N.Y.; Tragle, *Southampton Slave Revolt*, 69; William M. Atkinson to R. R. Gurley, September 10, 1831, in American Colonization Society Papers.

Slaves could never long put aside knowledge of the wrath that awaited them on account of the missteps of their fellows as well as of themselves. Joseph Riddick of North Carolina no doubt was correct in concluding, upon disclosure of a slave plot in 1802, that slaves seemed more alarmed at the news than did the whites, for in times of rumored conspiracy, slaves were rounded up with little discrimination and condemned on the flimsiest of grounds, and fear gave license to unprovoked violence.[36]

The hysteria and violence surrounding conspiracy alarms generally came only at long intervals. In ordinary times, the principal source of friction with white persons other than the slaves' owners lay in the imposition of the patrols, the community police force that usually was manned by the neighborhood's small farmers. Folklore as well as slave narratives fully illustrate the slaves' irritation with these men who had authority to intrude into their homes and interfere with their leisure-time activities. Slaves would have resented them in any event, but their resentment was greater because patrollers sometimes could not resist the opportunity to tyrannize over blacks and with little or no excuse to inflict cruelties both large and small. By doing so, however, they risked reprisals. In 1802 at Powhatan, Virginia, defiant slaves declared the patrols "had already been permitted to go on too long but that it should not be long before a Stop should be put to them," and in 1798 in Bertie County, North Carolina, a band of slaves "did attack, pursue, knock down and lay prostrate the patrollers of said county."[37]

But such bold defiance was highly unusual, for most slaves must have known they had little chance to get the better of this official arm of the state. The most they could expect to do was to trick, humiliate, and sometimes inflict pain. Still, these incidents did not represent moves in a parlor game of wits. The frequent, petty, interracial clashes that occurred in the course of the patrols' carrying out their assignments may be regarded as incidents in the smoldering warfare waged between blacks and nonslaveholders, racial warfare that characterized the antebellum South. "Many negro slaves are allow'd by their owners to Raise and keep dogs . . . that do great injury to our stocks and if we kill these dogs they will kill our dog,

36. Riddick to Benjamin Williams, June 18, 1802, in Governors' Papers, North Carolina Division of Archives and History.
37. Horatio Turpin to James Monroe, January 22, 1802, in Executive Papers, Virginia State Library; Called Court, May 31, 1798, in Bertie County Slave Papers, 1800–1805.

our horse, or our Cow," complained a group of nonslaveholding farmers in 1830.[38] The slaves' interference with the patrol struck a blow, however slight, against slavery itself, for the patrollers were the slaveholders' surrogates, carrying out measures thought essential to maintain the social and economic order. The functions assigned the patrol and the pay they received helped bind them to the slaveholder and assure their continued support.

Slaves were not resourceless in the conflict, as the aggrieved small farmers learned. Yet since law and society intended the blacks' subservience, whites were in a position to inflict severe retaliatory injury with only moderate risk to themselves. How common such offenses were is difficult to say, but evidence from South Carolina extending over four decades suggests their prevalence. From Charleston in 1792 came a complaint of indiscriminate mob violence directed against blacks in the wake of insurrectionary alarm: "Whilst we wish to punish the disorderly we cannot but reprobate the inhuman practice of murdering the peaceable and inoffensive." Existing laws are "entirely inadequate to prevent the prevailing crime of murdering negroes, whereby our land is becoming stained with blood, and the pages of our records crowded with instances of unexpiated murder," reported a Kershaw grand jury in 1808.[39]

Ten years later, residents of the same district again complained of the "inadequacy of the punishment attached to the crime, in preventing persons of malignant dispositions from murdering slaves." At the same time, a grand jury in Fairfield called attention to "the great and growing evil" of "many instances of murder and cruel treatment of Slaves in this District and other parts of the State." And again, in 1819 petitioners from Kershaw warned of a "fast increasing" evil—"slaves wantonly abused and crippled by loose and licentious men."[40]

Perhaps as a response to these and similar complaints, the state legislature in 1821 imposed punishment for murder of slaves, but a grand jury in Richland nine years later found that the offense still was considered "nearly nominal, no instance having yet occurred in

---

38. Quoted in Johnson, *Ante-bellum North Carolina*, 556.

39. Grand Jury Presentments from Charleston District, September 21, 1792, and from Kershaw District, November 14, 1808, both in Grand Jury Presentments, South Carolina Department of Archives and History.

40. Grand Jury Presentments from Kershaw District, April 14, 1818, and November 19, 1819, *ibid*; Grand Jury Presentment from Fairfield District, November, 1818, *ibid*.

which the penalty has been enforced, although many and increasing instances have occurred characterized with the deepest guilt." In light of the data from South Carolina, Frederick Law Olmsted's report of 1860 becomes more believable. Olmsted wrote of meeting a slaveholder in Mississippi who boasted as evidence of his unusual virtue that he had never shot one of his slaves.[41]

It is not clear whether the offenses against blacks of the sort that appear to have been so flagrant in parts of South Carolina were at the hands of their owners or of other persons. But the retributions that commonly followed slave violence almost certainly can be charged for the most part to nonslaveholders in whom festered a malignant dread of blacks and, perhaps, envy and resentment toward their masters.

If the lowest class of white persons disliked both master and slave, the feeling was mutual. Narratives of fugitive slaves, often written under abolitionist tutelage, and recollections of elderly former slaves frequently allude to the contempt blacks felt for "poor whites." These degraded persons, it appears, fell under the scorn of slaves and southern gentry alike. In expressing derogatory opinion of an entire social class whose culture and deprivations in some respects resembled their own, slaves only mirrored attitudes of their masters—and these were attitudes calculated to strengthen slavery by discouraging the creation of interracial bonds.[42]

Planters had good reason to look down upon poor whites and to encourage blacks to do the same. They were scorned by planters less for shiftlessness and lack of social grace than because their lowly status suggested they might someday become allies of slaves, as they narrowly had missed doing in colonial days. Indeed, in spite of social pressure, a few of them still manifested such meager racial pride as to associate on terms of near equality with free blacks and slaves to whom they sometimes offered aid and comfort. The aid was reciprocated. A number of elderly blacks in the 1930s remembered slavery days when poverty-stricken white persons had appealed to their parents for food and other kinds of assistance.[43] Planters felt compelled to check these inclinations, for they signified

41. Grand Jury Presentment from Richland District, October, 1830, *ibid.*; Frederick Law Olmsted, *A Journey in the Back Country* (New York, 1860), 62–63.

42. See Eugene D. Genovese, "'Rather Be a Nigger than a Poor White Man': Slave Perceptions of Southern Yeomen and Poor Whites," in Hans L. Trefousse (ed.), *Toward a New View of America: Essays in Honor of Arthur C. Cole* (New York, 1977), 79–96.

43. Rawick (ed.), *American Slave*, II, 87; George P. Rawick *et al.* (eds.), *American Slave: Supplement, Series I*, Vol. II, pp. 135–36, and Vol. V, p. 320.

a break, however slight, in white solidarity and to that extent undermined slavery. The fostering of prejudice in both poor whites
and slaves helped reduce the possibility of the two groups ever
coalescing.

Slaves only feebly resisted their owners' effort to drive a wedge
between them and the group whose sympathy could have provided
strength to both. Most slaves fell into the trap their owners designed; they commonly joined the masters in holding poor whites in
contempt. Probably most never questioned why they did so, but a
few pondered the matter and found an explanation. Many years after emancipation, Tom Woods still remembered the "white folks
[who] wasn't much better off dan we was. Dey had to work hard and
dey had to worry 'bout food, clothes and shelter, and we didn't. Lots
of slave owners wouldn't allow dem on deir farms among deir slaves
without orders from de overseer. I don't know why unless he was
afraid dey would stir up discontent."[44]

While slaveowners were defining poor whites as members of a
subordinate caste scarcely on a level even with slaves, they also
tried to persuade blacks that they themselves were inferior beings
suited for no other role than that of slave.[45] The effort was utili-
tarian. Obviously slavery would be made more stable if blacks could
be convinced of their limitations and come to view their servile
status as being appropriate to persons of their small capacity. When
slaves adopted as their own the masters' view of the poor whites,
they thereby also conceded the masters' view of their own inferiority. Anyone willing to associate with blacks on terms of familiarity
and equality is thereby rendered contemptible—so ran the thought
process. "Anyone as poor as I am and as lacking in all that the world
honors is not worth my regard," the slaves were supposed to feel.
Their contempt for poor whites was a manifestation of self-con-
tempt nurtured by planters for their own purposes.

But just as slaves never altogether relinquished ties with poor
whites, neither did they fully accept as valid the allegation of their
own hopeless inferiority. Their religion, with its gospel of worth and
redemption, and the positive roles and relationships that the slave
community afforded, tended to promote a feeling of self-worth suf-

44. Rawick (ed.), *American Slave*, VII, 354.
45. Rawick *et al.* (eds.), *American Slave: Supplement, Series I*, Vol. II, pp. 167, 169;
Blassingame, *Slave Community*, 177, 202–203. On the ideas masters sought to incul-
cate in slaves, see Thomas L. Webber, *Deep Like the Rivers: Education in the Slave
Quarter Community, 1831–1865* (New York, 1978), 27–58.

ficient to counteract efforts to denigrate them. In any event, slaves saw that despite the pretensions to superiority by masters and overseers, the whites were, after all, human beings much like themselves, whose judgment in practical matters did not always exceed their own and whose individual strength was no greater.[46] Their masters, too, made mistakes, suffered misfortune, became ill, and died. The mystique in which whites tried to cloak themselves, if not transparent, was easily rent. Thus the authority and position of whites depended chiefly upon force, and this was an element that slaves, too, could muster. Resistance to impositions made by one's equal—or inferior—was tempting; although risky, it also was easy and sometimes successful. From Bradley and Drew counties in Arkansas came word in 1858 that "the slaves are refusing to be flogged, and much trouble is apprehended." Similar accounts of slaves who refused to be disciplined and got away with it are plentiful.[47]

Recalcitrance of this sort apparently increased in the 1850s and thus coincided with menacing northern political developments. Less extreme instances of slave resistance and jousting for position probably occurred on practically every plantation. Planters lived in fear that such commonly witnessed evidences of initiative would grow, be coordinated, and spread beyond control. In reality, however, the means by which slaves could organize resistance were severely limited. Plantations were scattered, slaves were closely watched, and, perhaps most important of all, the majority of white southerners of every social degree—despite troublesome defections—combined to support the planters' authority. So severe were the sanctions against extending aid and sympathy to slaves that few white southerners chose to champion their cause. Nevertheless, the possibility remained alive. And here and there, especially in the upper South, antislavery voices continued to be heard.

For a long time, abolitionists shied away from even the prospect of attempting to intervene in the southern racial conflict. Indeed, as we have seen, they advised slaves to moderate their resistance and wait for moral suasion to work its emancipating effect. Throughout the 1830s they refrained from any attempt to reach into the South, to make contact with slaves, or to encourage their resistance. They

46. [Brown], *Slave Life in Georgia*, 204–205; Webber, *Deep Like the Rivers*, 91–101. For an example of slaves ignoring work instructions they judged faulty, see Jack P. Greene (ed.), *Diary of Colonel Landon Carter*, I, 568.

47. Blassingame, *Slave Community*, 317–20; Corydon Fuller Journal, June 4, 1858, in William L. Clements Library, University of Michigan, Ann Arbor.

remained uncommitted in the ongoing struggle that took place on most plantations and in most southern communities. Whatever discontent abolitionist activities aroused in blacks was unintended and was seldom exploited. "The weapons of our warfare are not carnal," insisted the abolitionist Simeon S. Jocelyn in 1834. "Palsied be the arm that would unsheathe the sword of violence."[48]

Surprisingly, in view of the vigor and frequency of statements in that vein, abolitionist attitudes toward slaves rapidly underwent transformation beginning in the late 1830s, until by the 1850s a number of prominent abolitionists had renounced pacifism as a tactic and unabashedly begun to urge slaves to act in concert with them to promote emancipation.

The easy abandonment of pacifism and nonengagement by a dynamic abolitionist element is readily accounted for. Slaves amply proved to northerners their desire to be free, both by running away and by resisting their owners' impositions. Although the Southampton revolt of 1831 was never repeated, evidence of slave restiveness accumulated on a scale sufficiently large to demonstrate its destructive potential to the slave system. At the same time, growing numbers of abolitionists judged their program of moral suasion a failure. They had not broken the South's will to maintain and extend slavery. Neither had they converted a northern majority to their program. But their own determination to end slavery remained undiminished, even grew. The conjunction of these phenomena soon led abolitionists to reconsider their policy of disengagement from slaves and, with scarcely a pang, to abandon it. If the white population would not end slavery peacefully, then blacks, always eager for freedom, might be encouraged to end it themselves by force.

48. American Anti-Slavery Society, *First Annual Report*, 21.

10

●●●●●●●●●●●●●●●●●●●●●●●●●●●●●●●●●●●●

Toward an Abolitionist-
Slave Alliance

After the Southampton revolt in 1831, no large-scale slave uprising devastated any part of the American South. But that good fortune brought less relief than one might expect, for on individual plantations unrest and slave escapes appeared on a scale large enough to warn of their destructive potential and possible acceleration. Revolt might be brewing anywhere. Planters liked to profess complete confidence in the loyalty and docility of the slave population. They boasted of sleeping with doors unlocked and of old ladies left alone in remote plantation houses.[1] Yet the insurrectionary panics that periodically swept parts of the South belied the vaunted self-assurance.

There was good reason not to be truly confident, for even if most of the rumored conspiracies turned out to have no basis, a haunting reality still could not be shrugged off: Acts of violence continued to be directed at owners and overseers, and slaves persisted in exploiting every opportunity to gain advantage within the slave system. They ran away as they always had done, some for a limited time to nearby woods and swamps, some to southern cities, some to northern free states or to Mexico or Canada. Such experiences confronted planters with almost daily demonstration of their vulnerability,

---

1. Charleston *Courier* cited in *Liberator*, March 24, 1845; Scarborough (ed.), *Diary of Edmund Ruffin*, I, 556–57.

lending to antislavery agitation a menacing aspect quite unrelated to its moral censoriousness. The abundant evidence of discontent influenced abolitionists as well, leading some of them to reexamine their policy of disengagement from slaves.

A particularly dramatic event on the high seas hastened the reconsideration. In June, 1839, a slave ship flying the Portuguese flag landed in Cuba with a cargo of newly captured Africans. There some of them were transferred to the Spanish vessel *Amistad* and then launched toward an unspecified destination. During the passage, the slaves mutinied, killed several white crewmen, and took control of the vessel. They tried to sail the ship home to Africa, but surviving white crew members managed to thwart the plan and instead maneuvered the boat into Long Island Sound.[2]

There the blacks were seized and imprisoned. At once began a lengthy court battle over disposition of the captives, with a committee of abolitionists directing efforts to prevent their being delivered to Spanish authorities. Massive publicity surrounded the affair as the case eventually made its way to the Supreme Court, which ordered the captives freed and returned to Africa. Not only did these complex legal maneuvers bring much favorable attention in the North to the antislavery cause, but the court battles also gave many abolitionists for the first time an opportunity to defend the rights of black people in a practical rather than a theoretical way. The special circumstance that allowed them to aid these slaves could not be brushed away—it was mutiny and murder that brought the *Amistad's* human cargo into northern waters. Blacks themselves, with no prompting from white allies, thus projected the issue of violence into the foreground of abolitionist concern. Mutiny aboard the *Amistad* confronted abolitionists with the fact of black rebellion. In that manner, they were given opportunity to condone violence in the movement against slavery, to accept its creative possibilities, and—perhaps still more important—to make common cause with blacks. But for the moment, despite their acquiescence in the slaves' forceful escape from bondage, most abolitionists still distinguished between the slaves' resort to violence through their own choice and abolitionists' use or advocacy of it. Most also seem not yet to have recognized the utility to their cause of an abolitionist-slave alliance.

Abolitionist response to the *Amistad* affair nevertheless suggests

2. For an account of the entire episode, see Howard Jones, *Mutiny on the "Amistad": The Saga of a Slave Revolt and Its Impact on American Abolition, Law, and Diplomacy* (New York, 1986).

how lightly held and easily relinquished was the ideal of nonresistance. Few condemned the blacks for what they had done. On the contrary, abolitionists accepted and justified the mutiny as they marshaled all their resources to prevent the rebels' return to slavery. Among the leaders in the campaign that eventually sent the mutineers as free men to Africa was Lewis Tappan, the well-known evangelical abolitionist, who happened also to be one of the most confirmed of nonresistants. Tappan easily bent his principles to accommodate rebellion in the cause of freedom. If he recognized the inconsistency, it did not appear to trouble him. His example was by no means an isolated one.[3]

Two and a half years later, in November, 1841, mutiny on the *Creole*, a brig transporting slaves from Virginia to Louisiana, provided abolitionists with a similar though less celebrated opportunity to defend the cause of black rebels. After seizing command of the vessel, the mutineers sailed to Nassau, where authorities released most of them. Furious at British disregard of American property rights, southerners talked of war. Abolitionists ridiculed the prospect. Gamaliel Bailey's *Philanthropist* drew a ludicrous picture of the threatened conflict. If the nation decided to fight over the incident, the editor wrote, slaveholders would be forced to stay "at home to protect their families against the slaves," while antislavery "northern freemen" would be called upon to fight "for the coastwise slave trade."[4] Again abolitionists reproached the South for its military weakness in the face of an enslaved "internal enemy," and again they defended rebellious slaves.

As abolitionist response to the *Amistad* and *Creole* mutinies made clear, the consensus for nonresistance, fragile from the start, displayed unmistakable signs of fracture by the 1840s. For many, pacifism, even in its most earnestly proclaimed phase, had been only a chosen strategy designed to fit the times rather than a matter of deep conviction. When circumstances changed, strategy could be changed, too, with no resultant pangs of conscience. Especially among those abolitionists eager to translate antislavery fervor into direct political action, nonresistance was lightly held and easily relinquished. Its passing would have grave consequence for slaveholders.

Some of the same abolitionists who in the late 1830s led the move-

3. Wyatt-Brown, *Lewis Tappan*, 205–20.
4. The incident aroused far less interest than did the *Amistad* mutiny, but see William Ellery Channing, *The Duty of the Free States; or, Remarks Suggested by the Case of the Creole* (Boston, 1842), and *Philanthropist*, January 5, 1842.

ment to transfer antislavery from the sphere of moral reform into the arena of party politics were among the first to alter their stance toward slaves and slave resistance. Those politically disposed reformers, who were more likely to be lawyers, editors, or businessmen than clergymen, held commonplace attitudes with respect to power and its uses. They viewed slaveholders and "the slave power" as political enemies to be confronted by ordinary worldly means and defeated. If southerners would not relinquish slavery in response to moral influence exerted through persuasion and prayer, then they would be deprived of their slaves by earthly instruments of coercion. If slavery could not be ended peacefully, with consent of the owners, it would be ended in some other way. Political power offered itself as the coercive means most readily at hand and the most attractive way to effect this goal. Individuals hostile to the South on account of the policies of its congressional political leaders likewise found in antislavery activity a weapon congenial to their needs. For some of them, the encouragement of slave violence was not out of the question.[5]

The abolitionists' entrance into party politics did not lead inevitably to encouragement of slave resistance or to efforts to forge an alliance with slaves. But as nonresistants readily understood, the decision to resort to politics and thus to coercion meant that such strategies no longer were theoretically precluded. "We dread the tendency to ballots," wrote Garrison in 1843. "They are but one remove from bloodshed."[6] As Garrison realized, behind majority rule lay force, the power to coerce minorities and to destroy dissenters.

The trend toward direct action notably strengthened in the late 1830s, when abolitionists came to view southerners less as erring fellow citizens than as overt enemies. In their eyes, the sharp resistance manifested toward abolitionist efforts in that turbulent decade rapidly transformed slaveholders from being misguided fellow countrymen into stubborn foes. The violence encountered by nonresistant abolitionists invited violence in return. Northern mobs aroused intense hatred in some. It was hard to remain a forbearing and forgiving Christian in the face of disrupted lectures, wrecked

5. Larry Gara, "Slavery and the Slave Power: A Crucial Distinction," *Civil War History*, XV (1969), 4–18; Bretz, "Economic Background of the Liberty Party," 250–64; Richard H. Sewell, *Ballots for Freedom: Antislavery Politics in the United States, 1837–1860* (New York, 1976), 3–23.
6. *Liberator*, September 22, 1843.

newspaper presses, a murdered editor, a burned Pennsylvania Hall, battered slaves.[7]

White abolitionists seldom thought of fighting slaveholders themselves, but some began to consider the possibility of encouraging slaves, the planters' natural enemies, to do so. Abolitionists who frequently had justified their program as offering the only means to avoid interracial warfare began in the late 1830s to view insurrection in a different light. Rather than recoiling from the prospect, they were attracted by it. Insurrection came to be welcomed as the ultimate means, perhaps the only means, of ending slavery and destroying the power of slaveholders.

Jabez Delano Hammond of Cherry Valley, New York, was one of the earliest white advocates of deliberately fomenting rebellion as an antislavery device. Such extremism came unexpectedly from that source. Hammond fit no pattern for the malcontented of that or any age. He was not an obscure, downtrodden figure; there was nothing in the biographical record to show alienation or dogged sense of failure; neither can his easy marriage with violence be credited to the impetuosity of youth or to romantic desperation. Hammond was a respected Otsego County judge and past the age of sixty when he revealed his militant program. Earlier he had served unremarkably as a member of the Fourteenth Congress of the United States and as a New York state senator. A serious student of politics as well as an experienced politician, he soon would write an acclaimed and still-consulted political history of New York. Oddly enough, despite his unbounded hatred for the South, Hammond was not usually identified at the time as an abolitionist, though his wife wore the badge of that fellowship.[8]

The prospect of voluntary emancipation by slaveholders had disappeared, Hammond decided as early as 1839, and he saw little more reason to anticipate the "spread of correct views" in the North. "The only way in which slavery at the South can be abolished is by force," he concluded. Hammond proposed that abolition-

7. See the impassioned statements in Alvan Stewart to Samuel Webb, May 28, 1838, and June 25, 1840, in Alvan Stewart Papers, New-York Historical Society, New York, N.Y. A strand in Quaker thought, and perhaps in other Protestant thought as well, insisted on the need for retributive justice for slaveholders. See Josiah F. Polk to R. R. Gurley, December 17, 1829, in American Colonization Society Papers.

8. Allan Johnson and Dumas Malone (eds.), *Dictionary of American Biography* (New York, 1928–36), VII, 205–206; Wesley Bailey to Gerrit Smith, March 6, 1845, in Gerrit Smith Papers.

ists establish two military academies patterned after West Point, one in Upper Canada and another at Matamoras in Mexico, both centers of southern black refugees and both beyond easy interference by slaveholders or the United States government. From these academies, black youths trained in the art of war would be dispatched to infiltrate the South. There they would blend into the slave population, encourage sabotage, and foment slave uprisings. Such military agents, said Hammond, in a phrase disposing of the conventional agents of moral suasion, would prove "the most successful Southern missionaries."[9]

At first Hammond revealed his unorthodox views only in private correspondence, perhaps to no one except his radical New York neighbor Gerrit Smith. But Hammond's violent proposals represented no passing mood, and before another decade passed, he had published a version of them in the form of a fictionalized slave autobiography, *Julius Melbourne*. Its pages repeated his advice of 1839: Philanthropists should begin to recruit black armies instead of "raising funds to pay abolition lecturers." With undisguised relish, he pictured the day "when the rich rice and cotton fields of the south will be drenched with human gore . . . and when the gorgeous palaces which now adorn the southern plantations will be enveloped in flames."[10]

Few abolitionists were so forward or so bloodthirsty as Hammond. Most conscientiously shied from such livid scenes and continued to insist that their activity was designed to prevent violence rather than promote it. Yet prospects for a peaceful end to slavery through the agency of repentant white Americans continued to recede. Blacks, both North and South, taught white abolitionists a surer way.

Beginning in the late 1830s, the arrival in the North of growing numbers of fugitive slaves acquainted abolitionists with the eagerness of slaves to free themselves independent of outside advice or agency. The behavior of northern free blacks likewise was instructive. Few of them, as it turned out, adhered to nonresistance. White abolitionists found that free blacks, from whose consciousness the fact of slavery could never long be absent, were ready on their own initiative to take up arms to defend fugitives—and themselves—

9. Jabez Delano Hammond to Gerrit Smith, May 18, 1839, in Gerrit Smith Papers.
10. [Jabez Delano Hammond], *Life and Opinions of Julius Melbourne* . . . (Syracuse, N.Y., 1847), 237.

from slave catchers and from authorities who would enforce the fugitive slave laws. In several northern cities they formed vigilance committees, sometimes in cooperation with whites, to safeguard runaways and prevent kidnappings. In the course of their risky pursuits, members on occasion used force, broke the law, and otherwise resisted authority.[11] No one absorbed in such desperate activity was likely to stop for very long in order to ponder its implication for the future of nonresistance theory. Thus the enterprise of aiding runaways ineluctably moved its advocates forward to new positions, with free blacks conspicuously in the vanguard. It was but a short step from helping fugitives elude the clutches of the law in the North to urging them to escape from the South.

White abolitionists thus awoke to both the propensity of slaves to free themselves and the eagerness of free blacks to help them in doing so. Abolitionists, white and black alike, soon learned to exploit these developments, not alone for their humanitarian purpose, but also for their utility in arousing northern antislavery sympathies. Accordingly, they made the fugitive an important adjunct to their cause on the lecture platform and in their publications.

But abolitionists also learned from fugitives a threefold practical lesson that extended well beyond propaganda value. First, each successful escape freed at least one slave and, by demonstrating to both owner and bondsman the vulnerability of slavery, weakened the entire system; second, these were the accomplishments of direct action, not of moral suasion; third, they undeniably were the work of slaves themselves. Only in an indirect way, if at all, could they be credited to the abolitionists' influence.

Even white abolitionists who continued to be nonresistants would find themselves uncomfortable if they asked the victimized slaves or free blacks to follow their own pacific example. The trend instead was toward justifying and even encouraging black resistance rather than continuing to voice old pleas for patience. By adding their support, abolitionists now assumed a major role in the campaign slaves and free blacks already had initiated to destroy slavery.

The flight of slaves in the 1840s and 1850s was viewed as a serious problem, especially by owners in the upper South, who found that the ease of escape significantly weakened their control. For the present, the erosion in absolute numbers could be borne, but the facility

11. Jane H. Pease and William H. Pease, *They Who Would Be Free: Blacks' Search for Freedom, 1830–1861* (New York, 1974), 206–12.

with which escapes took place forecast a time when the loss would become ruinous. Abolitionists appeared to be ready to hasten that day. A few—whites and free blacks alike—already had carried their hatred of slavery and their willingness to defy the law to the point of entering slave states themselves and helping slaves escape. These well-publicized incidents, with the prison literature some of them engendered, made an important contribution to the romanticizing of abolitionism.[12] Of greater significance to the evolution of northern relationships to slaves, however, were less dramatic events taking place in state legislatures. At the same time that individual northern citizens on their own initiative were aiding slaves to escape and to elude would-be captors, some northern states enacted personal liberty laws denying the use of state facilities and the aid of state officials for the enforcement of the federal fugitive slave law.[13] The implication of such legislation for the plantation South could not be missed. Northern states had unmistakably put themselves in the position of being accessories to the South's racial conflict, even when waged on remote plantations, and had become committed partisans of the slave.

It may have been his understanding of these implications of the fugitive slave issue that persuaded the New York philanthropist Gerrit Smith, with whom the radical Judge Hammond was in frequent correspondence, to prepare his "Address to the Slaves of the United States" for presentation to a Liberty party convention held at Peterboro, New York, in January, 1842. The address generally has been ignored by historians of the antebellum United States; yet because of its shift away from the policies of pacifism and disengagement that had been written into the platform of the American Anti-Slavery Society, Smith's work stands as a milestone in the process that would lead to the destruction of slavery. It was in some respects a declaration of war against the South in the vein made familiar by Lord Dunmore's proclamation of November, 1775, to the slaves of Virginia, inviting them to escape. Unlike most earlier abolitionists, Smith recognized slaves as active participants in the struggle for emancipation. His address proclaimed a hitherto unacknowledged

<hr/>

12. Notable examples of this genre are Joseph C. Lovejoy, *Memoir of Rev. Charles T. Torrey, Who Died in the Penitentiary of Maryland, Where He Was Confined for Showing Mercy to the Poor* (New York, 1847); Daniel Drayton, *Personal Memoir of Daniel Drayton, for Four Years and Four Months a Prisoner (for Charity's Sake) in Washington Jail* (Boston, 1855); George Thompson, *Prison Life and Reflections . . .* (Hartford, 1854).

13. Thomas D. Morris, *Free Men All: The Personal Liberty Laws of the North, 1780–1861* (Baltimore, 1974), 107–29.

alliance between abolitionists and slaves and set forth radically new roles for both groups.

Smith announced his abandonment of the "almost universally held" conviction "that the friends of the slave have no right to communicate with him." Instead, it was the abolitionists' duty to be the slaves' "advisors, comforters, and helpers." Their obligation extended well beyond sympathy and rhetoric. Duty also required them to take direct, aggressive action against the slave system. According to Smith, "the abolitionist has a perfect moral right to go into the South, and use his intelligence to promote the escape of ignorant and imbruted slaves from their prison-house." Slaves had a parallel responsibility: They were duty-bound to run away. The day of prayer and persuasion had passed; now both parties—slaves and abolitionists—should *act* in the cause of freedom.[14]

The address counseled against violence. Smith did not suggest, as his friend Hammond had done, that slaves murder and burn in a strike for freedom. Nevertheless he insisted on their right to take from their masters or other white persons food, clothing, horses, boats—whatever they needed to make good their escape. Few abolitionists could object to Smith's urging slaves to run away, though the antislavery Virginian Samuel M. Janney thought the advice unnecessary. But they found it hard to approve his counsel to steal, especially to steal even from persons in the free states. Despite objection, Smith's address was endorsed by the Liberty party convention in New York and by antislavery groups in Illinois and elsewhere.[15]

Yet acceptance of the revolutionary principles of direct action against slavery and alliance with slaves did not come easily for all. Gamaliel Bailey, for one, entered his protest: "Our business is simply with the master." In this respect, the Cincinnati editor wrote, he would continue to stand firmly on the principles of the American Anti-Slavery Society as Garrison formulated them in 1833. Reformers, thought Bailey, ought to avoid taking positions too far in advance of public opinion. Bailey interpreted Smith's address as a call for slave rebellion. To appear to sanction violence, he warned, would further close the minds of southerners while it also impeded the growth of antislavery sentiment in the free states. A still

14. *National Anti-Slavery Standard*, February 24, 1842.
15. Samuel M. Janney to J. Miller McKim, December 1, 1843, in Antislavery Collection, Cornell University, Ithaca, N.Y.; Alice Eliza Hamilton to Gerrit Smith, September 22, 1842, in Gerrit Smith Papers; Minutes of the Illinois State Anti-Slavery Society, May 26, 1842, Chicago Historical Society, Chicago; Sewell, *Ballots for Freedom*, 90.

more serious matter: If abolitionist advice encouraged slaves to revolt, the result might be extermination of the race rather than its
liberation.[16]

Opposition in this vein did not bury Smith's proposal. On the contrary, his advice soon was repeated. In 1843 the New England Anti-
Slavery Convention endorsed a similar address to the slaves written
and presented by no less a confirmed nonresistant than William
Lloyd Garrison. The event proved that some New England abolitionists, too, now were prepared to accept the logic of their relationship with slaves. They would abandon their earlier policy of disengagement and attempt to forge an open slave-abolitionist coalition.

Garrison's address, like Smith's, warned slaves to attempt no
insurrections, not because revolt was wrong or unjustified, but
because it would fail. Instead of fighting hopeless battles on their
masters' plantations, Garrison advised, slaves should make every
effort to escape to the North. In reaching that conclusion, however,
Garrison moved closer than had Smith to justifying, even encouraging, the use of violence. "By precept and example," wrote Garrison, slaveholders "declare that it is both your right and duty to
wage war against them, and to wade through their blood, if necessary, to secure your own freedom."[17] Despite such language, Garrison remained a pacifist himself, but he neither expected nor advised
slaves to follow his example.

Both Smith's and Garrison's addresses represent a major compromise of the principle of moral suasion. And both closely resemble
the policy followed in the eighteenth century by foreign enemies
of English America, who planned to use slaves as instruments in
struggle for empire. Through their ostensibly peaceful nineteenth-
century prose echo the Spanish king's proclamation directed to
Anglo-American slaves in 1733 and Lord Dunmore's proclamation
of 1775 as well as Admiral Cochrane's less famous proclamation
during the War of 1812.

The white abolitionists' change in policy paralleled that of northern free blacks as they, too, consciously moved toward open alliance
with slaves. After escape to the North, some fugitives managed to

16. *Philanthropist*, February 9, April 6, and August 27, 1842. See also *ibid.*, September 22, 1841.

17. *Address of the New England Anti-Slavery Convention to the Slaves of the United
States with an Address to President Tyler, Faneuil Hall, May 31, 1843* (Boston, 1843),
3–13. The address is also in *Liberator*, June 2, 1843. On Garrison's authorship, see
Henry Wilson, *History of the Rise and Fall of the Slave Power in America* (Boston,
1872–77), I, 563.

maintain ties with family and friends in the slave states. For many, these perhaps represented no more than ordinary bonds of human sympathy, but others made the crucial ideological leap of extending personal relationships to embrace an entire people. From such expanded consciousness came resolve to destroy the institution that kept most blacks in bondage and degraded all of them. Northern free blacks, even though resident in ostensibly free states, early recognized that to the existence of slavery must be charged the prejudice and discrimination that burdened every aspect of their lives.

In the growing northern cities, particularly in Boston, New York, and Philadelphia, but also in smaller places such as Detroit, Pittsburgh, and Columbus, a community of free blacks had developed parallel to the slave community in the South. The functions of the two were similar. In each instance, an oppressed and exploited people, barred by law and custom from equal participation in society and the economy, had come together for mutual aid and support. In each instance, too, the formation of the community and its import were largely ignored by white people.

Members of the slave community helped each other in their psychological resistance to slavery. The community fostered in its members a sense of self-worth in the face of calculated efforts at degradation. It offered support against the cruelties and burdens that were inseparable from slavery. The slave community thus was a self-help organization that made it possible for blacks to survive the ordeal of slavery and through whose collective action members sometimes extorted from masters and overseers concessions that individual effort would not likely have achieved.[18]

Free-black communities in the North offered their members much the same kind of aid and support, necessarily tailored, however, to the North's market economy, which had only the most primitive representation in the rural South. Their free-state location allowed them to act more openly in their own behalf than was possible for slaves. It also provided the added opportunity to speak freely against slavery with little fear of retribution and with the possibility of influence. Further, the northern setting allowed them more openly to disturb slavery by providing refuge for fugitives and defending them from slave catchers, though blacks in the South did these things, too.

At least as early as 1796, Boston blacks founded the African Soci-

18. The most thorough treatment is Blassingame, *Slave Community*.

ety, principally for mutual aid and charity, but almost inevitably one of its chief concerns came to be abolition. In 1808 it published a formal antislavery statement. Members of Boston's African Masonic Lodge, a fraternal order whose purpose was racial solidarity and mutual aid, likewise periodically listened to condemnations of slavery: The noted black leader Prince Hall, for example, delivered an antislavery oration before the lodge in 1797. Free blacks in the North, as in the South, stood in the vanguard of opposition to proposals by the American Colonization Society to send them to Africa, and in doing so, they proclaimed ties with slaves that white southerners could only view as ominous. In 1817 black Philadelphians responded to colonization plans by resolving that "we never will separate ourselves voluntarily from the slave population of this country; they are our brethren by the ties of consanguinity, of suffering, and of wrong." Free-black intransigence on this subject, when borrowed by Garrison, became basic to the abolitionist program of the 1830s. As the fugitive slave issue grew in political prominence after the 1830s, urban blacks throughout the North formed vigilance committees to help runaways and, especially, to protect them from recapture. Thus by the time organized antislavery activity among white northerners achieved prominence, northern free blacks already had created an antislavery tradition that closely tied them to the southern slave community, thereby lending to their activity strength and authenticity difficult for white abolitionists to equal. Northern blacks and white abolitionists joined forces in the moral suasionist antislavery campaign of the 1830s, but under stress of urgencies that white reformers were not likely to experience, black abolitionists more readily than their co-workers soon moved from pacifism, with its faith in moral power, reason, and good will, toward advocacy of direct antislavery action.[19]

In the late 1820s, a group of black youths, students in the New York African Free Schools, talked of schemes "for the freeing and upbuilding of our race." They made a solemn pact, one of them remembered, "that when we had educated ourselves we would go South, start an insurrection and free our brethren in bondage." Although none of the band ever quite fulfilled that youthful pledge, one of them, Henry Highland Garnet, came near to doing so when

19. Horton and Horton, *Black Bostonians*, 28–29, 30, 54, 58; Aptheker (ed.), *Documentary History*, I, 71; Pease and Pease, *They Who Would Be Free*, 8–12, 171.

in the 1840s he ventured to commit northern black leadership to alliance with slaves and advocacy of black revolt.[20]

Northern blacks on several occasions had answered mob violence with counterviolence, as in riots at Cincinnati in 1829 and Philadelphia in 1832, and again in fugitive-slave rescues in the 1840s and 1850s. Especially noteworthy among these incidents was a martial encounter at Christiana, Pennsylvania, in 1851, when free blacks and their white sympathizers repulsed a posse called out to capture fugitives and in the process killed the fugitives' owner.[21] Such response did more than confirm familiar observation that human beings under physical attack commonly try to defend themselves and may strike back. Those demonstrations of black prowess in defense of rights flew in the face of the vulgar contention that blacks were specially qualified for slavery and meekly accepted it. They should be placed near the extreme of the continuum of well-thought-out black response to oppression that extends from the self-help organizations of the 1790s to military service in the Civil War. These dramatic illustrations of determination to defend freedom against further encroachment formed the background for the bold policy statements enunciated by black spokesmen in the 1840s. At a convention of blacks held at Buffalo in 1843, the issue of slave violence revealed its political face as black spokesmen proclaimed impatience with moral suasion and drafted incendiary messages addressed to their still-enslaved brethren in the South.

Much of the Reverend Samuel Davis' address opening the proceedings at Buffalo took the form of a sustained paraphrase of Patrick Henry's famous prerevolutionary speech in the Virginia House of Burgesses in which Henry proclaimed the futility of verbal protest against British policy and the expediency of resort to arms. Davis compared black military action in the cause of freedom with recent, much-admired revolts in Greece and Poland. In support of European rebels, Davis observed: "Money, as well as arms and ammunition, were sent out from our own land. And not only these, many of freedom's noblest sons largely volunteered their own services, risking their lives and fortunes to the dangerous chances of

20. Alexander Crummell, *The Eulogy of Henry Highland Garnet, D.D., Presbyterian Minister . . .* (Washington, D.C., 1882), 25–26; Pease and Pease, *They Who Would Be Free,* 238.

21. Jonathan Katz, *Resistance at Christiana: The Fugitive Slave Rebellion, Christiana, Pennsylvania, September 11, 1851* (New York, 1974), 81–103.

war with the infidel, tyrant Turks." The lesson was obvious: Northern blacks should encourage and welcome revolt in the South, and when revolt began, they should join forces with embattled slaves. "No other hope is left us," said Davis, "but in our own exertions and an 'appeal to the God of armies!' "[22]

The militant tone of the convention having been set, it was Garnet's turn to speak. For an hour and a half, he exhorted delegates to support a slave uprising. "Brethren, arise, arise!" he cried. "Strike for your lives and liberties. Now is the day and hour." Despite his choice of language, the tactics Garnet advocated were not those of Nat Turner, whose men had massacred indiscriminately, but instead resembled those of a general strike. No one, said Garnet—echoing advice given earlier by David Walker—should consent to be a slave. Slaves should resolve to be slaves no longer. They should confront their owners with the pronouncement that they wanted "their liberty and had come to ask for it, and if the masters refused it, to tell them, then we shall take it, let the consequence be what it may."[23] Violence certainly would be the result, but Garnet maintained a shred of nonresistance principles when he pointed out that, under his plan, the violence would be initiated by masters, not by slaves. In any event, the end sought now required new modes of action. Freedom would not come in that generation, thought Garnet, without the shedding of blood.

Frederick Douglass, who recently had fled from slavery in Maryland and still was identified with the nonresistant Garrisonians, spoke eloquently against Garnet's counsel. He favored "trying the moral means a little longer." He "wished in no way to have any agency in bringing about" insurrection. Convention delegates from Cincinnati joined Douglass in deploring a course certain to lead to violence. Garnet's plan, said one of them, "would be fatal to the safety of the free people of color of the slave States, but especially so to those who lived on the borders of the free States." Such an opinion must have had powerful impact on persons who knew of the terrible retribution often visited on blacks in time of suspected conspiracy. Not surprisingly, a majority of delegates refused to authorize the printing of Garnet's address as representing the sentiments of the convention, though a motion to do so failed by only one vote.[24]

22. *Minutes of the National Convention of Colored Citizens Held at Buffalo on the 15th, 16th, 17th, 18th and 19th of August, 1843* . . . (New York, 1843), 6.
23. *Ibid.,* 12–13; Aptheker, *Documentary History,* I, 226–33.
24. *Minutes of the National Convention,* 13–19.

As the narrowness of defeat suggests, Garnet's address would not be set aside and forgotten. It too accurately reflected the mood and wishes of growing numbers of abolitionists, white as well as black, to be ignored for long. Four years later a national convention of blacks held at Troy, New York, ordered it printed in a slightly modified version, and in 1849 a convention in Ohio agreed to publish an edition of five hundred copies, together with *Walker's Appeal*, its ideological ancestor.[25]

Further evidence of the weakened hold of pacifism and moral suasion on free-black leaders appeared in 1847, when Charles Remond, who had strongly opposed Garnet's sentiments at the Buffalo convention, reversed himself and in an address at Abington, Massachusetts, advised slaves to rise in insurrection. Although the abolitionist press chose to minimize Remond's about-face, the influential Boston *Daily Whig* gave his views much hostile attention. The newspaper was ready to accept slave revolt if slaves themselves determined on that course, but it could not tolerate a northern abolitionist—particularly not a black abolitionist—urging them to the act. Remond was "a traitor to the country, to the Constitution, to Humanity." Some white abolitionists, too, had difficulty accepting such bold attempts to interfere in the South's domestic affairs. The Boston politician Ellis Gray Loring complained to Garrison and demanded that the American Anti-Slavery Society disavow Remond's sentiments, but even as he did so, he admitted to suspecting that pacifism's sun was setting. In the confrontational atmosphere of the 1840s, views like Remond's could not be repressed. Loring had "no doubt that (like the doctrines of Young Ireland) they are destined to gain a certain currency."[26]

Their currency among black abolitionists was not to be denied. By 1849 Douglass, who more than anyone else could take credit for the early rejection of Garnet's address, now openly advocated slave revolts. Sentiment favorable to insurrection continued to grow. In the late summer of 1850, a convention of some fifty fugitive slaves and a number of well-known radical abolitionists, both black and white, met at Cazenovia, New York. The gathering was occasioned by passage of the hateful new Fugitive Slave Law as well as by the imprisonment at Washington, D.C., of the abolitionist William L. Chaplin for the crime of aiding slaves to escape and supplying them

25. Pease and Pease, *They Who Would Be Free*, 239.
26. Boston *Daily Whig*, July 3, 1847. See also *ibid.*, July 9, 1847, for a defense of slave violence by "J. C."; Loring to Garrison, June 28, 1847, *Liberator*, July 9, 1847.

with weapons. Talk of violence and insurrection and consolidating an abolitionist-slave alliance dominated the sessions.[27]

The delegates pledged to help fugitives and advised them to use arms against would-be captors rather than be returned to slavery. But the Cazenovia convention did not limit its concern to blacks who had fled to the North, and by focusing on slaves, its members clearly intended to inaugurate an intensified stage in the interracial struggle. The delegates went far beyond merely encouraging slaves to flee to the North, the course Smith and Garrison had recommended a few years earlier. Slaves were held as prisoners of war "in an enemy's country," said the delegates, and thus had "the fullest liberty to plunder, burn and kill" to make good their escape. Along with its advocacy of open revolt, the convention proclaimed a political and military alliance between northern and southern blacks. "When the insurrection of the Southern Slaves shall take place, as take place it will," so ran their message to slaves, "the great mass of the colored men of the North . . . will be found by your side, with deep-stored and long-accumulated revenge in their hearts, and death-dealing weapons in their hands." The new militant spirit spread well beyond the abolitionists of central New York to sweep away pacifism in unexpected places. Soon after the Cazenovia convention adjourned, the nonresistant Parker Pillsbury, addressing, as he supposed, a nonresistant Garrisonian gathering at Salem, Ohio, found himself instead speaking to an assembly of whites and blacks now determined to arm themselves to fight slavery. Not even Pillsbury's eloquence could persuade them to resume their more moderate former course.[28]

Few prominent white abolitionists before the late 1850s could bring themselves to endorse slave insurrection, still less to advocate white participation. Nonetheless they, too, were irresistibly attracted to the prospect of violent overthrow of slavery, few more so than Garrison himself, once the very figurehead of nonresistance theory. Garrison depicted for slaves earlier and perhaps more easily accomplished emancipation than most hitherto had thought possible. "Your blood is the cement which binds the American Union together," he wrote in 1843; "your bodies are crushed beneath the massy weight of this Union; and its repeal or dissolution would ensure the downfall of slavery." The South was able to maintain its

27. *National Anti-Slavery Standard*, August 29, September 5 and 12, 1850.
28. *Ibid.*, October 10, 1850.

institutions, Garrison continued, only because "the whole military power of the nation is pledged to suppress all insurrections."[29]

Startling as Garrison's idea may have seemed in the 1840s, it was far from being new. As early as 1820, John Quincy Adams, starting from the same assumption, had predicted that secession would be followed by civil war, slave rebellion, and the consequent end of slavery. When Benjamin Lundy presented a similar forecast to New England audiences during his lecture tour in 1828, Garrison heard the idea, probably for the first time. In an early demonstration of his marvelous receptivity to radical thought, Garrison adopted Lundy's view as his own. "What protects the South from instant destruction?" asked Garrison in 1832. "OUR PHYSICAL FORCE. Break the chain which binds her to the Union, and the scenes of St. Domingo would be witnessed throughout her borders."[30] It was an attractive prospect for the radical abolitionist, beautiful in its simplicity and ease of accomplishment, satisfying for its embodiment of merited retribution. In 1832 the prediction that slave violence would follow in the wake of disunion also could be read as a political warning addressed to southern leaders not to make good their threats of nullification and secession. The writings of Samuel Cornish soon afterward must have held even greater pertinence for southerners fearful not only of slave revolt but also of the disruptive effect of class divisions in white society. Dissolution of the Union, the black editor predicted in 1837, would allow slaves to join oppressed "honest white laborers" in an uprising marked by "anarchy, bloodshed and rapine."[31]

Implicit in Garrison's notorious disunionist proposals of the 1840s and 1850s was the expectation that slave revolt would follow secession. Garrisonian disunionism, often dismissed as a visionary, nonresistant device whereby scrupulous persons sought to separate themselves from evil, thus presented a practical, militant aspect. Hidden behind its pacific countenance lay the means for promoting slave rebellion and assuring its success. Slavery, Garrison continued to believe, could not long survive withdrawal of federal support. When antislavery politicians in the mid-1840s called upon the na-

---

29. *Liberator*, June 2, 1843.

30. Adams (ed.), *Memoirs of John Quincy Adams*, V, 210; Garrison to Editor of the Boston *Courier*, August 11, 1828, in Walter M. Merrill and Louis Ruchames (eds.), *The Letters of William Lloyd Garrison* (Cambridge, Mass., 1971–81), I, 65; *Liberator*, June 7, 1832. See also *Liberator*, November 10, 1831, and March 10, 1832.

31. *Colored American*, September 2, 1837.

tional government to sever all its ties with slavery, they perhaps had uppermost in mind this political outcome rather than merely the austere goal of promoting national moral purity.

The movement in the 1840s for national disassociation from slavery gained momentum from proposals to annex Texas. That issue, more than any other, rendered the Union intolerable to many antislavery northerners. Texas constituted a long-standing problem for both abolitionists and slaveholders. Its attractions had been obvious for many years, and failure of the Adams-Onis Treaty of 1819 to include the region within United States boundaries was an omission later diplomats and politicians would much regret and seek to remedy.

The fact that Texas was not a United States possession did not prevent American citizens from wishing to settle there. Americans moving into the Mexican state in the 1820s found an undeveloped, nearly uninhabited region admirably suited to plantation agriculture and slave labor. But to their dismay, they also discovered that they had placed themselves under a regime in which, unlike the United States, the revolutionary impulse toward emancipation had not been checked. In 1829 the Mexican government proclaimed the end of slavery, no matter the interests of settlers in Texas who came from slave states and fully expected to surround themselves with familiar institutions. Mexican policy proved hardly less dismaying to Americans left at home. White southerners could not face with equanimity the prospect of a free-labor state growing up on their western border. It would constitute a barrier to the further westward advance of slavery with consequent build-up in the East of an explosive servile population. Its mere existence would encourage unrest in the neighboring black belt and offer another refuge to fugitives.[32]

Texans' pleas and fervid representations to the Mexican government brought them special exemption to the ban against slavery, but they understood its provisional character. They never felt secure about the permanency of the exemption they had been granted. When in the early 1830s Mexican officials began a process of political centralization, American settlers faced loss of most of the autonomy they until then enjoyed. Americans in Texas proved as devoted to "states' rights" as did southern planters, and for much the

32. Phillips (ed.), *Plantation and Frontier*, II, 250; Stephen F. Austin to Mary Austin Holley, August 2, 1835, in Eugene C. Barker (ed.), *The Austin Papers, October 1834–January 1837* (Austin, Texas, 1927), III, 102.

same reason. They protested the consolidating tendencies under way in Mexico and the consequent lessening of local control, for they dreaded being governed by an antislavery Mexican majority. The resultant friction between state and central government—between Texan minority and Mexican majority—led first to protests and then to revolution and the establishment of the Republic of Texas. It would be hard to exaggerate the role of slavery in bringing about these events.[33]

As the revolutionary movement in Texas proceeded, encouraged and aided by persons in the United States, many of them in the South, abolitionists launched a full-scale campaign against annexation. Their efforts received a favorable response, for whatever persuasive arguments might be advanced in support of acquiring Texas, impossible to hide from northern voters was the fact that addition of so vast a region would considerably increase southern political influence while also assuring continued growth of slavery. And to a people whose economic interests diverged so sharply from those of the South these seemed consequences worth resisting.

Anti-Texas northerners also summoned to their support the same spirit of nationalism that a generation earlier had proved so fertile a source of opposition to the spread of slavery into the Louisiana Purchase. Slavery, they again argued, produced internal dissension and military weakness; it embittered intersectional relations; it invited invasion and insurrection. Acquisition of new slaveholding areas would enfeeble the nation. Annexation, wrote the sanguinary Judge Hammond, "should be resisted unto blood."[34]

All these were prospective, intangible, perhaps imaginary dangers. In contrast, southerners found in an independent Texas real and immediate threats. Under the rule of an antislavery, Mexican majority, Texas would have proved an intolerable neighbor for the great planters of Mississippi and Louisiana, but still more widely objectionable in the South was the prospect of a feeble, independent Texas falling within the orbit of a hostile European power. The Ten-

33. Paul D. Lack, "Slavery and the Texas Revolution," *Southwestern Historical Quarterly*, LXXXIX (1985), 181–202. For a quite different interpretation of the background of the Texas Revolution and the war with Mexico, see Eugene C. Barker, "The Influence of Slavery in the Colonization of Texas," *Mississippi Valley Historical Review*, XI (1924), 3–36, and Seymour V. Connor and Odie B. Faulk, *North America Divided: The Mexican War, 1846–1848* (New York, 1971), 3–32.

34. Hammond to Gerrit Smith, March 15, 1836, in Gerrit Smith Papers. "Every addition of a slave state increases the danger of foreign invasion, and domestic insurrection, and thereby weakens the nation." *Signal of Liberty*, April 6, 1842.

nessee jurist John Catron alluded to a pressing consideration: the unpleasant fact that Texas touched "our great 'Slave and Indian border'" and thus in unsympathetic hands offered potential for inciting unbearable disorder throughout the South. Catron's hope that "our relations with Texas . . . may be so settled as to leave no further cause of apprehension from the poor Mexicans, or the (much to be dreaded) *English*" was shared by other southern statesmen in the 1830s, who anxiously watched the fortunes of the infant republic.[35]

The government of Texas proved stable enough to meet most southern expectations as it followed the United States model in its development as a slaveholding republic. But diplomatic trends soon presented new worries to western-border watchers. England appeared to be gaining influence within Texas; even British acquisition of the republic seemed not out of the question. Southerners found this prospect far more menacing than Mexican control ever had been. Long dreaded by slaveowners—but admired by blacks—as home of destructive antislavery influences, England now was rumored to have projected schemes for emancipation on a hemispheric scale. England planned to free the slaves in Cuba and Brazil by force, wrote a Washington editor, "and when she has accomplished her purpose . . . she will be prepared to enforce the same principle as to us."[36]

All this was an old story for southerners, made no less disturbing by familiarity. Once again, the South apparently faced the situation that so often in times past had menaced its interests—the presence of a strong, hostile power on its border. If Texas were abolitionized through English influence, slaveholders would find themselves in an absolutely untenable position. Bordered on north and west by aggressive enemies offering haven for runaways, slavery would be so unstabilized as to be doomed. If by some miracle planters escaped that fate, another—equally dreaded—eventually would overtake them: Barred from further expansion to the west, the ever-growing slave population would decline in value and eventually become an explosive force to the ruin of the South.

35. John Catron to Andrew Jackson, June 8, 1836, in Bassett (ed.), *Correspondence of Andrew Jackson*, V, 401.
36. David M. Pletcher, *The Diplomacy of Annexation: Texas, Oregon, and the Mexican War* (Columbia, Mo., 1973), 79–84, 120–25; Washington *Semi-Weekly Union*, September 4, 1845.

Southern annexationists in the 1840s did not try to cloak their concern or hide their motives as they confronted the prospect of Texas slipping out of their control forever. Texas must be secured by the United States in order to safeguard slavery where it already existed and to clear the path for its continued diffusion into the West.[37] Northern politicans made political capital out of the obvious. The "Real object" of Texas annexation, said Henry Waldron, a commission merchant from Hillsdale, Michigan, and later Radical Republican congressman, was "perpetuation of Slavery and the political power of the Slave States."[38]

By annexing Texas, the United States annexed a war, for the government of Mexico never had acknowledged the independence of its rebellious state and had always vowed to reconquer it. But expansionist-minded Americans did not allow this fact to check their ambition. The desire to acquire other Mexican territory in the West—California and New Mexico—also was strong, as was the urge to punish the unstable Mexican government for its various transgressions against United States citizens. Hardly less compelling was the widespread popular desire to confront England and frustrate her schemes to interfere in hemispheric concerns. War with Mexico in 1846 thus became surrogate for war with England, the more welcome for its prospect of rich territorial reward on the Pacific coast as well as increased security for slavery.

Some persons at the time more than half-expected England to enter the war in support of Mexico and in so doing to utilize a timeworn tactic against the United States. "The English in case of war, would doubtless do all they could to make the slaves rise and would supply them with the necessary arms and ammunition to make them really formidable," predicted William Tecumseh Sherman. If the thought made the soldier uneasy, abolitionists welcomed the prospect. Samuel May, facing the war he had opposed, decided amidst all the gloom that "one ray of hope shines through. If England engages with Mexico in a war against the U.S., *Slavery must fall*." The abolitionist Abby Kelley indulged in wilder fantasy as she envisioned a million slaves "ready to rise at the first tap of the

37. Washington *Semi-Weekly Union*, October 23, 1845. See also John C. Calhoun's Fort Hill Letter, May 15, 1845, in *Niles' Weekly Register*, LXVIII (June 4, 1845), 232.
38. Hillsdale (Mich.) *Whig Standard*, September 15, 1846. See also Joshua R. Giddings to Joseph A. Giddings, April 28, 1844, in Joshua Giddings Papers, Ohio Historical Society, Columbus.

drum." They, together with the twenty thousand blacks in Canada, would join with Mexicans and hostile Indians to overwhelm the United States Army.[39]

Although when war began, slaves in Texas tried to take advantage of the conflict by fleeing to Mexico—a course Texans believed Mexican authorities encouraged—the potential for revolt across the South could not be realized. The campaigns were staged far from the centers of slave population, and the early success of United States forces prevented invasion by Mexican armies whose commanders might have exploited slave discontent much as the British had done with such effect during both the Revolution and the War of 1812. Yet the conflict entailed risks, as planters understood. Southerners warned of the consequence of sending too many white men to combat. Residents of Pensacola, Florida, believed slaves there intended to rebel "as soon as a sufficient number of the white men went off to war," and South Carolinians experienced similar apprehensions. Although the war brought slaves little opportunity to change their condition, those living close to Mexico followed the fortunes of the armies and dreamed of the benefits defeat of the Unted States might bring. In Louisiana, the former slave Solomon Northup remembered, slaves cheered news of Mexican victories and mourned Mexican defeats.[40] But nowhere, except in Texas itself, did the war occasion an unusual degree of slave restiveness, still less a strike for freedom.

The war's destructive effect on slavery came indirectly. Conquest of Mexico provoked intense political struggle between North and South for control of the newly acquired area. The Wilmot Proviso of 1847 set the premise for years of bitter debate. Slavery, Representative David Wilmot had resolved, should forever be barred from any territory acquired from Mexico. Although political compromise in 1850 put the issue in abeyance for a time, the Kansas-Nebraska Act of 1854 renewed the controversy in still more virulent form. By its repeal of a portion of the Missouri Compromise, all the Louisiana Purchase lay open to the advance of slavery and the plantation system. Free-soil political groups bent upon containing—and thus ul-

39. Sherman to John Sherman, January 4, 1846, in Rachel Sherman Thorndike (ed.), *The Sherman Letters* (New York, 1894), 29; May to J. B. Estlin, May 30, 1846, in Antislavery Collection, Boston Public Library; *Liberator*, May 22, 1846.

40. *Liberator*, June 5, 1846; Steven A. Channing, *Crisis of Fear*, 54; Solomon Northup, *Narrative of Solomon Northup: Twelve Years a Slave . . .* (Auburn, N.Y., 1853), 248.

timately destroying—the slaveholding South mobilized to resist this development, with warfare in the new Kansas Territory the most celebrated result.

By the late 1850s, the South faced in the new Republican party a political force determined to check southern power and southern expansion and to dominate the Union for its own purposes. It could be counted on to exclude plantation interests from effective participation in national affairs and to enact legislation designed to carry out its leaders' declared intention to put slavery on a course toward "ultimate extinction."

An external enemy now menaced the South as none had done since 1815. By appeal to principles of human rights, northerners would justify to themselves and to others their intention to destroy southern power. To protest that Republicans, their abolitionist partners, and slaveowners all were fellow Americans did not hide the truth. Republicans were avowed enemies of planter interest; through enactment in the 1840s and 1850s of the personal liberty laws designed to protect fugitive slaves, northern states had made themselves partisans of the South's "internal enemy." Abolitionists had declared themselves not merely advocates of the freedom of blacks but their allies in an ongoing struggle for liberation. In that manner, slave-master discord in southern households, workplaces, and plantations became linked still more closely to sectional rivalries, and evidence of even apparently minor class antagonisms among white southerners assumed major import as they acquired association with the larger conflict.

11

Intimations of Violence

Organization of the Liberty party in 1839 and of its successors, the Free Soil party in 1848 and the Republican party in 1854, signaled the emergence of a northern political force antagonistic to slavery and to planter influence. For the first time since elimination of French, Spanish, and English power in North America, the slave states faced grave external danger. Moral-based opposition to the South and to slavery, once associated almost solely with zealous religious reformers, now unmistakably was bound to power in the form of northern political parties.

For the moment, the role slaves might play in the new situation remained unsettled. Although by the 1850s abolitionists showed little reluctance to welcome and even encourage slave resistance as an adjunct to their efforts, political party spokesmen—whether Liberty, Free Soil, or Republican—never acknowledged ties to the slaves and never spoke of joining with them to overthrow the southern planters. Republican leaders, seeking the widest possible support, customarily denied having abolitionist goals and shunned association with proclaimed abolitionists as well as with blacks. But the logic of the politicians' antisouthern position made their stance unconvincing and, as it proved, short-lived. Southerners, in any event, thought they protested too much. The planters never disguised their suspicion of a party that harbored and rewarded such consistent opponents of the South as the outspoken politicians

Henry Wilson, Charles Sumner, Joshua Giddings, and Benjamin Wade. Politicians of that brand, thought a South Carolinian, were not "the representatives of the Northern abolitionists—they are simply the tools of the latter."[1] Antislavery, one might argue, had become the motive force in northern politics.

A political force hostile to southern legislative policies and territorial ambitions, as the Republicans were, could not be expected to remain forever unsympathetic to abolitionist intent. As southerners understood, the politicians' disavowal of abolitionism could not hide either their antislavery or antisouthern purpose. Neither, when the time was right, would it prevent them from combining with slaves in efforts to hasten the South's downfall. Slaves then would assume both a political and military role in a power struggle among white Americans.

At an early date, some abolitionists acknowledged that a majority of white voters were unlikely to accept essential features of their program. Slaveholding southerners surely could not be expected to do so. Even though by sentiment northerners inclined toward both antislavery and antisouthern positions, racial bias and desire for national tranquillity prevented majority endorsement of abolitionism. Thus some abolitionists despaired of ever creating a consensus favorable to the ending of slavery. Slavery, they decided, was not likely to be ended by rational, peaceful means. Violence alone, it appeared, could "cut the Gordian knot," and that kind of initiative would come most effectively and appropriately from slaves themselves.[2]

At the middle of the nineteenth century, the peace movement and nonresistance had lost authority nearly everywhere. Honored in theory though such principles still were, few accomplishments could be credited to their influence. On the contrary, as daily news revealed, it was force and violence that moved the peoples of Europe toward the valued goals of national unification and parliamentary

1. Thomas H. Seymour to Milledge Luke Bonham, December 30, 1859, in Milledge Luke Bonham Collection, South Caroliniana Library, University of South Carolina, Columbia.
2. Jabez Delano Hammond to Gerrit Smith, May 18, 1839, and Artemas V. Bentley to Gerrit Smith, November 8, 1852, both in Gerrit Smith Papers; Alvan Stewart to Samuel Webb, June 25, 1840, in Alvan Stewart Papers; Gerrit Smith to Frederick Douglass, August 28, 1854, in Gerrit Smith, *Speeches of Gerrit Smith in Congress* (New York, 1856), 401; Abraham Lincoln to George Robertson, August 15, 1855, in Roy P. Basler *et al.* (eds.), *Collected Works of Abraham Lincoln* (New Brunswick, N.J., 1953–55), II, 318.

democracy. Recent revolutions in the Germanies, Italy, and France had made a mockery of pacifism. For that generation, the conclusion seemed inevitable: Persons who sought to change the political or social order must resort to worldly weapons in order to translate ideals into reality. Moral suasion remained useful for creating a public opinion favorable to reform, but after minds had been changed, an entrenched old order still must be overthrown before the new order could take its place. "Garrisonians . . . would & yet will plant the wilderness of this world with the rose of Sharon," wrote a New England abolitionist in the late 1850s, "but there needs a rough breaking up team to prepare the way. The ugly dragons heads must be cut off & their necks singed & their dens destroyed."[3] Such bloody procedure would not be the work of moral suasionists.

When in the 1830s abolitionists were subjected to mob violence made possible by the unwillingness or inability of local governments to protect them, they took strong stands in support of "law and order" and self-righteously condemned those who violated them. Yet in more tranquil moments, they admitted to an ambivalence toward the value of both and toward the legitimacy of the devices used to maintain them. They were likely to reject man-made law when it conflicted with their principles and to appeal for sanction instead to the Higher Law. After all, slavery was fully supported by statute, and order as it existed in the United States embraced the bondage and subordination of black people. The state obviously was competent to enforce wicked laws as well as good ones and could maintain evil as well as beneficent institutions. Benjamin Drew, a Boston journalist and abolitionist, recognized the paradox. Government, he concluded, is the instrument by which privilege maintains its dominion. Therefore violence against the state may be the only means for shifting power relationships. "A strong police must watch the motions of the oppressed," he wrote. "This system of police usually answers its atrocious purpose very well. It wields the lash against offenders, and instills into the oppressed the fear requisite to suppress any overt act toward their rights as human beings. In-

---

3. Daniel Mann to Lysander Spooner, January 16, 1859, in Antislavery Collection, Boston Public Library; Edmund Quincy believed moral reform would succeed when its converts resorted to "ballot-boxes . . . Senates . . . battlefields." Massachusetts Anti-Slavery Society, *Nineteenth Annual Report* (Boston, 1851), 83. See also Charles Burleigh's statement in Cincinnati *Gazette*, April 29, 1852, and the curious program in John M. Spear, *Twelve Discourses on Government; Purported to Have Been Delivered in Boston, Massachusetts, December, 1852, by Thomas Jefferson of the Spirit World* (Hopedale, Mass., 1853), 36, 40–41.

cidentally, it hinders the commission of crimes, prevents mobs . . . and keeps the streets quiet, and is so far beneficent in its actions. Yet it cannot be denied that the cause of liberty in the world has been much indebted to mobs." As a means of advancing a righteous cause, Drew concluded, abolitionists might properly defy the laws and institutions through which the dominant maintain oppression.[4]

Even though some abolitionists tried, no counterinfluence managed to halt or even slow the trend toward acceptance of force in the slavery controversy. As sectional political disputes drove North and South further apart in the 1850s, old zealots persisted in their call for violent overthrow of slavery, and new ones came forth to join them. At the same time, some northern black abolitionists, together with a few discouraged whites, concluded that the United States offered black people no hope of justice and that emigration to Africa or perhaps Haiti was their only recourse. Others, however, resolved not to advise blacks to abandon the sharpening struggle by fleeing the country. Instead, they boldly advocated physical defense of personal rights and early overthrow of the South's institutions. Blacks in several northern cities supplemented their venerable vigilance committees with military companies, ostensibly for their own protection against kidnappers, and in 1857 delegates to a black convention in Ohio resolved to study military tactics and "to become more proficient in the use of arms." "The time is not far distant when the slave must be free," said Mary A. Darnes as she presented the Attucks Blues of Cincinnati with a company flag, and she added "if not by moral and intellectual means it must be done by the sword." In 1859 Martin R. Delany, sometimes called the Father of Black Nationalism, began serial publication of his militant novel *Blake; or, The Huts of America*, whose main theme was the organization by a slave of a slave rebellion throughout the South. "I am for war," Delany wrote, "—war upon the whites."[5]

Jabez Delano Hammond, the bellicose New York county judge, continued to beat the drum for military invasion of the South as the most effective means to end slavery. Ten thousand men bearing arms and ammunition sufficient to equip five times as many slave

---

4. Drew, *A North-Side View of Slavery*, 7.
5. Pease and Pease, *They Who Would Be Free*, 217–19; Howard H. Bell, "Expressions of Negro Militancy in the North, 1840–1860," *Journal of Negro History*, XLV (1960), 11–20; George W. Williams, *History of the Negro Race in America from 1619 to 1880* (New York, 1883), II, 145–46; Martin R. Delany, *Blake; or, The Huts of America* (Boston, 1970), xxiii.

recruits could sweep through the South and liberate every slave, he wrote. Hammond's greatest regret, as he explained in the sixteen-page letter outlining his scheme, was that he himself was then too old to lead such an invasion and slave revolt.[6]

Perhaps few other white northerners dreamed of martial plans of the sort Hammond designed. Yet the growing inclination to prepare for military encounter was undisguised. A coterie of abolitionists supported warfare in Kansas in the mid-1850s, and in 1855 citizens in Grand Rapids, Michigan, founded a military company "for the protection of Northern rights and Northern men." Its leaders announced their intent to organize similar companies "in every city, town, and village north of Mason and Dixon's line."[7] The most striking evidence of the altered view toward force was the change that took place in the 1850s among ostensibly nonresistant Garrisonian abolitionists. At the formation of the American Anti-Slavery Society in 1833, no member demurred from the society's official policies of barring violence as a tactic, counseling against slave resistance, and focusing persuasive efforts solely on whites. Less than a quarter century later, abolitionist conventions renounced each of these positions and endorsed its opposite.

A group of abolitionists in the late 1850s proclaimed an alliance with slaves, justified and encouraged slave insurrections, and announced their readiness to aid rebels. They thus confessed their belief in the bankruptcy of moral reform as well as in the strength of racial bias. The barriers that white Americans had erected against abolitionism and racial justice, they believed, could be breached only by blacks themselves and only by violent means.

In October, 1857, a biracial National Disunion Convention meeting at Cleveland endorsed slave rebellion. The membership included, among others, the blacks Charles Remond and his sister Sarah and William Wells Brown, and white radicals Susan B. Anthony, Abby Kelley, Charles C. Burleigh, Parker Pillsbury, and Aaron Powell—all of them identified with the Garrisonian wing of the antislavery movement. But the language of their resolutions made that relationship hardly credible. "It is the duty of the slaves to strike down their tyrant masters by force and arms," agreed the delegates, "whenever the blow, however bloody, can be made effec-

6. Jabez Delano Hammond to Gerrit Smith, February 28, 1852, in Gerrit Smith Papers.
7. *Liberator*, July 20, 1855.

tive to that end." And, they continued, "whenever we behold them in the battle-field of Freedom, we will give them every aid and comfort in our power."[8]

So alluring, especially to certain New Englanders, was the prospect of insurrection that the Massachusetts Anti-Slavery Society's convention in January, 1857, devoted most of its sessions to discussing the possibility.[9] On that occasion, one speaker after another proclaimed the right of slaves to rebel and the duty of northerners to aid them. Garrison entered the discussion, not in doctrinaire support of nonresistance, but in oblique endorsement of rebellion, a position for which association with militant blacks perhaps had prepared him. "A man has no right to consent to be a slave," said Garrison, echoing both David Walker's *Appeal* written nearly thirty years earlier and Henry Highland Garnet's Buffalo address of 1843. "He is bound in duty to seek freedom," Garrison continued, "and he must seek it in a manner accordant with his own ideas of right, deciding that point for himself." Parker Pillsbury, who seven years earlier had been shocked by the northern blacks' propensity to violence, concurred with Garrison, but asserted the duty of rebellion even more starkly: "It is as well a sin to be a slave as to hold a slave."

Garrison's close friend Henry C. Wright, a name once inseparable from nonresistance, now stepped forward to join Garrison in urging the opposite principle. "It is the right and duty of the people of the North, themselves being witnesses, to incite the slave to insurrection," said Wright, "and to furnish them with arms and ammunition to carry out their purpose." The Boston orator Wendell Phillips endorsed Wright's counsel: "If a negro kills his master to-night, write his name by the side of Warren: say that he is a William Tell in disguise. . . . I want to accustom Massachusetts to the idea of insurrection, to the idea that every slave has a right to seize his liberty on the spot."

The view of slavery as warfare rather than as a paternalistic relationship had been expressed considerably earlier by some abolitionists, especially by those who had firsthand experience with the institution. "Some men go for the abolition of Slavery by peaceful means," said the former slave Frederick Douglass in 1848. "So do I; I am a peace man but I recognize in the Southern States at the mo-

---

8. *Ibid.*, November 6, 1857. See also American Anti-Slavery Society, *Annual Reports for 1857 and 1858* (New York, 1858), 183.
9. Most of the proceedings are in *Liberator*, February 13, 1857.

ment . . . a *state* of war." But it was Richard Hildreth, novelist and historian, who most fully set forth the concept. Africans had been captured in war, he wrote, "sold upon the coast of Guinea to a certain Yankee slave-trader," transported to America, and resold to the planters. "Slavery then is a continuation of the state of war. It is true that one of the combatants is subdued and bound; but the war is not terminated."[10] Abolitionists who abandoned nonresistance only reluctantly may have found advocacy of violence easier if they could believe, with Hildreth, that they did not initiate conflict, but only recognized a battle already under way. Perhaps it was her awareness of this struggle of conscience that led Abby Kelley, a birthright member of the Society of Friends, to assure fellow abolitionists that the "question is not whether we shall counsel the slaves to forsake peace, and commence war; *the war exists already*, and has been waged unremittingly ever since the slave has been in bondage."[11]

All this talk of violence, however bold, was solely a matter of theory. The convention that heard abolitionists voice their militant sentiments proposed no plans for implementing them. Instead, after expressing encouragement, they waited for slaves to take the initiative and rise in open revolt.

At this point, abolitionists confronted a problem. Such slave initiative, without assurance of outside material aid, was not likely to be taken, for slaves knew as accurately as did their masters that revolt had no more chance of success in the 1850s—perhaps less—than it had under Nat Turner's leadership in 1831. Slaves generally lacked arms and ammunition, but even with them, so the former slave Solomon Northup believed, revolt would mean "certain defeat, disaster and death."[12] But this rational appraisal could have done little to reassure southern whites as they read abolitionists' inciting remarks, saw slaves escape into the North, and watched the growth of antisouthern political forces. The numerous southern newspaper reports of servile plots and violence in the 1850s served

10. Philip S. Foner (ed.), *The Life and Writings of Frederick Douglass* (New York, 1950–55), II, 115; Richard Hildreth, *Despotism in America: An Inquiry into the Nature, Results, and Legal Basis of the Slave-Holding System in the United States* (Boston, 1854), 35–36. See also Frederick Law Olmsted, *A Journey through Texas; or, A Saddle-Trip on the Southwestern Frontier* (New York, 1857), 123: "In Texas, the state of war in which slavery arises, seems to continue in undertone to the present."

11. *Liberator*, February 13, 1857.

12. Northup, *Narrative*, 248–49; Olmsted, *Journey in the Back Country*, 474–75. See Chancellor Harper's explanation for the slaves' failure to revolt in E. N. Elliott, *Cotton Is King, and Pro-Slavery Arguments . . .* (Augusta, Ga., 1860), 607–609.

as reminders of the insecurities inherent in a slaveholding society. These accounts chart the rising temper of slaves, but they also trace the deepening concern of southern whites, who now faced opposition not only from relatively powerless—and familiar—abolitionist reformers but also from potent antislavery, antisouthern politicians.

When the newly organized Republican party entered national politics in 1856 by running John C. Fremont, a dashing figure of antislavery reputation, as its first presidential candidate, southern politicians freely charged Republicans with planning abolition, even insurrection. In that way, those slaves who had access to newspapers or political discussion gained the impression that their freedom was at stake in the election. Fremont's defeat dashed their hopes for early deliverance. The result was a wave of loose talk among slaves, especially in the upper South, of how they might secure the liberty the polls had denied them. That the rash of alleged conspiracies in Tennessee in the fall of 1856 had firmer grounding in reality seems unlikely, for all evidence suggests that, except in the rarest, most desperate circumstance, slaves made rational calculation of the probable results of their acts.[13] They could not help but know by the 1850s that resort to open warfare was all but certain to fail. Northern aid for runaways was readily at hand, but material support for revolt remained highly unlikely.

Most slaves in the 1850s who found bondage intolerable fled from it instead of fighting to alter or abolish it. "Flight not fight is the slaves' ultima ratio," wrote the abolitionist J. Miller McKim in 1857. "An antislavery movement has crossed the line." Flight, in itself, somewhat changed the institution. On plantations from which slaves made good their escape, the remaining slaves gained satisfaction and hope. A traveler in Chicot County, Arkansas, found in 1857 that "all the slaves looked sorrowful, and displeased" when they saw a captured runaway led back to his master. It was commonly thought, too, that slaves in the upper South were treated with greater consideration on account of the ease of escape and that slaves in southern Texas near the Mexican border enjoyed similar indulgence.[14]

13. Charles B. Dew, "Black Ironworkers and the Slave Insurrection Panic of 1856," *Journal of Southern History*, LXI (1975), 321–38.

14. McKim to Maria Weston Chapman, November 19, [1857], in Antislavery Collection, Boston Public Library; Corydon Fuller Journal, May 6, 1857; Olmsted, *Journey through Texas*, 266; Harrison A. Trexler, *Slavery in Missouri, 1804–1865* (Baltimore, 1914), 97; Rawick *et al.* (eds.), *American Slave: Supplement*, Series I, Vol. II, p. 121; Berlin, *Slaves Without Masters*, 351–52.

Fugitives absolutely must be captured, an overseer advised, or all plantation discipline would be lost, an impression that suggests the destructive potential of northern encouragement to runaways. Successful escapes encouraged further escapes. In 1845 John Thom of Berryhill Plantation near Stevensburg, Virginia, advertised for John Roberts, his twenty-five-year-old blacksmith and shoemaker, who "no doubt will attempt to go to the North, and has, likely, free papers." Thom gave his version of why his slave had fled: "Several have left the county; and he will no doubt attempt to follow." In some plantation areas bordering free states, flight became epidemic. From Martinsburg, Virginia, in 1847 came word that "slaves are absconding from Maryland and this portion of Virginia in gangs of tens and twenties and the moment they reach the Pennsylvania line, all hopes of their redemption are abandoned." And three years later, slaves in Montgomery and Prince George counties in Maryland were said to be running away "in droves."[15]

The increasing tempo of the "nullifying flights" meant that owners in some areas now held their property in uneasy tenure. Proximity to the free states made escapes from the upper South more likely to succeed, but even in the lower South success was by no means unknown. Slaves in Louisiana, Arkansas, and Texas had access to the Indian nations and to Mexico. In Texas in the 1850s, slaveowners on their own account several times organized armed bands to invade the Mexican state of Coahuila in pursuit of runaways. In 1855 three companies of Texas militia, acting under the governor's order, raided Mexico for the same purpose. Texans suspected persons of Mexican extraction of sympathizing with slaves and aiding their flight across the border, a situation that perhaps contributed to the Anglo-Texans' long-lasting scorn for the Mexicans who lived among them.[16]

The apparently increased restlessness of slaves in the 1850s and their demonstrated eagerness to escape to the North encouraged two radical northerners to project schemes designed to effect im-

15. Bassett, *Southern Plantation Overseer*, 54, 65; Washington *Semi-Weekly Union*, October 2, 1845; Charles J. Faulkner to John C. Calhoun, July 15, 1847, in Chauncey S. Boucher and Robert P. Brooks (eds.), *Correspondence Addressed to John C. Calhoun, 1837–1849*, Vol. II of American Historical Association, *Annual Report . . . for the Year 1929* (Washington, D.C., 1930), 386; James C. Jackson to Gerrit Smith, September 8, 1850, in Gerrit Smith Papers.

16. Corydon Fuller Journal, July 27, 1858; J. Fred Rippy, *The United States and Mexico* (New York, 1931), 173–74, 179; Olmsted, *Journey through Texas*, 106, 257, 323–27, 456, 502–503.

mediate emancipation. They would move plans beyond discussion in antislavery conventions by carrying them into the South. Although John Brown secretly developed his conspiracy, Lysander Spooner, a Boston lawyer, was less discreet. He published his plan in 1858.

Spooner's analysis of southern class structure closely resembled the one Hinton Rowan Helper of North Carolina recently had set forth in his *The Impending Crisis of the South: How to Meet It*. Like Helper, Spooner depicted economic and social conflict between the South's slaveholders and nonslaveholders. Spooner's aim was to detach small farmers from their long-standing alliance with the planter class. He would launch military forces into the South at several points and appeal to nonslaveholding southerners as well as slaves to join them. "The state of slavery is a state of war," he declared, echoing the new abolitionist orthodoxy. He urged nonslaveholding whites to seize slaveowners and hold them as hostages for the good treatment of slaves: "Man may rightfully be constrained to do justice," he explained. But he advised slaves to attempt no general insurrection until northern white armies "go down, to take part in it, in such numbers as to insure a certain and easy victory."[17]

Late in 1858, Spooner sent drafts of his plan to a few prominent abolitionists, inviting their endorsement and financial aid. Shortly afterward, it was published in the Boston *Courier* and by that means came to southern attention. Almost no one who received his appeal offered any encouragement at all. Wendell Phillips thought the scheme "a good one if it were only practicable," but cautioned that too few would take part to save it "from being ridiculous" and from being crushed by government forces. Francis Jackson, one of Garrison's closest associates, too polite to make light of the project, refused support on the ground he already had fully committed his resources to other modes of abolitionism. Both Benjamin S. Hedrick, recently discharged from the faculty of the University of North Carolina on account of his free-soil sympathies, and Helper dismissed the plan as absurd. "*Immature—impractical—impolitic*," wrote Helper, adding that the abortive Lopez filibustering expedition to Cuba would be ranked "a brilliant triumph compared with the result your plan would have." Only Daniel Mann, a New Englander temporarily living in Ohio, endorsed Spooner's proposal

17. The plan exists in several drafts in the Antislavery Collection, Boston Public Library.

without reservation. It exactly met his desire for bold, coercive action. "I want the bullies & desperadoes of slavery to be taught that the champions of freedom are ready for the contest in any form, civil or savage," he wrote, and added, "My trust in God is stronger when I put some trust in myself, & keep my powder dry."[18] But Mann's enthusiasm was not enough. Thoroughly rebuffed, Spooner made no effort to put his scheme into operation, the essential element—northern white support—being absent. John Brown suffered no such inhibitions.

Although it was Brown who moved beyond rhetoric in an overt attempt to consummate the abolitionist-slave alliance, the road he took to Harpers Ferry clearly had been prepared by others. His association with certain militant blacks, among whom Henry Highland Garnet and Frederick Douglass were the most prominent, and with radical white abolitionists, including Gerrit Smith and Thomas Wentworth Higginson, confirmed his determination to act boldly rather than merely to pray and speak against slavery. For many years, Brown had brooded on schemes to free slaves by enlarging operations of the Underground Railroad. His exploits during the guerrilla war in Kansas in the 1850s taught him military techniques that he believed might effectively further the emancipationist cause.[19]

Brown gained the confidence of several prominent white abolitionists who encouraged him and supplied financial aid without perhaps fully understanding exactly what he intended to do. He also conferred with northern blacks whose support he regarded as being crucial to his plan. It was they, or the men they could influence, whom he expected to fill the ranks of his invading force and to help fund it. "There are thousands of dollars in the Canadian Provinces which are ready for the use of the insurrectionists," wrote one of Brown's confidants. At Chatham, Ontario, in the spring of 1858, thirty-three blacks and twelve whites under Brown's leadership or-

18. Boston *Courier*, January 28, 1859; New York *Tribune*, January 31, 1859; Wendell Phillips to Lysander Spooner, July 16, 1858, Francis Jackson to Spooner, December 3, 1858, Hinton Rowan Helper to Spooner, December, 1858, Daniel Mann to Spooner, January 16, 1859, all in Antislavery Collection, Boston Public Library. See also Theodore Parker to Spooner, November 30, 1858, and Thomas Wentworth Higginson to Spooner, November 30, 1858, *ibid*. A different interpretation of Phillips' view is in James Brewer Stewart, *Wendell Phillips, Liberty's Hero* (Baton Rouge, 1986), 199–200.

19. Stephen B. Oates, *To Purge This Land with Blood: A Biography of John Brown* (New York, 1970), 48–65, 126–228 *passim.*; James Redpath, *The Roving Editor; or, Talks with Slaves in the Southern States* (New York, 1859), 286–87, 306.

ganized a provisional government whose main function would be to conduct guerrilla warfare in the South. Yet the rather fanciful project Brown outlined seemed little more than playacting. When months passed and nothing more happened, support among the Canadian blacks faded away. Only one of the Chatham thirty-three followed Brown to Harpers Ferry.[20]

Brown's efforts to organize support among blacks in the northern United States proved little more productive. Black leaders could not fail to sympathize with his goal, but few believed the time had come when his particular scheme could succeed. Such was the conclusion of Henry Highland Garnet, who a few years earlier had been so open in calling upon northern blacks to support slave revolt. In the summer of 1859, the Reverend Jarmain Loguen of Syracuse did what he could to assist by organizing blacks in Canada into "Liberty Leagues," but he finally told Brown that these people lacked the financial means to travel to the intended base of operations on the North-South border. Harriet Tubman, the black fugitive from Maryland who managed to lead scores of slaves out of the South, apparently favored Brown's plan and perhaps intended to join him at Harpers Ferry, but at the last moment did not do so. Frederick Douglass was in steady communication with Brown. Brown desperately wanted support of such an able and effective leader and believed he had it, but Douglass, too, finally declined Brown's appeal to join him in western Virginia, where his help was needed to "hive the swarming bees."[21]

Although Brown aimed at sharing his plans with only a very few trusted friends, eastern abolitionists learned his intent, at least in a general way, months before he attempted to put it into effect. In January, 1859, at a convention of the Massachusetts Anti-Slavery Society, Richard J. Hinton, a British-born newspaper correspondent who had visited Brown in Kansas, read to the delegates Brown's letter of greeting in which he proclaimed the start of a "new era in the Anti-Slavery movement." Hinton explained the pattern Brown saw in recent events: "The rifle that laid low the first victim in Kansas, has rung the death-knell of slavery on this continent." By attacking free-state settlers, Hinton continued, southerners had inaugurated an intersectional war that would destroy slavery. Brown

20. Benjamin Quarles, *Allies for Freedom: Blacks and John Brown* (New York, 1974), 43–51.
21. Benjamin Quarles (ed.), *Blacks on John Brown* (Urbana, Ill., 1972), 29–30; Oates, *To Purge This Land*, 241, 247–48, 282–83.

viewed his own plans as an essential campaign in a war already under way.[22]

Hinton went on to advise the assembled Garrisonians, some of whom still clung to nonresistance, that "the terrible Logic of History teaches plainly that no great wrong was ever cleansed without blood." The lesson taught by guerrilla warfare in Kansas, he said, "was the mode and manner by which the most vulnerable point of slavery, that of Insurrection may be reached. Kansas has done this and it has also educated men for the work." Hinton presented abolitionists with scenes of carnage and the use of weapons that only recently they had believed their life's work was designed to avoid: "For one, believing in the right of resistance for myself, I extend the same to my African brother and stand ready at any time to aid in the overthrow of slavery by any and all means—the rifle or revolver, the dagger or torch."

Thomas Wentworth Higginson, a romantic young preacher who, as befitted a confidant of Brown, long had talked of revolution, joined Hinton in advocating a scheme to promote slave revolt. In doing so, he almost disclosed Brown's plan. Brown's recent raid into Missouri to free slaves, Higginson explained, was "an indication of what may come before long." Not long before, Higginson, like most other abolitionists, looked to the Underground Railroad as the most effective aid to slaves. He put that tactic behind him now. Slaves, declared Higginson, desired "not as formerly to go to freedom but to have freedom come to them. And who knows how speedily a morning may arise to show us that it has come?" The question hinted at impending events, for as Higginson knew, Brown already had designated himself as the agent who would carry freedom to the slaves.

Brown's plan coincided exactly with strategy outlined by James Redpath, a Scottish-born reporter who, like Hinton, had spent some time with Brown in Kansas. Redpath, then in his mid-twenties, was fascinated by revolution, particularly by black revolution. Slaves, he believed, were ready for the experience. Redpath claimed to have interviewed numerous black people, slave and free, during extended recent travels through Virginia, the Carolinas, Georgia, and Alabama. Almost without exception he found them eager to free themselves through insurrection. But they needed information, weapons, and—above all—assurance that northern whites would actively

22. Quarles, *Allies*, 72–80. The convention proceedings are in *Liberator*, February 4, 1859.

support them in the attempt. Slaves, wrote Redpath, possessed an "underground telegraph" that sped news the length and breadth of the South. A northern-led strike for liberty at any point along the southern border would bring mass desertion by the slaves and, probably, a violent servile uprising.[23]

On October 16, 1859, John Brown and his small band attacked the United States arsenal at Harpers Ferry in western Virginia in a futile attempt to start the rebellion that Redpath and a number of other abolitionists desired and believed imminent. Brown displayed little skill as a tactician, and slaves did not respond as he had been led to expect. There was only a thin slave population in the immediate area. At no time had Brown made any effort to acquaint even those few persons with his plan or what he expected of them. No slaves fled their masters to join Brown's band. Neither did nonslaveholding white Virginians cooperate as Lysander Spooner, and probably Brown too, had believed they would. The isolated conspirators were besieged and captured by government armed forces before Redpath's "underground telegraph" could do its work.[24]

Despite the total failure of his undertaking, Brown and those who shared his fascination with revolt made no error in their assessment of the slaves' desire for freedom. Events during the Civil War would prove, too, that they were not mistaken in believing many slaves would welcome invaders who came to sweep away the dominion of their masters. But they were wrong when they assumed that slaves would blindly undertake rebellion at the behest of white radicals whose talent for the undertaking was untested and whose goals and methods remained for the most part unknown to them. Slaves would not heed appeals to trust whites and accept their leadership simply because they lived in the North rather than the South. In the late summer of 1860, when "Mr. Ford" informed some slaves in South Carolina that "a man would come along between then & Christmas to set them free—with arms and would they fight," no answer was forthcoming. The slaves politely put him off: "They told him they would see about it."[25] Slaves had been in bondage for a

23. Redpath, *Roving Editor*, 286.
24. Oates, *To Purge This Land*, 290–306. Brown's plans may have embraced arming whites in western Virginia. See Craig M. Simpson, *A Good Southerner: The Life of Henry A. Wise of Virginia* (Chapel Hill, N.C., 1985), 208. For attitudes of white residents of Harpers Ferry, see Scarborough (ed.), *Diary of Edmund Ruffin*, I, 373.
25. Slave Trial, October 11, 1860, Pendleton/Anderson District, Court of Magistrates and Freeholders, Trial Papers, South Carolina Department of Archives and History, Columbia.

long time. They were willing to wait awhile longer for deliverance. They would judge matters for themselves and not let others determine the time, the place, or the occasion for their casting off of slavery.

Slaves understood the great preponderance of power that lay with white southerners. Among the enslaved blacks were individuals as brave—and sometimes as cowardly—as members of other races, and as willing to take risks, but through generations of subjection to force and terror, they had learned lessons in caution that would not be set aside casually. Experience and determination to survive caused them to heed the same internal command that prompted Garrison in 1859 to warn of the possible disastrous outcome of the stampede toward violence. Garrison remained unconvinced that it would be better to end slavery in a holocaust than to see its continuance. He did not believe that southern blacks would be better off dead than enslaved. "Where there is no life, there are no rights," he said.[26] Blacks who had seen countless of their fellow slaves sold, maimed, hanged, and burned for resisting bondage would have understood the wisdom of Garrison's words perhaps better than did the northern reformers to whom he addressed them.

Free blacks in the North, like white abolitionists, welcomed Brown into the lean ranks of the truly great as a martyr to the cause of liberty. Since few slaves had known anything of Brown's plans, it is not strange that little evidence appears of their concern for his fate. Yet impressions of his significance soon spread among them. When the slave William Summers fled from Charleston in the spring of 1862, he carried as one of his few treasures a picture of John Brown; some slaves in far-off Missouri knew of Brown's raid; and in Arkansas, Piomer Harshaw's mistress whipped her for singing a song about Brown.[27]

Although Brown's efforts brought almost no immediate slave response and were readily contained, his raid set new waves of fear in motion. It was easy to believe that this incident, itself trivial, heralded the doom of slavery. Papers found in Brown's possession suggested that his plans for slave revolt were not limited to northwestern Virginia but extended even to South Carolina, Georgia, and Florida.[28] Brown was dead, but others would follow, one might sup-

26. *Liberator*, February 4, 1859.
27. Blassingame (ed.), *Slave Testimony*, 700; Rawick *et al.* (eds.), *American Slave*: *Supplement, Series I*, Vol. VI, p. 2, and Vol. XII, p. 170.
28. Steven A. Channing, *Crisis of Fear*, 19–20, 268n.

pose, and with greater success. Harpers Ferry forecast the fate that awaited the South if abolitionists continued their agitation and if the Republican party gained ascendancy. Abortive though it was, Brown's raid made a large contribution to the crisis atmosphere that enveloped the section in 1860, the year of the nation's most fateful presidential contest.

Abraham Lincoln's election brought dissolution of the Union, an event that some northerners had convinced themselves never would take place. Continued faith in the likelihood of slave insurrection encouraged some in the North to discount the possibility that the southern states would dare make good their oft-repeated threat to secede. Abolitionists—or Republicans—might drive the South out of the Union, but rebellious slaves would force them to hurry back in for the sake of federal protection. Thomas Willis predicted that southern whites "would prove inadequate to defend themselves from the knife, and the torch, and the poison in the hands of their own slaves, and would come back like the prodigal son, to be re-admitted under the parental roof." Perhaps some southerners, too, felt misgivings as they considered the domestic consequences of secession. "In case of a *separation* . . . we may have some fighting to do at home," wrote Thomas H. Seymour just before he learned that his home state of South Carolina finally had left the Union.[29]

Such qualms, though real enough, soon were set aside, for Lincoln's election convinced southerners that they faced an ultimate crisis. Particularly in South Carolina, for years the center of southern disaffection, and in Alabama and Mississippi, politicians argued that Republican electoral triumph made the Union untenable. With much reason, they equated Republicans with abolitionists. For safety's sake, secession must come. It must come quickly, and it must be carried through with little debate. Discussion "in field and fireside," warned the Clayton (Alabama) *Banner* shortly before election day, "will only end in servile insurrections. Already the mere Presidential canvass is provoking them everywhere. The direct question of Union or Division . . . will inevitably give them birth."[30]

Lincoln's election proved that the slave states had declined to the

29. Burton Alva Konkle, *The Life and Speeches of Thomas Williams . . . 1806–1872* (Philadelphia, 1905), II, 428; Thomas H. Seymour to Milledge Luke Bonham, December 30, 1859, in Milledge Luke Bonham Collection. For doubts of the loyalty of poorer whites, see Scarborough (ed.), *Diary of Edmund Ruffin*, II, 187–89.

30. Quoted in William L. Barney, *The Secessionist Impulse: Alabama and Mississippi in 1860* (Princeton, N.J., 1974), 206.

position of being a hopeless minority within the nation. Henceforth they could not expect to set federal policy or to protect themselves for long against hostile legislation. Under Republican control, the Union no longer offered the South tangible advantage. On the contrary, it now posed a threat more menacing than any yet encountered, for the young, aggressive Republican party might be expected to extend its organization throughout the South. By use of the patronage, the Lincoln administration would create a Republican party in the slave states. Who could doubt that the material for such a structure lay readily at hand in the form of nonslaveholders who would trade allegiance to the planters—and slavery—for office and preferment? Behind the anxieties such a prospect generated lay the slaves who could not be kept in subjection and at work once division over fundamental issues erupted among the white population.[31]

Omens emerged during the presidential campaign. As the election of 1860 drew near, slaves, who long had followed the course of national events, came to see their future at stake in the contest. In testimony given at Spartanburg, South Carolina, on October 11, 1860, Robert Ott's slave Anderson was accused of "talking about being set free—said he expected the black people would have to fight and he would fight if he was obliged to." Ellis was still more eager; he "was going to get him a revolver and would be good for six white men." Dave told John that "the North was going to set all the Negroes free, and seemed to feel certain of the fact."[32]

Republican victory appeared to heighten both slave expectations and white apprehensions. In the spring of 1861, a vigilance committee in northern Alabama "ferreted out a most hellish insurrectionary plot among the slaves." By means of torture, authorities at Trion extracted confessions leading them to conclude that slaves believed "Lincoln is soon going to free them all, and they are everywhere making preparations to aid him when he makes his appearance." Near Petersburg, Virginia, slaves assumed that the election of Lincoln was the equivalent of emancipation. Following his inauguration, seventeen of them marched away from the plantation after announcing to their master that they were free. They soon were captured, however, and then sold out of the state.[33]

31. Eric Foner, "The Causes of the American Civil War: Recent Interpretations and New Directions," *Civil War History*, XX (1974), 209–10.

32. Slave Trial, October 11, 1860, Pendleton/Anderson District, Court of Magistrates and Freeholders, Trial Papers, South Carolina Department of Archives and History.

33. Clement Eaton, *A History of the Southern Confederacy* (New York, 1954), 245; *Liberator*, May 24, 1861.

Southerners could not believe that slaves would hold such ideas without artful indoctrination by outsiders. In 1860, at the height of the presidential campaign, rumor sped through the South of abolitionist agents infiltrating the section and inciting slaves to acts of vengeance. Originating in Texas and spreading across the entire South were reports of mounting slave discontent. To a dynamic group of southerners confronting that menace and long bent on revolution, secession appeared the only recourse. Secession admittedly could not guarantee the slaves' docility or end subversion, but it could make abolitionists and slaveholders citizens of separate nations, foreigners no longer bearing responsibility for the acts of their former countrymen. No longer would either group be subject to tyrannical imposition from the other.

Further, secession might offer a means to strengthen wavering sectional loyalties. In particular, it might halt the apparent movement of states in the upper South, most notably Kentucky and Maryland, into the ranks of the free states. The concern was not new. As early as 1821, a Georgia editor noted what appeared to him to be the lessening support for slavery in Virginia and Maryland. Will they not eventually "assume the tone of the northern states?" he asked. Might they not "at some remote period, join in a general crusade against the South?" The apprehension continued. "How long will Maryland, western Virginia, Kentucky, Eastern Tennessee and even the Western Part of North Carolina feel it their interest to retain slaves?" worried a South Carolinian in 1848. In 1859 a Mississippi jurist explained that Georgia, Alabama, and Mississippi in the early 1830s had enacted laws regulating the interstate slave trade because "it was feared that if these border States were permitted to sell us their slaves . . . *they too* would unite in the wild fanaticism of the day, and render the institution . . . thus reduced to a few Southern States, an easy prey to its wicked spirit."[34] Secession would promote southern solidarity. By associating slavery with a nation, southerners would restore to the institution the legitimacy it had lost throughout nearly all the western world. If separation risked much, as some asserted, and solved no fundamental problem, as others admitted, remaining in the Union offered only danger and enforced humility.

The course of the South toward secession was not in every in-

---

34. *Georgia Journal*, December 4, 1821, in Phillips (ed.), *Plantation and Frontier*, II, 69; David Johnson to John C. Calhoun, October 18, 1848, in Boucher and Brooks (eds.), *Correspondence Addressed to John C. Calhoun*, 482; Catterall (ed.), *Judicial Cases*, III, 361.

stance marked by such careful deliberation. The irrational note in the movement and evidence of its desperation can be discerned in emotion-distorted lines written by Representative Lawrence M. Keitt of South Carolina, whose brother recently had been murdered by the slaves on his Florida plantation: "If Lincoln is elected—what then? I am in earnest. I'd cut loose through fire and blood if nescessary [*sic*]—See—poison in the wells in Texas and fire for the Houses in Alabama—Our Negroes are being enlisted in politics—with poison and fire how can we stand it? I confess this new feature alarms me more than even everything in the past."[35] The prospect of a Republican-slave alliance was too much for Keitt and many other southerners to bear.

Countless rumors of slave plots and of actual revolts, presumably in response to the Republican victory, did indeed disturb the South in the weeks following the November election. A newspaper in the Alabama black belt reported that "most" slaves in the area "had heard that Lincoln was elected, and took for granted that they were to be free." The most venturesome among them were said to have declared their intention to join "Lincoln's army" as soon as he sent it south. It was generally agreed, too, that slaves had measured the fear sweeping the South and that even in tranquil neighborhoods slaves believed insurrections elsewhere either were planned or already were taking place.[36]

President James Buchanan gave official stamp to this concern in his fourth annual message on December 3, 1860, when he declared that "the increased and violent agitation of the slavery question" had produced a "malign influence on the slaves and inspired them with vague notions of freedom. Hence a sense of security no longer exists around the family altar. This feeling of peace at home has given place to apprehensions of servile insurrections."[37]

But the dreaded revolt did not come. In its place came intersectional war, with results fully as devastating to the South and its institutions.

35. Lawrence M. Keitt to James H. Hammond, September 10, 1860, in Steven A. Channing, *Crisis of Fear*, 269. On the murder of William J. Keitt, see C. Vann Woodward and Elisabeth Muhlenfeld (eds.), *The Private Mary Chesnut: The Unpublished Civil War Diaries* (New York, 1984), 181, 182.

36. Barney, *Secessionist Impulse*, 210–11; Aptheker, *American Negro Slave Revolts*, 355–58; Steven A. Channing, *Crisis of Fear*, 272.

37. Richardson (ed.), *Messages and Papers*, VII, 3157–58.

12

❦❦❦❦❦❦❦❦❦❦❦❦❦❦❦❦❦❦❦❦❦❦❦❦❦❦❦❦❦

The War of the Rebellion
1861–1865

The war that began with the Confederate shelling of Fort Sumter on April 12, 1861, was designated three days later by Abraham Lincoln as rebellion, and so by official usage it would be known. Union authorities chose not to view the conflict as a civil war, a "war between the states," or a "war for southern independence." Instead, according to them, it resulted from a combination of dissident individuals rebelling against the authority of the United States. But despite official sanction, the name never caught on—even Lincoln would speak of a "great civil war" in his Gettysburg Address of November 19, 1863. Yet "War of the Rebellion" acquires aptness extending beyond its origin in Lincoln's political theory when the conflict is viewed in its other, less familiar aspect. The war was not only a rebellion of white southerners against the Union. It also was a rebellion of slaves against masters or, more exactly, a rebellion of slaves against bondage.

The war assumed the character of a slave uprising, not at all in the horrific manner some had predicted, but gradually, with little overt violence on the part of slaves, and with such inevitability as rarely to provoke comment outside the Confederacy. Indeed, few in the North equated the conduct of blacks during the Civil War with insurrection. The lack of remark became the equivalent of popular acceptance of a great folk movement that occurred spontaneously without need for prompting or direction.

Slave revolt was more or less expected to follow withdrawal of federal authority from the South, or if not at that moment, then surely as soon as invading Union armies appeared. For obvious, prudential reasons, Confederate leaders chose not to dwell on this danger but simply denied its possibility: "Of themselves—moving by themselves—I say history does not chronicle a case of negro insurrection," Jefferson Davis had told the United States Congress on January 10, 1861. Northerners, however, and especially abolitionists, made much of the perilous situation secessionists created for themselves when they decided to dispense with federal protection. "Well, the time has come to expect a slave insurrection at any moment," wrote Garrison, and he promised it his "warmest sympathies."[1]

No doubt Garrison envisioned secession as producing an upheaval similar to the one that long ago had devastated Saint-Domingue. But Garrison would have trouble identifying slave behavior during the Civil War with his notion of revolt, for no blood-drenched uprising followed hard upon secession. From first to last, the slaves' response to war and invasion produced little of the lurid drama and practically none of the insurrectionary horror that for so long had been predicted.

Yet the conflict was hardly under way when slaves began to take advantage of the situation by shaking off white control and setting themselves free. Some did not join the movement until late in the war, and as happens in all revolutions, some took no part at all. The process of self-emancipation was most evident wherever Union armies appeared; it was least evident far from military action. In such places, slaves were likely to continue their usual routine almost as though a revolutionary war was not under way. Many remained in their master's service until the very end (thus providing basis for the "loyal Negro" tradition), while others, willingly or under coercion, aided the Confederate war effort as military laborers or in other capacities.[2] However much longed for, emancipation seemed to some an unreachable goal. "Us heard talk 'bout de war, but us didn't pay no 'tention," one former slave remembered. "Us

1. Dunbar Rowland (ed.), *Jefferson Davis, Constitutionalist: His Letters, Papers and Speeches* (Jackson, Miss., 1923), V, 30; *Liberator*, May 24, 1861.
2. For a comprehensive account, see Bell I. Wiley, *Southern Negroes, 1861–1865* (New Haven, Conn., 1938). Pertinent documents appear in Ira Berlin *et al.* (eds.), *The Destruction of Slavery* (New York, 1985); Vol. 1 of Berlin *et al.* (eds.), *Freedom: A Documentary History of Emancipation, 1861–1867, Series I*, 2 vols. to date.

never dreamed dat freedom would come."[3] The maintenance of traditional patterns of behavior while society crumbled and distant armies decided their fate no doubt in some instances reflected ignorance as much as it did lethargy and unconcern. But except in areas reached by the Union army, even slaves who desperately wanted to be free and who understood the import of the war could not easily find a practical alternative to remaining in bondage. Although gravely weakened by invasion, the same forces that maintained slavery in peacetime continued to operate in wartime.

As war began, southern state governments moved to lessen the disruptive impact hostilities were expected to have on master-slave relationships. Despite urgent requests from Confederate headquarters for additional men and arms, some state governors early in 1861 decided to retain a home guard and a store of arms and ammunition under their exclusive control for use within the state, much as had been done during the Revolution and the War of 1812. So extensive was this precautionary policy during the first months of war that it produced shortages in the Confederate armies and weakened their fighting capacity.[4]

Even though state officials probably understood the military consequence of their decision, they nevertheless had to balance local exigencies with national needs. Pressure to yield to local concern was hard to resist. Nervous citizens in Mississippi urged the governor not to allow Confederate authorities to remove militia or volunteers. In Georgia, citizens planned to request officials to leave enough forces at home "as will be sufficient to keep our colored population under supervision and control. . . . And also a force sufficient to give assurance and confidence of protection."[5] The same considerations may have hindered recruitment as well. Confronted by the dual threats of slave unrest and Yankee invasion, one Missis-

---

3. Rawick (ed.), *American Slave*, VI, 131. See also Rawick *et al.* (eds.), *American Slave: Supplement, Series I*, Vol. X, pp. 2022–23, 2070.

4. Frank Lawrence Owsley, *State Rights in the Confederacy* (Chicago, 1925), 6; Eaton, *History of the Southern Confederacy*, 263; Steven A. Channing, *Crisis of Fear*, 272. Armstead Robinson, "In the Shadow of Old John Brown: Insurrection Anxiety and Confederate Mobilization, 1861–1863," *Journal of Negro History*, LXV (1980), 279–97.

5. Clement Eaton, *Freedom of Thought in the Old South* (Durham, N.C., 1940), 105–106; C. C. Jones to R. Q. Mallard, November 30, 1861, in Robert M. Myers (ed.), *Children of Pride: A True Story of Georgia and the Civil War* (New Haven, Conn., 1972), 804. For the role of Georgia blacks in the war, see Clarence L. Mohr, *On the Threshold of Freedom: Masters and Slaves in Civil War Georgia* (Athens, Ga., 1986).

sippi resident set "to thinking where I could be of the most service to my County *at home* or *in the army* you will see nothing but eternal Vigilance will keep down the enemy at home as well as *at* our frontier."[6]

As white citizens became soldiers, civilians believed, slavery perceptibly changed. A warning reached the Mississippi governor from Jackson in August, 1861, that if more men were taken from the county, "we may as well give it to the negroes . . . now we have to patrole every night to keep them down." Even patrols did not always prove effective. In July, 1862, at Harrisonville, Georgia, citizens petitioned the governor to quarter soldiers in the county. Fifty-one slaves—"traitors . . . the worst of spies"—had run to the Federals. The petitioners understood why: "The temptation of *cheap goods, freedom, and paid labor* cannot be withstood."[7]

Despite such disruption, means still were at hand in most places for maintenance of the slave system. Especially during the first half of the war, soldiers sometimes remained temporarily in camps within the state while they were being assembled prior to transfer to the field. Since these men now were organized in military units and were armed, their capacity to maintain order was enhanced rather than diminished by their absence from home. While soldiers could not punish the slaves' ordinary day-to-day infractions, they could be deployed as needed to crush any coordinated outbreak.[8]

Regular slave patrols for the most part ceased to function in the summer of 1861, when the men who filled their ranks joined the armies. Thus the principal force that always had impeded free movement of slaves disappeared, but the efforts of very young men and of men beyond military age partly made up the deficiency. In plantation regions such persons, organized as home guards, mounted pickets, and vigilance committees took the place of slave patrols and helped prevent unauthorized movement and assembly of slaves. While evidence was plentiful that slave dissidence increased, the white population generally succeeded in containing it within manageable limits, even resorting to ruthless means to do so.

6. J. D. L. Davenport to Governor J. J. Pettus, May 14, 1861, quoted in Aptheker, *American Negro Slave Revolts*, 364; Eaton, *Freedom of Thought*, 105–106.

7. Wiley, *Southern Negroes*, 36; C. C. Jones to C. C. Jones, Jr., July 10, 1862, in Myers (ed.), *Children of Pride*, 929–30.

8. Bassett, *Slavery in the State of North Carolina*, 108–109; Eaton, *History of the Southern Confederacy*, 245–46.

Brutal reprisals against defiant slaves continued as before the war, thereby restating the old lesson that white power was not to be flouted. "There is a great disposition among the Negroes to be insubordinate, and to run away and go to the federals," reported a Confederate official at Natchez in 1862. "Within the last 12 months we have had to hang some 40 for plotting an insurrection, and there has been about that number put in irons." A Louisiana planter wrote: "Things are just now beginning to work right—the negroes hated to go to work again. Several have been shot and probably more will have to be."[9] Those slaves had tested the planters' power and determination and found them still strong. Thus, except in places where the presence of Union armies effectively counterbalanced southern military power, slaves remained under coercion. They had little more chance of freeing themselves than before war began. Not until outside support appeared could revolt in the form of mass desertion occur.

The presence of a foreign foe always had provided the acid test of slavery, as southerners learned during the Revolution and again in the War of 1812. The effect of invasion proved no less severe in 1861. With the advance of Union armies, thousands of slaves, often in family units, deserted their owners to seek protection in the camps of the invaders, thereby becoming, in General Benjamin F. Butler's odd phrase, "contraband of war."[10] Distance from Union forces was a powerful obstacle to flight but not an insuperable one, as a slaveholder in the hills of northwestern Georgia revealed when he advertised for three runaways who he believed were heading west to join the Yankees at Corinth. Most slaves located so far from Union lines risked no such perilous journeys. Instead, they stayed where they were, though they still might manifest disloyalty by performing their prescribed duties reluctantly or not at all. Uncle Tom in Alabama provided an example of such behavior. When Union soldiers arrived at the plantation, he first led them to the horses and mules he had helped his master hide and then joined the soldiers in ran-

9. Herbert Aptheker, "Notes on Slave Conspiracies in Confederate Mississippi," *Journal of Negro History*, XXIX (1944), 76; John H. Ransdell to Governor Thomas O. Moore, May 26, 1863, in G. P. Whittington (ed.), "Concerning the Loyalty of Slaves in Northern Louisiana in 1863: Letters from John H. Ransdell to Governor Thomas O. Moore, Dated 1863," *Louisiana Historical Quarterly*, XIV (1931), 494.

10. On the origin of the term, see James G. Randall and David Donald, *The Civil War and Reconstruction* (2nd ed., rev.; Lexington, Mass., 1969), 371n.

sacking the plantation house. "He hadn't been much good to massa since de war commenced," a former slave remembered. "Lay off in de swamp mos' of de time."[11]

The mass flight of slaves from plantations to Union lines, an acceleration of the folk movement that abolitionists and northern free blacks had encouraged for years, was in itself rebellion, even though little violence accompanied it. Blacks in effect declared themselves free and, usually without raising a hand against their owners, simply walked away from slavery. The significance of this movement—its equivalence to rebellion—was not lost on slaveholders. The Reverend Charles C. Jones in Georgia speculated on a possible remedy in the form of harsh legal sanctions: "Could their overt rebellion in the way of casting off the authority of their masters be made by construction insurrection?" he asked.[12] Perhaps it was at Jones's urging that a committee in Liberty County, Georgia, requested officials to extend martial law to runaway slaves. "The negroes constitute a part of the body politic in fact," they reasoned, "and should be made to know their duty; that they are perfectly aware that the act which they commit is one of rebellion against the power and authority of their owners and the Government under which they live."[13] But such proposals were at best quixotic, for the time had nearly passed when law or even the threat of summary punishment could do much toward maintaining in blacks the attitudes essential to slavery. Paternalism had had its day.

By their willingness to serve the invaders as guides, spies, informers, laborers, and—as soon as Union policy allowed—soldiers, the contrabands left no doubt about their rejection of their former owners and their owners' government. By the third summer of war, southern white soldiers found themselves facing armed blacks, most of them former slaves, wearing uniforms of the Union army. At the moment northern blacks and southern contrabands took up arms against the military forces of their former masters, the Civil War unquestionably assumed the character of controlled, black insurrection.

All this happened, it must be noted, almost solely at the initiative

---

11. Rome *Weekly Courier*, September 19, 1862, cited in Paul D. Escott, "The Context of Freedom: Georgia's Slaves During the Civil War," *Georgia Historical Quarterly*, LVIII (1974), 84; Rawick (ed.), *American Slave*, VI, 78.

12. Jones to C. C. Jones, Jr., July 21, 1862, in Myers (ed.), *Children of Pride*, 935.

13. *The War of the Rebellion: A Compilation of the Official Records of the Union and Confederate Armies* (130 vols.; Washington, D.C., 1880–1901), Ser. IV, Vol. II, p. 37.

of slaves themselves. The Union government designed no policies aimed at producing such a response. At the start of hostilities, Lincoln's administration had drawn no plan to deprive planters of their labor and property, to incite social disorder within the South, or to arm slaves. But by the summer of 1862, it found itself doing each of these things, if only by indirection.

Every earlier enemy—the French, the Spanish, the English—had been quick to exploit slave discontent as a weapon to hamper and embarrass American military effort. Among all the foes American slaveholders ever faced, only the Union, as a matter of policy, declined to do this. The self-denial appears the more remarkable because, of all the planters' enemies, the Union was the only one with an antislavery reputation, the only one headed by the leader of an antislavery political party, the only one whose professed ideology might have been expected to produce an emancipationist policy as a matter of course.

Contradictions early became apparent. The decades of intersectional discord that preceded secession and war vested the northern invaders with an ideological quality absent from the South's earlier enemies. Southerners, black and white alike, viewed the Yankees as antislavery agents. But by no means did all Yankees view themselves that way. When Union commanders prepared to launch their first incursions into the Confederacy, Generals George B. McClellan and Robert Patterson undertook to remove any impression that they commanded armies of liberation. They issued proclamations assuring slaveholding Unionists of their lack of revolutionary purpose and of their readiness to put down the revolt their presence might encourage. They renounced any plan to forge political and military alliances with slaves, though the expediency of doing so must have been obvious to them. When General Butler marched his army from Annapolis to Washington in April, 1861, he, too, made his intent unmistakably clear. He informed the governor of Maryland of his readiness to help suppress slave uprisings in the state.[14]

With no trace of gratitude, Governor Thomas Hicks reported himself fully capable of controlling the situation without Yankee aid. Butler's message to Hicks produced intense editorial controversy in the North, thereby revealing support in some quarters for the instigation of slave revolt. Predictably, Garrison preached his customary

14. *Ibid.*, Ser. I, Vol. II, pp. 47–48, 662; *Liberator*, May 17, 1861; *War of the Rebellion*, Ser. I, Vol. II, p. 593.

editorial sermon in the *Liberator*—this time a reprimand—with Butler supplying the text. "General Butler supposes himself to be better than a negro slave," wrote Garrison. "He is no better. He assumes to have a better right to freedom: he has none. . . . Men who glory in Bunker Hill and Yorktown must not deny to the oppressed any of the means necessary to secure their freedom, whatever becomes of their oppressors."[15]

Such statements, though consistent with abolitionist principle, ignored long-standing and widely shared dread of black insurrection, but more important, they also ignored Lincoln's declared purpose in waging the War of the Rebellion. Lincoln had issued his call for seventy-five thousand volunteers to restore the Union, not to free the slaves or to ruin the planters. Although a dynamic element in the North long had sought any opportunity to end slavery and eliminate planter influence from national affairs, only slowly did Lincoln come to share its revolutionary intent.[16]

Lincoln earlier had voiced a commitment to place slavery on the road to ultimate extinction; yet the war he conducted bore in its first phase little relation to that end. War was an accident. It had been forced on the Union by the planters' rebellion and their subsequent aggression. Union armies in 1861 drove into the South with no further political aim than to suppress white Rebels and thereby make the Union operable. Had slaves at that time misunderstood Union policy and managed to rise in open revolt, Union forces, it is possible to believe, would have joined Confederates in restoring order, as Butler in fact had promised to do in Maryland. "The forlorn hope of insurrection among the slaves may as well be abandoned," wrote the northern black journalist Robert Hamilton in the summer of 1861. "They are too well informed and too *wise* to court destruction at the hands of the combined Northern and Southern armies."[17]

The limited goal of political restoration could be achieved more quickly and at less cost, administration leaders supposed, if in the

15. *Liberator*, May 24, 1861. This issue contains commentary from other newspapers.

16. George M. Fredrickson, "A Man but Not a Brother: Abraham Lincoln and Racial Equality," *Journal of Southern History*, XLI (1975), 39–58; Don E. Fehrenbacher, "Only His Stepchildren: Lincoln and the Negro," *Civil War History*, XX (1974), 293–310.

17. Quoted in James M. McPherson, *The Negro's Civil War: How American Negroes Felt and Acted During the War for the Union* (New York, 1965), 42. For an instance of Federal suppression of slave violence, see Louis S. Gerteis, *From Contraband to Freedman: Federal Policy Toward Southern Blacks, 1861–1865,* (Westport, Conn., 1973), 114–15.

process race relations were left undisturbed. In particular, slave-holding Unionists in border states—who had committed no political offense—should not be further alienated and perhaps driven to join the secessionists. Lincoln hesitated for a long time to accept the logic of the Union's position with respect to both planters and slaves. "What I do about slavery, and the colored race," he would write in 1862, "I do because it helps to save the Union; and what I forbear, I forbear because I do *not* believe it would help to save the Union."[18] Unacceptable as black and white abolitionists found that statement, it accurately expressed the president's priorities and his assessment of political necessity.

A war against slavery was politically impossible in 1861. Lincoln understood the complexities of public opinion better than did most antislavery radicals, who were prone to ignore or simplify them. Secession drew a political line between the sections; yet the line imperfectly demarked contrasting interests and ideologies. Lincoln could never ignore the sizable body of states' rights, antiabolitionist, anti-Negro thought that flourished in the North. Its presence must be taken into account when determining policy, and nothing must be done that might mobilize its influence against the war for the Union. Garrison, too, had grasped this fact well before the war began, though he did not allow that insight to compromise his antislavery zeal. "If we fight with actual slaveholders in the South," he had written in January, 1859, "must we not also fight with pro-slavery priests, politicians, editors, merchants, in the North? Where are we to begin?"[19] The Union's long delay in acknowledging emancipation as a war aim was the practical consequence flowing from the problem Garrison had identified.

With their hostility to slavery in no way compromised by political necessity, abolitionists held to a far different conception of the war and its revolutionary possibilities than did Lincoln. The slaveholders' decision to dissolve the Union had added to their numbers and determination. "Lawyers and laymen who have never been willing to own that they were abolitionists now publicly and privately avow themselves such and say slavery must die," observed an antislavery northerner shortly before hostilities began. Further, the North con-

---

18. Abraham Lincoln to Horace Greeley, August 22, 1862, in Basler *et al.* (eds.), *Collected Works of Abraham Lincoln*, V, 388–89. LaWanda Cox, *Lincoln and Black Freedom: A Study in Presidential Leadership* (Columbia, S.C., 1981), places Lincoln in the vanguard of the movement for emancipation and equal rights for blacks.

19. *Liberator*, February 4, 1859.

tained a dynamic element of persons, not self-defined as abolitionists, who nevertheless agreed that the welfare and destiny of the
nation required destruction of the planters' power. The most direct
means to this end, they believed, was emancipation. A group within
the Republican party, reflecting both antislavery idealism and antiplanter bias, worked consistently toward that end. They joined
free blacks and abolitionists in directing merciless criticism against
Lincoln for what they regarded as his narrow conception of the war
and his hesitancy to exploit its opportunities.[20]

Military operations and the conduct of slaves themselves had the
effect of supporting the critics' war aims rather than those of Lincoln, and in the end, his objections and reservations were swept
aside. Despite official rationale and political exigency, the Civil War
inevitably undermined slavery. But ideology and policy had less to
do with promoting this result than did slaves and the army itself,
and the result would have been much the same even had Lincoln
and the North not possessed an antislavery reputation well known
to many slaves.

Any "foreign" army operating on southern soil was certain to unsettle master-slave relationships, for the masters' enemies, whoever
they might be, were the slaves' friends. If invaders sought to "use"
slaves, slaves viewed invaders as instruments for accomplishing
their own purpose. But the Union army's disruptive effect and the
use resistant slaves could make of it became greater on account of
decisions made by some of its officers early in the war. In disregard
of Lincoln's hands-off policy toward slavery, a few military commanders took a position far in advance of his. The most conspicuous
dissident was General John C. Fremont, the Republican party's first
presidential candidate, who then commanded the Western Department. On August 30, 1861, Fremont proclaimed martial law in Missouri and declared the slaves of every Rebel in the state free.[21] The
action accorded with Fremont's own antislavery convictions; it also
was appropriate to an invader bent on wounding the enemy by resort to whatever weapon lay at hand. Lord Dunmore had acted simi-

20. E. Andrus to the secretary, American Missionary Association, April 1, 1861, in
American Missionary Association Archives; Kenneth M. Stampp, *"And the War
Came": The North and the Secession Crisis, 1860–1861* (Baton Rouge, 1950), traces the
influence of these groups. For their later activity, see T. Harry Williams, *Lincoln and
the Radicals* (Madison, Wis., 1965).
21. *War of the Rebellion*, Ser. I, Vol. III, pp. 466–67. For an assertion of the Union
Army's central role in emancipation, see Dwight Lowell Dumond, *America's Shame
and Redemption* (Marquette, Mich., 1965), 47–48, 90–93.

larly when confronting slaveholding rebels in Virginia in 1775, but Lincoln declined to be Lord Dunmore. He modified Fremont's proclamation in order to make it accord with Congress' First Confiscation Act of August 6, which held that only Rebel-owned slaves actually used in prosecution of the rebellion would be subject to confiscation, though not necessarily freed. When in May, 1862, General David Hunter, also acting well in advance of official policy, declared the slaves in South Carolina, Georgia, and Florida free, Lincoln countermanded the order.[22]

Despite these early signs of reluctance, the Union moved inexorably toward an emancipationist policy. By terms of the Second Confiscation Act, July 17, 1862, Congress declared slaves of Rebel masters "forever free" as soon as they entered Union lines, and on September 22, Lincoln issued his preliminary Emancipation Proclamation, which announced that on January 1, 1863, all slaves in the states still in rebellion would be "forever free."[23] Thus, gradually and without show of enthusiasm, Lincoln adopted a position consistent with his political role as head of a nation whose majority adhered to the principles of free soil, free labor, and free men. Yet no subsequent development quite removed the impression that the proclamation was primarily a political and military measure rather than an ideological and humanitarian one. It did not, for instance, apply to the loyal border slave states—or even to some parts of the seceded ones—any more than Dunmore's proclamation of 1775 to slaves in Virginia had applied to England's loyal slaveholding colonies in the West Indies.

Southern whites chose to interpret the Emancipation Proclamation as being a signal for slave insurrection.[24] Slaves, of course, did not respond in such fashion, and it should go without saying that Lincoln did not intend that they should. On the contrary, he recognized and attempted to counter the proclamation's potential for creating unmanageable servile unrest. Thus, included in the document

22. Abraham Lincoln to John C. Fremont, September 2, 1861, and September 11, 1861, in Basler *et al.* (eds.), *Collected Works of Abraham Lincoln*, IV, 506–507, 517–18; "Proclamation Revoking General Hunter's Order of Military Emancipation of May 9, 1862," May 10, 1862, *ibid.*, V, 222–23.

23. *Ibid.*, V, 433–36. John Hope Franklin, *The Emancipation Proclamation* (Garden City, N.Y., 1963); Hans Trefousse, *Lincoln's Decision for Emancipation* (Philadelphia, 1975).

24. Richmond *Enquirer*, October 1, 1862; James L. Roark, *Masters Without Slaves: Southern Planters in the Civil War and Reconstruction* (New York, 1977), 74–76; C. C. Jones, Jr., to C. C. Jones, September 27, 1862, in Myers (ed.), *Children of Pride*, 967.

was counsel to slaves to refrain from violence "unless in necessary self-defense," as well as admonition to work faithfully if reasonable wages were offered. By ruining the planters, emancipation would constitute revolution, but Lincoln did not intend it to produce anarchy. Neither the planters nor the staple-crop economy was to be destroyed in a reign of terror (if slaves had any such inclination), and emancipated slaves, it appeared, must work for others rather than possess the soil.

By the time Lincoln issued the Emancipation Proclamation, thousands of slaves already had stopped working on plantations and had associated themselves with Union military forces, either as laborers or as soldiers, a development that would have considerable political and military significance to both North and South. As soon as the war began, abolitionists and northern free blacks had called upon Congress to acknowledge the right of black men to enlist in the Union army. Blacks must take part, they argued, if the conflict were to lead to popular acceptance of their freedom and expanded rights. "Every race has fought for Liberty and its own progress," explained John A. Andrew, antislavery governor of Massachusetts. "If Southern slavery should fall by the crushing of the Rebellion, and colored men should have no hand and play no conspicuous part in the task, the result would leave the colored man a mere helot."[25] Arming of the blacks would recognize them as allies, if not equal partners, in war against the planters.

The cogency of the argument did not prevent objections. Critics pointed out especially the damaging effect black enlistment might be expected to have on the morale of white soldiers, who were assumed to be severely afflicted with racial prejudice, and they repeated allegations of the blacks' incapacity to fight. But looming as a large objection, too, was the prospect that their enlistment would incite insurrection. Upon seeing fellow blacks in arms, slaves would rise up in fury against the white population—so warned Senator Garrett Davis of Kentucky, who spoke of "insurrectionary war" as "a practical question." Blacks who in the 1850s commonly were depicted by slaveowners as docile and unthreatening became, in Davis' exposition, fiends. Figures of savagery laced his rhetoric. He spoke of the black's cruelty and of the "latent tiger fierceness

---

25. Quoted in James M. McPherson, *The Struggle for Equality: Abolitionists and the Negro in the Civil War and Reconstruction* (Princeton, N.J., 1964), 204.

in his heart . . . when he becomes excited by a taste of blood he is a demon."[26]

These were powerful arguments indeed, but Lincoln heeded them only to the extent of agreeing that enlistment of black troops would exploit southern fears and thus further damage Confederate morale. "The bare sight of fifty thousand armed, and drilled black soldiers on the banks of the Mississippi, would end the rebellion at once," he wrote. Military necessity, as Lincoln's comment suggests, eventually overcame all other considerations, and on July 17, 1862, Congress authorized the enlistment of blacks as soldiers. A month later, General Rufus Saxton, commander of the Department of the South, received permission to recruit five black regiments in the South Carolina Sea Islands. In March, 1863, the secretary of war authorized Adjutant General Lorenzo Thomas to recruit black regiments in the lower Mississippi Valley, and in May the War Department established the Bureau of Colored Troops to supervise the raising of black regiments in every part of the country. "By arming the negro we have added a powerful ally," commented General Ulysses S. Grant.[27] It was equally true that Negroes found in the Union army a powerful ally in their incessant struggle against enslavement.

By the time Congress allowed free blacks in the North to enlist, their martial enthusiasm—as well as that of the whites—had declined. Free black men did not rush to join the Union armies. By the midsummer of 1862, the war had entered a costly phase and much of its romance had vanished. The Emancipation Proclamation had not yet been issued, and it was by no means certain that the Union intended to end slavery. Discrimination in pay and perhaps in treatment further discouraged black enlistment, as did the prospect of serving under white officers. The Confederate government's threat to treat captured black soldiers as traitors and insurrectionists rather than as prisoners of war was another deterrent. It is likely, too, that to former slaves, army discipline and plantation discipline

26. McPherson, *Negro's Civil War*, 163–64; *Congressional Globe*, 37th Cong., 2nd Sess., Pt. 4, p. 3204. Garrison described the blacks as "not of a savage nature, but remarkably docile, patient, slow to wrath, reluctant to shed blood, forbearing and forgiving to a wonderful degree." *Liberator*, May 24, 1861.

27. Abraham Lincoln to Andrew Johnson, March 26, 1863, in Basler *et al.* (eds.), *Collected Works of Abraham Lincoln*, VI, 149–50; Grant to Abraham Lincoln, August 23, 1863, in McPherson, *Negro's Civil War*, 191. On proposals for the Union's promoting actual slave rebellion, see Wiley, *Southern Negroes*, 83, and Mohr, *On the Threshold of Freedom*, 218.

appeared so similar as to evoke unpleasant memories. The Georgia-born historian Ulrich Bonnell Phillips, while working at a United States Army camp in 1918, commented on the similarities of the life of blacks as soldiers and as slaves: "The negroes are not enslaved but drafted; they dwell not in cabins but in barracks; they shoulder the rifle, not the hoe."[28] There is every reason to suppose that blacks a half century or more before Phillips wrote also saw these resemblances, with resultant check to their martial fervor.

In the South, recruitment was more successful, for there in occupied territory Union commanders sometimes used their power to round up blacks and bring them into the army with little evidence of consent being required, a procedure that, according to General Saxton, produced "universal confusion and terror." Charlie Aarons in Mississippi remembered that he hid out in the swamps for fear of being impressed into the Union army.[29] Others, for much the same reason, may have decided to remain on the plantations and under their owner's control longer than they otherwise would have thought desirable.

After Congress instituted conscription in 1863, several northern state governments sent their own recruiting agents into the South in hopes of filling state troop quotas with blacks. The recruiters' successes were matched by their failures. Blacks sometimes showed little eagerness to accept the agents' offers. When an agent in Mississippi offered Berry Smith a chance to enlist, Smith remembered, "I tol' 'em I wasn't no rabbit to live in de woods." An Illinois agent reported similar rebuffs: "'Oh sir,' say some, 'I would rather be a slave all my days than go to war. I cant shoot nor I don't want to shoot Any Buddy. I cant fight.'" General William Tecumseh Sherman viewed the state agents much as blacks did—"as the new master that threatens him with a new species of slavery." Yet of the 178,975 blacks who served in the Union army, 99,337 were recruited within the Confederacy.[30]

Enlistment of blacks was thought to serve an indispensable mili-

28. McPherson, *Negro's Civil War*, 173–74; Phillips, *American Negro Slavery*, [ii].

29. Wiley, *Southern Negroes*, 309–10; Rufus Saxton to Edwin M. Stanton, December 30, 1864, in *War of the Rebellion*, Ser. III, Vol. IV, p. 1028; Rawick (ed.), *American Slave*, VI, p. 4; Gerteis, *From Contraband to Freedman*, 143.

30. Rawick *et al.* (eds.), *American Slave: Supplement, Series I*, Vol. X, p. 1981; John Hope Franklin (ed.), *Diary of James T. Ayres, Civil War Recruiter* (Springfield, Ill., 1947), 46; *War of the Rebellion*, Ser. I, Vol. XLVII, Pt. 2, p. 37; Frederick H. Dyer, *A Compendium of the War of the Rebellion Compiled and Arranged from Official Records . . .* (Des Moines, 1908), ll.

tary purpose. "All our increased military strength now comes from the negroes," wrote Gideon Welles, Lincoln's secretary of the navy, in January, 1863. Enlistment also lessened whatever possibility there was that the great numbers of blacks who had freed themselves or been freed from plantation discipline would become dangerously violent. Enrolling blacks in the army helped assure order by placing them again under white control.[31]

Most slaves, of course, experienced war as civilians, not as soldiers. War offered those not in the armies opportunity to gain advantage within the slave system, to escape from it, even to help destroy it, but in most instances the occasion for realizing these opportunities did not appear immediately. In early 1862, the slave Alek in South Carolina declared that "he was going to wait until all the men went away & he would do as he pleased." In large parts of the Confederacy, traditional authority persisted for a long time, a fact Alek evidently recognized, even as he felt the lessening of white-imposed pressure. When overseers and owners left for Confederate service, the absence of accustomed control invited a loosening of discipline. Slaves would not work without overseers, the governor of Florida warned Jefferson Davis: "The result will probably be insubordination and insurrection." The prediction was fulfilled in part, for though insurrection did not occur, the goals of production and profit, which had set the slaves' routine, receded from their lives. When white men rode away for the last time, slaves found it easier than before to conduct their daily affairs in ways pleasing to themselves. Common report held that under the supervision only of women, slaves worked less efficiently, became more insolent, and were harder to control. But male overseers, too, found their usual problems of exacting labor from unwilling bondsmen vastly greater than before.[32]

31. Howard K. Beale (ed.), *Diary of Gideon Welles, Secretary of the Navy Under Lincoln and Johnson* (New York, 1960), I, 324; Blassingame (ed.), *Slave Testimony*, 368; Gerteis, *From Contraband to Freedman*, 5, 72, 96, 146, 164–66; William F. Messner, "Black Violence and White Response: Louisiana, 1862," *Journal of Southern History*, XLVI (1975), 19–38.

32. Slave Trial, March 3, 1862, Pendleton/Anderson District, Court of Magistrates and Freeholders, Trial Papers, South Carolina Department of Archives and History; *War of the Rebellion*, Ser. IV, Vol. II, p. 401. The breakdown of plantation discipline is described in William Kauffman Scarborough, *The Overseer: Plantation Management in the Old South* (Baton Rouge, 1966), 138–57. See also Harvey Wish, "Slave Disloyalty Under the Confederacy," *Journal of Negro History*, XXIII (1938), 435–50, and Drew Gilpin Faust, *James Henry Hammond and the Old South: A Design for Mastery* (Baton Rouge, 1982), 368–70.

As a means of maintaining discipline and assuring crop production, the Confederate Congress on October 11, 1861, enacted legislation releasing and exempting from military service planters or their overseers supervising twenty or more slaves, a number later reduced to fifteen. The purpose, according to the act, was "to secure the proper police of the country." Under its terms, some three thousand men received exemptions. The extent to which the measure achieved its stated aim cannot be determined. What it certainly did do, however, was to supply a slogan for political dissidents. As the symbol of "a rich man's war and a poor man's fight," the exemption law made operative the class divisions that had long troubled persons aware of the necessity in a slaveholding society of maintaining white solidarity. The exemption law accompanied and justified faltering support for the Confederate cause.[33]

Even though the absence of white men from plantation areas encouraged shirking and "insolence" among slaves, their loose behavior amounted to little more than intensification of customary resistance. It rarely erupted into overt rebellion. Slaves might become insubordinate, substituting their own values for those of the masters, but until the Union army drew near, they could not easily abandon their owners. "We heard about de Yankees was fighten' to free us, but we didn't believe it until we heard about de fightin' at Vicksburg," recalled one former Mississippi slave.[34]

During much of the war, slaves far from Union lines could do little to hasten the coming day of freedom except to meet together away from the eyes of the nearby whites and pray for deliverance. But an earthly source of hope appeared in the form of news from the battlefield. Slaves took pleasure and encouragement from even small signs of Confederate difficulty and welcomed the South's reverses as opportunity to improve their own circumstance. Rumors of Confederate losses and evidence of political disaffection among whites imparted courage and thereby furthered slave resistance. In Lexington County, South Carolina, Confederates organized a "dog company," which used bloodhounds to track down army deserters, much as they tracked down fugitive slaves. The practice evidently was known to slaves in nearby Anderson County, where Alek was accused of "making a plan to raise an insurrection." The Yankees were winning, he told his friends, and the Confederate army had started

---

33. Eaton, *History of the Southern Confederacy*, 86. The standard treatment is Albert B. Moore, *Conscription and Conflict in the Confederacy* (New York, 1924).
34. Rawick *et al.* (eds.), *American Slave: Supplement, Series I*, Vol. X, p. 1986.

to crumble. Deserters were hiding out in the town of Anderson, white men schemed to evade military service, and "Dr. Hill" had been obliged to beat the bushes for more recruits. Confederate authorities planned to "Handcuff all that would not go & take them to Columbia . . . & take them to the army [and] they were going to give a man 100 lashes" if he failed to enlist. Alek thought that "if they were all gone they would see better times."[35] But whatever hopes such rumors brought, coordinated resistance by a still unarmed labor force that was divided among scattered plantations remained all but impossible. Even invasion and southerners' absorption in life-or-death conflict changed this circumstance only slowly.

From one point of view, the Civil War experience confirmed the wisdom of John C. Calhoun's prediction made many years earlier that during war slavery would be even more secure than in periods of peace. Lincoln, too, believed insurrection unlikely. "The society of the Southern States is now constituted on a basis entirely military," he told John Hay in November, 1863. "It would be easier now than formerly to repress a rising of unarmed and uneducated slaves." But, he added, should peace be restored and secession prove permanent, then slaves almost certainly would rebel.[36] These observations, however shrewd, proved largely irrelevant, for what both Lincoln and Calhoun overlooked was the change that military invasion produced in the slaves' attitudes.

Vital to slavery was the slave's recognition of the superior coercive power available to the master. That power disappeared when Union armies overran slaveholding areas. To the extent that slavery also depended upon the slave's recognition of the master's moral authority, that too was gone. Yankee guns now ruled. Union military force stripped the master of both physical authority and the right to command. He stood as naked before his enemy as the slave formerly had stood before him. He was master no longer, and without masters there can be no slaves. No military or political power would have been competent to restore prewar relationships.

When Union soldiers arrived in a plantation area, slaves saw that the ties that had bound them to their owners were severed. The

35. *Ibid.*, VI, 202, 249; Frank Wysor Klingberg, *The Southern Claims Commission* (Berkeley, Calif., 1955), 104; Slave Trial, March 3, 1862, Pendleton/Anderson District, Court of Magistrates and Freeholders, Trial Papers, South Carolina Department of Archives and History.

36. *Annals of Congress*, 12th Cong., 1st Sess., 480; Abraham Lincoln to John Hay, November 24, 1863, in Carl Sandburg, *Abraham Lincoln: The War Years* (New York, 1939), II, 27.

revelation first became evident early in November, 1861, with the arrival of a Union fleet off the Sea Islands of South Carolina. Master-slave relationships were immediately revolutionized in what had been one of the richest of all the South's plantation areas. The masters fled the islands. The slaves who remained behind looted the houses of their former masters and destroyed the cotton gins. The influence of that transformation extended beyond the area of actual Federal occupation to slaves in other parts of South Carolina and into Georgia as well.[37]

Events in the lower Mississippi Valley in 1862 and 1863 likewise illustrate the electric effect of this change. In August, 1862, the overseer at Magnolia Plantation in Louisiana boasted that not even "Horace Greeley could get up an insurrection among the negroes here." His confidence was short-lived. As soon as slaves learned that a Union army had occupied New Orleans and that another was advancing from the north, their former subservience gave way to what the overseer called "insolence." They set a new labor routine for themselves. They would work in the fields for a few hours in the morning, then stop for the afternoon. On October 14, the women at Magnolia Plantation confronted the overseer with their decision to do no more field work at all until he agreed to pay them ten dollars a month. A week later, the slaves built a gallows and gave "as an excuse for it that they are told they must drive their master . . . and Mr. Randall [the overseer] off the plantation, hang their master &c and that then they will be free." After slaves on a nearby plantation received arms from Union raiders, they drove the overseer away and "immediately rose and destroyed everything . . . in the house."[38]

Southern Louisiana came under Union control early in 1862, but a Confederate army still protected the rich plantations that lay in the central part of the state. These troops, together with an efficient home guard, kept most slaves at work under their owners' control. But when Union forces under General Nathaniel P. Banks reached Alexandria on May 6, 1863, great numbers of slaves immediately deserted the plantations and walked into town. Although the Union commanders accepted the fact of self-emancipation, they nevertheless set limits on acceptable behavior. Blacks might abandon their owners and to some extent even were encouraged to do so. They might appropriate property and—at least for a time—do as they pleased. But a campaign of retaliation against white civilians, had

37. Mohr, *On the Threshold of Freedom*, 68–70.
38. J. Carlyle Sitterson, "Magnolia Plantation, 1852–1862: A Decade of a Louisiana Sugar Estate," *Mississippi Valley Historical Review*, XXV (1938), 207–209.

one been projected, would not be tolerated. General Butler made this clear in his response to a report that insurrection had broken out near New Orleans and that white women had appealed to Union officers for protection. Attacks by blacks on white women and children, he announced, would be severely punished. As Butler's order suggests, Union officers maintained order and decorum among the black population, but their occasional attempts to bolster the planters' authority were less likely to succeed. Butler returned the blacks who ran away from David Pugh's plantation, but not even a general's command could make them slaves again. They refused to work and proceeded to assault both Pugh and his overseer.[39]

Such violent response was exceptional. White persons had little cause to fear physical attack from slaves during the Civil War. Their response to liberation generally took place within well-defined limits that excluded violence against persons except when whites attempted to restrain or coerce them, which had been Pugh's error.[40] Slaves doubtless harbored deep resentments toward their owners and perhaps toward other whites as well. Some evidently hated their oppressors, and in numerous instances bonds of interracial sympathy proved frail. Even trusted house servants whose owners had imagined them affectionate and loyal fled without the least show of regret and without saying good-bye. They were no respecter of persons. In June, 1862, Jefferson Davis announced the arrival of Mrs. Robert E. Lee in Richmond: "Her servants left her," he explained, "and she found it uncomfortable to live without them."[41] But the overriding motive among slaves was simply the desire to escape from slavery; few delayed their flight in order to inflict vengeance on whites. Even the most abused appear to have been satisfied merely to witness their owners' distress as Yankee armies approached. At last the tables were turned, and masters met a challenge too strong to hurl back. Blacks need not take part in the retribution in order to welcome it and reap its consequence.

39. *War of the Rebellion,* Ser. I, Vol. XV, p. 172; Benjamin F. Butler to Edwin M. Stanton, August 2, 1862, in Benjamin F. Butler, *Private and Official Correspondence of Benjamin F. Butler During the Period of the Civil War* (Norwood, Mass., 1917), II, 142.

40. When whites resorted to violence to restore slavery, blacks sometimes retaliated. See Blassingame (ed.), *Slave Testimony,* 359–60, and Gerteis, *From Contraband to Freedman,* 112–13. See also Bell I. Wiley, *The Plain People of the Confederacy* (Baton Rouge, 1943), 82.

41. Jefferson Davis to Mrs. Davis, June 13, 1862, in Rowland (ed.), *Jefferson Davis,* V, 278. Note the bitter postwar comment of a South Carolina planter: "The negros did not care as much about us as we did about them." Theodore Rosengarten, *Tombee: Portrait of a Cotton Planter, with the Journal of Thomas B. Chaplin 1822–1890* (New York, 1986), 348.

This does not mean that at the moment of liberation they could be counted on to remain stolid and, from the whites' point of view, well behaved. "The arrival of the advance of the Yankees alone turned the negroes crazy," wrote a Louisiana planter from south of Alexandria in 1863. "They became utterly demoralized at once and everything like subordination and restraint was at an end. All business was suspended and those that did not go on with the army remained at home to do *much worse*." What they did was not to turn on the whites who remained in the area, but rather to destroy the masters' property in the manner of primitive rebels, or else appropriate it for their own use. They stripped the plantation houses of furnishings, killed cattle, sheep, and hogs. They declared a holiday and wandered about the countryside. "No work was done and the place swarmed most of the time with negroes from other places," the Louisiana planter reported. Slaves on the rice plantations of South Carolina responded to Union invasion in virtually the same fashion.[42]

It would be a mistake to conclude from reports of such saturnalia that slaves always responded with jubilation or even approval to the Union presence. In an abstract sense, Yankee forces represented the idea of freedom and thus were the slaves' allies. Yet they came as conquerors and despoilers. Slaves could not easily identify freedom with the horsemen who rode through the countryside pillaging and violating their homes as well as great plantation houses. Besides being slaves and eager to be free, most blacks also were isolated rural people with strong attachment to place and property. Accordingly, they were likely to dread northern soldiers as aliens whose intentions they could not be certain of. Although they soon learned that Yankees would not sell them to Cuba, as their masters had warned, they still were slow to trust the invader. Northern men might be liberators, but that did not always make them friends. The soldiers' behavior sometimes did little to inspire confidence. When Union soldiers drove off the plantations' cows and horses and cleared storehouses of food, they left slaves as well as masters in want. They were as likely to appropriate the slaves' meager belongings as those of the masters. And Union soldiers sometimes abused slaves as outrageously as abolitionists charged was customary of southern whites. They also could be guilty of acts of wanton cruelty

42. Whittington (ed.), "Concerning the Loyalty of Slaves," 487–502. For similar reactions by South Carolina slaves, see Charles W. Joyner, *Down by the Riverside: A South Carolina Slave Community* (Urbana, Ill., 1984), 228–29, and Easterby (ed.), *South Carolina Rice Plantation*, 211.

that, though perhaps in themselves trivial, offended slaves and left an indelible impression on those who witnessed them. "When the soldiers got to the big road the flock of geese were crossing," Smith Simmons remembered long afterward. "Them soldiers shot every goose and left them there in the big road." Not even the passage of seventy years could blot out that sight.[43]

Violations of the blacks' sensibilities and autonomy were not always so haphazard, limited, and individualized as those mentioned. "There are to be *no more bondsmen and no more whippings*," was the army's welcome message to blacks in Georgia at war's end, but the limitations that hedged freedom soon were revealed. "A Yankee officer told the servants at the Creek this week," a planter's wife reported, "that they were to stay at home and work harder than they had ever done in their lives, and not run about and steal; that they had come to see that they behaved themselves." This Yankee demand for devotion to calling too closely resembled their masters' proscriptions to be received sympathetically. The blacks, Mrs. Buttolph continued, "were quite disgusted."[44]

As a matter of policy in some occupied regions, the army controlled the blacks' movement, confining them to plantations, forcing them to work, and punishing them for lapses of discipline, much as their former masters had done. Even in regions where official policy did not embrace army-managed plantations, Federal authorities sometimes provided support for a system of forced labor that closely resembled that of antebellum days. In Alabama, army officers and Freedmen's Bureau agents helped planters maintain order, even on some occasions detailing soldiers to restrain and punish recalcitrant laborers. When in the summer of 1865 Georgia planters found their efforts to produce a cotton crop threatened by "restless" blacks, they informed Federal authorities of the problem. Army headquarters at Albany responded: "Two Federals, in blue uniforms and armed, came out . . . and whipped every negro man reported to them, and in some cases unmercifully. . . . Another party visited Conquitt . . . and punished by suspending by the thumbs."

43. Franklin (ed.), *Diary of James T. Ayres*, 27; Charlotte Forten, "Life on the Sea Islands," *Atlantic Monthly*, XIII (May, 1864), 593; Joel Williamson, *After Slavery: The Negro in South Carolina During Reconstruction, 1861–1877* (Chapel Hill, N.C., 1965), 4, 13; Rawick *et al.* (eds.), *American Slave: Supplement, Series I*, Vol. II, p. 181, and Vol. X, pp. 1928, 2201; Escott, "The Context of Freedom," 92, 101; Bell I. Wiley, *The Life of Billy Yank, the Common Soldier of the Union* (Indianapolis, 1952), 114–15; Rawick *et al.* (eds.), *American Slave: Supplement, Series I*, Vol. X, p. 1940.

44. Laura E. Buttolph to Mary Jones, June 30, 1865, in Myers (ed.), *Children of Pride*, 1279.

The astounded blacks were heard to "whisper [that these were] only Southern men in blue clothes—that the true Yankee had not come yet." Doubtless both the disciplinary support given planters and the labor system Federal authorities established in some regions were designed to promote order and restore agricultural production, not primarily to repress blacks.[45] It also is true, however, that as a means of accomplishing the primary goals, repression was assumed to be both necessary and proper.

Impositions such as these destroyed neither the slaves' hopes for freedom nor their confidence in Lincoln as an emancipator. But how their hopes and confidence were to be realized remained uncertain. Blacks lived in terrible suspense throughout the war and Reconstruction. They saw everything around them being transformed, and with no more confidence than anyone else could they predict the form the new order would take. When the planters' world collapsed, so did that of the slaves. They simply did not know what to expect. Union victory assuredly had brought freedom, but no one, white or black, could say in 1865 exactly what that word meant.[46]

Few revolutions, as is well known, are all-embracing in their consequence. The new order contains survivals of the old. These remnants are modified and rearranged. Few altogether disappear. So it would be in the aftermath of the Civil War. The groups thrown on top may have supposed that they had won the privilege of sorting out from Old South survivals those that were to be accepted as consistent with the new order and those that were to be suppressed or allowed to die. But this was in large part illusion. Slavery had so profoundly affected everyone involved with it that its effects would endure well beyond the generation that saw its end. Thus the victors were not as free to mold the future immune from its influence as their triumph may have encouraged them to suppose. The freedmen and women had not been so abjectly crushed by bondage as their detractors and the detractors of their owners sometimes claimed, but it surely would be a mistake to claim that slavery had left no scars or that these were of no future consequence. Although blacks had cast off slavery, they had not managed to escape white domination. The freedmen soon discovered the rigid limits set on free-

45. Gerteis, *From Contraband to Freedman*, 100; Peter Kolchin, *First Freedom: The Response of Alabama's Blacks to Emancipation and Reconstruction* (Westport, Conn., 1972), 33; John Jones to Mary Jones, July 26, 1865, and August 21, 1865, in Myers (ed.), *Children of Pride*, 1282–83, 1292; Gerteis, *From Contraband to Freedman*, 96.

46. Rawick *et al.* (eds.), *American Slave: Supplement*, Series I, Vol. VII, p. 515, and Vol. X, pp. 2022–23, 2070. For conditions in one Confederate state, see John Cimprich, *Slavery's End in Tennessee, 1861–1865* (University, Ala., 1985), 118–31.

dom. In rising against their masters, they became clients of northern whites. Their revolt, it appeared, had served to advance the Union cause fully as much as it had advanced their own, and the interests of the two, as it proved, were considerably less than identical. Slaves were free, but they were still dependents. The old planters and others who thought like them had not been driven from the South, nor, for the most part, were their lands confiscated. Neither were they deprived for long of political power. The freedmen must find their place in a new free-labor system. They did not own the land, and no political policy was adopted to help them acquire it.

To blacks belonged a large share of credit for the defeat of the Confederacy.[47] As abolitionists had anticipated, they proved an indispensable auxiliary to the Union war effort. Black soldiers and military laborers gave the Union army vital support, lacking which the war almost certainly would have been prolonged and victory attained only at the expense of still greater sacrifice. But that was not the whole of their contribution. Especially in the first months of war, concern for slave discipline led southern state authorities to withhold men and supplies that might have gone to strengthen Confederate forces in the field. Later, as an expedient designed to maintain control over slaves, the Confederate congress exempted certain white men from military service, thereby weakening the Confederacy by antagonizing nonslaveholders and activating previously latent class conflict.[48] Further, the wartime derangements undergone by the slave system, and the common understanding by southern whites that restoration of the system was impossible, contributed to their sense that continued resistance had no purpose.

Important as these developments were in hastening the Confederate downfall, one might argue that they were more the consequence of the mere existence of slavery as an institution than of the slaves' will. But the calculated decisions of black men and women likewise contributed—and in a devastating way—to Confederate defeat. By rebelling against slavery and fleeing their owners, they crippled agricultural production, shattered the social structure, and destroyed the principal purpose for which secession was undertaken—the preservation of slavery and the status of slaveholders.

47. The themes presented in the next two paragraphs are developed fully in Armstead Robinson, "Day of Jubilo: Civil War and the Demise of Slavery in the Mississippi Valley, 1861–1865" (Ph.D. dissertation, University of Rochester, 1976).

48. Georgia Lee Tatum, *Disloyalty in the Confederacy* (Chapel Hill, N.C., 1939), is a state-by-state survey of dissension. See also Michael K. Honey, "The War Within the Confederacy: White Unionists of North Carolina," *Prologue*, XVIII (1986), 75–93.

With the disintegration of slavery white southerners had little that was tangible left to fight for and little reason to continue to support the Confederacy. Blacks thus contributed to the Confederacy's weakness while they added to the Union's strength.

But despite their essential contributions to Union victory, blacks were not in a position to make the choices that would shape the new regime. Northern whites would do that, and they had yet to decide how much influence to accord abolitionist principles of freedom and equality. One thing, however, soon became evident: The biracial alliance forged in wartime would carry little weight in designing the postwar settlement.

The Union's antislavery reputation, which had been fostered by white southerners as well as by abolitionists, led politically aware freedmen to anticipate more from their liberators than the liberators were prepared to give. A national government whose principles as well as facilities did not permit attempts at omnipotence could not carry out generous intentions through the vast expanse of the rural South. In the reconstructed South, as in antebellum days, race relations depended less on statutes than on private accommodation and the ability to coerce. Consequently, however generous and humane Republicans in Washington might wish to be, much that was cruel and exploitative occurred beyond their view or remedy, and freedom in the new South, as in the old, was defined less as the freedmen desired than in terms congenial to the interests of their white rulers. Given the aim, background, and power of the freedmen's former masters, and the freedmen's own economic weakness and political inexperience, and given the inadequacies of liberal ideology and the eventual exhaustion of northern will, it could not have been otherwise.

Slaves had viewed the Union government and its armies as allies in their generations-long war for freedom. White northerners, in turn, and for their own purposes, had exploited the blacks' desire to be free and to humble their oppressors, but from beginning to end, they had set rigid limits on black revolt and had controlled its results. They had made an alliance with the blacks, but no more than earlier enemies and invaders of the South had they recognized them as equal partners in the crusade that destroyed the system that enslaved and exploited them.

Conclusion

Slavery served white Americans well for nearly 250 years. Enslaved blacks joined with whites to perform the labor that transformed the North American wilderness into one of the world's flour-
ishing plantation regions. The crops they grew there not only
enriched slaveowners, they also contributed mightily to the development of the entire American economy and the economy of Europe
as well.

To those who visited them at any time before the Civil War, the
South's slave-cultivated farms and plantations were likely to seem
isolated and independent, and often they were so conceived by their
prideful owners. But their autonomy was in fact an illusion, for
however spatially remote the plantations might be, they were actually units in a far-flung system of capitalistic enterprise. Their economic fortune and, as it turned out, their fate were determined in
large part by faraway economic and political developments over
which their proprietors could exert scant control. Likewise the tensions and conflicts generated within the peculiar labor system that
accounted for the plantations' importance were not concerns only
of the men and women immediately involved with them, but were
closely related to the acts and ambitions of people located far from
the South.

Measured by its function as a labor system, slavery should be
judged a success. It fulfilled its intended purpose of controlling

labor and allowing for its transfer while at the same time it produced an abundance of valuable staples. But from first to last, these goals were accomplished only with pain and difficulty, and ultimately the effort could not be sustained. In order to realize its full potential as both an economic and social system, slavery needed to function as a nearly total institution. Slaves must be made to work like machines at tasks set for them by owners and overseers. Absolute discipline must be enforced, both for the sake of efficiency of production and of protecting the authority and safety of the slave-holding class. That was the ideal, but like most ideals, it could be achieved only in part. A problem was universally encountered. Far from being machines or acting like them, slaves turned out to be human beings very like their owners, having wills and ambitions and competencies that ill accorded with the goal of total subordination. Thus conflict, potentially severe, between owners and slaves always characterized southern labor relations. At the same time, a multitude of hostile influences originating outside the plantation also worked to impede the system. In the face of all of this, it is a tribute to the skill, determination, and ruthlessness of white Americans that they were able to keep the blacks enslaved for as long as they did.

Only with great difficulty could the slaves' discontent and their drive for autonomy be contained. Owners understood the significance of that fact. They recognized the rapidly growing slave population as the country's most severe potential for internal subversion. From at least the early eighteenth century, white southerners fretted about the danger presented by so explosive a labor force. Before the late antebellum period, when Romanticism and the "positive-good" defense of slavery transformed the popular image of blacks into meek, submissive beings, southern whites typically characterized them as their "internal enemy."

That portrayal should come as no surprise, for slaves were constantly restive. Along with examples of faithful labor and unexceptional behavior went examples of sullenness and disobedience, conspiracies, open revolt, and escapes. Instances of violence—assaults, murder, and arson—were common enough to awaken apprehensions for the future. White southerners and their governments nonetheless learned to cope with disorder, although its pervasiveness made the chief purpose of the slave system—profitable production—harder to achieve and generated suspicion that the resistance was encouraged if not induced by jealous or malevolent persons seeking the planters' ruin.

Slave discontent appeared to increase and its potential to be magnified at those times when political discord divided white society, as during the Missouri controversy, or when internal stress became evident, as in Virginia during the constitutional debates of the late 1820s and early 1830s. The appearance of alienation or disaffection among elements of the white population invited slave disorder. Thus nonslaveholders seldom were fully trusted; free blacks never were. External threats—and these were constant in the colonial period—magnified the problem. An early goal of United States diplomacy was the elimination of European powers from the continent, partly to make possible the westward expansion of slave-cultivated plantations and partly to stabilize slavery itself by removing a stimulus to discord. The goal was achieved, but only for a moment. Early in the nineteenth century, the North replaced England, France, and Spain as the South's major rival and enemy.

The fundamental explanation for the sectional enmity that marked antebellum decades doubtless lies in the contrasting lines of economic and social development then followed by North and South, the differing values and interests these produced, and the rival political measures they engendered. But the agents who articulated these differences (more often than not in the rhetoric of evangelical Protestantism) and gave them their emotive power were the abolitionists, a dedicated group of black and white men and women bent on destroying the South's labor system and on revolutionizing American values. Slaves, too, played a critical role in the deepening sectional conflict, influencing the actions of both abolitionists and southern statesmen. It was widely recognized that slaves were the subjects of hot debate. Less fully appreciated was the active part they took in driving the sections apart. The abolitionists' crusade coincided with what was interpreted in both North and South as increased slave unrest. Planters charged abolitionists with responsibility for the vexing problems they experienced in their fields and quarters. Slaves who rebelled and slaves who ran away may indeed have been encouraged to do so by northern antislavery activity. But just as important, abolitionism was stimulated—and justified—by the slave unrest for which rebels and swelling numbers of runaways supplied tangible evidence. Thus, slaves, planters, and abolitionists exercised reciprocal influence in the long process that moved the sections toward separation and war.

Slaves and free blacks certainly were antislavery in attitude, and insofar as slaveholders represented the South, blacks also were antisouthern. By fleeing to the North, slaves demonstrated their understanding that an antislavery, antisouthern North would offer them help and refuge exactly as the South's earlier enemies had done. The motive for northerners to do these things may have been humanitarian, or it may have been economic and political. Whatever its source, its effect was the same: The slaves had found a new ally, and slaveholders faced a new enemy.

When the abolitionists' program, or parts of it, became a force in electoral politics, as it manifestly had done by 1860, the slaveholding South faced a threat for which much in its political theory but nothing in its experience offered defense. The result was secession, and secession brought war. Civil War, with consequent military invasion at many points, provided slaves with powerful support in their perpetual plantation struggles. The disruption that slaves and the Union armies then brought to the South ended slavery and was the culmination of two and a half centuries of internal conflict.

Bibliography

I. Primary Sources

A. Published Reports, Letters, Memoirs, and Other Contemporary Material

Adams, Charles Francis, ed. *Letters of Mrs. Adams* . . . . 4th ed. Boston, 1848.
————, ed. *Memoirs of John Quincy Adams Comprising Portions of His Diary from 1795 to 1848.* 12 vols. Philadelphia, 1874–77.
————, ed. *The Works of John Adams, Second President of the United States, with a Life of the Author.* 9 vols. Boston, 1856.
Adams, John Quincy, and Lewis Condit. *Report of the Minority of the Committee on Manufactures, Submitted to the House of Representatives of the United States, February 28, 1833* (Boston, 1833).
Address of the New England Anti-Slavery Convention to the Slaves of the United States with an Address to President Tyler, Faneuil Hall, May 31, 1843. Boston, 1843.
Alden, John R. "John Stuart Accuses William Bull." *William and Mary Quarterly*, 3rd ser., II (1945), 315–20.
Ambler, Charles Henry, ed. *Correspondence of Robert M. T. Hunter, 1826–1876.* Vol. II of American Historical Association, *Annual Report . . . for the Year 1916.* Washington, D.C., 1918.
American Anti-Slavery Society. *First Annual Report . . . 1834.* New York, 1834.
————. *Annual Reports for 1857 and 1858.* New York, 1858.

American Convention for Promoting the Abolition of Slavery. *Minutes of the Proceedings of the Convention of Delegates . . . 1801*. Philadelphia, 1801.
———. *Minutes of the Proceedings of the Convention of Delegates . . . 1805*. Philadelphia, 1805.
American State Papers, Class VII: Post Office Department. 1834.
Andrews, Ethan Allen. *Slavery and the Domestic Slave Trade in the United States*. Boston, 1836.
Annals of Congress. 1st Cong., 2nd Sess.; 3rd Cong., 2nd Sess.; 6th Cong., 1st Sess.; 8th Cong., 1st Sess.; 9th Cong., 1st Sess., 2nd Sess.; 12th Cong., 1st Sess., 2nd Sess.; 13th Cong., 3rd Sess.; 14th Cong., 2nd Sess.; 15th Cong., 1st Sess., 2nd Sess.; 16th Cong., 1st Sess.
Aptheker, Herbert, ed. *A Documentary History of the Negro People in the United States*. 2 vols. New York, 1951.
Archives of Maryland: Proceedings and Acts of the General Assembly of Maryland, October 1678–March 1683. Baltimore, 1889.
[Ball, George]. *Fifty Years in Chains; or, The Life of an American Slave*. New York, 1858.
Barker, Eugene C., ed. *The Austin Papers*. Vol. II, Pt. 1 of American Historical Association, *Annual Report . . . for the Years 1919 and 1922*. Washington, D.C., 1924–28.
———, ed. *The Austin Papers*. Vol. III. Austin, Texas, 1927.
Basler, Roy P., *et al.*, eds. *Collected Works of Abraham Lincoln*. 9 vols. New Brunswick, N.J., 1953–55.
Bassett, John Spencer, ed. *Correspondence of Andrew Jackson*. 7 vols. Washington, D.C., 1926–35.
———, ed. *The Southern Plantation Overseer as Revealed in His Letters*. Northampton, Mass., 1925.
Beale, Howard K., ed. *Diary of Gideon Welles, Secretary of the Navy under Lincoln and Johnson*. 3 vols. New York, 1960.
Berlin, Ira, ed. "After Nat Turner: A Letter from the North." *Journal of Negro History*, LV (1970), 144–51.
Berlin, Ira, *et al.*, eds. *The Destruction of Slavery*. New York, 1985. Vol. I of Berlin et al., eds., *Freedom: A Documentary History of Emancipation, 1861–1867, Series I*.
Billings, Warren, ed. *The Old Dominion in the Seventeenth Century: A Documentary History of Virginia, 1606–1689*. Chapel Hill, N.C., 1975.
[Bishop, Abraham]. "Rights of Black Men." *American Museum*, XII (1792), 299–300.
Blassingame, John W., ed. *Slave Testimony: Two Centuries of Letters, Speeches, Interviews, and Autobiography*. Baton Rouge, 1977.
Blodgett, Samuel. *Economica: A Statistical Manual for the United States of America*. Washington, D.C., 1806.
[Blunt, Joseph]. *An Examination of the Expediency and Constitutionality of Prohibiting Slavery in the State of Missouri*. New York, 1819.
Boucher, Chauncey S., and Robert P. Brooks, eds. *Correspondence Addressed*

to John C. Calhoun, 1837–1849. Vol. II of American Historical Association, *Annual Report . . . for the Year 1929.* Washington, D.C., 1930.

Bowers, Claude G., ed. *The Diary of Elbridge Gerry, Jr.* New York, 1927.

Boyd, Julian P., ed. *The Papers of Thomas Jefferson.* 20 vols. to date. Princeton, N.J., 1950–.

Branagan, Thomas. *The Penitential Tyrant: A Juvenile Poem. . . .* Philadelphia, 1805.

———. *The Penitential Tyrant; or, Slave Trader Reformed. . . .* 2nd ed. New York, 1807.

Brock, R. A., ed. *Official Records of Robert Dinwiddie, Lt. Gov. of the Colony of Virginia, 1751–1758.* 2 vols. Virginia Historical Society Collection, n.s., III and IV. Richmond, 1883–84.

[Brown, John]. *Slave Life in Georgia: A Narrative of the Life, Sufferings, and Escape of John Brown, a Fugitive Slave, Now in England.* London, 1855.

Brunhouse, Robert L., ed. "David Ramsay, 1749–1815: Selections from His Writings." *Transactions of the American Philosophical Society*, n.s., LV, Pt. 4 (1965).

Butler, Benjamin F. *Private and Official Correspondence of Benjamin F. Butler During the Period of the Civil War.* 5 vols. Norwood, Mass., 1917.

Candler, Allen D., ed. *The Colonial Records of Georgia.* 26 vols. 1904; rpr. New York, 1970.

Cappon, Lester J., ed. *The Adams-Jefferson Letters: The Complete Correspondence Between Thomas Jefferson and Abigail and John Adams.* 2 vols. Chapel Hill, N.C., 1959.

Carter, Clarence E., ed. *The Territory of Orleans, 1803–1812.* Washington, D.C., 1940. Vol. IX of Carter, ed. *The Territorial Papers of the United States.* 28 vols.

Catterall, Helen T., ed. *Judicial Cases Concerning American Slavery and the Negro.* 5 vols. Washington, D.C., 1924–26.

Channing, William Ellery. *The Duty of the Free States; or, Remarks Suggested by the Case of the Creole.* Boston, 1842.

Clark, Elmer T., *et al.*, eds. *The Journal and Letters of Francis Asbury.* 3 vols. London, 1958.

Congressional Globe, 37th Cong., 2nd Sess.

Correspondence of Mr. Ralph Izard of South Carolina, from the Year 1774 to 1804. New York, 1844.

Cralle, Richard K., ed. *Speeches of John C. Calhoun. . . .* 6 vols. New York, 1853.

Crummell, Alexander. *The Eulogy of Henry Highland Garnet, D.D., Presbyterian Minister. . . .* Washington, D.C., 1882.

Davis, Edwin A., ed. *Plantation Life in the Florida Parishes of Louisiana, 1836–1846, as Reflected in the Diary of Bennet H. Barrow.* New York, 1943.

Delany, Martin R. *Blake; or, The Huts of America.* Boston, 1970.

Dew, Thomas R. *Review of the Debate in the Virginia Legislature of 1831 and 1832.* Richmond, 1832.

Donnan, Elizabeth, ed. *Papers of James A. Bayard, 1796–1815.* Vol. II of American Historical Association, *Annual Report . . . for the Year 1913.* Washington, D.C., 1915.

Drayton, Daniel. *Personal Memoir of Daniel Drayton, for Four Years and Four Months a Prisoner (for Charity's Sake) in Washington Jail.* Boston, 1855.

Drew, Benjamin. *A North-Side View of Slavery: The Refugee; or, The Narratives of Free Slaves in Canada. . . .* Boston, 1856.

Dwight, Timothy. *An Oration Spoken Before the Connecticut Society for the Promotion of Freedom and the Relief of Persons Unlawfully Holden in Bondage.* Hartford, 1794.

Dyer, Frederick H. *A Compendium of the War of the Rebellion Compiled and Arranged from Official Records. . . .* Des Moines, 1908.

[Earle, Thomas]. *Life, Travels, and Opinions of Benjamin Lundy.* Philadelphia, 1847.

Easterby, James Harold, ed. *The South Carolina Rice Plantation, as Revealed in the Papers of Robert F. W. Allston.* Chicago, 1945.

Elliot, Jonathan, ed. *The Debates in the Several State Conventions, on the Adoption of the Federal Constitution. . . .* 5 vols. Philadelphia, 1907.

Elliott, E. N. *Cotton Is King, and Pro-Slavery Arguments. . . .* Augusta, Ga., 1860.

Evans, Emory G., ed. "A Question of Complexion: Documents Concerning the Negro and the Franchise in Eighteenth-Century Virginia." *Virginia Magazine of History and Biography,* LXXI (1963), 411–415.

Fawcett, Benjamin. *A Compassionate Address to the Christian Negroes in Virginia.* London, 1756.

Fitzpatrick, John C., ed. *The Writings of George Washington.* 39 vols. Washington, D.C., 1931–44.

Foner, Eric. *Nat Turner.* Englewood Cliffs, N.J., 1971.

Foner, Philip S., ed. *The Life and Writings of Frederick Douglass.* 4 vols. New York, 1950–55.

Foote, William Henry. *Sketches of Virginia, Historical and Biographical, 2nd Series,* 2nd ed. Philadelphia, 1856.

Ford, Paul Leicester, ed. *The Writings of Thomas Jefferson.* 10 vols. New York, 1892–99.

Ford, Worthington C., ed. *Letters of William Lee.* 3 vols. Brooklyn, N.Y., 1891.

Ford, Worthington C., et al., eds. *Journals of the Continental Congress, 1774–1789.* 34 vols. Washington, D.C., 1904–37.

Forten, Charlotte. "Life on the Sea Islands." *Atlantic Monthly,* XIII (May, 1864), 587–96.

Franklin, John Hope, ed. *Diary of James T. Ayres, Civil War Recruiter.* Springfield, Ill., 1947.

Goodell, William. *Slavery and Anti-Slavery: A History of the Great Struggle in Both Hemispheres with a View of the Slavery Question in the United States.* New York, 1852.

Greene, Jack P., ed. *The Diary of Colonel Landon Carter of Sabine Hall, 1752–1778.* 2 vols. Charlottesville, Va., 1965.

Hamer, Phillip M. *et al.*, eds. *The Papers of Henry Laurens.* 11 vols. to date. Columbia, S.C., 1968–.

Hamilton, J. G. de Roulhac, ed. *The Papers of Thomas Ruffin.* 4 vols. Raleigh, N.C., 1918–20.

Hamilton, Stanislaus, ed. *The Writings of James Monroe.* 7 vols. New York, 1893–1903.

[Hammond, Jabez Delano]. *Life and Opinions of Julius Melbourne. . . .* Syracuse, N.Y., 1847.

Harlan, Louis R., ed. *The Booker T. Washington Papers.* 13 vols. Urbana, Ill., 1972–84.

Hening, William Waller, comp. *The Statutes at Large, Being a Compilation of All the Laws of Virginia. . . .* 13 vols. Richmond, 1810–23.

Higginbotham, Don, ed. *The Papers of James Iredell.* 2 vols. Raleigh, N.C., 1976.

Hildreth, Richard. *Despotism in America: An Inquiry into the Nature, Results, and Legal Basis of the Slave-Holding System in the United States.* Boston, 1854.

Hints for the Consideration of the Friends of Slavery, and Friends of Emancipation. Lexington, Ky., 1803.

Horsmanden, Daniel. *The New York Conspiracy; or, A History of the Negro Plot, with the Journal of the Proceedings Against the Conspirators at New York in the Years 1741–42. . . .* 2nd ed. New York, 1810.

Hurd, John Codman. *The Law of Freedom and Bondage in the United States.* 2 vols. Boston, 1858.

Hutchinson, William T., and William M. E. Rachal, eds. *The Papers of James Madison.* 16 vols. to date. Chicago, 1962–.

Jameson, J. Franklin, ed. *Correspondence of John C. Calhoun.* Vol. II, Pt. 2 of American Historical Association, *Annual Report . . . for the Year 1899.* Washington, D.C., 1900.

Janson, Charles William. *The Stranger in America, Containing Observations Made During a Long Residence in That Country. . . .* London, 1807.

Killens, John Oliver, ed. *The Trial Record of Denmark Vesey.* Boston, 1970.

Klingburg, Susan M., ed. *Records of the Virginia Company of London.* 4 vols. Washington, D.C., 1906–35.

The Lee Papers . . . 1754–1800. 4 vols. New-York Historical Society Collections, 1871–1874. New York, 1872–75.

Levering, Robert E. H. *The Kingdom of Slavery. . . .* Circleville, Ohio, 1844.

Lipscomb, Andrew A., ed. *The Writings of Thomas Jefferson.* 20 vols. Washington, D.C., 1903–1904.

Lovejoy, Joseph C. *Memoir of Rev. Charles T. Torrey, Who Died in the Penitentiary of Maryland, Where He Was Confined for Showing Mercy to the Poor.* New York, 1847.

Massachusetts Anti-Slavery Society. *Nineteenth Annual Report*. Boston, 1851.

Merrill, Walter M., and Louis Ruchames, eds. *The Letters of William Lloyd Garrison*. 6 vols. Cambridge, Mass., 1971–81.

Merriwether, Robert L., *et al.*, eds. *The Papers of John C. Calhoun*. 17 vols. to date. Columbia, S.C., 1959–.

[Methodist Episcopal Church]. *The Address of the General Conference of the Methodist Episcopal Church, to All Their Brethren and Friends in the United States, Baltimore, May 23, 1800*. N.p., n.d.

Minutes of the National Convention of Colored Citizens Held at Buffalo on the 15th, 16th, 17th, 18th and 19th of August, 1843. . . . New York, 1843.

Monroe, Haskell M., Jr., and James T. McIntosh, eds. *The Papers of Jefferson Davis*. 5 vols. to date. Baton Rouge, 1971–.

Mullin, Michael, ed. *American Negro Slavery: A Documentary History*. New York, 1976.

Myers, Robert M., ed. *The Children of Pride: A True Story of Georgia and the Civil War*. New Haven, Conn., 1972.

Northup, Solomon. *Narrative of Solomon Northup: Twelve Years a Slave. . . .* Auburn, N.Y., 1853.

O'Kelley, James. *Essay on Negro Slavery*. Philadelphia, 1789.

Olmsted, Frederick Law. *A Journey in the Back Country*. New York, 1860.

———. *A Journey Through Texas; or, a Saddle-Trip on the Southwestern Frontier*. New York, 1857.

Palmer, William, Sherwin McRae, and H. W. Flournoy, eds. *Calendar of Virginia State Papers and Other Manuscripts, 1652–1869, Preserved at the Capitol in Richmond*. 11 vols. Richmond, 1875–93.

Paul, Nathaniel. *An Address, Delivered on the Celebration of the Abolition of Slavery in the State of New York, July 5, 1827*. Albany, N.Y., 1827.

[Paulding, James K.]. *Letters from the South, Written During an Excursion in the Summer of 1816*. 2 vols. New York, 1817.

Pease, William H., and Jane H. Pease. "Walker's *Appeal* Comes to Charleston: A Note and Documents." *Journal of Negro History*, LIX (1974), 289–92.

"People of Colour." *Port Folio*, I (May 23, 1801), 163–64.

Phelps, Amos A. *Lectures on Slavery and Its Remedy*. Boston, 1834.

Phillips, Ulrich B., ed. *Correspondence of Robert Toombs, Alexander H. Stephens, and Howell Cobb*. Vol. II of American Historical Association, *Annual Report . . . for the Year 1911*. Washington, D.C., 1913.

———, ed. *Plantation and Frontier, 1649–1863*. 2 vols. Cleveland, 1909.

Quarles, Benjamin, ed. *Blacks on John Brown*. Urbana, Ill., 1972.

Rankin, John. *Letters on American Slavery Addressed to Mr. Thomas Rankin. . . .* Newburyport, Mass., 1837.

Rawick, George P., ed. *The American Slave: A Composite Autobiography*. 19 vols. Westport, Conn., 1972.

Rawick, George P., *et al.*, eds. *The American Slave: A Composite Autobiography: Supplement, Series I*. 12 vols. Westport, Conn., 1977.

Redpath, James. *The Roving Editor; or, Talks with Slaves in the Southern States*. New York, 1859.

Review of *The Tenth Annual Report of the American Society for Colonizing the Free People of Colour. . . . Southern Review*, I (1828), 219–32.

Rice, David. *Slavery Inconsistent with Justice and Good Policy. . . .* Philadelphia, 1792.

Richardson, James D., ed. *A Compilation of the Messages and Papers of the Presidents*. 20 vols. Washington, D.C., 1896.

Rose, Willie Lee, ed. *A Documentary History of Slavery in North America*. New York, 1976.

Rowland, Dunbar, ed. *Jefferson Davis, Constitutionalist: His Letters, Papers and Speeches*. 10 vols. Jackson, Miss., 1923.

————, ed. *Official Letter-Books of W. C. C. Claiborne, 1801–1816*. 6 vols. Jackson, Miss., 1917.

Ruchames, Louis, ed. *The Abolitionists: A Collection of Their Writings*. New York, 1963.

Scarborough, William Kauffman, ed. *The Diary of Edmund Ruffin*. 3 vols. Baton Rouge, 1972–89.

Seybert, Adam. *Statistical Annals: Embracing Views of the Population, Commerce, Navigation, Fisheries . . . of the United States of America. . . .* Philadelphia, 1818.

Shea, Deborah, ed. "Spreading Terror and Devastation Wherever They Have Been: A Norfolk Woman's Account of the Southampton Slave Insurrection." *Virginia Magazine of History and Biography*, XCV (1987), 65–74.

Silliman, Benjamin. "Some of the Causes of National Anxiety." *African Repository*, VIII (August, 1832), 161–87.

Smith, Gerrit. *Speeches of Gerrit Smith in Congress*. New York, 1856.

Smith, Margaret Bayard. *The First Forty Years of Washington Society*. New York, 1906.

Sparks, Edwin Earle, ed. *The Lincoln Douglas Debates of 1858*. Springfield, Ill., 1908.

Spear, John M. *Twelve Discourses on Government; Purported to Have Been Delivered in Boston, Massachusetts, December, 1852, by Thomas Jefferson of the Spirit World*. Hopedale, Mass., 1853.

Starobin, Robert S., ed. *Blacks in Bondage: Letters of American Slaves*. New York, 1974.

"Summary of Trial Proceedings of Those Accused of Participating in the Slave Uprising of January, 1811." *Louisiana History*, XVIII (1977), 472–73.

Sutcliff, Robert. *Travels in Some Parts of North America in the Years, 1804, 1805, and 1806*. Philadelphia, 1812.

Taylor, John. *Arator; Being a Series of Agricultural Essays, Practical and Political*. 2nd ed. Georgetown, 1814.

Thompson, George. *Prison Life and Reflections.* . . . Hartford, 1854.

[Thompson, John]. *Life of John Thompson, a Fugitive Slave.* . . . Worcester, Mass., 1856.

Thorndike, Rachel Sherman, ed. *The Sherman Letters.* New York, 1894.

Tragle, Henry Irving. *The Southampton Slave Revolt of 1831.* Amherst, Mass., 1971.

[Tucker, St. George]. *A Letter to a Member of the General Assembly of Virginia on the Subject of the Late Conspiracy.* . . . Baltimore, 1801.

[Turnbull, Robert J.]. *The Crisis; or, Essays on the Usurpations of the Federal Government.* Charleston, S.C., 1827.

Turner, Frederick Jackson, ed. *Correspondence of the French Ministers to the United States, 1791–1797.* Vol. II of American Historical Association, *Annual Report . . . for the Year 1903.* Washington, D.C., 1904.

U.S. Bureau of the Census. *Historical Statistics of the United States, Colonial Times to 1970.* 2 vols. 1975.

————. *Negro Population, 1790–1915.* 1918.

U.S. Department of State. *State Papers and Correspondence Bearing upon the Purchase of the Territory of Louisiana.* 1903.

The War of the Rebellion: A Compilation of the Official Records of the Union and Confederate Armies. 130 vols. Washington, D.C., 1880–1901.

[Warner, Samuel]. *Authentic and Impartial Narrative of the Tragical Scene Which Was Witnessed in Southampton County (Virginia) on Monday the 22nd of August Last.* . . . [New York, 1831].

Whittier, John Greenleaf. *The Works of John Greenleaf Whittier.* 7 vols. New York, 1892.

Whittington, G. P., ed. "Concerning the Loyalty of Slaves in Northern Louisiana in 1863: Letters from John H. Ransdell to Governor Thomas O. Moore, Dated 1863." *Louisiana Historical Quarterly,* XIV (1931), 487–502.

Windley, Lathan A., comp. *Runaway Slave Advertisements: A Documentary History from the 1730s to 1790.* 4 vols. Westport, Conn., 1983.

Winthrop Sargent to "Sir," November 16, 1800. Printed broadside. N.p. N.d. Ohio Historical Society.

Woodward, C. Vann, and Elisabeth Muhlenfeld, eds. *The Private Mary Chesnut: The Unpublished Civil War Diaries.* New York, 1984.

B. Newspapers

Abolition Intelligencer (Shelbyville, Ky.), 1822.

Boston *Courier,* January 28, 1859.

Boston *Daily Whig,* July 3 and 9, 1847.

Charleston *City Gazette and Daily Advertiser,* October 22, 1800, and September 27, 1822.

Cincinnati *Gazette,* April 29, 1852.

Colored *American* (New York), September 2, 1837.

Connecticut Courant (Hartford), December 12, 1796.

The Emancipator (Complete), Published by Elihu Embree, Jonesborough, Tennessee, 1820. Rpr. Nashville, 1932.
Freedom's Journal (New York), 1827–29.
Genius of Universal Emancipation (Mt. Pleasant, Ohio, and other cities), 1821–39.
Genius of Universal Emancipation and Baltimore Courier, 1825–26.
Hillsdale (Mich.) *Whig Standard,* September 15, 1846.
Liberator (Boston), 1831–65.
National Anti-Slavery Standard (New York), 1842 and 1850.
New York *Evening Post,* February 19 and 20, 1811.
New York *Tribune,* January 31, 1859.
Niles' Weekly Register (Baltimore), I (1812)–LXVIII (1845).
Philanthropist (Cincinnati), 1841–42.
Richmond *Enquirer,* October–December, 1862.
Signal of Liberty (Ann Arbor, Mich.), April 6, 1842.
Washington *Semi-Weekly Union,* September–October, 1845.

C. Manuscripts

Amistad Research Center, Tulane University, New Orleans
    American Home Missionary Society Papers.
    American Missionary Association Archives.
Boston Public Library, Boston
    Antislavery Collection.
Chicago Historical Society, Chicago
    Minutes of the Illinois State Anti-Slavery Society.
Cornell University Library, Ithaca, N.Y.
    Antislavery Collection.
Duke University Library, Durham, N.C.
    Enfield, Gertrude Dixon, ed. "Life and Letters of Christopher Houston."
    Typescript.
Georgia State Archives, Atlanta
    Executive Papers.
Historic New Orleans Collection, New Orleans
    Villeré, Jacques Philippe. Papers.
Historical Society of Pennsylvania, Philadelphia
    Pennsylvania Abolition Society Papers.
Manuscripts Division, Library of Congress, Washington, D.C.
    American Colonization Society Papers.
    Monroe, James. Papers (microfilm).
New-York Historical Society, New York, N.Y.
    Miscellaneous Manuscripts.
    Stewart, Alvan. Papers.
New York Public Library
    Peters Family Letters.

North Carolina Division of Archives and History, Raleigh
   Bertie County Slave Papers, 1800–1805.
   Gates County Slave Records, 1783–1867.
   Governors' Papers.
   Jacocks, Charles W. Papers.
   Legislative Papers. Petitions, 1800–59.
   Turner, James. Papers.
   Mordecai, Pattie. Collection.
   Onslow County Miscellaneous Records.
   Perquimans County Slave Papers, 1759–1864.
   Wayne County Records.
Ohio Historical Society, Columbus
   Giddings, Joshua. Papers.
   Sherman, William Tecumseh. Papers.
South Carolina Department of Archives and History, Columbia
   Governors' Messages, 1791–1800.
   Governors' Papers.
   Grand Jury Presentments.
   Legislative Papers, Slavery Petitions, 1800–30.
   Pendleton/Anderson District. Court of Magistrates and Freeholders. Trial
      Papers.
South Caroliniana Library, University of South Carolina, Columbia
   Aiken County Records.
   Ball Family Papers.
   Blanding, William. Papers.
   Bonham, Milledge Luke. Collection.
   Izard, Ralph. Papers.
   Manigault Family Papers.
   Pinckney, Charles. Papers.
   Read, Jacob. Papers.
Southern Historical Collection, University of North Carolina, Chapel Hill
   Kimberly, John. Papers.
   Mason, Nathaniel. Papers.
Syracuse University Library, Syracuse
   Smith, Gerrit. Papers.
Virginia State Library, Richmond
   Executive Papers.
William L. Clements Library, University of Michigan, Ann Arbor
   Fuller, Corydon. Journal.
   Van Deventer, Christopher. Papers.

II. Secondary Sources

Abzug, Robert H. "The Influence of Garrisonian Abolitionists' Fears of Slave
   Violence on the Antislavery Argument, 1829–1840." *Journal of Negro History*, LV (1970), 14–28.

Alden, John R. *The First South*. Baton Rouge, 1961.

Ambler, Charles Henry. *Sectionalism in Virginia from 1776 to 1861*. Chicago, 1910.

Ammon, Harry. *The Gênet Mission*. New York, 1973.

Aptheker, Herbert. *American Negro Slave Revolts*. New York, 1943.

——. *The American Revolution, 1763–1783*. New York, 1980.

——. *Nat Turner's Slave Rebellion*. New York, 1966.

——. "Notes on Slave Conspiracies in Confederate Mississippi." *Journal of Negro History*, XXIX (1944), 75–79.

——. *"One Continual Cry": David Walker's "Appeal to the Colored Citizens of the World," 1829–1830, Its Setting, and Its Meaning*. New York, 1965.

Ballagh, James Curtis. *A History of Slavery in Virginia*. Baltimore, 1902.

Banner, James M., Jr. *To the Hartford Convention: The Federalists and the Origins of Party Politics in Massachusetts, 1798–1818*. New York, 1970.

Barker, Eugene C., "The Influence of Slavery in the Colonization of Texas." *Mississippi Valley Historical Review*, XI (1924), 3–36.

Barney, William L. *The Secessionist Impulse: Alabama and Mississippi in 1860*. Princeton, N.J., 1974.

Barnhart, John D. "Sources of Southern Migration into the Old Northwest." *Mississippi Valley Historical Review*, XXII (1935), 49–62.

Bassett, John Spencer. *Slavery in the State of North Carolina*. Baltimore, 1899.

Bell, Howard H. "Expressions of Negro Militancy in the North, 1840–1860." *Journal of Negro History*, XLV (1960), 11–20.

Berlin, Ira. *Slaves Without Masters: The Free Negro in the Antebellum South*. New York, 1974.

——. "Time, Space, and the Evolution of Afro-American Society in British Mainland North America." *American Historical Review*, LXXXV (1980), 44–78.

Betts, Albert Deems. *History of South Carolina Methodism*. Charleston, S.C., 1952.

Blassingame, John W. *The Slave Community: Plantation Life in the Antebellum South*. Rev. ed. New York, 1979.

Boles, John B. "Tension in a Slave Society: The Trial of the Reverend Jacob Gruber." *Southern Studies*, XVIII (1979), 179–97.

Boney, F. N. *Southerners All*. Macon, Ga., 1984.

Brackett, Jeffrey R. *The Negro in Maryland: A Study of the Institution of Slavery*. Baltimore, 1889.

Breen, Timothy H. "A Changing Labor Force and Race Relations in Virginia, 1660–1710." *Journal of Social History*, VII (1973), 3–25.

Bretz, Julian P. "The Economic Background of the Liberty Party." *American Historical Review*, XXXIV (1929), 250–64.

Brewer, James H. "Negro Property Owners in Seventeenth-Century Virginia." *William and Mary Quarterly*, 3rd ser., XII (1955), 575–80.

Bruce, William Cabell. *John Randolph of Roanoke, 1773–1833*. 2 vols. New York, 1922.

Cassell, Frank A. "Slaves of the Chesapeake Bay Area and the War of 1812." *Journal of Negro History*, LVII (1972), 144–55.

Channing, Steven A. *Crisis of Fear: Secession in South Carolina*. New York, 1970.

Charlton, Walter G. "A Judge and a Grand Jury." In *Papers of the 31st Annual Session of the Georgia Bar Association . . . 1914*. Macon, Ga., 1914.

Childs, Frances S. *French Refugee Life in the United States, 1790–1800: An American Chapter of the French Revolution*. Baltimore, 1940.

Cimprich, John. *Slavery's End in Tennessee, 1861–1865*. University, Ala., 1985.

Connor, Seymour V., and Odie B. Faulk. *North America Divided: The Mexican War, 1846–1848*. New York, 1971.

Cooper, William J., Jr. *Liberty and Slavery: Southern Politics to 1860*. New York, 1983.

———. *The South and the Politics of Slavery, 1828–1856*. Baton Rouge, 1978.

Cox, LaWanda. *Lincoln and Black Freedom: A Study in Presidential Leadership*. Columbia, S.C., 1981.

Craven, Avery O. *The Coming of the Civil War*. New York, 1942.

———. "Poor Whites and Negroes in the Antebellum South." *Journal of Negro History*, XV (1930), 14–25.

Craven, Wesley Frank. "Twenty Negroes to Jamestown in 1619?" *Virginia Quarterly Review*, LVII (1971), 416–20.

———. *White, Red, and Black: The Seventeenth-Century Virginian*. Charlottesville, Va., 1971.

Crow, Jeffrey J. *The Black Experience in Revolutionary North Carolina*. Raleigh, N.C., 1973.

Davis, David Brion. *The Problem of Slavery in the Age of Revolution, 1770–1823*. Ithaca, N.Y., 1975.

———. *The Slave Power Conspiracy and the Paranoid Style*. Baton Rouge, 1969.

Davis, Thomas J. *A Rumor of Revolt: The "Great Negro Plot" in Colonial New York*. New York, 1985.

Dawidoff, Robert. *The Education of John Randolph*. New York, 1979.

De Conde, Alexander. *The Quasi-War: The Politics and Diplomacy of the Undeclared War with France, 1797–1801*. New York, 1966.

———. *This Affair of Louisiana*. New York, 1976.

Degler, Carl N. *The Other South: Southern Dissenters in the Nineteenth Century*. New York, 1974.

———. "Slavery and the Genesis of American Race Prejudice." *Comparative Studies in Society and History*, II (1959), 49–66.

Demos, John. "The Antislavery Movement and the Problem of Violent 'Means.'" *New England Quarterly*, XXXVII (1964), 501–26.

Dew, Charles B. "Black Ironworkers and the Slave Insurrection Panic of 1856." *Journal of Southern History*, LXI (1975), 321–38.

Dillon, Merton L. *The Abolitionists: The Growth of a Dissenting Minority*. DeKalb, Ill., 1974.

————. *Benjamin Lundy and the Struggle for Negro Freedom*. Urbana, Ill., 1966.

————. *Elijah P. Lovejoy, Abolitionist Editor*. Urbana, Ill., 1961.

————. "Three Southern Antislavery Editors: The Myth of the Southern Antislavery Movement." *East Tennessee Historical Society's Publications*, No. 42 (1970), 47–56.

Dorman, James H. "The Persistent Specter: Slave Rebellion in Territorial Louisiana." *Louisiana History*, XVIII (1977), 393–404.

Drake, Thomas E. *Quakers and Slavery in America*. New Haven, Conn., 1950.

Dumond, Dwight Lowell. *America's Shame and Redemption*. Marquette, Mich., 1965.

Eaton, Clement. "A Dangerous Pamphlet in the Old South." *Journal of Southern History*, II (1936), 1–12.

————. *Freedom of Thought in the Old South*. Durham, 1940.

————. *A History of the Southern Confederacy*. New York, 1954.

Escott, Paul D. "The Context of Freedom: Georgia's Slaves During the Civil War." *Georgia Historical Quarterly*, LVIII (1974), 79–104.

Faust, Drew Gilpin. *James Henry Hammond and the Old South: A Design for Mastery*. Baton Rouge, 1982.

Fehrenbacher, Don E. "Only His Stepchildren: Lincoln and the Negro." *Civil War History*, XX (1974), 293–310.

Feldstein, Stanley. *Once a Slave: The Slaves' View of Slavery*. New York, 1971.

Fladeland, Betty L. *James G. Birney: Slaveholder to Abolitionist*. Ithaca, N.Y., 1955.

————. *Men and Brothers: Anglo-American Antislavery Cooperation*. Urbana, Ill., 1972.

Foner, Eric. "The Causes of the American Civil War: Recent Interpretations and New Directions." *Civil War History*, XX (1974), 197–214.

————. *Free Soil, Free Labor, Free Men: The Ideology of the Republican Party Before the Civil War*. New York, 1970.

Foner, Philip S. *History of Black Americans*. 3 vols. Westport, Conn., 1975–83.

Fordham, Monroe. "Nineteenth-Century Black Thought in the United States: Some Influences of the Santo Domingan Revolution." *Journal of Black Studies*, VI (1975), 115–26.

Franklin, John Hope. *The Emancipation Proclamation*. Garden City, N.Y., 1963.

————. *The Free Negro in North Carolina, 1790–1860*. New York, 1969.

————. *The Militant South*. Cambridge, Mass., 1956.

Fredrickson, George M. *The Black Image in the White Mind: The Debate on Afro-American Character and Destiny, 1817–1914*. New York, 1971.

————. "A Man But Not a Brother: Abraham Lincoln and Racial Equality." *Journal of Southern History*, XLI (1975), 39–58.

Freehling, Alison Goodyear. *Drift Toward Dissolution: The Virginia Slavery Debate of 1831–1832*. Baton Rouge, 1982.

Freehling, William W. "The Editorial Revolution, Virginia and the Coming of the Civil War: A Review Essay." *Civil War History*, XVI (1970), 64–72.

———. "Denmark Vesey's Peculiar Reality." In *New Perspectives on Race and Slavery in America: Essays in Honor of Kenneth M. Stampp*, edited by Robert H. Abzug and Stephen E. Maizlish. Lexington, Ky., 1986.

———. *Prelude to Civil War: The Nullification Controversy in South Carolina, 1818–1836*. New York, 1966.

Frey, Sylvia R. "Between Slavery and Freedom: Virginia Blacks in the American Revolution." *Journal of Southern History*, XLIX (1983), 375–98.

Galenson, David W. *White Servitude in Colonial America: An Economic Analysis*. Cambridge, Eng., 1981.

Gara, Larry. "Slavery and the Slave Power: A Crucial Distinction." *Civil War History*, XV (1969), 4–18.

Garrison, Wendell Phillips, and Francis Jackson Garrison. *William Lloyd Garrison, 1805–1879*. 4 vols. Boston, 1885–89.

Gatell, Frank Otto. "Postmaster Huger and the Incendiary Publications." *South Carolina Historical Magazine*, LXIV (1963), 193–201.

Genovese, Eugene D. *From Rebellion to Revolution: Afro-American Slave Revolts in the Making of the Modern World*. Baton Rouge, 1979.

———. "'Rather Be a Nigger Than a Poor White Man': Slave Perceptions of Southern Yeomen and Poor Whites." In *Toward a New View of America: Essays in Honor of Arthur C. Cole*, edited by Hans L. Trefousse. New York, 1977.

———. *Roll, Jordan, Roll: The World the Slaves Made*. New York, 1974.

———. "Yeoman Farmers in a Slaveholding Democracy." *Agricultural History*, XLIX (1975), 331–42.

Gerteis, Louis S. *From Contraband to Freedman: Federal Policy Toward Southern Blacks, 1861–1865*. Westport, Conn., 1973.

Gewehr, Wesley M. *The Great Awakening in Virginia, 1740–1790*. Durham, N.C., 1930.

Greene, Lorenzo J. *The Negro in Colonial New England, 1620–1776*. New York, 1942.

Halasz, Nicholas. *The Rattling Chains: Slave Unrest and Rebellion in the Antebellum South*. New York, 1968.

Hamer, Phillip M. "Great Britain, the United States, and the Negro Seamen Acts, 1822–1848." *Journal of Southern History*, I (1935), 3–28.

Harris, J. William. *Plain Folk and Gentry in a Slave Society: White Liberty and Black Slavery in Augusta's Hinterlands*. Middletown, Conn., 1985.

Hoffman, Ronald. *A Spirit of Dissension: Economics, Politics, and the Revolution in Maryland*. Baltimore, 1973.

Honey, Michael K. "The War Within the Confederacy: White Unionists of North Carolina." *Prologue*, XVIII (1986), 75–93.

Horton, James Oliver, and Lois E. Horton. *Black Bostonians: Family Life and Community Struggle in the Antebellum North*. New York, 1979.

Hunt, Alfred N. *Haiti's Influence on Antebellum America: Slumbering Volcano in the Caribbean*. Baton Rouge, 1988.

Isaac, Rhys. "Evangelical Revolt: The Nature of the Baptists' Challenge to the Traditional Order in Virginia, 1765–1773." *William and Mary Quarterly*, 3rd ser., XXXI (1974), 345–68.

Jacobs, Donald M. "David Walker, Boston Race Leader, 1825–1830." *Essex Institute Historical Collections*, CVII (January, 1971), 94–107.

James, C. L. R. *The Black Jacobins: Toussaint L'Ouverture and the San Domingo Revolution.* Rev. ed. New York, 1963.

Johnson, Guion Griffis. *Ante-Bellum North Carolina: A Social History.* Chapel Hill, N.C., 1937.

Johnston, James Hugo. *Race Relations in Virginia and Miscegenation in the South, 1776–1860.* Amherst, Mass., 1970.

Jones, Bobby Frank. "A Cultural Middle Passage: Slave Marriage and Family in the Ante-Bellum South." Ph.D. dissertation, University of North Carolina, Chapel Hill, 1965.

Jones, Howard. *Mutiny on the Amistad: The Saga of a Slave Revolt and Its Impact on American Abolition, Law, and Diplomacy.* New York, 1986.

Jordan, Winthrop D. *White over Black: American Attitudes Toward the Negro, 1550–1812.* Chapel Hill, N.C., 1968.

Joyner, Charles W. *Down by the Riverside: A South Carolina Slave Community.* Urbana, Ill., 1984.

Kaplan, Sidney. "The 'Domestic Insurrections' of the Declaration of Independence." *Journal of Negro History*, LXI (1976), 243–55.

Katz, Jonathan. *Resistance at Christiana: The Fugitive Slave Rebellion, Christiana, Pennsylvania, September 11, 1851.* New York, 1974.

Kerber, Linda. *Federalists in Dissent: Imagery and Ideology in Jeffersonian America.* Ithaca, N.Y., 1970.

Klingberg, Frank Wysor. *The Southern Claims Commission.* Berkeley, Calif., 1955.

Kolchin, Peter. *First Freedom: The Response of Alabama's Blacks to Emancipation and Reconstruction.* Westport, Conn., 1972.

Konkle, Burton Alva. *The Life and Speeches of Thomas Williams . . . 1806–1872.* 2 vols. Philadelphia, 1905.

Lack, Paul D. "Slavery and the Texas Revolution." *Southwestern Historical Quarterly*, LXXXIX (1985), 181–202.

Lefebvre, Georges. *The Great Fear of 1789: Rural Panic in Revolutionary France.* New York, 1973.

Lemmon, Sarah McCulloh. *Frustrated Patriots: North Carolina and the War of 1812.* Chapel Hill, N.C., 1973.

Lofton, John. *Insurrection in South Carolina: The Turbulent World of Denmark Vesey.* Yellow Springs, Ohio, 1964.

Logan, Rayford W. *The Diplomatic Relations of the United States with Haiti, 1776–1891.* Chapel Hill, N.C., 1941.

Lynd, Staughton. *Class Conflict, Slavery, and the United States Constitution.* Indianapolis, 1967.

Maier, Pauline. "The Charleston Mob and the Evolution of Popular Politics in Revolutionary South Carolina, 1765–1784." *Perspectives in American History*, IV (1970), 173–98.

Mathews, Donald G. "The Methodist Mission to the Slaves, 1829–1844." *Journal of American History*, LI (1965), 615–31.

———. *The Methodists and Slavery: A Chapter in American Morality, 1780–1845*. Princeton, N.J., 1965.

———. *Religion in the Old South*. Chicago, 1977.

McColley, Robert. *Slavery and Jeffersonian Virginia*. Urbana, Ill., 1964.

———. "Slavery in Virginia, 1619–1660: A Reexamination." In *New Perspectives on Race and Slavery in America: Essays in Honor of Kenneth M. Stampp*, edited by Robert H. Abzug and Stephen E. Maizlish. Lexington, Ky., 1986.

McLeod, Duncan. *Slavery, Race, and the American Revolution*. London, 1974.

———. "Toward Caste." In *Slavery and Freedom in the Age of Revolution*, edited by Ira Berlin and Ronald Hoffman. Charlottesville, Va., 1983.

McManus, Edgar J. *A History of Negro Slavery in New York*. Syracuse, N.Y., 1966.

———. *Black Bondage in the North*. Syracuse, N.Y., 1973.

McMaster, John Bach. *A History of the People of the United States from the Revolution to the Civil War*. 8 vols. New York, 1915.

McPherson, James M. *The Negro's Civil War: How American Negroes Felt and Acted During the War for the Union*. New York, 1965.

———. *The Struggle for Equality: Abolitionists and the Negro in the Civil War and Reconstruction*. Princeton, N.J., 1964.

Meriwether, Robert L. *The Expansion of South Carolina, 1729–1765*. Kingsport, Tenn., 1940.

Messner, William F. "Black Violence and White Response: Louisiana, 1862." *Journal of Southern History*, XLVI (1975), 19–38.

Miles, Edwin A. "The Mississippi Slave Insurrection Scare of 1835." *Journal of Negro History*, XLII (1957), 48–60.

Miller, John C. *The Wolf by the Ears*. New York, 1977.

Milligan, John D. "Slave Rebelliousness and the Florida Maroon." *Prologue*, VI (1974), 4–18.

Mohr, Clarence L. *On the Threshold of Freedom: Masters and Slaves in Civil War Georgia*. Athens, Ga., 1986.

Moore, Albert B. *Conscription and Conflict in the Confederacy*. New York, 1924.

Moore, George Henry. *Notes on the History of Slavery in Massachusetts*. New York, 1866.

Moore, Glover. *The Missouri Controversy, 1819–1821*. Lexington, Ky., 1953.

Morgan, Edmund S. *American Slavery, American Freedom: The Ordeal of Colonial Virginia*. New York, 1975.

Morgan, Philip D., and George D. Terry. "Slavery in Microcosm: A Conspiracy Scare in Colonial South Carolina." *Southern Studies*, XXI (1982), 121–45.

Morison, Samuel Eliot. *Life and Letters of Harrison Gray Otis, Federalist 1765–1848*. 2 vols. Boston, 1913.

Morris, Thomas D. *Free Men All: The Personal Liberty Laws of the North, 1780–1861*. Baltimore, 1974.

Mullin, Gerald W. *Flight and Rebellion: Slave Resistance in Eighteenth-Century Virginia*. New York, 1972.

———. "Religion, Acculturation, and American Negro Slave Rebellions: Gabriel's Insurrection." In *American Slavery: The Question of Resistance*, edited by John H. Bracey, Jr., August Meier, and Elliott Rudwick. Belmont, Calif., 1971.

Mullin, Michael, ed. *American Negro Slavery: A Documentary History*. New York, 1976.

Mutersbaugh, Bert M. "The Background of Gabriel's Conspiracy." *Journal of Negro History*, LXVIII (1983), 209–11.

Nash, Gary B. *Forging Freedom: The Formation of Philadelphia's Black Community, 1720–1840*. Cambridge, Mass., 1988.

Norton, Mary Beth. "'What an Alarming Crisis Is This': Southern Women and the American Revolution." In *The Southern Experience in the American Revolution*, edited by Jeffrey J. Crow and Larry E. Tise. Chapel Hill, N.C., 1978.

Nye, Russell B. *Fettered Freedom: Civil Liberties and the Slavery Controversy, 1830–1860*. East Lansing, Mich., 1949.

Oakes, James. "The Political Significance of Slave Resistance." *History Workshop*, No. 22 (Autumn, 1986), 89–107.

———. *The Ruling Race: A History of American Slaveholders*. New York, 1982.

Oates, Stephen B. *The Fires of Jubilee: Nat Turner's Fierce Rebellion*. New York, 1975.

———. *To Purge This Land with Blood: A Biography of John Brown*. New York, 1970.

Ohline, Howard A. "Slavery, Economics, and Congressional Politics, 1790." *Journal of Southern History*, XLVI (1980), 335–60.

Olwell, Robert A., "'Domestick Enemies': Slavery and Political Independence in South Carolina, May 1775–March 1776." *Journal of Southern History*, LV (1989), 21–48.

Owens, Leslie Howard. *This Species of Property: Slave Life and Culture in the Old South*. New York, 1976.

Owsley, Frank Lawrence. *State Rights in the Confederacy*. Chicago, 1925.

Palmer, Paul C. "Servant into Slave: The Evolution of the Legal Servitude of the Negro Laborer in Colonial Virginia." *South Atlantic Quarterly*, LXV (1966), 355–70.

Pargellis, Stanley M. "Braddock's Defeat." *American Historical Review*, XLI (1936), 253–69.

Patrick, Rembert Wallace. *Florida Fiasco: Rampant Rebels on the Georgia-Florida Border, 1810–1815*. Athens, Ga., 1954.

Pease, William H., and Jane H. Pease. *They Who Would Be Free: Blacks' Search for Freedom, 1830–1861*. New York, 1974.

Phillips, Ulrich Bonnell. *American Negro Slavery: A Survey of the Supply,*

Employment and Control of Negro Labor as Determined by the Plantation Regime. New York, 1918.

Pletcher, David M. *The Diplomacy of Annexation: Texas, Oregon, and the Mexican War.* Columbia, Mo., 1973.

Porter, Kenneth Wiggins. "Negroes on the Southern Frontier, 1670–1763." *Journal of Negro History,* XXXIII (1948), 53–78.

Quarles, Benjamin. *Allies for Freedom: Blacks and John Brown.* New York, 1974.

———. "Lord Dunmore as Liberator." *William and Mary Quarterly,* 3rd ser., XV (1958), 494–507.

———. *The Negro in the American Revolution.* Chapel Hill, N.C., 1961.

Raboteau, Albert J. *Slave Religion: The "Invisible Institution" in the Antebellum South.* New York, 1978.

Rachleff, Marshall. "David Walker's Southern Agent." *Journal of Negro History,* LXII (1977), 100–103.

Randall, James G., and David Donald. *The Civil War and Reconstruction.* 2nd ed., rev. Lexington, Mass., 1969.

Rankin, Hugh F. *The North Carolina Continentals.* Chapel Hill, N.C., 1971.

Ratner, Lorman. *Powder Keg: Northern Opposition to the Antislavery Movement, 1831–1840.* New York, 1968.

Remini, Robert V. *Andrew Jackson and the Course of American Empire, 1763–1821.* New York, 1977.

Richards, Leonard L. *"Gentlemen of Property and Standing:" Anti-Abolitionist Mobs in Jacksonian America.* New York, 1970.

Rippy, J. Fred. *The United States and Mexico.* New York, 1931.

Roark, James L. *Masters Without Slaves: Southern Planters in the Civil War and Reconstruction.* New York, 1977.

Robert, Joseph C. *The Road from Monticello: A Study of the Virginia Slavery Debate of 1832.* Durham, N.C., 1941.

Robinson, Armstead. "Day of Jubilo: Civil War and the Demise of Slavery in the Mississippi Valley, 1861–1865." Ph.D. dissertation, University of Rochester, 1976.

———. "In the Shadow of Old John Brown: Insurrection Anxiety and Confederate Mobilization, 1861–1863." *Journal of Negro History,* LXV (1980), 279–97.

Robinson, Donald L. *Slavery in the Structure of American Politics, 1765–1820.* New York, 1971.

Rogers, George C., Jr. *Charleston in the Age of the Pinckneys.* Norman, Okla., 1969.

Rose, Willie Lee. *Slavery and Freedom.* New York, 1982.

Rosengarten, Theodore. *Tombee: Portrait of a Cotton Planter, with the Journal of Thomas B. Chaplin, 1822–1890.* New York, 1986.

Rothman, David. *The Discovery of the Asylum: Social Order and Disorder in the New Republic.* Boston, 1971.

Sandburg, Carl. *Abraham Lincoln: The War Years.* 4 vols. New York, 1939.

Sayre, Robert Duane. "The Evolution of Early American Abolitionism: The American Convention for the Abolition of Slavery and Improving the Condition of the African Race, 1794–1837." Ph.D. dissertation, Ohio State University, 1987.

Scarborough, William K. *The Overseer: Plantation Management in the Old South*. Baton Rouge, 1966.

Schaper, William A. "Sectionalism and Representation in South Carolina." In Vol. I of American Historical Association, *Annual Report . . . for the Year 1900*. Washington, D.C., 1901.

Schmidt, Fredrika Teute, and Barbara Ripel Wilhelm. "Early Proslavery Petitions in Virginia." *William and Mary Quarterly*, 3rd ser., XXX (1973), 133–46.

Schwarz, Philip J. "Gabriel's Challenge: Slaves and Crime in Late Eighteenth-Century Virginia." *Virginia Magazine of History and Biography*, XC (1982), 283–309.

Sellers, Charles Grier, Jr., ed. *The Southerner as American*. Chapel Hill, N.C., 1960.

Sewell, Richard H. *Ballots for Freedom: Antislavery Politics in the United States, 1837–1860*. New York, 1976.

Shore, Laurence. "Making Mississippi Safe for Slavery: The Insurrectionary Panic of 1835." In *Class, Conflict, and Consensus: Antebellum Community Studies*, edited by Orville Vernon Burton and Robert C. McMath, Jr. Westport, Conn., 1982.

Shortreed, Margaret. "The Antislavery Radicals: From Crusade to Revolution, 1840–1868." *Past and Present*, XVI (November, 1959), 65–87.

Simpson, Craig M. *A Good Southerner: The Life of Henry A. Wise of Virginia*. Chapel Hill, N.C., 1985.

Sitterson, J. Carlyle. "Magnolia Plantation, 1852–1862: A Decade of a Louisiana Sugar Estate." *Mississippi Valley Historical Review*, XXV (1938), 197–210.

Smith, Julia Floyd. *Slavery and Rice Culture in Low Country Georgia, 1750–1860*. Knoxville, Tenn., 1985.

Smith, Page. "Anxiety and Despair in American History." *William and Mary Quarterly*, 3rd ser., XXVI (1969), 416–24.

Stampp, Kenneth M. *"And the War Came": The North and the Secession Crisis, 1860–1861*. Baton Rouge, 1950.

Stegmaier, Mark J. "Maryland's Fear of Insurrection at the Time of Braddock's Defeat." *Maryland Magazine of History*, LXXVI (1976), 467–83.

Stewart, James Brewer. "Evangelicalism and the Radical Strain in Southern Antislavery Thought During the 1820s." *Journal of Southern History*, XXXIX (1973), 379–96.

———. *Wendell Phillips, Liberty's Hero*. Baton Rouge, 1986.

Stoddard, T. Lothrop. *The French Revolution in San Domingo*. Boston, 1914.

Strickland, John Scott. "The Great Revival and Insurrectionary Fears in North Carolina: An Examination of Antebellum Southern Society and

Slave Revolt Panics." In *Class, Conflict, and Consensus: Antebellum Southern Community Studies*, edited by Orville Vernon Burton and Robert C. McMath, Jr. Westport, Conn., 1982.

Strickland, William P. *The Life of Jacob Gruber*. New York, 1860.

Szasz, Ferenc M. "The New York Slave Revolt of 1741: A Re-examination." *New York History*, XLVIII (1967), 215–30.

Tatum, Georgia Lee. *Disloyalty in the Confederacy*. Chapel Hill, N.C., 1939.

Terry, George. "A Study of the Impact of the French Revolution and the Insurrection in Saint-Domingue upon South Carolina, 1790–1805." M.A. thesis, University of South Carolina, 1975.

Thomas, John L. *The Liberator, William Lloyd Garrison: A Biography*. Boston, 1963.

Trefousse, Hans. *Lincoln's Decision for Emancipation*. Philadelphia, 1975.

Trexler, Harrison A. *Slavery in Missouri, 1804–1865*. Baltimore, 1914.

Ver Steeg, Clarence L. *Origins of a Southern Mosaic: Studies of Early Carolina and Georgia*. Athens, Ga., 1975.

Wade, Richard C. "The Vesey Plot: A Reconsideration." *Journal of Southern History*, XXX (1964), 143–61.

Walker, James W. St. G. *The Black Loyalists: The Search for a Promised Land in Nova Scotia and Sierra Leone, 1783–1870*. London, 1975.

Webb, Stephen Saunders. *1676: The End of American Independence*. New York, 1984.

Webber, Thomas L. *Deep Like the Rivers: Education in the Slave Quarter Community, 1831–1865*. New York, 1978.

Whitfield, Theodore M. *Slavery Agitation in Virginia, 1829–1832*. Baltimore, 1930.

Wiecek, William M. "The Statutory Law of Slavery and Race in the Thirteen Mainland Colonies of British America." *William and Mary Quarterly*, 3rd ser., XXXIV (1977), 258–80.

Wikramanayak, Marina. *A World in Shadow: The Free Black in Antebellum South Carolina*. Columbia, S.C., 1973.

Wiley, Bell I. *The Life of Billy Yank, the Common Soldier of the Union*. Indianapolis, 1952.

———. *The Plain People of the Confederacy*. Baton Rouge, 1943.

———. *Southern Negroes, 1861–1865*. New Haven, Conn., 1938.

Williams, George W. *History of the Negro Race in America from 1619 to 1880*. 2 vols. New York, 1883.

Williams, T. Harry. *Lincoln and the Radicals*. Madison, Wisc., 1965.

Williamson, Joel. *After Slavery: The Negro in South Carolina During Reconstruction, 1861–1877*. Chapel Hill, N.C., 1965.

Willis, William S., Jr. "Anthropology and Negroes on the Southern Colonial Frontier." In *The Black Experience in America: Selected Essays*, edited by James C. Curtis and Lewis L. Gould. Austin, Texas, 1970.

———. "Divide and Rule: Red, White, and Black in the Southeast." *Journal of Negro History*, XLVIII (1963), 157–76.

Wilson, Henry. *History of the Rise and Fall of the Slave Power in America.* 3 vols. Boston, 1872–77.

Wish, Harvey. "Slave Disloyalty Under the Confederacy." *Journal of Negro History,* XXIII (1938), 435–50.

Wood, Peter H. *Black Majority: Blacks in Colonial South Carolina from 1670 Through the Stono Rebellion.* New York, 1974.

———. "Nat Turner: The Unknown Slave as Visionary Leader." In *Black Leaders of the Nineteenth Century,* edited by Leon Litwack and August Meier. Urbana, Ill., 1988.

Wyatt-Brown, Bertram. *Lewis Tappan and the Evangelical War Against Slavery.* Cleveland, 1969.

———. "William Lloyd Garrison and Antislavery Unity: A Reappraisal." *Civil War History,* XIII (March, 1967), 5–24.

Young, Tommy R., II. "The United States Army and the Institution of Slavery in Louisiana, 1803–1815." *Louisiana Studies,* XIII (1974), 201–22.

Zorn, Roman. "The New England Anti-Slavery Society: Pioneer Abolitionist Organization." *Journal of Negro History,* XLIII (1957), 157–76.

Index